THE CAMBRIDGE COMPANION TO
EVANGELICAL THEOLOGY

Evangelicalism, a vibrant and growing expression of historic Christian orthodoxy, is already one of the largest and most geographically diverse global religious movements. This Companion offers an up-to-date articulation of evangelical theology that is both faithful to historic evangelical convictions and in dialogue with contemporary intellectual contexts and concerns. In addition to original and creative essays on central Christian doctrines such as Christ, the Trinity, and Justification, it breaks new ground by offering evangelical reflections on issues such as gender, race, culture, and world religions. This volume also moves beyond the confines of Anglo-American perspectives to offer separate essays exploring evangelical theology in African, Asian, and Latin American contexts. The contributors to this volume form an unrivalled list of many of today's most eminent evangelical theologians and important emerging voices.

TIMOTHY LARSEN is Professor of Theology at Wheaton College, Illinois. He is author of *Crisis of Doubt: Honest Faith in Nineteenth-Century England* (2006) and editor of the *Biographical Dictionary of Evangelicals* (2003).

DANIEL J. TREIER is Associate Professor of Theology at Wheaton College, Illinois. He is author of *Virtue and the Voice of God: Toward Theology as Wisdom* (2006) and associate editor of the *Dictionary for Theological Interpretation of the Bible* (2005).

CAMBRIDGE COMPANIONS TO RELIGION

A series of companions to major topics and key figures in theology and religious studies. Each volume contains specially commissioned chapters by international scholars which provide an accessible and stimulating introduction to the subject for new readers and non-specialists.

Other titles in the series

THE CAMBRIDGE COMPANION TO CHRISTIAN DOCTRINE
edited by Colin Gunton (1997)
ISBN 0 521 47118 4 hardback   ISBN 0 521 47695 x paperback

THE CAMBRIDGE COMPANION TO BIBLICAL INTERPRETATION
edited by John Barton (1998)
ISBN 0 521 48144 9 hardback   ISBN 0 521 48593 2 paperback

THE CAMBRIDGE COMPANION TO DIETRICH BONHOEFFER
edited by John de Gruchy (1999)
ISBN 0 521 58258 x hardback   ISBN 0 521 58781 6 paperback

THE CAMBRIDGE COMPANION TO LIBERATION THEOLOGY
edited by Christopher Rowland (1999)
ISBN 0 521 46144 8 hardback   ISBN 0 521 46707 1 paperback

THE CAMBRIDGE COMPANION TO KARL BARTH
edited by John Webster (2000)
ISBN 0 521 58476 0 hardback   ISBN 0 521 58560 0 paperback

THE CAMBRIDGE COMPANION TO CHRISTIAN ETHICS
edited by Robin Gill (2001)
ISBN 0 521 77070 x hardback   ISBN 0 521 77918 9 paperback

THE CAMBRIDGE COMPANION TO JESUS
edited by Markus Bockmuehl (2001)
ISBN 0 521 79261 4 hardback   ISBN 0 521 79678 4 paperback

THE CAMBRIDGE COMPANION TO FEMINIST THEOLOGY
edited by Susan Frank Parsons (2002)
ISBN 0 521 66327 x hardback   ISBN 0 521 66380 6 paperback

THE CAMBRIDGE COMPANION TO MARTIN LUTHER
edited by Donald K. McKim (2003)
ISBN 0 521 81648 3 hardback   ISBN 0 521 01673 8 paperback

THE CAMBRIDGE COMPANION TO ST. PAUL
edited by James D. G. Dunn (2003)
ISBN 0 521 78155 8 hardback   ISBN 0 521 78694 0 paperback

THE CAMBRIDGE COMPANION TO POSTMODERN THEOLOGY
edited by Kevin J. Vanhoozer (2003)
ISBN 0 521 79062 x hardback   ISBN 0 521 79395 5 paperback

THE CAMBRIDGE COMPANION TO JOHN CALVIN
edited by Donald K. McKim (2004)
ISBN 0 521 81647 5 hardback   ISBN 0 521 01672 x paperback

THE CAMBRIDGE COMPANION TO HANS URS VON BALTHASAR
edited by Edward T. Oakes, SJ and David Moss (2004)
ISBN 0 521 81467 7 hardback   ISBN 0 521 89147 7 paperback

THE CAMBRIDGE COMPANION TO REFORMATION THEOLOGY
edited by David Bagchi and David Steinmetz (2004)
ISBN 0 521 77224 9 hardback   ISBN 0 521 77662 7 paperback

THE CAMBRIDGE COMPANION TO AMERICAN JUDAISM
edited by Dana Evan Kaplan (2005)
ISBN 0 521 82204 1 hardback   ISBN 0 521 52951 4 paperback

THE CAMBRIDGE COMPANION TO KARL RAHNER
edited by Declan Marmion and Mary E. Hines (2005)
ISBN 0 521 83288 8 hardback   ISBN 0 521 54045 3 paperback

THE CAMBRIDGE COMPANION TO FRIEDRICH SCHLEIERMACHER
edited by Jacqueline Mariña (2005)
ISBN 0 521 81448 0 hardback   ISBN 0 521 89137 x paperback

THE CAMBRIDGE COMPANION TO THE GOSPELS
edited by Stephen C. Barton (2006)
ISBN 0 521 80766 2 hardback   ISBN 0 521 00261 3 paperback

THE CAMBRIDGE COMPANION TO THE QUR'AN
edited by Jane Dammen McAuliffe (2006)
ISBN 0 521 83160 1 hardback   ISBN 0 521 53934 x paperback

THE CAMBRIDGE COMPANION TO JONATHAN EDWARDS
edited by Stephen J. Stein (2007)
ISBN 0 521 85290 0 hardback   ISBN 0 521 61805 3 paperback

Forthcoming

THE CAMBRIDGE COMPANION TO ISLAMIC THEOLOGY
edited by Tim Winter

THE CAMBRIDGE COMPANION TO THE VIRGIN MARY
edited by Sarah Boss

THE CAMBRIDGE COMPANION TO ANCIENT CHRISTIANITY
edited by Rebecca Lyman

THE CAMBRIDGE COMPANION TO

EVANGELICAL THEOLOGY

Edited By Timothy Larsen and Daniel J. Treier

CAMBRIDGE
UNIVERSITY PRESS

CAMBRIDGE UNIVERSITY PRESS
Cambridge, New York, Melbourne, Madrid, Cape Town, Singapore, São Paulo

Cambridge University Press
The Edinburgh Building, Cambridge CB2 8RU, UK

Published in the United States of America by Cambridge University Press, New York

www.cambridge.org
Information on this title: www.cambridge.org/9780521609746

First published 2007

Printed in the United Kingdom at the University Press, Cambridge

A catalogue record for this publication is available from the British Library

ISBN 978-0-521-84698-1 hardback
ISBN 978-0-521-60974-6 paperback

For Mark A. Noll
Scholar, mentor, and friend

Contents

List of contributors   *page* xi
Acknowledgments and note on references   xiv
A note on the cover image   xvi

1   Defining and locating evangelicalism   1
TIMOTHY LARSEN

Part I *Evangelicals and Christian doctrine*   15

2   The triune God of the gospel   17
KEVIN J. VANHOOZER

3   Scripture and hermeneutics   35
DANIEL J. TREIER

4   Jesus Christ   51
JOHN WEBSTER

5   The human person in the Christian story   65
CHERITH FEE NORDLING

6   Justification and atonement   79
D. STEPHEN LONG

7   The Holy Spirit   93
TERRY L. CROSS

8   Conversion and sanctification   109
MIYON CHUNG

9   The church in evangelical theology and practice   125
LEANNE VAN DYK

Part II *The contexts of evangelical theology*   143

10   Evangelical theology and culture   145
WILLIAM A. DYRNESS

11   Evangelical theology and gender   161
ELAINE STORKEY

12 Race and the experience of death: theologically
    reappraising American evangelicalism   177
    J. KAMERON CARTER

13 Evangelical theology and the religions   199
    VELI-MATTI KÄRKKÄINEN

14 Evangelical theology in African contexts   213
    TITE TIÉNOU

15 Evangelical theology in Asian contexts   225
    SIMON CHAN

16 British (and European) evangelical theologies   241
    STEPHEN R. HOLMES

17 Evangelical theology in Latin American contexts   259
    C. RENÉ PADILLA

18 Evangelical theology in North American contexts   275
    TIMOTHY GEORGE

    Index   293

Contributors

J. Kameron Carter is Assistant Professor of Theology and Black Church Studies, Duke University Divinity School, Durham, North Carolina. His forthcoming book is entitled *Race: A Theological Account*.

Simon Chan is Ernest Lau Professor of Systematic Theology, Trinity Theological College, Singapore. His books include *Pentecostal Theology and the Christian Spiritual Tradition* (2000).

Miyon Chung is Lecturer in Systematic Theology, Torch Trinity Graduate School of Theology, Seoul, Korea. She is currently working on a book in which she will use Ricoeurian narrative theory to explore Augustine's theology of grace.

Terry L. Cross is the Dean of the School of Religion and Professor of Theology, Lee University, Cleveland, Tennessee. He is an editor of *The Spirit and the Mind: Essays in Informed Pentecostalism* (2000) and the author of *Dialectic in Karl Barth's Doctrine of God* (2001).

William A. Dyrness is Professor of Theology and Culture, Fuller Theological Seminary, Pasadena, California. His recent publications include *Reformed Theology and Visual Culture: The Protestant Imagination from Calvin to Edwards* (2004).

Timothy George is the Dean, Beeson Divinity School, Samford University, Birmingham, Alabama. His numerous editorial commitments include serving as an executive editor of *Christianity Today*, and his recent books include *Mr Moody and the Evangelical Tradition* (2004).

Stephen R. Holmes is Lecturer in Theology, University of St Andrews. He is the managing editor of the *International Journal of Systematic Theology* and his publications include *Listening to the Past: The Place of Tradition in Theology* (2002).

Veli-Matti Kärkkäinen is Privatdozent of Ecumenics, University of Helsinki, Finland, and Professor of Systematic Theology, Fuller Theological Seminary,

Pasadena, California. His recent books include *Trinity and Religious Pluralism: The Doctrine of the Trinity in Christian Theology of Religions* (2004).

Timothy Larsen is Professor of Theology, Wheaton College, Wheaton, Illinois, and a Visiting Fellow, Trinity College, Cambridge, for the Lent and Easter terms, 2007. His work as an editor includes the *Biographical Dictionary of Evangelicals* (2003), and his most recent monograph is *Crisis of Doubt: Honest Faith in Nineteenth-Century England* (2006).

D. Stephen Long is Associate Professor of Systematic Theology, Garrett-Evangelical Theological Seminary, Evanston, Illinois. His most recent books include *John Wesley's Moral Theology: The Quest for God and Goodness* (2005).

Cherith Fee Nordling is Co-Director of Christian Formation and Adjunct Professor of Theology, Calvin College, Grand Rapids, Michigan. Her publications include the *Pocket Dictionary of Theological Terms* (2000).

C. René Padilla is Director of Publications and President Emeritus, Fundación Kairos, Argentina, and a widely respected, leading evangelical voice over the past several decades. His recent publications include *Terrorism and the War in Iraq: A Christian Word from Latin America* (2004).

Elaine Storkey is Senior Research Fellow, Wycliffe Hall, Oxford University. In addition to being the author of the landmark study, *What's Right With Feminism* (1985), she has recently authored *Created or Constructed? The Great Gender Debate* (2001).

Tite Tiénou is Senior Vice President and Academic Dean, Trinity Evangelical Divinity School, Deerfield, Illinois, and was formerly President and Dean of the Faculté de Théologie Evangélique de l'Alliance, Abidjan, Côte d'Ivoire. His work includes *The Theological Task of the Church in Africa* (1990).

Daniel J. Treier is Associate Professor of Theology, Wheaton College, Wheaton, Illinois. He is an associate editor of the *Dictionary for Theological Interpretation of the Bible* (2005) and the author of *Virtue and the Voice of God: Toward Theology as Wisdom* (2006).

Leanne Van Dyk is Academic Dean and Professor of Reformed Theology, Western Seminary, Holland, Michigan. Her recent publications include *A More Profound Alleluia: Theology and Worship in Harmony* (2005).

Kevin J. Vanhoozer is Research Professor of Systematic Theology, Trinity Evangelical Divinity School, Deerfield, Illinois. His work as an editor includes the *Cambridge Companion to Postmodern Theology* (2003) and his recent monographs include *The Drama of Doctrine: A Canonical-Linguistic Approach to Christian Theology* (2005).

John Webster is Professor of Systematic Theology, University of Aberdeen; formerly he served as Lady Margaret Professor of Divinity, Oxford University. His work as an editor includes *The Cambridge Companion to Karl Barth* (2000) and his recent books include *Confessing God: Essays in Christian Dogmatics II* (2005).

Acknowledgments

Evangelical theology centers on grace, and so it is especially fitting for us to acknowledge the divine gifts that have made this book possible. "What do you have that you did not receive?" (1 Cor. 4:7) Indeed.

We dedicate the project to Mark Noll, the renowned evangelical historian who – just prior to this writing – has announced his departure from Wheaton College and will represent evangelical Protestants at the University of Notre Dame. Mark's teaching and encouragement have initiated and sustained Tim Larsen's career from his undergraduate days onward. Mark's famous book *The Scandal of the Evangelical Mind* had direct and deeply personal bearing on Dan Treier's calling to theological scholarship. Both of us rejoiced at the opportunity to be Mark's colleagues, and we have reveled in the continual support and guidance he offers. The public knows of his outstanding scholarship, as evidenced for example in the magnum opus *America's God: From Jonathan Edwards to Abraham Lincoln*, a standard for stewardship of intellectual gifts that neither of us can hope to attain. We also can attest, however, what you might only know by reading between the lines: Mark Noll is an unfailingly humble person of deep conviction, global awareness, and gentle good cheer; he is also a very capable theologian on the side.

Many other colleagues at Wheaton are unfailingly supportive as well. Among our fellow theologians in particular, we especially thank Steve Spencer for advice and friendship that made this book better. Barry Jones, soon to depart from our student ranks, generously provided text editing, research, and bibliographical preparation at the same time he was finalizing his Ph.D. thesis. Michael Allen kindly helped to prepare the indexes. Our dean, Jill Peláez Baumgaertner, has also been generous in helping us to find the time for this work.

Originally, two additional contributors were part of this project. We regret not having represented in this volume another evangelical voice from the Church of England, Canon Dr. Christina Baxter CBE, Principal,

St. John's College, Nottingham. But we understand that, when it becomes necessary to choose, her ecclesiastical, administrative, and ministry commitments should rightly take priority. We were also honored that Stanley J. Grenz, Pioneer McDonald Professor of Theology, Carey Theological College, Vancouver, and a preeminent evangelical theologian, had consented to write for this volume. We mourn his death on 12 March 2005 and can only pray that God will raise up other theologians of such caliber in our midst.

It remains to acknowledge our families, who raised us in the heritage of evangelical Christian faith and who sustain us with constant support. Our wives, Jane Larsen and Amy Black Treier, believe in our scholarly pursuits and love us in spite of how much energy we spend on projects such as this. Both are testimonies to God's grace in our lives.

NOTE ON REFERENCES

Unless otherwise stated, the New Revised Standard Version (NRSV) is normally the Bible translation used.

A note on the cover image

THE ESSA CROSS

Towards the end of the last century Gert Swart was commissioned to make a cross for the Evangelical Seminary of Southern Africa (ESSA), a multicultural seminary drawing students from many countries in Africa. ESSA's campus, a small but significant example of urban renewal, is situated in the South African city of Pietermaritzburg, the capital of KwaZulu-Natal.

The complex symbolism of the cross was carefully selected to convey several messages including the suffering of many South Africans in the turbulent, violent years before the birth of our democracy, the suffering of countless others in what must be one of the bloodiest centuries in the history of the world, and, crucially, one of redemption, reconciliation, and hope.

Gert used images of his hands, each with a finger on the trigger of a gun directed at the Lamb to contextualize the cross – in a province known as the "killing fields of Natal" in the 80s – and as a comment on the complicity of each one of us in the brutal execution of Christ on the cross.

As people gathered to dedicate the cross on 11 September 2001 news was filtering through of the audacious and devastating attacks on the World Trade Towers and the Pentagon. So it was that while the USA reeled, a small assembly intimately acquainted with terror and tragedy exuberantly celebrated the arrival of the ESSA Cross, a beacon of hope on a dark day in a dark world.

Gert and Istine Swart

1 Defining and locating evangelicalism

TIMOTHY LARSEN

An evangelical is:

1. an orthodox Protestant
2. who stands in the tradition of the global Christian networks arising from the eighteenth-century revival movements associated with John Wesley and George Whitefield;
3. who has a preeminent place for the Bible in her or his Christian life as the divinely inspired, final authority in matters of faith and practice;
4. who stresses reconciliation with God through the atoning work of Jesus Christ on the cross;
5. and who stresses the work of the Holy Spirit in the life of an individual to bring about conversion and an ongoing life of fellowship with God and service to God and others, including the duty of all believers to participate in the task of proclaiming the gospel to all people.

This definition has been specifically devised for this volume. As I have tried it out on colleagues, they have jokingly referred to it as "the Larsen Pentagon," which is a compliment to the standard definition of evangelicalism, the Bebbington Quadrilateral. The British historian, David Bebbington, in his seminal study, *Evangelicalism in Modern Britain: A History from the 1730s to the 1980s* (1989), defined evangelicalism by identifying its four distinguishing marks: conversionism, activism, biblicism, and crucicentrism – that is, evangelicals emphasize conversion experiences; an active laity sharing the gospel and engaged in good works; the Bible; and salvation through the work of Christ on the cross.[1] Bebbington's definition is routinely employed to identify evangelicalism; no other definition comes close to rivaling its level of general acceptance. It is the definition used by numerous scholars who have studied aspects of evangelicalism.[2] For example, it is employed by the two main works of reference comprised of evangelical biographies that have been published since 1989, Donald M. Lewis, *The Blackwell Dictionary of Evangelical Biography* and my own *Biographical Dictionary of Evangelicals.*[3]

The eminent American historian of evangelicalism, Mark Noll, has repeatedly commended the quadrilateral as "the most serviceable general definition" in existence.[4] A leader of evangelicalism in Britain, Derek Tidball (whose current positions include chairing the council of the Evangelical Alliance in the United Kingdom), has testified concerning this definition: "[Bebbington's] suggestions have met with a ready response from across the spectrum of evangelicals and has quickly established itself as near to a consensus as we might ever expect to reach."[5] My five-point definition is not intended to supplant Bebbington's. The quadrilateral has the important advantage of being quite short, while the pentagon is far too long to be easily deployed in many contexts where a definition is needed. Indeed, I imagine that most reviewers of this *Cambridge Companion* will not want to expend some 125 words of their valuable space in order to quote it in full.

Nevertheless, the pentagon does bring out important contextual information that Bebbington was able either to assume (given the geographical and chronological scope of his study as identified in its title) or to develop explicitly elsewhere in his book. Without such additional context, the term "evangelical" loses its utility for identifying a specific Christian community. For example, if no context is made explicit, an argument could be made that St. Francis of Assisi was an evangelical. St. Francis, after all, had a clear, dramatic conversion experience; he was so committed to activism that he pioneered friars out itinerating amongst the people, preaching the gospel, and ministering to physical needs rather than being cloistered monks; his biblicism was so thorough that his *Rule* was made up mostly of straight quotations from Scripture; his crucicentrism was so profound that it reached its culmination in the stigmata. For all I know, St. Francis might have been a better Christian and more committed to the distinctives of the quadrilateral (generically conceived) than any evangelical as defined in this chapter who ever lived, but a definition of evangelicalism that would include medieval Roman Catholic saints would not be serviceable for delineating the scope of scholarly projects.

Accordingly, the goal of this chapter is merely to find a definition that clearly identifies a distinct Christian community that can then be discussed. This is decidedly not an attempt to judge the actual identity or status of any individuals who happen to fall outside or inside those functional boundaries. Specifically, this working definition is not intended to challenge anyone's right to use "evangelical" as an appropriate self-description. To take an obvious example, the word "evangelical" functions in some contexts, especially European ones, as a synonym for "Protestant." This is a perfectly legitimate usage: it is just not the one being employed here. Etymologically, "evangelical" is derived from the Greek word, *euangelion*, meaning "good news" or "gospel," and many not intended when the term is used in this volume would quite rightly consider themselves to be people of the gospel. Likewise, the pentagon is not meant to violate anyone's right to refuse to be co-opted into the evangelical camp. Any individual or group who finds the label unwelcome can simply reply to this message and say so; they will have their address removed from the mailing list promptly and without question. More to the point, I have made an effort in this chapter to quote doctrinal statements only from organizations that self-identify as evangelical. Hence this working definition should not be misconstrued as an effort to impose a reality to which people are expected to conform, and to use for deciding whom they can accept as believers of the same ilk with whom they could cooperate. Its only purpose is to mark off a coherent scope for a scholarly project.

On the other hand, this definition is intended to locate an actual, self-identified "evangelical" Christian community in existence. While "evangelical" can be used in many ways, the definition being advanced here articulates what might be meant when this term is used in numerous real-life contexts such as the Association of Evangelical Theological Education in Latin America, the *Africa Journal of Evangelical Theology*, the *Journal of Asian Evangelical Theology*, the Evangelical Alliance of the United Kingdom, the Korea Evangelical Theological Society, the Evangelical Fellowship of Pakistan, the Fellowship of European Evangelical Theologians, the Evangelical Theological Seminary in Cairo, the Romanian Evangelical Alliance, the National Association of Evangelicals in America, the National Council of Evangelical Churches in Papua New Guinea, and the Nairobi Evangelical Graduate School of Theology. While the word "evangelical" will undoubtedly not mean exactly the same thing in such diverse locations, the members of these organizations are indeed part of a cross-pollinating international movement. It is routine for an individual in good standing with one of these groups (or numerous more that have not been named) to be sought after for service in any of the others, thus revealing the sense that they are fellow believers of the same species, local variations notwithstanding. Let us therefore explore the defining boundaries being established for this work.

(i) AN ORTHODOX PROTESTANT

Evangelicals are a subset within historic, orthodox Christianity. In particular, they are Trinitarians whose doctrines of God and Christ are in line with the ones articulated at the councils of Nicaea (AD 325) and Constantinople (AD 381). Many evangelicals explicitly accept the Apostles' Creed and the Nicene Creed. There are some evangelicals, however, who reject all creedal statements in principle, interpreting the Protestant principle of *sola Scriptura* to mean that Christians should have "no creed but the Bible." This instinct has often been expressed, for example, in restorationist churches such as those arising from the Stone–Campbell movement.⁶ An individual who rejected the ecumenical Christian creeds on such grounds might still be identifiable as an evangelical if her understanding of what the Bible teaches on the Trinity and the nature of Christ correlated with the teaching of the Nicene Creed. More than one evangelical leader has claimed that the historic creeds should have no place in matters of faith and instead embarked upon a project to find the teaching of the Bible directly from scratch, but has nevertheless come away from the Scriptures after such an effort with doctrinal convictions identical to the rulings of the early ecumenical councils. On the other hand, some groups are indeed excluded by this point – the fact notwithstanding that they bear a striking resemblance in other ways to those defined as evangelicals here. Oneness Pentecostals would be an obvious example of a group whose church life and worship would correlate strongly in many ways to that of those identified here as evangelicals, but whose lack of a Trinitarian theology positions them beyond the focus of this study.⁷ In short, the doctrine of evangelicals accords with Nicene orthodoxy.

Evangelicalism is also a form of Protestantism. Historically, much of the Christian community being identified here has often cultivated an explicitly anti-Catholic stance, not infrequently in ways that make for painful reading. Indeed, a significant prompt (but not the only one) for the founding in 1846 of the Evangelical Alliance in Britain was a desire to create a united front against Roman Catholicism. The eminent Scottish divine, Thomas Chalmers, hoped at the time of its founding that the Evangelical Alliance would be a "great anti-Popish Association."⁸ It would not be hard to compile a long list from across multiple nations and centuries of self-identified evangelicals attacking Catholicism. Recently, efforts to communicate respect for other orthodox Christians have become so energetic for some conservative Protestants that it is sometimes viewed as bad manners to define the evangelical camp in a way that excludes Roman Catholic and Eastern Orthodox believers. Such politeness, however, has the liability of being apt to confuse the uninitiated. A former colleague of mine is an ordained Presbyterian minister. He is also a Benedictine oblate who has served on the board of the

American Benedictine Academy. The fact that the Benedictines would receive him in this way shows that they are not animated by anti-Protestant sentiments. Nevertheless, his case notwithstanding, the clearest way to define "Benedictine" would be as a particular community within Roman Catholicism. Likewise, a desire for methodological clarity prompts me to acknowledge that the term "evangelical" as it is being used here is normed by the wider category of Protestantism. Moreover, this volume concerns evangelical *theology*. Although readers of this volume might know personally people who are a hybrid of evangelicalism and Roman Catholicism or Orthodoxy, to date, I do not think that one can point to significant theological work that has been done by someone who is simultaneously both Catholic or Orthodox and also recognized by any of the self-identified "evangelical" organizations listed above as an evangelical theologian.

(2) WHO STANDS IN THE TRADITION OF THE GLOBAL CHRISTIAN NETWORKS ARISING FROM THE EIGHTEENTH-CENTURY REVIVAL MOVEMENTS ASSOCIATED WITH JOHN WESLEY AND GEORGE WHITEFIELD

The purpose of this point is, first, to demarcate the chronological scope of the movement and, second, to identify a particular social network. In other words, it provides the context that explains why this volume is not referring to Augustine, John Chrysostom, Catherine of Siena, Martin Luther, or Richard Baxter when it speaks of "evangelicals," however much evangelicals as defined here might admire these figures and appreciate their theological contributions. The network under consideration in this volume began in the cross-pollinating revivalistic and evangelistic atmosphere of Britain and North America in the 1730s, together with links and parallels to Pietists in continental Europe. Leaders such as the Englishmen John Wesley and George Whitefield were avidly collaborating with like-minded believers across Britain, in North America, in Europe, and sometimes beyond.[9] Their names serve well to identify a particular network of believers that has continued ever since, though other names from that first generation might have also performed this function (such as Jonathan Edwards in Massachusetts or Howell Harris in Wales).

Wesley and Whitefield express well the other points of the pentagon. The fact that Wesley was an Arminian and Whitefield a Calvinist notwithstanding, their views on Scripture, the work of Christ on the cross, the work of the Spirit, and the duties of believers corresponded to this definition. From the generation of Wesley and Whitefield to the present, believers who hold these convictions have worked together to pursue common goals. They have also successfully spread their convictions. This spreading influence has resulted in the network taking root in every corner of the globe: only the Roman Catholic Church can rival the extent to which evangelicalism is truly and profoundly a global religious movement. This identifiable, worldwide Christian network has also influenced many different denominational contexts and provided the impetus for creating a wide array of new ones. It is this network to which the word "evangelical" refers.

Origin is not destiny, however. The reference to Wesley and Whitefield should not be misconstrued as norming today's evangelicalism by narrowly Western standards. To find out what is meant in this volume by an evangelical today, one would be better off observing Pentecostals in Korea than Methodists in England, despite the fact that British Methodists look to John Wesley as their institutional founder. In this study, "evangelical" does not mean whatever historically evangelical institutions or groups have become. Rather, this definition recognizes that historically evangelical groups can change their theological convictions and Christian practices in ways that move them beyond the scope of this study. This could also happen to any of the organizations mentioned earlier with the word "evangelical" in their titles. One prominent way this has happened in the past is when individuals or groups have imbibed theologically liberal or Modernist doctrinal convictions to the point where evangelical distinctives are muted. When such theological influences lead one to deny the unique authority of the Bible, to find an emphasis on the atoning work of Christ no longer central to Christian proclamation, or to dispense with the practice of evangelism and an expectation of conversion, then such a person no longer falls within the scope of this study. Many British Methodists, of course, are evangelicals in the sense being advanced here, but one cannot infer this automatically from their denominational identity (for that matter, being a Korean Pentecostal does not make one *ipso facto* an evangelical either, and that tradition could develop in non-evangelical ways in the future). Conversely, many groups that are not historically evangelical now have members that are evangelicals. For example, some believers in Christian communities that pre-date the 1730s, such as the Mennonites, have been influenced by the evangelical movement, accepted its core traits, and chosen to build relationships in the context of the wider evangelical network. Although it began in the 1730s, an individual believer or a whole Christian group might join this international evangelical network and become truly evangelical – even become a supreme current example of evangelicalism – the fact that their Christian tradition does not have historic links to it notwithstanding.

As long as a network continues to exist that expresses the theology and practice articulated in the other points of the pentagon, then there will still be evangelicalism in the sense used in this book, however much the network might change or shift its center of gravity in terms of denominational, ethnic, cultural, or geographical contexts. In short, evangelicalism is a *network* that reflects particular *distinctives of doctrine and Christian practice.* This study is not interested in gathering up people outside an identifiable, self-described, "evangelical" network who happen to share these doctrinal distinctives and insisting that they are evangelicals whether they know it or not, whether they would resent being so labeled or not. On the other hand, this study also rejects the notion that evangelicalism is whatever once-central parts of such an identifiable network might become: if they depart from the distinctives of doctrine and Christian practice outlined in the other four points of the pentagon, then they are no longer evangelicals in its sense.

(3) WHO HAS A PREEMINENT PLACE FOR THE BIBLE IN HER OR HIS CHRISTIAN LIFE AS THE DIVINELY INSPIRED, FINAL AUTHORITY IN MATTERS OF FAITH AND PRACTICE

The Bible is central to evangelicals as a point of doctrine, as the authority by which they defend all their theological convictions, and as a fundamental component of their Christian practice. In terms of the latter, a widespread devotional pattern in evangelicalism is the practice of daily Bible reading. The expectation of regular, private Bible reading is for the whole literate community – both the laity and the clergy, both the young and the old, both new believers and mature ones. Devotional Bible reading is more foundational to evangelical piety than the rosary is to Roman Catholic piety. Innumerable aids have been continually written to guide evangelicals in the systematic reading of Scripture (schemes for reading the Bible through yearly are one standard model). In addition, evangelicals often see the sermon as the high point of corporate worship. They generally expect the sermon to be an exposition of a specific text of Scripture or an account of what the Bible says on a particular theme. Evangelicals often gather in small groups and/or Sunday school classes for Bible study. Evangelical spiritual formation frequently includes the memorization of portions of Scripture. Evangelical missionary work to unreached people groups characteristically prioritizes the translation of the Bible into indigenous languages.

Such Christian practice reflects doctrinal convictions regarding the nature of Scripture. Foundational to this stance is the Protestant principle of *sola Scriptura*. Unlike some liberal Protestants, evangelicals reject the notion that a modern awareness of religious pluralism undermines belief in the Bible as an uniquely divine text, or that modern biblical criticism has compromised the Bible as a reliable source of truth, and so forth. Evangelicals believe that the Bible is uniquely the word of God written. The whole of the Bible is authoritative and no other documents possess this exclusive level of authority. Therefore, all other doctrinal statements must be tested against the teaching of Scripture. It is common for statements of faith written by evangelicals to place Scripture references in parentheses behind each point. Evangelicals believe that human beings are judged by the Bible and called to change in the light of it, rather than standing in judgment over the Bible and rejecting those parts that are not in line with their own sensibilities. It would be unevangelical to claim that what the Bible teaches is actually a deceptive understanding of the nature of God. In the last hundred years, many evangelicals have used the word "inerrancy" to express these convictions regarding the nature of Scripture. Other evangelicals have shied away from that word, protesting that it is not a historic term, suspecting that it might be overdetermined, and worrying that it could divert the community into concentrating on explaining relatively trivial discrepancies in the text. A strong case can be made that inerrancy is an apt term for the way that the church historically has often viewed the Bible, the medieval Catholic theologian St. Bernard of Clairvaux no less than the twentieth-century, American, evangelical, theologian Carl F. H. Henry, for example.[10] Regardless, that debate should be kept in proportion: there is a strong, confident, uniform evangelical consensus on the inspiration, authority, uniqueness, and sufficiency of Scripture, as well as on its complete trustworthiness in matters of Christian faith and practice.

A globally comprehensive, formal evangelical organization is the World Evangelical Fellowship (now Alliance). Its statement of faith, written in 1951 and still in use, has as its first point (of seven): "The Holy Scriptures as originally given by God, divinely inspired, infallible, entirely trustworthy; and their supreme authority in all matters of faith and practice."[11] The Evangelical Alliance in Britain has revised its statement of faith twice – most recently in 2005 – since its founding in 1846. The point on the doctrine of Scripture from these three versions is as follows: "The divine Inspiration, Authority and Sufficiency of the Holy Scriptures" (1846); "The divine inspiration of the Holy Scripture and its consequent trustworthiness and supreme authority in all matters of faith and conduct" (1970); "The divine inspiration and supreme authority of the Old and New Testament Scriptures, which are the written Word of God – fully trustworthy for faith and conduct" (2005).[12] The Association of Evangelicals in Africa has as the first point of its eight-point statement of faith: "The Holy Scriptures of the Old and New Testament (a total of 66 Books) are the Word of God. It is divinely inspired, infallible, inerrant, entirely trustworthy and serves as a supreme authority in all matters of faith and conduct (2 Tim. 3:16–17)."[13] Numerous other evangelical statements could be cited from across the centuries and the nations that would illustrate this point of the pentagon.

(4) WHO STRESSES RECONCILIATION WITH GOD THROUGH THE ATONING WORK OF JESUS CHRIST ON THE CROSS

Evangelicals are people of the gospel, and the gospel they preach is that human beings can have their sins forgiven and be reconciled to God through the atoning work of Christ on the cross. This is Bebbington's "crucicentrism." Repeatedly, when theologians reflecting other traditions have moved the center of gravity in Christian thought toward doctrines such as the incarnation, the life and teaching of Christ, or the Fatherhood of God, evangelicals have insisted, as P. T. Forsyth put it, on *The Cruciality of the Cross*.[14] Overwhelmingly, evangelicals have viewed the nature of the work of Christ on the cross as vicarious and/or substitutionary. Thus, the statement of faith of the National Association of Evangelicals in America confesses a belief in Christ's "vicarious and atoning death through His shed blood."[15] "Vicarious and atoning" is also the wording in the statement of faith of the World Evangelical Alliance, and numerous bodies across the globe such as the Evangelical Fellowship of India and the Evangelical Association of the Caribbean also accept this wording.[16] The current statement of the Evangelical Alliance of the United Kingdom affirms a belief in: "The atoning sacrifice of Christ on the cross: dying in our place, paying the price of sin and defeating evil, so reconciling us with God."[17] Words and concepts such as "substitutionary," "propitiation," and "penal" have sometimes been found problematic by some evangelicals. While there are intra-evangelical discussions about the exact nature of the atonement and the best way to express this doctrine in language, all evangelicals agree that Christ's work on the cross has made possible the only hope, plan, and way of reconciliation with God that human beings have. For evangelicals, "Christ and him crucified" (1 Cor. 2:2) is at the heart of gospel.

(5) AND WHO STRESSES THE WORK OF THE HOLY SPIRIT IN THE LIFE OF AN INDIVIDUAL TO BRING ABOUT CONVERSION AND AN ONGOING LIFE OF FELLOWSHIP WITH GOD AND SERVICE TO GOD AND OTHERS, INCLUDING THE DUTY OF ALL BELIEVERS TO PARTICIPATE IN THE TASK OF PROCLAIMING THE GOSPEL TO ALL PEOPLE

An overarching and unifying theme can be discerned in several features of evangelicalism that are often discussed separately, notably Bebbington's "conversionism" and "activism." The theme that binds them together is the work of God through the Holy Spirit in the lives of individuals. From a starting point at the beginning of the twentieth century, Pentecostal and charismatic expressions of Christianity have gone on to exert a particularly strong influence on global evangelicalism. This influence has increased the prominence of pneumatology in evangelical thought. Nevertheless, an emphasis on the work of the Spirit has always been a distinguishing mark of evangelical Christian life, not least in the first generation of Wesley and Whitefield. At its founding in 1846, the Evangelical Alliance in Britain had as its seventh point in a pithy nine-point doctrinal basis of faith: "The work of the Holy Spirit in the Conversion and Sanctification of the sinner." The National Association of Evangelicals in America has as the fourth and fifth points in its even briefer seven-point statement of faith: "We believe that for the salvation of lost and sinful people, regeneration by the Holy Spirit is absolutely essential. We believe in the present ministry of the Holy Spirit by whose indwelling the Christian is enabled to live a godly life." Likewise, the Association of Evangelicals in Africa has an eight-point statement. The fifth point includes the affirmation that human beings receive salvation "through regeneration by the Holy Spirit" and the fourth point declares: "The Holy Spirit is God. As the third Person in the Godhead, He indwells every believer upon conversion and enables the believer to live a holy life; to witness in power; and to work for the Lord Jesus Christ (Acts 5:3–4; Matt. 28:19; Acts 1:8)."[18] A historic gathering of global evangelical leaders happened in 1974 at the International Congress on World Evangelization in Lausanne, Switzerland. With leaders from more than 150 nations attending, it was a truly global gathering to an extraordinary degree by the standards of any movement or organization. This International Congress agreed on a fifteen-point statement, the Lausanne Covenant, all related in some way to the task of evangelism. Here is the fourteenth point, on "The Power of the Holy Spirit":

> We believe in the power of the Holy Spirit. The Father sent his
> Spirit to bear witness to his Son; without his witness ours is futile.
> Conviction of sin, faith in Christ, new birth and Christian growth
> are all his work. Further, the Holy Spirit is a missionary spirit; thus
> evangelism should arise spontaneously from a Spirit-filled church.
> A church that is not a missionary church is contradicting itself and
> quenching the Spirit. Worldwide evangelization will become a
> realistic possibility only when the Spirit renews the Church in truth
> and wisdom, faith, holiness, love and power. We therefore call upon
> all Christians to pray for such a visitation of the sovereign Spirit of
> God that all his fruit may appear in all his people and that all his gifts
> may enrich the body of Christ. Only then will the whole world become
> a fit instrument in his hands, that the whole earth may hear his voice.[19]

Evangelicalism is a community that emphasizes conversion. The Holy Spirit draws sinful individuals to God. Many evangelicals believe that the decisive moment of turning from darkness to light can happen at a specific, emotionally charged point in time. While evangelicals recognize that people can also be truly drawn to Christ over a long period of time and without any dramatic turning point, the evangelical tradition is thick with testimonies in which believers recount a specific, euphoric day when they experienced conversion and their life was changed for ever. Conversion leads to an ongoing life of fellowship with God. Evangelicals often speak of their relationship with God in very intimate terms. As the refrain of "In the Garden," a gospel song beloved by many evangelicals, expresses it: "And He walks with me, and He talks with me, and He tells me I am His own; and the joy we share as we tarry there, none other has ever known."[20] For outsiders, popular evangelical piety can seem disconcertingly sentimental, gushy, and all-pervasive. However dignified they might be culturally, all evangelicals – when they are true to their tradition – possess a firm conviction that God hears their prayers, cares about their daily needs and trials, and desires to receive their love and worship and use them to fulfill divine purposes.

Therefore, this relationship with God, through the work of the Holy Spirit, leads on to what Bebbington calls "activism." Evangelicalism is a tradition marked by a mobilized laity as well as a highly energized clergy. This activism has produced a rich tradition of social action, including, for example, the movement in Britain guided by the evangelical William Wilberforce to abolish the slave trade and the work among the poor of the evangelical organization, the Salvation Army.[21] A particularly distinct form of evangelical activism is evangelism. Evangelicals believe that every individual should be given the opportunity to hear the gospel and be challenged to accept it. Their hope is that these efforts, through the work of the Spirit, will lead on to genuine conversions. All believers are called to participate in this task. This commitment is often expressed simultaneously in both radically global ways (such as supporting missions in remote places on the other side of the world) and in radically local ways (such as speaking to one's immediate neighbors and relatives about whether or not they have faith in Jesus Christ). Evangelicalism has spawned innumerable evangelistic and mission organizations and efforts. Many of the people that the evangelical tradition recognizes as its greatest leaders, exemplars, or heroes have been primarily evangelists or missionaries – from the evangelist John Wesley in the first generation of evangelicalism, to the global evangelist Billy Graham into the twenty-first century. Empowered by the Spirit, evangelicals work to address the spiritual, physical, and other needs of a sinful, lost, broken, and hurting world.

Further reading

Bebbington, D. W. *Evangelicalism in Modern Britain: A History from the 1730s to the 1980s.* London: Unwin Hyman, 1989.

Elwell, Walter A. (ed.). *Evangelical Dictionary of Theology.* Grand Rapids, MI: Baker, 1984.

Larsen, Timothy (ed.). *Biographical Dictionary of Evangelicals.* Leicester: InterVarsity, 2003.

Marsden, George M. *Understanding Fundamentalism and Evangelicalism.* Grand Rapids, MI: Eerdmans, 1991.

Noll, Mark A. *The Rise of Evangelicalism: The Age of Edwards, Whitefield, and the Wesleys.* Downers Grove, IL: InterVarsity, 2003.

Olson, Roger E. *The Westminster Handbook to Evangelical Theology.* Louisville, KY: Westminster John Knox, 2004.

Packer, J. I., and Thomas C. Oden. *One Faith: The Evangelical Consensus*. Downers Grove, IL: InterVarsity, 2004.

Padilla, C. René (ed.). *The New Face of Evangelicalism: An International Symposium on the Lausanne Covenant*. Downers Grove, IL: InterVarsity, 1976.

Randall, Ian, and David Hilborn. *One Body in Christ: The History and Significance of the Evangelical Alliance*. Carlisle: Paternoster, 2001.

Tidball, Derek. *Who Are the Evangelicals? Tracing the Roots of the Modern Movements*. London: Marshall Pickering, 1994.

Notes

1. D. W. Bebbington, *Evangelicalism in Modern Britain: A History from the 1730s to the 1980s* (London: Unwin Hyman, 1989), pp. 2–17.

2. For a fuller demonstration of the unrivaled position of Bebbington's definition, see Timothy Larsen, "The Reception Given *Evangelicalism in Modern Britain* since Publication," in Michael Haykin and Kenneth J. Stewart (eds.), *Continuities in Evangelical History: Interactions with David Bebbington* (Downers Grove, IL: InterVarsity, forthcoming).

3. Donald M. Lewis (ed.), *The Blackwell Dictionary of Evangelical Biography* (Oxford: Blackwell, 1995); Timothy Larsen (ed.), *Biographical Dictionary of Evangelicals* (Leicester: InterVarsity, 2003).

4. See, e.g., Mark A. Noll, *American Evangelical Christianity: An Introduction* (Oxford: Blackwell, 2001), p. 185; Mark A. Noll, *America's God: From Jonathan Edwards to Abraham Lincoln* (New York: Oxford University Press, 2002), p. 5.

5. Derek Tidball, *Who Are the Evangelicals? Tracing the Roots of the Modern Movements* (London: Marshall Pickering, 1994), p. 14.

6. For recent scholarship on this movement, see Douglas A. Foster (ed.), *The Encyclopedia of the Stone–Campbell Movement* (Grand Rapids, MI: Eerdmans, 2004).

7. For an insider account of Oneness Pentecostalism, see Arthur L. Clanton, *United We Stand: A History of Oneness Organizations* (Hazelwood, MO: Pentecostal Publishing House, 1970). For a theological critique of this movement, see Gregory A. Boyd, *Oneness Pentecostals and the Trinity* (Grand Rapids, MI: Baker, 1992).

8. John Wolffe, "The Evangelical Alliance in the 1840s: An Attempt to Institutionalise Christian Unity," in W. J. Sheils and Diana Wood (eds.), *Voluntary Religion* (Oxford: Basil Blackwell [for the Ecclesiastical History Society], 1986), p. 340.

9. For an accessible account of this first-generation of evangelicals and their links with one another, see Mark A. Noll, *The Rise of Evangelicalism: The Age of Edwards, Whitefield, and the Wesleys* (Downers Grove, IL: InterVarsity, 2003). For a more technical treatment that particularly develops the continental Pietist contribution, see W. R. Ward, *The Protestant Evangelical Awakening* (Cambridge: Cambridge University Press, 1992).

10. Arguably the leading American evangelical theologian of his generation, Carl F. H. Henry's *magnum opus* was *God, Revelation and Authority*, 6 vols. (Waco, TX: Word, 1976–83).

11. See their website www.worldevangelical.org.

12. Ian Randall and David Hilborn, *One Body in Christ: The History and Significance of the Evangelical Alliance* (Carlisle: Paternoster, 2001), pp. 358–61; www.eauk.org (accessed 19 December 2005).

13. Nairobi Evangelical Graduate School of Theology accepts the statement of faith of the Association of Evangelicals in Africa and I have accessed it from their website: www.negst.edu/statement_of_faith.htm (accessed 19 December 2005).

14. P. T. Forsyth, *The Cruciality of the Cross* (London: Independent, 1909); also germane is his *The Work of Christ* (London: Hodder and Stoughton, 1910).

15. See its website: www.nae.net (accessed 19 December 2005).

16. For the Evangelical Fellowship of India, see www.efionline.org; for the Evangelical Association of the Caribbean, see www.caribevangelical.org.

17. www.eauk.org

18. www.eauk.org; www.nae.net; www.negst.edu.

19. John Stott, *The Lausanne Covenant – An Exposition and Commentary* (Minneapolis, MN: World Wide Publications, 1975), p. 33.

20. This hymn was written in 1913 by Charles Austin Miles (1868–1946). I have copied the lyrics from Alfred A. Smith (ed.), *Inspiring Hymns: A choice of Hymns and Gospel Songs for singing in Church* (Wheaton, IL: Singspiration, 1951), p. 268.

21. For an account of evangelicalism's historic commitment to social action in an American context, see Donald W. Dayton, *Discovering An Evangelical Heritage* (Peabody, MA: Hendrickson, 1976); the British context is explored in John Wolffe (ed.), *Evangelical Faith and Public Zeal: Evangelicals and Society in Britain, 1780–1980* (London: SPCK, 1995).

Part I

Evangelicals and Christian doctrine

2 The triune God of the gospel

KEVIN J. VANHOOZER

"Evangelicals are gospel people"[1]

AN INTRODUCTORY PARADOX: THE DIFFICULT, DIFFIDENT EVANGELICAL DOCTRINE OF GOD

Evangelicals are a people of the gospel (*evangel*). The good news about what God has done in Jesus Christ for the world presupposes two key theological truths: (1) *God has acted* (there is something good to report); (2) *God has spoken* (the news comes from God and so it is utterly reliable). There is no gospel, neither Christological content nor biblical form, apart from the speech and act of God. It therefore stands to reason that evangelicals enthusiastically affirm the God of the gospel, and on one level this is true.

A cursory examination of evangelical theology thus finds nothing exceptional to report: evangelicals agree with the orthodox consensus of the church that God exists, reveals himself in word and deed, and is able to accomplish his gracious purposes. The very logic of the gospel – the declaration that God enables believers to relate to God the Father in Jesus Christ through the Spirit – implies the divinity of the Son and Spirit as well. Hence evangelicals concur with the Trinitarian formula produced by the church fathers in 325 AD – the Nicene Creed – professing belief in one God: Father, Son, and Spirit.

One nevertheless detects a certain malaise in evangelical theology. Though evangelicals did not depart from orthodox affirmations, the doctrine of God languished through much of the twentieth century, mired in a deep funk. John Frame notes that "we live in an age in which the knowledge of God is rare"[2] and David Wells laments the "weightlessness of God" in many contemporary churches.[3] One important reason for this malaise was the tendency to treat the doctrine of the Trinity (when it *was* treated rather than neglected) in a merely notional way rather than as the operative concept of the distinctly Christian God of the gospel.

A second possible explanation is the fault-line running through the history of evangelicalism that stems from its dual allegiance to head and heart.[4] While it would be wrong simply to identify the scholastic "head" with Calvinism and the pietist "heart" with Wesleyan-Arminianism – for each tradition wants both to know *and* to love God – there is a popular perception that the former emphasizes divine sovereignty and the latter divine love.[5] In fact, all evangelicals profess both, though the precise meaning of these divine attributes remains in some dispute. The ultimate challenge for any doctrine of God is rightly to distinguish, and to relate, God's transcendence or "beyondness" and immanence or "nearness." Given their mixed (e.g., scholastic and pietist) heritage, then, evangelicals have to work especially hard to preserve the delicate balance between the truth of God's absolute otherness from creation and the gospel truth that God relates to creatures personally.[6]

The malaise in evangelical theology is most apparent not in academic textbooks but in Christian life and worship. It is easier to be deceived into worshiping what is not God when knowledge of God is in short supply. Ancient Israel was influenced by the plausibility structures of its neighbors and consequently "the worship of Baal began to seem natural and normal."[7] North American evangelicals are similarly coming under the influence of contemporary culture and thought forms. Meeting our felt needs is not necessarily the same as meeting God. Marva Dawn worries about the "dumbing down" of worship in some evangelical churches: "The only means for keeping worship free of idolatries is to keep God the subject."[8]

Worship involves a conception of the one to which our praise and prayers are directed. The nature and quality of our worship is an index of theological understanding, a measure of our apprehension of God's "worth-ship."[9] Our worship thus transmits our vision of ultimate reality. So do our patterns of everyday life. Evangelicals too often look and act like everyone else. In an American context this culturally compliant practice may reflect deeper affinity with the civil religion of "Moralistic Therapeutic Deism":[10] the belief that God wants people to be nice and to feel good. This diluted doctrine of God fits hand in glove with the dumbed-down worship that characterizes some evangelical churches.

The label "evangelical" is the statement of an ambition – to correspond to the gospel – rather than an achievement. Similarly, "God of the gospel" names a project, not a finished product. It also pinpoints the major challenge for an evangelical doctrine of God: to think about God biblically, according to the Scriptures that attest Jesus Christ, rather than following cleverly devised conceptual or cultural myths. Accordingly, we begin our survey of the doctrine by asking where evangelicals have obtained their view of God: from the gospel, Greek philosophy, or both.

CONSERVING: WHOSE THEISM? WHICH TRADITION?

Most evangelical theology textbooks present the doctrine of God in roughly the same order: the existence, knowledge, nature, and attributes of God, followed by the Trinity and the works of God (e.g., creation; providence).[11] Where did this order come from and what is its significance?

Classical theism: a fusion of biblical and Greek horizons

"Evangelical theologians live in the house that Thomas built." While this is too simplistic, it is true that most evangelical theologians embrace some form of classical theism of which Thomas Aquinas was the leading medieval exponent. Classical theism began when Christian apologists of the second century somewhat necessarily used then-dominant concepts of Greek philosophy to commend the faith, and the Scriptures, to the cultured despisers of religion.[12] Theists define God as a being of infinite perfection: all-holy, all-powerful, all-knowing, and everywhere present.[13]

Classical theism refers to what has long been presumed as a synthesis worked out in the ancient and medieval church between biblical Christianity and Greek philosophy, and in particular between "God" and Aristotle's notion of the "Unmoved Mover" (or Uncaused Cause). The Unmoved Mover is a perfect being: self-sufficient, eternal, and pure actuality (*actus purus*). From the latter – that God has no unrealized potential – Aristotle deduced that the Unmoved Mover must be immutable, because any change would be either for better or worse, and a perfect being is already as good as it can, and will for ever, be. God must not therefore have a body, because all bodies can be moved, so God is not material but immaterial. So: God sets the world into motion yet nothing moves God.

Thomas Aquinas did not appropriate Aristotle's Unmoved Mover wholesale. He realized that philosophy (a.k.a. "natural theology") takes us only so far. Reason yields knowledge concerning the world of nature and, by extension, its Creator, but only revelation gives knowledge of the realm of grace and hence of the Son and Spirit. Nevertheless, by employing

Aristotelian categories (e.g., substance, form, essence) and by conceding some knowledge of God to reason alone, the die of classical theism was arguably cast.

The first part of Aquinas's *Summa* discusses the "one God" (*de Deo Uno*) and treats themes accessible to natural reason – doctrines that would be held in common by Christians, Jews, and Arabs alike. Here we find discussions of God's existence, unity, nature, and attributes. Aquinas treats the "three persons" (*de Deo Trino*) second, when he turns to the truths of revelation. He consequently presents the divine attributes before he even begins referring to the Incarnation and passion of the Son; in brief, he has been read as thinking about God apart from the gospel.

Seven hundred years later Charles Hodge would define theism in a way that seems to recall Aquinas: God is the *ens perfectissimum* ("most perfect being") and theism is "the doctrine of an extra-mundane, personal God, the creator, preserver, and governor of the world."[14] Hodge also cites the Westminster Catechism, which gives what is "[p]robably the best definition of God ever penned by man":[15] "God is a Spirit, infinite, eternal, and unchangeable, in his being, wisdom, power, holiness, justice, goodness, and truth."

The Reformation protest: *sola scriptura; sola Christus*

Though the main focus of the Reformers was on salvation, they were also concerned to make Scripture, not what they saw as Greek philosophy, the supreme criterion for theology, including the doctrine of God.[16] It was therefore important to Luther and Calvin, as it is to contemporary evangelicals, to bring the traditional theistic descriptions of God's being and attributes into line with the biblical portrait of God as personal and covenantal.

A perfect being has properties rather than personality traits.[17] Persons, unlike things, have histories because, as agents, they say and do things. For example, in Exodus 3:14 God speaks to Moses out of the burning bush and names himself. Yet this very name – "I am that I am" – encouraged theologians to relate Yahweh to the perfect being of Greek philosophy, despite Pascal's contrast between the God of Abraham, Isaac, and Jacob and the god of the philosophers.

Several divine attributes that feature prominently in classical theism also have biblical support; take, for example, the notions that God is immaterial ("God is Spirit" [John 4:24]) and perfect ("Be ye perfect, as your heavenly Father is perfect" [Matt. 5:48]). Jesus' statement in John 5:26 ("The Father has life in himself") gives credence to the notion of divine aseity[18] and one can even find proof texts for divine immutability ("I am the Lord and I change not" [Mal. 3:6]). As for biblical passages that go against classical theism by appearing to ascribe a certain changeableness to God – "And the Lord was sorry that he had made man" (Gen. 6:6); "And the Lord regretted that he had made Saul king" (1 Sam. 15:35) – classical theists retort that such language is anthropomorphic: the change is not in God but in humanity's relation to God.

The pertinent question to ask here is methodological: is the Bible really the supreme source and authority for our doctrine of God if such passages are read through someone's idea as to what the perfect being *must* be like?[19] Luther in particular protested what he thought was Aquinas's use of Aristotelian categories as a hermeneutical framework for reading Scripture. In so doing, he anticipated what would later become a flash point for evangelical theologians: whether to explicate the biblical narrative in light of some concept of "most perfect being" or to revise the concept of perfect being even further so that it conforms to the biblical depiction of God.[20]

Luther insisted that Jesus Christ was the supreme revelation of God. He went so far as to speak of God wrapped in swaddling clothes, even of the crucified God, and to distinguish the "theology of glory" (namely, what philosophy can find out about God) from the "theology of the cross" (namely, what we can only know about God by contemplating Jesus Christ). Luther insisted that what God reveals of himself in Christ *confounds* the wisdom – especially the philosophers! – of this world. And, while Calvin affirmed a general revelation of God available apart from Jesus Christ, he too insisted that we cannot ultimately obtain true knowledge of God apart from Scripture's "spectacles of faith" and the illumination of the Holy Spirit.[21]

Early modern theism: the rise of philosophical theology and worldviews

Though the Reformers questioned the biblical pedigree of classical theism, in the end they revised rather than rejected it. In so doing, they kept focus on God as the supreme rather than the distinctively triune being. The eclipse of trinitarian theology became almost total when, in the face of rational objections to the existence of God, philosophers and theologians began to fight back with their opponents' weapons.

Where medieval theologians sought understanding, their seventeenth-century counterparts had to contend with the natural sciences, for which explanation was the desired end: "During the seventeenth and eighteenth centuries, the word 'god' came to be used, for the first time, to name the ultimate explanation of the system of the world."[22] In the context of early modern philosophy and Newtonian science, God came to be thought of in terms of "an immaterial substance, single subject, and first cause" – in short, as "a rational causative substance."[23]

The Reformers' emphasis on God's sovereign will, combined with a Newtonian mechanistic view of science, resulted in arguments over whether God's will was the efficient cause of everything that happened in the world, including the purportedly free acts of human beings. Natural scientists and theologians alike became intent "on identifying the causal order in a series of determined events."[24] God came to be seen as the efficient cause of creaturely effects – a principle of metaphysical explanation more than a person to be adored. The question with which evangelical theists were left to struggle is whether this picture of "a timeless immaterial substance, whose absolute subjectivity is the predetermining cause of all things"[25] faithfully represents the God of the gospel.

REACTING: DEFENDING (AND TWEAKING) CLASSICAL THEISM IN RESPONSE TO MODERN CHALLENGES

Evangelical theologians in the nineteenth and twentieth centuries paid relatively little attention to the doctrine of God until Friedrich Schleiermacher and his liberal progeny challenged the tradition. In the age of immanence, modern theologians constructed their doctrine of God with the mud and straw of human experience. The best rubric under which to describe North American evangelical theology during this period is not "always reforming" but "always reacting."

Saving the revelation of the sovereign God

The main issue that exercised evangelical theologians for much of the twentieth century was revelation and the knowledge of God. Schleiermacher conceded Kant's point that we cannot know God in himself, but only God as he is experienced by us. Schleiermacher, and liberals in general, viewed the Bible not as God's word but as an expression of human religious experience. Neo-orthodoxy, with its claim that God reveals *himself* (in Jesus Christ), not *information about himself*, represented yet another perceived threat to the "Scripture principle" that posited a direct identity between the human words of the Bible and the word of God.

The most significant work on God in North American evangelical theology during the latter half of the twentieth century was Carl F. H. Henry's six-volume *God, Revelation, and Authority*,[26] a response to liberal and neo-orthodox challenges to the traditional view that God reveals himself verbally and conceptually in the biblical text. Henry argued that revelation is cognitive and propositional and that the system of truth revealed in Scripture is superior, intellectually and existentially, to all other worldviews. What Henry called "biblical theism" rests on two axioms: the ontological axiom of the living God ("God exists") and the epistemological axiom of divine revelation ("God speaks and shows").

Saving the sovereignty of the revealed God

As one of its most insightful critics, Edward Farley, has demonstrated, the Scripture principle ultimately relies on the "royal metaphor," namely, the assumption that God can work his will in the world (and thus in the human words of the Bible).[27] With the Protestant exception of Karl Barth, evangelicals found themselves alone, a theological remnant, with regard to the issue of divine sovereignty. In light of the horrendous evils of the twentieth century (e.g., the Holocaust), a number of Christian theologians abandoned theism for panentheism's alternate picture of the God–world relation that emphasized divine intimacy, not supremacy.[28]

So-called "process" theologians maintain that God is not "above" the world but "alongside" it, developing his, and its, potential. God's perfection is a function not of his "apartness" but "relatedness." It is precisely because God is related to all that is that he is able to influence the world for good. Process theologians claim to have "solved" the problem of evil, at the cost of giving up the notion that God is all-powerful. God's loving will is not sovereign, but persuasive; God does not coerce or rule the world but woos it.

Evangelicals by and large have defended theism from all its competitors – atheism, Deism, and now panentheism – on the grounds that the God of infinite perfection is substantially the same as the God of Abraham, Isaac, and Jacob. Evangelical philosophers have rushed to theism's defense as well: "analytic theology" – an alliance of evangelical philosophers, philosophical theologians, and systematic theologians – continues to clarify, defend, and in some cases significantly adjust, classical theism's portrait of God as the infinitely perfect being.[29]

One area in which many evangelicals are inclined toward revision concerns God's emotions. According to the classical view, God's perfection demands that he be unable to change or be affected as we are by anything outside himself. More than a few evangelical theologians have difficulty imagining how humans can enter into a genuinely personal relation with such a being. Accordingly, they qualify divine immutability, a key plank in the classical theist platform, to mean that God is unchanging in being, character, knowledge, and purposes, but not in his relations and responses to creatures.[30]

RETHINKING: CONTEMPORARY ISSUES AND PROPOSALS

The closing years of the twentieth century saw significant changes in the evangelical doctrine of God. The fault-line between divine transcendence and immanence – and the underlying Calvinist and Arminian tectonic plates – shifted under increasing pressure from both biblical scholarship and contemporary cultural sensibilities. The result: a hybrid form of "open" theism.

Two other developments continue to pose challenges to the evangelical doctrine of God: first, the rise of religious pluralism; second, the expansion of evangelicalism to the non-Western world. Those challenges, however, may be offset by an even more significant development of great value to the long-term health of evangelical theology, namely, the recovery of Trinitarian theology.

Rereading Scripture: the "openness" of God

Much of the contemporary impetus in evangelical theology today proceeds from the desire to rethink the classical theistic picture of God as "self-contained and all-sufficient, impassible, supremely detached from the world of pain and suffering"[31] in order to reconcile it with the biblical picture of a God who loves the world supremely. However, in 1994 a group of five evangelicals put forward a new paradigm in a co-authored book entitled *The Openness of God: A Biblical Challenge to the Traditional Understanding of God.*[32]

Open theists claim that their classical counterparts subscribe to a sub-biblical view of God that is detrimental to Christian piety. Greek philosophical ideas about God's immutability have skewed the way subsequent theologians have interpreted the Bible, leading them to dismiss as anthropomorphic language about God relating and responding personally to human beings: "How long do theologians intend to permit the Hellenic-biblical synthesis to influence exegesis?"[33] Open theists want to take seriously (by which they mean literally) the biblical depiction of God's give-and-take relationship with humans. On their view, God is not an "aloof monarch" but a wise and "caring parent": "His sovereignty is not the all-determining kind, but an omnicompetent kind."[34] God grants humans real freedom to respond or to reject his initiatives; such is the cost of a *genuine* personal relationship. Indeed, "persons in loving relation" is the central rubric for open theism.[35]

Two controversial claims follow from the model of God in "genuine" (e.g., mutual and reciprocal) relation to human beings: first, God limits his knowledge of how people will use their freedom in the future (otherwise human freedom would be determined and therefore compromised); second, God's providence or care for the world, precisely because it is not deterministic but respectful of human freedom, is risky. Open theists do not deny divine omniscience and omnipotence but understand these attributes differently in light of their control belief in God's loving self-limitation. The Evangelical Theological Society in 2001 declared its own mind on the matter when it passed a resolution affirming that the Bible teaches God's exhaustive foreknowledge.[36]

Clark Pinnock, the public face and elder statesman of open theism, acknowledges that modern culture is "more congenial to dynamic thinking about God than is the Greek portrait"[37] and has allowed us to rediscover the original biblical witness.[38] Though Pinnock confesses that "God has used process thinkers"[39] to lead him to revise theism in such a way that it conforms more to the biblical model, he is careful to distinguish open from process theism.[40] The most important difference: open theists hold to "an asymmetrical view of the relationship of God and the world" whereby the world depends on God for its being but not vice versa.[41]

The conservative backlash has been nevertheless quick and fierce, ranging from caustic comments to critical, book-length commentaries.[42] The stakes, and rhetoric, were raised even higher when some critics, most of them Reformed, hinted that the underlying problem was a certain unchecked, thorough-going Arminianism in which libertarian freedom, not divine sovereignty, became the control belief and chief hermeneutical principle.[43] The waters were muddied somewhat when Pinnock was invited to give the keynote address at the 1997 annual meeting of the Wesleyan Theological Society, and by Pinnock's suggestion that the more dynamic model of God's nature was "intimated also in Wesley's thinking."[44] Still, most critics acknowledge that traditional Arminians affirm God's exhaustive foreknowledge.

Retrieving tradition: rediscovering the Trinity

The most important task of the doctrine of God is to identify the God of the gospel who has revealed himself in Jesus Christ through the Scriptures.

It is therefore surprising that the bulk of evangelical treatments have been given over to discussions of the existence, nature, and attributes of God – *that* God is and *what* God is – rather than to God's identity or *who* God is, even though Scripture itself identifies God by what he says and by what he does: "I am the Lord your God, who brought you out of the land of Egypt" (Exod. 20:2). When it comes to personal identity, actions speak louder than words, even when that word is *perfect being.*[45]

One of the most significant recent developments is the renaissance in Trinitarian theology.[46] Ironically, the doctrine's recovery owes more to Karl Barth and other non-evangelicals (e.g., Jürgen Moltmann, Karl Rahner, Robert Jenson, John Zizioulas) than to any evangelical theologian. Perhaps, in light of Barth's achievement, the outstanding story of twentieth-century evangelical theology is its benign neglect of the Trinity. Only in the closing years of the century did evangelicals begin to rediscover it.[47]

Of course, it was not as if the doctrine of the Trinity had been lost. All evangelical theology textbooks have a section on the three persons (*de Deo Trino*). Yet the Trinity was often tacked on as a kind of appendix to the doctrine of God, as it was (literally) in Schleiermacher's *The Christian Faith.*[48] These textbooks end up speaking of God's nature and attributes *without adequate focus on the way he has made himself known in Jesus Christ and the Spirit* (what Irenaeus calls the "two hands" of God). As Barth insisted, however, the only God Christians know and confess is the God who has revealed himself as Father, Son, and Spirit. The Trinity is not merely the appendix to the doctrine of God, then, but the primary and distinctive way in which Christians should think about God.

The doctrine of the Trinity is not abstract speculation but the church's response to the revelation of God in history and Scripture. We best come to know other persons not through charts that list their personality traits, properties, or vital statistics, but by listening to stories about what they have said and done or, better yet, by watching them in action. The gospel is an account of something God has said and done. Hence the key insight behind the renaissance of Trinitarian theology: God's nature must not be deduced from anything other than the narrative of his own revelatory and redemptive acts.[49]

Though the technical term "Trinity" is not explicit in Scripture, the doctrine is "so clearly implied by all that Scripture says and by the logic of the incarnation of God in Jesus Christ that it is a necessary implication of and protective concept of the Christian gospel itself."[50] Furthermore, the renaissance of Trinitarian theology affects not only the doctrine of God, but the whole of Christian theology inasmuch as it offers a framework through which to read Scripture and to understand other doctrines as well.[51]

Reforming and regrouping: from Greek concepts to global contexts

The doctrine of God may be largely informed by Greek categories, but God himself surpasses any one culture's interpretative framework. Here I can only mention two illustrations, one owing to the continuing attempt to free Christian theology from categories of the modern West, the other owing more to increasing global awareness of other religions and to evangelicalism's growth in the non-Western world.

Some evangelicals draw connections between the postmodern emphasis on community and the being of the triune God as "community" in order to advocate social Trinitarianism. Stanley Grenz then argues from God's being as communion to the conclusion that we should view human beings, made in God's image, not in terms of individual rational substances (as Aristotle and modern thinkers would have it) but in terms of interpersonal relations.[52] Miroslav Volf proposes something similar with regard to the church.[53] And LeRon Shults identifies what he calls the "turn to relationality" as a new paradigm for understanding not only divine and human personhood but the nature of reality itself.[54] As evangelicals continue coming to grips with the passing of modernity, the doctrine of the Trinity affords new resources for rethinking not only the traditional loci of systematic theology, but being itself in terms of relations rather than substances.[55]

A second point. As globalization has brought Westerners face-to-face with people from other ethnicities, traditions, and religions, the numerical center of evangelical gravity has shifted to the non-Western world. These changes pose two challenges for the doctrine of God. John Hick states the first: "Does God have many names?" Hick, like other religious pluralists, argues that all world religions are culturally conditioned responses to the same divine reality. Note that the religious pluralist goes beyond political correctness: he or she does not merely respect religious differences but smoothes them out. This way the bland generic god of moral-therapeutic Deism lies.

The challenge for evangelicals in the non-Western world is somewhat different. It concerns how to relate to a doctrine of God formulated with foreign (e.g., ancient Greek and Western) concepts far removed from the lived experience of the majority of those who inhabit the southern hemisphere today. Kwame Bediako suggests that traditional religion can do for

African Christianity what Greek philosophy has done for the West, namely, serve as "preparation" for the gospel.[56] Other evangelical African theologians, however, worry that such an approach could lead to unbiblical syncretism. Ironically, this is precisely the worry that open theists have with regard to classical theism, which is itself only a "local" (i.e., Western) theology.

Still other African evangelicals are as concerned to relate African Christianity to its catholic as to its cultural and religious heritage.[57] It is not enough to ask "how may African Christianity become more authentically African? It must also insistently be asked how African Christianity may become more authentically Christian."[58] The same humble, dialogical strategy ought to characterize every other ethnic evangelical theology as well. The way forward is to recover the *catholic* heritage of the church in *local* contexts. After all, Yahweh is no mere tribal deity, for there is but one God, the triune maker of heaven and earth.[59]

The crucial question, then, with regard to global evangelical theology, is this: will it stay Trinitarian? Will it continue to recite the Nicene creed?[60] Some may object that the creed was forged in a specific historical-cultural location, and that is true. Concepts such as *homoousios* (the Son "of the same substance" with the Father) were not mined direct from Scripture. Yet the judgment about who the Son is that underlies that Greek concept is thoroughly biblical. One hopes, then, that non-Western evangelical doctrines of God will display the same biblical judgments as those reflected in the Nicene Creed, even if the particular terms and concepts are not those of Nicea.[61]

Evangelicals can meet both of the above challenges by focusing not on the divine "what" but the divine "who." The God of the gospel is not a generic deity but has spoken and acted in concrete ways, revealing his identity in history with Israel and ultimately in the history of Jesus Christ. The way forward for global evangelicals, therefore, is to use canon-sense and catholic sensibility: for the best evangelical (e.g., gospel-centered) theology is a canonic (i.e., biblical), catholic (i.e., Trinitarian) theology.[62]

CONCLUSION: THE DIVINE COMEDY'S TRIUNE ACTOR

The major issue in theology is the identity of the God whom we worship. Worship equips us to see God, the world, and ourselves as we really are and equips us to live rightly with others before God. If the above account has a moral, it is that one must not move too hastily from the God of the gospel to culturally conditioned ideas about the most perfect being; after all, it was the core of the gospel, the cross of Christ, that led the apostle Paul to contrast the way and wisdom of God with worldly wisdom (1 Cor. 1:18–25).

God has acted; God has spoken – this is the good news. Consequently, if evangelicals are to conform their thinking to the gospel, they would do well to avoid thinking of Christianity as a philosophy or a system of morality. Christianity is first and foremost a theo-drama: an account of what God – Father, Son, and Spirit – has said and done in creation and redemption.[63] Drama highlights the importance of God as a *who* rather than a *what* and, in so doing, privileges the category of communicative action over that of impersonal causality.[64] God is a sovereign speech agent, whose Word does not return empty (Isa. 55:11) because it is efficaciously conveyed and accompanied by his Spirit.

God is the triune actor in the drama of redemption; the doctrine of God ultimately involves all that God says and does on the stage of world history. A theo-dramatic conception of God combines the best parts of the evangelical heritage – scholastic (intellectual), pietistic (heart), and activist (will) theology alike – in order to embody Christian wisdom and to demonstrate what it means to know and love God in individual and communal forms of life. Evangelicals in different cultures may formulate and "perform" the doctrine of God in different ways, each suited to their respective contexts and cultural scenes, yet the theological judgments underlying these ways are rooted in the one biblical script and the one gospel: one Lord, one faith, one baptism.[65]

The good news is that humans have not been excluded from the divine comedy but invited to join in. The people of God have important roles to play, both speaking and acting parts. The doctrine of God thus ultimately has a pastoral function: to direct believers to participate in the life and mission of God, glorifying and enjoying him for ever.[66] We can do no less for the triune God of the gospel, the Father who reaches out with both hands – Son and Spirit – in order to lift us up to himself.

Further reading

Bloesch, Donald G. *God the Almighty: Power, Wisdom, Holiness, Love.* Christian Foundations. Downers Grove, IL: InterVarsity, 1995.

Bray, Gerald. *The Doctrine of God.* Downers Grove, IL: InterVarsity, 1993.

Frame, John. *The Doctrine of God.* Phillipsburg, NJ: P. & R., 2002.

Grenz, Stanley J. *Rediscovering the Triune God: The Trinity in Contemporary Theology.* Minneapolis, MN: Fortress, 2004.

The Named God and the Question of Being: A Trinitarian Theo-Ontology. Louisville, KY: Westminster John Knox, 2005.

Kärkkäinen, Veli-Matti. *The Doctrine of God: A Global Introduction.* Grand Rapids, MI: Baker Academic, 2004.

Metzger, Paul (ed.). *Trinitarian Soundings in Systematic Theology.* Edinburgh: T. & T. Clark, 2006.

Olson, Roger E. and Christopher A. Hall. *The Trinity.* Guides to Theology. Grand Rapids, MI: Eerdmans, 2002.

Packer, J. I. *Knowing God.* Downers Grove, IL: InterVarsity, 1973.

Richards, Jay Wesley. *The Untamed God: A Philosophical Exploration of Divine Perfection, Simplicity, and Immutability.* Downers Grove, IL: InterVarsity, 2003.

Shults, F. LeRon. *Reforming the Doctrine of God.* Grand Rapids, MI: Eerdmans, 2005.

Vanhoozer, Kevin J. (ed.). *The Trinity in a Pluralistic Age: Theological Essays on Culture and Religion.* Grand Rapids, MI: Eerdmans, 1997.

Notes

1. Douglas Sweeney, *The American Evangelical Story* (Grand Rapids, MI: Baker, 2005), p. 17.
2. John Frame, *The Doctrine of God* (Phillipsburg, NJ: P. & R., 2002), p. 1.
3. David Wells, *God in the Wasteland* (Grand Rapids, MI: Eerdmans, 1994), pp. 88–117.
4. One of the best examples of an evangelical theologian who gets the head/heart balance right is J. I. Packer, *Knowing God* (Downers Grove, IL: InterVarsity, 1973).
5. Calvinist or "Reformed" theologians stress the sovereignty of God, especially with regard to God's provision for salvation: believers choose God because God first chooses us. Wesleyan-Arminian theologians, by contrast, argue that the reason God chooses some to save and not others is because they have freely chosen to believe. Both traditions acknowledge the need for God's grace, though they disagree on the particulars of its distribution.
6. Cf. Roger Olson's comment that "If evangelical theology in general has its own spin on traditional Christian belief in God, it may be an emphasis on God's personal nature" (*The Westminster Handbook to Evangelical Theology* [Louisville, KY: Westminster John Knox, 2004], p. 188).
7. David Wells, "Introduction: The Word in the World," in John H. Armstrong (ed.), *The Compromised Church* (Wheaton, IL: Crossway, 1998), p. 23.
8. Marva Dawn, *Reaching Out Without Dumbing Down: A Theology of Worship for the Turn-of-the-Century Culture* (Grand Rapids, MI: Eerdmans, 1995), p. 285.
9. See Kevin J. Vanhoozer, "Worship at the Well: From Dogmatics to Doxology (and Back Again)," *Trinity Journal* 23 (2002): 3–16.
10. The term comes from Christian Smith's *Soul Searching: The Religious and Spiritual Lives of American Teenagers* (Oxford: Oxford University Press, 2005).
11. See, for example, the standard systematic theologies of Charles Hodge, Louis Berkhof, Augustus Strong, and Millard Erickson. Even Wayne Grudem, whose theology self-consciously strives to be biblical, follows this order.

12. Several church fathers regarded Greek philosophy as a divine preparation of the gospel (see Gerald Bray, *The Doctrine of God* [Downers Grove, IL: InterVarsity, 1993], p. 30).

13. There are, of course, exceptions. Donald Bloesch argues for "a biblical theism that must be radically differentiated from classical theism" (*God the Almighty* [Downers Grove, IL: InterVarsity, 1995], p. 14).

14. Charles Hodge, *Systematic Theology*, 3 vols. (Grand Rapids, MI: Eerdmans, 1979), vol. I, p. 204.

15. *Ibid.*, p. 367.

16. What held the Reformers' interest were not questions about God's being but his will. Indeed, to some extent, Calvin reassigned the God-making properties that the medievals associated with God's nature to God's will, a move that explains his successors' preoccupation with predestination and the divine decree: that eternal, sovereign, immutable will of God.

17. Neoplatonists called God *to on* ("that which is") but Christians, knowing that God is personal, called him *ho on* ("he who is"). Paul Jewett contrasts the philosophers' abstract idea of God with evangelicals' emphasis on God's concrete, personal self-revelation (*God, Creation, and Revelation: A Neo-Evangelical Theology* [Grand Rapids, MI: Eerdmans, 1991], pp. 174–77). Whereas Greek philosophers speak of "the Absolute," Jesus and the New Testament authors cry "Abba" (Mark 14:36; Rom. 8:15; Gal. 4:6).

18. From the Latin *a se* = "from himself."

19. The issue concerns the relative priority of biblical narrative and metaphysics, that branch of philosophy concerned with the nature of ultimate reality. For a contemporary evangelical theologian who responds to classical theism by claiming to adhere consistently to *sola scriptura*, see Frame, *The Doctrine of God*, esp. pp. 7–13. In Frame's view, the Bible presents God not as perfect being but as covenant Lord.

20. Instead of seeing classical theism as a hermeneutical framework through which one interprets and orders the Bible's talk of God, some see it as an attempt to clarify the intrinsic logic of the biblical text itself. In other words, classical theism may be less like metaphysical than analytic philosophy. Alternately, one may see the attempt to employ categories of Greek thought to interpret the biblical stories as "another way of contextualizing the gospel" (Veli-Matti Kärkkäinen, *The Doctrine of God: A Global Introduction* [Grand Rapids, MI: Baker, 2004], p. 81).

21. Calvin believes the project of natural theology is rotten at the core, namely, the sinful human heart: "They do not apprehend God as he offers himself . . . but measure him by the yardstick of their own carnal stupidity [and] imagine him as they have fashioned him in their own presumption" – which is as incisive a critique of conceptual idolatry as anything postmoderns have produced! (John Calvin, *Institutes of the Christian Religion*, ed. John T. McNeill, trans. Ford Lewis Battles, Library of Christian Classics *XX* and *XXI* [Philadelphia, PA: Westminster, 1960], 1:47; order slightly amended).

22. Nicholas Lash, *Holiness, Speech and Silence: Reflections on the Question of God* (Aldershot: Ashgate, 2004), p. 9.

23. F. LeRon Shults, *Reforming the Doctrine of God* (Grand Rapids, MI: Eerdmans, 2005), p. 9.

24. *Ibid.*, p. 67.

25. *Ibid.*, p. 1.

26. Carl F. H. Henry, *God, Revelation, and Authority*, 6 vols. (Waco, TX: Word, 1976–83).

27. Edward Farley, *Ecclesial Reflection: An Anatomy of Theological Method* (Philadelphia, PA: Fortress, 1982).

28. According to panentheism, the world is in God but God is greater than the world. It follows for panentheists that God and the world exist in a relation of mutual interdependence, so much so that some suggest that the world is God's "body" while God is the "mind" of the world.

29. For an example of a contribution from analytic philosophical theology, see Jay Wesley Richards, *The Untamed God: A Philosophical Exploration of Divine Perfection, Simplicity, and Immutability* (Downers Grove, IL: InterVarsity, 2003).

30. John S. Feinberg professes himself dissatisfied with classical and process theism alike. The self-sufficient, immutable sovereign God of classical theism is "too domineering, too austere, and too remote to be at all religiously adequate" (*No One Like Him: The King Who Cares*, Foundations of Evangelical Theology [Wheaton, IL: Crossway, 2001], p. 31) yet the changing, empathetic, power-sharing (and at the limit, impotent) God of process theology is not strong enough to sustain hope that all things shall be well. Accordingly, Feinberg proposes a third model: the king who cares (p. 32). However, as J. I. Packer points out, the depiction of the God of classical theism as detached and uncaring is something of a caricature (J. J. Packer, "God the Image-Maker," in Mark A. Noll and David F. Wells (eds.), *Christian Faith and Practice in the Modern World: Theology from an Evangelical Point of View* [Grand Rapids, MI: Eerdmans, 1988], pp. 27–50).

31. Bloesch, *God the Almighty*, p. 21.

32. Clark Pinnock, et al., *The Openness of God* (Downers Grove, IL: InterVarsity, 1994).

33. Clark Pinnock, *Most Moved Mover: A Theology of God's Openness* (Grand Rapids, MI: Baker, 2001), p. 63.

34. Clark Pinnock, "God Limits His Knowledge," in David and Randall Basinger (eds.), *Predestination and Free Will: Four Views of Divine Sovereignty and Human Freedom* (Downers Grove, IL: InterVarsity, 1986), pp. 145–46.

35. Progressive evangelicals are not the only ones reluctant to throw in their theological lot with classical theism. J. I. Packer comments: "Western Christian theism as generally received today is a blend of philosophical and exegetical reasoning, the former appearing to constitute the frame into which the latter has to fit" ("God the Image-Maker," p. 33). Packer ultimately argues not for abandonment but an "*aggiornamento*" ("update") of traditional theism.

36. For an open theist perspective on divine omniscience, see Gregory Boyd, "The Open-Theism View," in James K. Beilby and Paul R. Eddy (eds.), *Divine Foreknowledge: Four Views* (Downers Grove, IL: InterVarsity, 2001), pp. 13–47, and Gregory Boyd, *God of the Possible* (Grand Rapids, MI: Baker, 2000). For an open theist perspective on divine providence, see John Sanders, *The God who Risks: A Theology of Providence* (Downers Grove, IL: InterVarsity, 1998).

37. Pinnock (ed.), *Openness of God*, p. 107.

38. Even our greater awareness of the world as "an interconnected ecosystem" helps us to imagine God's openness to the world (Pinnock [ed.], *Openness of God*, p. 112).

39. Pinnock, "Between Classical and Process Theism," in Ronald Nash (ed.), *Process Theology* (Grand Rapids, MI: Baker, 1987), p. 317.

40. See especially Pinnock, *Most Moved Mover*, pp. 140–50.

41. *Ibid.*, p. 145.

42. For example, one critic described open theism as "a dangerous trend within evangelical circles of creating God in man's image" (Norman Geisler, *Creating God in the Image of Man* [Minneapolis, MN: Bethany House, 1997], p. 11). See also John Piper, Justin Taylor, and Paul Kjoss Helseth (eds.), *Beyond the Bounds: Open Theism and the Undermining of Biblical Christianity* (Wheaton, IL: Crossway, 2003) and Millard Erickson, *What Does God Know and When Does He Know It?* (Grand Rapids, MI: Zondervan, 2003). Donald Bloesch includes an appendix critical of open theism in his *God the Almighty*, pp. 254–60.

43. See John Frame, *No Other God: A Response to Open Theism* (Phillipsburg, NJ: P. & R., 2001).

44. "Evangelical Theologians Facing the Future: Ancient and Future Paradigms," *Wesleyan Theological Journal* 33 (1998): 12–13. Barry L. Callen claims that Pinnock's relational theism represents a "Wesley-sensitive school of thought" ("From TULIP to ROSE: Clark H. Pinnock on the Open and Risking God," *Wesleyan Theological Journal* 36 [2001]: 160–86, esp. p. 160).

45. Richard Bauckham develops the notion of divine identity into a fascinating account of the deity of Jesus Christ in his *God Crucified: Monotheism and Christology in the New Testament* (Grand Rapids, MI: Eerdmans, 1998).

46. For a full account, see Stanley J. Grenz, *Rediscovering the Triune God* (Minneapolis, MN: Fortress, 2004). According to Grenz, the rebirth of Trinitarian theology is "one of the most far-reaching theological developments of the [twentieth] century" (p. 1).

47. One exception to the rule is Cornelius Van Til. It is also interesting to note that the Evangelical Theological Society decided to add belief in the triune God, along with biblical inerrancy, as the only two requirements for membership.

48. In fairness, it should be said that Western theology typically has been read as presenting the one God before turning to the three persons.

49. One of the most important identifying acts in the biblical narrative is God's self-naming. For a recent evangelical attempt to think through the relation of God's triune naming to the traditional concept of perfect being, see Stanley Grenz, *The Named God and the Question of Being: A Trinitarian Theo-Ontology* (Louisville, KY: Westminster John Knox, 2005), esp. ch. 8.

50. Roger Olson and Christopher Hall, *The Trinity* (Grand Rapids, MI: Eerdmans, 2002), p. 2.

51. This, at least, is the premise behind the essays in Paul Metzger (ed.), *Trinitarian Soundings in Systematic Theology* (Edinburgh: T. & T. Clark, 2006).

52. Stanley Grenz, *The Social God and the Relational Self* (Louisville, KY: Westminster John Knox, 2001). Other evangelicals, however, worry that the social analogy leads to tritheism, the heretical belief in three gods.

53. Miroslav Volf, *After Our Likeness: The Church as the Image of the Trinity* (Grand Rapids, MI: Eerdmans, 1998).
54. Shults, *Reforming the Doctrine of God.*
55. There is a possibility that theologians espousing this new conceptuality have simply exchanged masters; "relationality" may simply be the new "substance"! Paul Molnar cautions against allowing some principle other than God to define the meaning of relationality. See *Divine Freedom and the Doctrine of the Immanent Trinity* (Edinburgh: T. & T. Clark, 2002), pp. 126–46.
56. See Kwame Bediako, *Theology and Identity: The Impact of Culture upon Christian Thought in the Second Century and in Modern Africa* (Oxford: Regnum, 1992).
57. See Tite Tiénou, *The Theological Task of the Church in Africa*, 2nd edition (Achimota, Ghana: Africa Christian Press, 1996).
58. Paul Bowers, "African Theology," *Africa Journal of Evangelical Theology* 21 (2002): p. 123.
59. See also Aida Besançon Spencer and William David Spencer (eds.), *The Global God: Multicultural Evangelical Views of God* (Grand Rapids, MI: Baker, 1998), which argues that churches in every culture have something to contribute to the church's knowledge of the one God.
60. Gerald Bray rightly stresses the importance of the Trinity in any future evangelical doctrine of God (*Doctrine of God*, pp. 246–51).
61. For the distinction between judgments and concepts, see David Yeago, "The New Testament and the Nicene Dogma," in Stephen Fowl (ed.), *The Theological Interpretation of Scripture* (Oxford: Blackwell, 1997), pp. 87–100.
62. For a further development of this proposal, see my "'One Rule to Rule them All?' Theological Method in an Era of World Christianity," in Craig Ott and Harold Netland (eds.), *Globalizing Theology: Christian Belief and Practice in an Era of World Christianity* (Grand Rapids, MI: Baker, 2006).
63. See Michael Horton, *Covenant and Eschatology: The Divine Drama* (Louisville, KY: Westminster John Knox, 2002).
64. Kevin J. Vanhoozer, *First Theology* (Downers Grove, IL: InterVarsity, 2002), ch. 4.
65. See Kevin J. Vanhoozer, *The Drama of Doctrine* (Louisville, KY: Westminster John Knox, 2005).
66. Cf. Paul Fiddes, *Participating in God: A Pastoral Doctrine of the Trinity* (Louisville, KY: Westminster John Knox, 2000) and Packer's citation of a Puritan (John Perkins) who defines theology as "the science of living blessedly forever" ("God the Image-Maker," p. 28).

3 Scripture and hermeneutics

DANIEL J. TREIER

Evangelicals understand themselves as confessionally orthodox Protestants oriented to piety that is personal. Therefore they claim to embrace not only the Trinitarian and Christ-centered biblical doctrine expressed in the Nicene Creed, but also the basic understanding of Scripture's authority that was held by the church fathers – in a Protestant way.

The Eastern Orthodox churches respect the authority of Scripture as a (foundational) subset of the church's great Tradition; the Roman Catholic communion respects Scripture as the ultimate written source of God's Revelation in Jesus Christ, but grants to Tradition (via the magisterial teaching office of the church) a decisive role in its interpretation.[1] The Protestant distinctive of *sola scriptura*, "Scripture alone," rejects the "coincidence" and "supplementary" views of Tradition's relation to Scripture in favor of an "ancillary" view:[2] contrary to popular misconceptions of *nuda scriptura*, tradition plays a vital role when understanding God's revelation via Scripture, but the role is "ministerial" rather than magisterial.[3] Scripture is the final authority over, but not the sole source of, Christian belief and practice. Evangelicals have used underlying concepts from the Protestant Reformation to support this theological sufficiency: "the priesthood of all believers" and "the clarity of Scripture." The former suggests not that individual Christians may use the Bible apart from other teachers, as if they were alone with God on an island, but that with the "due use of ordinary means"[4] they can understand Scripture's basic message centered on the gospel of Jesus Christ. The latter then suggests not only that this basic message is clear, but also that it can be used to interpret more difficult details in particular biblical passages; in fact, by this "analogy of faith" and "analogy of Scripture," clearer biblical texts can enlighten others on any given difficulty, at least setting interpretative boundaries.

That these doctrines, while liable to misuse (perhaps especially in the individualistic context of Western democratic ideals), do not neglect or reject the churchly context of biblical interpretation is clear in the early

Protestants: they strongly supported and undertook catechesis of their church members, while opposing anti-ecclesiastical forms of "enthusiasm"; they were only providing the clear scriptural message to believer-priests via translations in the first place – which already involved interpretation by church teachers – and they did so for personal reading but not for public interpretation or instruction.

Nevertheless, evangelical identity regarding the authority of Scripture has a history since the early days of Protestantism. This history introduces two other qualifiers or contrasts. First, evangelicals are oriented to piety that is personal. Their heritage stems not merely from those who opposed Orthodox and Catholic clericalism or hierarchy, but also from those who sought renewal of what they judged to be dead or dying Protestant state churches later on. Evangelicals hear and read the Bible for application and guidance not just doctrine, at home as well as in church – expecting to encounter the living God when doing so. Second, evangelicals are confessionally orthodox, rejecting "liberal" theologies and anti-supernaturalist approaches to the Bible. Accordingly, they view themselves – whether in free-standing churches or inside mainline denominations working for renewal – as the true heirs of the Protestant Reformation. The spread of Christianity within the global South admittedly complicates this picture, with shades of gray concerning how closely some "evangelicals" think they dwell to the classic Protestant "house of authority."[5] Moreover, questions about the viability of such an intellectual foundation within the Western academy, coupled with ever-increasing theological vitality and internal variability, make evangelicalism a very shadowy figure indeed. Nevertheless, we can still trace the outlines of an "evangelical" approach to Scripture around three major points: two themes regarding the nature of the Bible, and then (ideally productive) tension regarding the nature of its interpretation.

SCRIPTURE'S INSPIRATION

Evangelicals take seriously the Bible's own testimony to its nature.[6] Besides the view of Jesus himself, the most central passage is 2 Timothy 3:16–17: "All scripture is inspired by God and is useful for teaching, for reproof, for correction, and for training in righteousness, so that everyone who belongs to God may be proficient, equipped for every good work" (NRSV). Biblical inspiration is not a matter of romantic or ecstatic genius, a genus of the species enjoyed by artists. Rather, the term *theopneustos* has also been rendered recently as "God-breathed" (NIV). Sacred writings come, as it were, from God's mouth as divine speech and, lest this category of "Scripture" be limited to 2 Timothy's direct reference – roughly the Old Testament – 2 Peter 3:16 demonstrates its possible extension to writings included in the New Testament. Speaking in Scripture,[7] God makes us wise for salvation in Christ Jesus (2 Tim. 3:15) and for sanctification resulting in good works (2 Tim. 3:16–17).

Evangelicals accept the Protestant "canon" that collects the thirty-nine books known traditionally as the Old Testament together with the twenty-seven books known traditionally as the New Testament. They continue to reject the "Apocrypha" accepted by Roman Catholics, although popularly they perhaps neglect the legitimate value of these books more than they should. For the books listed as Scripture to be "canonical" means that as one book (the "Bible") they rule over Christian belief and practice.

It is important to note that evangelicals recognize the Bible as God's Word in a particular way. Scripture itself identifies God's Son Jesus Christ as the final, ultimate divine Word or speech (Heb. 1:1–3) – the Logos who reveals God the Father (John 1:1–18). Because this revelation makes truth claims with cognitive content, it is "propositional." Against the so-called "neo-orthodox" theologians who described revelation in "personal" or otherwise non-propositional terms, American evangelicals sometimes vociferously emphasized its propositional character during the middle of the twentieth century. At the dawn of the twenty-first, evangelicals realize that Scripture being God's Word in written form means it bears corresponding witness to the incarnate Logos and in another sense becomes God's contemporary speech dynamically through the power of the Holy Spirit.[8] The propositional aspect of revelation conveys its central message personally, and these are not mutually exclusive.

For evangelicals, the inspiration of Scripture is often understood as "verbal" and "plenary." It is verbal because the words of the Bible themselves "count as,"[9] indeed are, God's speech. Of course the words are not magical in isolation from each other, but convey a message together. Yet, on the other hand, it is not some idealized message that can be abstracted from the Bible, to the neglect of certain particular words within Scripture, which becomes authoritative. Understanding God's speech requires attending to the details of how every word does, or does not, distinctively help to communicate the message of divine revelation; inspiration is plenary because it extends fully to using all the words.

More qualifications are of course in order. While it is fair to say that evangelicals take an oracular view of the Bible as Scripture, this is true only in the sense that they view its authoritative message in terms of the model of divine speech. Consistently (though with some aberrations in popular practice), evangelicals reject a "dictation" theory of inspiration, in which God simply and directly communicates every word of the Bible without reference to human authorship, as if the writers were nothing more than impersonal divine pens. Evangelicals affirm the importance of Scripture's human authors: God communicates through their investigation and structuring of material (e.g., Luke 1:1–4); linguistic styles (e.g., compare Mark and Hebrews); personalities and histories (e.g., psalms, apocalypses, and prophetic writings); and so on. For many, an analogy between the "living Word" Jesus Christ and the written Word is helpful: the Son of God was fully God yet embraced full humanity; so also the Bible's fully divine revelation is spoken by fully embracing human forms of communication.

SCRIPTURE'S INFALLIBILITY . . . AND INERRANCY?

The comprehensiveness of the Bible's inspiration, or perhaps its significance in light of Scripture's humanity, became a matter of intra-evangelical debate, late in the 1800s and then again in the middle of the twentieth century. "Infallible" had been a Protestant characterization of Scripture for some time. The Word of God does not return void but accomplishes its divine purposes (Isa. 55:11). Of course, this had been noteworthy as a characterization exclusive to Scripture, in comparison with Roman Catholic ascription of infallibility also to the Pope, which became official at Vatican Council I in 1870.[10]

With the rise of so-called "higher" biblical criticism and various theological accommodations to culture, "Modernism" infiltrated Protestant denominations with the tendency to reject supernatural claims and thus orthodox Christian teaching. The controversy gave rise to the reaction of "fundamentalism," which at first simply designated those who reaffirmed belief in the fundamentals of biblical Christianity rather than reinterpreting them. Labels aside, theologians at Princeton Seminary defended the Bible as without error and, in the face of scholarly ideals from the new German universities, further developed an understanding of theology as an inductive science that arranged biblical facts. Hardly naive or obscurantist, they interacted with the natural sciences quite openly; contrary to caricature, for example, at least one of them was open to Darwinian evolutionary theory as being compatible with Scripture.[11]

From these roots many conservative Protestants became committed to the Bible's "inerrancy," which continued as the self-understanding of new "evangelicals" such as Carl F. H. Henry when, in the 1940s, they revived that label in an effort to reinvigorate and redirect fundamentalism. Controversy ensued in the early 1960s, however, when the flagship evangelical seminary, Fuller, revised its doctrinal statement to be open to limited inerrancy – Scripture is infallible on matters of faith and practice, but might be in error concerning details of history, science, and the like. Karl Barth was influential: while "neo-orthodox" may be an unfair label, Barth's position was not the traditional one. He saw the Bible as indirectly the Word of God, a witness to God's Revelation, Jesus Christ, which only becomes the Word of God in events of personal encounter via the Holy Spirit.[12] Thus the Bible in its humanity might err, yet God was inextricably bound to Scripture as the form of divine witness to Revelation. In the 1970s, as the "battle for the Bible" intensified, Jack Rogers of Fuller and Donald McKim asserted that a form of this limited inerrancy, or infallibility without inerrancy, position was in fact the closest contemporary heir of traditional Protestantism.[13] John Woodbridge of Trinity Evangelical Divinity School (revitalized in the 1960s as an academically rigorous, inerrantist alternative to Fuller) responded with a strong historical rejection of their work:[14] while biblical inerrancy was undoubtedly modern language responding to historical-critical controversies, it seemed to perpetuate commitments expressed by ancient and Protestant fathers. Meanwhile, the International Council on Biblical Inerrancy produced the "Chicago Statement" that defined this aspect of the doctrine of Scripture for many American evangelicals over the ensuing decades.[15]

The inerrancy of Scripture means "that when all the facts become known, they will demonstrate that the Bible in its original autographs and correctly interpreted is entirely true and never false in all it affirms, whether that relates to doctrine or ethics or to the social, physical, or life sciences."[16] Most would say that inerrancy does not require the Bible to speak with scientific precision and technical vocabulary; to have equal relevance for today in all portions; to contain verbatim quotation of the Old Testament in the New or literalist agreement between parallel accounts of events; or to lack unclear passages, the recording of sinful acts or errant claims, quotations from non-inspired authors, or historical investigation and perspective.[17] The inerrancy of the Bible certainly does not extend to interpretations of Scripture, and therefore does not imply that evangelicals will presently know all the answers to challenging historical-critical questions. But biblical inerrancy does entail that there can finally be no outright internal contradictions in Scripture's teaching (when rightly interpreted in canonical context), and no external contradictions between Scripture and genuine science or other forms of human knowledge (often associated with the concept of "general revelation," as opposed to "special revelation" via Jesus Christ, the Bible, and so on). Thus, "context, context, context" becomes the hermeneutically paramount rule for implementing commitment to biblical inerrancy in interpretative practice; special attention must be paid to the diverse ways that literary genres relate to truth claims.

Conflict over scriptural inerrancy has not defined evangelicalism elsewhere as it did in the United States.[18] British and other non-American evangelicals, for example, have held various other versions of a "high" view of Scripture.[19] Even among Americans, some Reformed Christians have retained the classic Protestant language of biblical infallibility without taking a more specific position. Some non-Reformed Christians have rejected much of the controversy as a fixation on epistemology to the detriment of more holistic concerns in theological methodology and beyond. Many recent evangelicals have felt the need to distinguish carefully between a particular philosophical understanding of rationality or approach to apologetics using the Bible, and commitment to the trustworthiness of Scripture itself.

If, confessing Scripture's inspiration, one holds to a fairly direct relation between the Bible and the revealed Word of God, then a viewpoint approximating biblical inerrancy follows as a matter of course. God speaks truly. The question concerns whether the focus of Scripture's purpose – which clearly concerns faith and practice according to 2 Timothy 3:16–17, among other passages – exempts certain aspects or affirmations of the Bible from truly being the Word of God in the sense implied by verbal, plenary inspiration. Or instead, as inerrantists claim, should Scripture's saving and sanctifying purpose focus our interpretative efforts on finding what the Bible as God's Word truly means?

BIBLICAL INTERPRETATION AND THE SPIRIT'S ILLUMINATION

Indeed, stories of evangelical biblical interpretation range from the awe-inspiring to the absurd. While the aberrations of some biblical inerrantists[20] have given way to the steady increase of competent and even influential biblical scholarship by various evangelicals, there is still progress to make. Following up the Chicago Statement, the International Council on Biblical Hermeneutics of the 1980s was not very successful, and trickle-down effects from scholarship to the pews – and pulpits – have been modest. At worst, evangelicals must confess popular weaknesses such as the influence of the apocalyptic *Left Behind* novels; at best, they can claim the creative and academically influential work of scholars such as N. T. Wright, as well as the theological scholarship of non-Western Christians. In between, they can claim a long heritage of faithful saints who have loved to learn and live out basic biblical teaching.

Probably the chief evangelical tension over biblical hermeneutics concerns the contemporary work of the Holy Spirit in the reader(s), relative to Scripture's communication as written text(s). To what extent is the latter fixed by the Holy Spirit's already-completed witness to God's final Word having been spoken in Jesus Christ? That is, how do the implications of the Bible's inspiration set parameters for the Holy Spirit's work of "illumination"? Practical questions follow from this doctrinal tension. Do biblical scholars seemingly aspire to function as a Protestant papacy or magisterium, ruling on acceptable versus unacceptable uses of Scripture to the exclusion of "the priesthood of all believers"? Do such scholars and perhaps trained clergy (who have been to "cemetery," as seminaries are sometimes called) often eclipse the spiritual power of the biblical text in their own lives and for others, by dogmatically insisting on the "scientific" pursuit of Scripture's single "meaning" to restrain lay people in practice? For, since the rise of evangelical biblical scholars in recent decades, their dominant hermeneutical approach (in the West) has typically followed E. D. Hirsch, Jr.:[21] re-describing the author's intention is the initial goal of valid interpretation, gaining understanding of the text's meaning. This must be distinguished from, and determinative for, the many possible applications, or "significance," of the text. If this distinction is not observed – if the Spirit's illumination can continually grant new cognitive insight into a text's meaning – then can biblical interpretation be public or shareable or even reliable? Any individual could idiosyncratically claim the Spirit's leading for interpretations of Scripture that are private (at best), or even dangerous and dishonoring to the gospel (at worst). Democracy means disunity.

This tension relates to doctrinal trends more generally. Increasing emphasis upon the diversity of biblical material, especially its literary genres, has resulted in recognition of different models for Scripture's authority within the texts themselves.[22] Address to God in the second-person, such as in the Psalms, functions differently than omniscient narrative that may describe God in the third-person, which is different still from the oracular model of God as first-person speaker in the

Prophets. Using the oracular model simplistically for all Scripture, flattening its variety into one model of translating propositional revelation into theological concepts, does injustice to the "whole counsel" of divine speech and, ironically, to the evangelical conviction regarding Scripture's unity.[23]

Moreover, contemporary theologians have felt the need to emphasize more the Holy Spirit and the present relative to the Logos and the past, when constructing a doctrine of revelation. This trend suggests a less narrow focus on Scripture's authority, as statically construed around its subject matter or cognitive content, with more emphasis on its "functioning" dynamically by the Holy Spirit to sanctify readers and shape communal identity.[24] The work of David Kelsey is particularly challenging for evangelicals regarding the variety – legitimate and illegitimate – of theologians' actual practices in appealing to the Bible.[25] Accordingly, whereas traditional evangelical theologies tended to place the doctrine of Scripture at the front, among "prolegomena" or introductory words justifying the task of theology along the lines of a scientific methodology, recently Stanley Grenz has placed the doctrine toward the end, under the community-forming work of the Holy Spirit.[26] Such a move is consistent with the third article of the Nicene Creed.

More generally, evangelicals today are beginning to profit from greater attention to Trinitarian theology. Efforts to locate understanding of Scripture "in the economy of salvation"[27] and with respect to "sanctification" as the work of the triune God will pay dividends in more balanced understandings of "revelation" and "inspiration,"[28] even as such older formulations are also being defended and revitalized.[29] Often in these discussions, evangelicals are interacting with, and substantially contributing to, more general philosophical and literary hermeneutics at the same time.[30] Yet they are doing so while making more consistent use of the resources within Trinitarian thought, partly at the instigation of Barth, rather than defensively borrowing from outside the Christian faith.[31]

Evangelical reasons for giving increased attention to the Holy Spirit's illumination, then, sometimes appear "postmodern," recognizing the inescapable and important role of interpretative communities or perhaps realizing that such generalities describe what was already true of evangelical piety in the first place.[32] More doctrinally, the concern is one of balance in Trinitarian theology. However, evangelicals will not be able to agree in detail on the relationship of Word and Spirit. For evangelicalism is a form of ecumenical Protestantism, within which specific doctrinal traditions (or even communities undefined by formal theology) differ on precisely that point.

Moreover, an underlying and increasing cause of evangelical diversity and hermeneutical tension could be framed either in terms of culture or ethics. Two cases of this deserve mention. First, evangelicals realize acutely their failure in America, and as Protestants generally despite the legacy of William Wilberforce, to recognize the evil of slavery while they held cultural power. That is putting it mildly: indeed, many evangelicals argued from the Bible to justify slavery and racial division.[33] Contemporary Western "culture wars," then, especially regarding gender roles and sexual practices seem to present a case that could be analogous in some way.[34] Often the issue is framed in terms of either fidelity to the inspired words of the Bible (labeled by opponents a "static" hermeneutic), or a "redemptive movement" approach that follows the "trajectory" of the "spirit" of the text – away from its apparent toleration or tacit endorsement of an unjust structure (slavery or patriarchy) and toward an "ideal" or "ultimate ethic" based on broader biblical principles.[35] The latter approach is labeled by opponents as "liberal" or unfaithful to the text itself.

These are the hermeneutical debates of evangelicals in the West, especially North America, and indeed they affect the lives and vocations of real people. But a second and more significant reality is the rise and spread of global Christianity. Well chronicled by Philip Jenkins and Andrew Walls among others, this expansion of communities with connections to "evangelicals" will have theological implications for their ecclesiastical culture. It is symptomatic of the current situation, however, that most sources cited in this essay are Western and even American. Partly that is due to the present author's limitations. Yet research coupled with help from colleagues in the World Evangelical Alliance theological list-serv did unearth some other resources. Much of the non-Western evangelical literature on Scripture, though, is not translated into English, is unavailable for ready Western distribution, or else it has not been definitive for the "evangelical" identity treated in academic theology. However, that situatedness in part begs the question of what a globally evangelical approach to Scripture and hermeneutics could or should be. For, indeed, the Western evangelical literature on Scripture, despite all its biblical sophistication, is also the product of a very local and particular set of conversational interests, as is the set of biblical passages on which Westerners typically focus. Yet those with the cultural power to define "evangelical" theology often have not been very attentive to these realities.

A fairly early example of global evangelical engagement with hermeneutical issues comes from the Context and Hermeneutics in the Americas Conference, which was sponsored by the Theological Students Fellowship and the Latin American Theological Fraternity in Mexico in 1983. Occurring partly in response to liberation theology's influence, its proceedings demonstrate the possibility of genuinely global conversation engaging hermeneutics via doctrine, biblical case studies, and practical theological issues.[36] The World Evangelical Alliance has also fostered such dialogues on a variety of questions. Of recent hermeneutical import is the report of a working group on "The Interpretation of Scripture as the Word of God in the Plurality of Cultures and Church." As part of its affirmations in addition to the doctrine of Scripture, the report calls evangelicals to the "task of dynamic contextualization (or inculturation) of the message of the Bible," before detailing under various headings the cultural challenges pointed out here.[37]

"Contextualization" has become a fairly popular way for evangelicals to describe their theological encounter with Scripture in culture(s), consistent with their persistent commitment to Bible translation. The translation/contextualization model has undeniable virtues; perhaps most appealing is its consistency with a traditional doctrine of Scripture since it suggests something fixed or stable (the "timeless truth" of the Bible's meaning) and something variable upon reception (application or cultural significance and its effect even on linguistic form). Nevertheless, this model also maintains an undeniable power differential that can favor the status quo of the "translator."[38] That may be simply one instance of a broader phenomenon about which non-Western evangelicals rightly complain: appeals to hermeneutical theory, even in dealing with questions of culture, have been socially conservative, not sufficiently challenging to open the eyes of Western Christians regarding questions of justice. Only such global concern brings an adequate range of alternative possibilities for reading Scripture into view.[39]

Somewhat ironically, then, our hermeneutical tour of culture brings us back to the horizon of tradition. Global evangelicals along with some Western theologians have renewed interest in pre-critical, spiritual practices of reading Scripture[40] and in the hermeneutical role of the ancient Christian creeds. Certainly evangelicalism needs to improve its historical rootedness in the very orthodoxy (with attendant priority upon the church) that it claims to maintain for Protestants. An especially important classical retrieval may be the role of oral/aural culture, whereby some non-Western cultures today are much closer to the biblical audiences and to traditional church practices than are "literate" and image-saturated Westerners.[41] Besides classic practices and confessional beliefs, other "traditions," such as evangelicalism's approach to Scripture, have an appropriately foundational status for many of its Western institutions. Taken too far, though, such traditions can occlude openness to the illumination of the Spirit taking place via engagement with Scripture on the part of all global Christians. Thus, increased attention to the work of the Spirit in and through the Word of God does not settle hermeneutical concerns but newly crystallizes their form: the relative importance of corporate institutions and traditions vis-à-vis individual or cultural illumination, and how these affect evangelical understanding of God's authoritative teaching in the Bible.

No conclusion could predict the future on this subject; at best, one can point fingers in promising directions. Evangelicals will have to work out the hermeneutical implications of their existing commitments dialogically,[42] by careful listening to Scripture and to each other. Careful listening to Scripture requires paying attention to how the Bible itself addresses the relation of letter and Spirit, perhaps especially in the New Testament's use of the Old.[43] Careful listening to each other suggests we need a theme for theological authority that addresses community generally and globally along with cultural density specifically. Various themes are possible that could orient this conversation to shared resources in Scripture, but "wisdom" may be particularly suggestive. Not only is it highlighted in the context of 2 Timothy 3 (v. 15); it embraces the dynamics of Word and Spirit, institution and illumination, plus corporate and individual. Furthermore, wisdom also holds together tradition and time, as well as creation and redemption.[44] Ultimately, wisdom is found in Jesus Christ (e.g., Col. 2:3), and gives hope by reemphasizing that God's action precedes and undergirds our own. As evangelicals seek to fulfill the promise of their heritage to engage fully the world God has made and redeemed, they need wisdom to hear God and others ever more faithfully.

Further reading

Bacote, Vincent E., Laura C. Miguélez, and Dennis L. Okholm (eds.). *Evangelicals and Scripture: Tradition, Authority and Hermeneutics.* Downers Grove, IL: InterVarsity, 2004.

Carson, D. A., and John D. Woodbridge (eds.). *Scripture and Truth.* Grand Rapids, MI: Baker, 1992.

Hermeneutics, Authority and Canon. Reprint. Grand Rapids, MI: Baker, 1995.

Goldingay, John. *Models for Scripture.* Grand Rapids, MI: Eerdmans, 1994.

Henry, Carl F. H. *God, Revelation, and Authority.* Waco, TX: Word, 1976–83.

Noll, Mark A. *Between Faith and Criticism: Evangelicals, Scholarship, and the Bible in America.* New York: Harper and Row, 1986.

Packer, J. I. *God Has Spoken: Revelation and the Bible.* 3rd edition. Grand Rapids, MI: Baker, 1994.

Stackhouse, John G., Jr. (ed.). *Evangelical Futures: A Conversation on Theological Method*. Grand Rapids, MI: Baker, 2000.

Vanhoozer, Kevin J. *The Drama of Doctrine: A Canonical-Linguistic Approach to Theology*. Louisville, KY: Westminster John Knox, 2005.

Work, Telford. *Living and Active: Scripture in the Economy of Salvation*. Sacra Doctrina. Grand Rapids, MI: Eerdmans, 2002.

Wright, N. T. *The Last Word: Beyond the Bible Wars to a New Understanding of the Authority of Scripture*. San Francisco: Harper, 2005.

Notes

1. It has become common to suggest that in the 1960s the Second Vatican Council introduced a shift from a two-source theory of Scripture and Tradition (in which Tradition could be a somewhat independent source of doctrine or practice) to an interpretation of the Council of Trent that made a one-source theory possible (in which Tradition's authority is subordinate to Scripture, as its interpreter, from which no doctrine can be undergirded independently). See, e.g., Charles Colson and Richard John Neuhaus (eds.), *Your Word is Truth: A Project of Evangelicals and Catholics Together* (Grand Rapids, MI: Eerdmans, 2002), especially the essays by Timothy George and Avery Cardinal Dulles, S. J. See also *Catechism of the Catholic Church*, 2nd edition (Washington, DC: United States Catholic Conference, 1997), pp. 26–27, esp. paras. 80–83.

2. Anthony N. S. Lane, "Tradition," in Kevin J. Vanhoozer (gen. ed.), *Dictionary for Theological Interpretation of the Bible* (Craig G. Bartholomew, Daniel J. Treier, N. T. Wright, assoc. eds.; Grand Rapids, MI: Baker Academic, and London: SPCK, 2005), pp. 809–12.

3. See Kevin J. Vanhoozer, "Scripture and Tradition," in Kevin J. Vanhoozer (ed.), *Cambridge Companion to Postmodern Theology* (Cambridge: Cambridge University Press, 2003), p. 168. Henri Blocher suggests a few factors that lead evangelical Protestants to this position: "*assessment of the effects of human sinfulness*"; "emphasis on *divine transcendence*"; a "*view of time*" emphasizing particular events more than "continuous flow"; and, ultimately, "the very *understanding of salvation*" as focused on the problem of guilt rather than the change of human nature ("Scripture and Tradition: An Evangelical Response," *Evangelical Review of Theology* 21. 2 [April 1997]: 121–27, pp. 125–26). See also the theme issue "Scripture and Tradition," *Evangelical Review of Theology* 19. 2 (April 1995).

4. The Westminster Confession of Faith, ch. I, para. VII.

5. The phrase is Edward Farley's, from *Ecclesial Reflection: An Anatomy of Theological Method* (Philadelphia, PA: Fortress, 1982).

6. As evident perhaps especially in D. A. Carson and John D. Woodbridge (eds.), *Scripture and Truth* (Grand Rapids, MI: Baker, 1992); *Hermeneutics, Authority and Canon*, reprint (Grand Rapids, MI: Baker, 1995); J. I. Packer, *God Has Spoken: Revelation and the Bible*, 3rd edition (Grand Rapids, MI: Baker, 1994).

7. The Westminster Confession of Faith speaks of "the Holy Spirit speaking in the Scripture" (ch. I, para. X).

8. Kevin J. Vanhoozer, "God's Mighty Speech-Acts: The Doctrine of Scripture Today," in Philip E. Satterthwaite and David F. Wright (eds.), *A Pathway into the Holy Scripture* (Grand Rapids, MI: Eerdmans, 1994), pp. 143–81.

9. Following the recent use of speech-act theory by many, including Nicholas Wolterstorff, *Divine Discourse: Philosophical Reflections on the Claim that God Speaks* (Cambridge: Cambridge University Press, 1995), as one philosophical explanation of how this could be so.

10. This applies when the Pope speaks *ex cathedra*, from his representative throne making a definitive pronouncement on faith or morals for the whole church – which has only happened twice since.

11. So B. B. Warfield, according to Mark A. Noll, *Between Faith and Criticism: Evangelicals, Scholarship, and the Bible in America* (New York: Harper and Row, 1986), p. 38. See B. B. Warfield, *Evolution, Scripture, and Science: Selected Writings*, ed. with an introduction by Mark A. Noll and David N. Livingstone (Grand Rapids, MI: Baker, 2000).

12. For a more recent understanding, with nuance, of Barth's position vis-à-vis the evangelical view, see Bruce McCormack, "The Being of Holy Scripture Is in Becoming: Karl Barth in Conversation with American Evangelical Criticism," in Vincent E. Bacote, Laura C. Miguélez, and Dennis L. Okholm (eds.), *Evangelicals and Scripture: Tradition, Authority and Hermeneutics* (Downers Grove, IL: InterVarsity, 2004), pp. 55–75. An evangelical who has appropriated Barth significantly is Donald G. Bloesch; see esp. *Holy Scripture: Revelation, Inspiration and Interpretation*, Christian Foundations 2 (Downers Grove, IL: InterVarsity, 1994).

13. Harold Lindsell, *The Battle for the Bible* (Grand Rapids, MI: Zondervan, 1976); Jack B. Rogers and Donald K. McKim, *The Authority and Interpretation of the Bible: An Historical Approach* (San Francisco: Harper and Row, 1979).

14. John Woodbridge, *Biblical Authority: A Critique of the Rogers/McKim Proposal* (Grand Rapids, MI: Zondervan, 1982).

15. The Evangelical Theological Society and many other institutions use "Chicago" officially or unofficially to guide their confessional understanding.

16. Paul D. Feinberg, "Bible, Inerrancy and Infallibility of," in Walter A. Elwell (ed.), *Evangelical Dictionary of Theology*, 2nd edition (Grand Rapids, MI: Baker, 2001), p. 156.

17. This list was influenced by Carl B. Hoch, Jr.

18. A survey of evangelical doctrinal statements confirms the variety described in this paragraph. The National Association of Evangelicals (American) begins, "We believe the Bible to be the inspired, the only infallible, authoritative Word of God" (see www.nae.net). The World Evangelical Alliance likewise begins with a statement on the Holy Scriptures, "as originally given by God, divinely inspired, infallible, entirely trustworthy; and the supreme authority in all matters of faith and conduct" (see www.worldevangelical.org). The global Lausanne Covenant (1974) is more detailed, but deals with the Bible after an article on God: "We affirm the divine inspiration, truthfulness and authority of both Old and New Testament Scriptures in their entirety as the only written Word of God, without error in all that it affirms, and the only infallible rule of faith and practice" (at www.lausanne.org).

19. The British branch of the International Fellowship of Evangelical Students (the InterVarsity movement) makes the following statement on Scripture: "The Bible, as originally given, is the inspired and infallible Word of God. It is the supreme authority in all matters of belief and behaviour" (at www.uccf.org.uk).

20. A notable example was the idea that the time markers of the Gospels must be understood with literal precision, and since they apparently conflicted, Peter must have denied Jesus six times rather than three (e.g., Lindsell, *Battle for the Bible*, pp. 174–76).

21. E. D. Hirsch, Jr., *Validity in Interpretation* (New Haven, CT: Yale University Press, 1967).

22. John Goldingay, *Models for Scripture* (Grand Rapids, MI: Eerdmans, 1994); *Models for Interpretation of Scripture* (Grand Rapids, MI: Eerdmans, 1995).

23. For further discussion and sources, see Daniel J. Treier, "Canonical Unity and Commensurable Language: On Divine Action and Doctrine," in Bacote, Miguélez, and Okholm (eds.), *Evangelicals and Scripture*, pp. 211–28; "Scripture, Unity of," in *Dictionary for Theological Interpretation of the Bible*, pp. 731–34.

24. Again, for further discussion and sources, see Daniel J. Treier, "Theological Hermeneutics, Contemporary," in Vanhoozer (gen. ed.), *Dictionary for Theological Interpretation of the Bible*, pp. 787–93; *Virtue and the Voice of God: Toward Theology as Wisdom* (Grand Rapids, MI: Eerdmans, 2006), esp. ch. 7.

25. See David H. Kelsey, *The Uses of Scripture in Recent Theology* (Philadelphia: Fortress, 1975), reissued as *Proving Doctrine* (Harrisburg, PA: Trinity Press International, 1999); the responses in Robert K. Johnston (ed.), *The Use of the Bible in Theology: Evangelical Options* (Atlanta, GA: John Knox, 1985) are only partially satisfying. Most recently, see Kevin J. Vanhoozer, *The Drama of Doctrine: A Canonical-Linguistic Approach to Theology* (Louisville, KY: Westminster John Knox, 2005).

26. Stanley Grenz, *Theology and the Community of God* (Nashville, TN: Broadman and Holman, 1994); for his recent methodological statements, see Stanley J. Grenz and John R. Franke, *Beyond Foundationalism: Shaping Theology in a Postmodern Context* (Louisville, KY: Westminster John Knox, 2001).

27. Telford Work, *Living and Active: Scripture in the Economy of Salvation*, Sacra Doctrina (Grand Rapids, MI: Eerdmans, 2002). See also the earlier Richard Lints, *The Fabric of Theology: A Prolegomenon to Evangelical Theology* (Grand Rapids, MI: Eerdmans, 1993), and, popularly, N. T. Wright, *The Last Word: Beyond the Bible Wars to a New Understanding of the Authority of Scripture* (San Francisco: Harper, 2005).

28. John Webster, *Holy Scripture: A Dogmatic Sketch*, Current Issues in Theology (Cambridge: Cambridge University Press, 2003).

29. E.g., Timothy Ward, *Word and Supplement: Speech Acts, Biblical Texts, and the Sufficiency of Scripture* (Oxford: Oxford University Press, 2002).

30. E.g., Kevin J. Vanhoozer, *Is There a Meaning in This Text? The Bible, the Reader, and the Morality of Literary Knowledge* (Grand Rapids, MI: Zondervan, 1998); *First Theology: God, Scripture, Hermeneutics* (Downers Grove, IL: InterVarsity, 2002); the "Scripture and Hermeneutics" series led by Craig Bartholomew (Grand Rapids, MI: Zondervan/Carlisle: Paternoster); and several works by Anthony C. Thiselton. In general, Hirsch is less dominant, while interaction with Hans-Georg Gadamer, Paul Ricoeur, and certain "postmodern" theorists is on the rise.

31. The Word-centered yet somewhat rationalistic legacy of Carl F. H. Henry emphasizing propositional revelation (in his six-volume *God, Revelation, and*

Authority [Nashville, TN: Word, 1976–83]) still stands, but is more balanced with another stream of thinking via Bernard Ramm (see, e.g., *The Evangelical Heritage*, reprint [Grand Rapids, MI: Baker, 2000] and *Special Revelation and the Word of God* [Grand Rapids, MI: Eerdmans, 1961]) that has interacted more constructively with Barth. Both Vanhoozer and Grenz seek to appropriate the legacy of Ramm, as their essays show in John G. Stackhouse, Jr. (ed.), *Evangelical Futures: A Conversation on Theological Method* (Grand Rapids, MI: Baker, 2000).

32. In addition to various works by Grenz, see, e.g., James Callahan, *The Clarity of Scripture: History, Theology, and Contemporary Literary Studies* (Downers Grove, IL: InterVarsity, 2001).

33. See, e.g., Mark A. Noll, *America's God: From Jonathan Edwards to Abraham Lincoln* (Oxford: Oxford University Press, 2002), chs. 18–19.

34. See, e.g., Kevin Giles, "The Biblical Argument for Slavery: Can the Bible Mislead? A Case Study in Hermeneutics," *Evangelical Quarterly* 66. 1 (1994): 3–17.

35. William J. Webb, *Slaves, Women and Homosexuals: Exploring the Hermeneutics of Cultural Analysis* (Downers Grove, IL: InterVarsity, 2001).

36. Mark Lau Branson and C. René Padilla (eds.), *Conflict and Context: Hermeneutics in the Americas* (Grand Rapids, MI: Eerdmans, 1986).

37. See "Faith and Hope for the Future: Towards A Vital And Coherent Evangelical Theology For The 21st Century: Summary Reports of the Working Groups," *Evangelical Review of Theology* 21. 1 (January 1997): 5–40, esp. pp. 5–7.

38. Although, in various works, Lamin Sanneh has emphasized the ways in which Bible translation (perhaps unintentionally) destabilized Western cultural hegemony and cultivated indigenous leadership.

39. A solid overview and some assessment of such hermeneutical models for doing theology can be found in David K. Clark, *To Know and Love God: Method for Theology*, Foundations of Evangelical Theology (Wheaton, IL: Crossway, 2003).

40. See "Faith and Hope for the Future," p. 6; Daniel J. Treier, "The Superiority of Pre-Critical Exegesis? *Sic et Non*," *Trinity Journal* 24 ns no. 1 (Spring 2003): 77–103; more broadly, D. H. Williams, *Retrieving the Tradition and Renewing Evangelicalism: A Primer for Suspicious Protestants* (Grand Rapids, MI: Eerdmans, 1999).

41. See, e.g., Paul Griffiths, *Religious Reading: The Place of Reading in the Practice of Religion* (Oxford: Oxford University Press, 1999).

42. A major theme from retrieval of Mikhail Bakhtin, dialogism suggests that voices may speak truly without speaking comprehensively – for the full truth, all the genuinely insightful voices must be spoken and heard together.

43. A recent example, though only one possibility, for working out such implications is I. Howard Marshall, *Beyond the Bible: Moving from Scripture to Theology* (Grand Rapids, MI: Baker Academic, 2004).

44. See Daniel J. Treier, "Wisdom," in Vanhoozer (gen. ed.), *Dictionary for Theological Interpretation of the Bible*, pp. 844–47; *Virtue and the Voice of God.*

4 Jesus Christ

JOHN WEBSTER

Along with the Scripture principle, the axiom of *solus Christus* has been a hallmark of theologies in the Reformation tradition. The first indicates the priority of divine revelation over tradition, speculation, or immediate experience; the second acknowledges the sovereignty of divine grace in incarnation and redemption over against apparently synergistic conceptions of its mediation through church, sacrament, or the moral acts of Christian existence. The perfection of Christ – the integrity and completeness of his person as the God-man, and the non-transferability of his offices – is Christologically and soteriologically fundamental. For much of Protestant theological history, the incarnational and Trinitarian metaphysics underpinning these commitments were taken for granted as non-controversial. In the post-Reformation confessional period, disagreements emerged between Lutheran and Reformed over the relation of the divine and human natures of the incarnate one, partly in relation to eucharistic controversies over the ubiquity of Christ's humanity. Lutherans emphasized that the humanity of the ascended Christ shares the divine property of omnipresence, and so is present in the eucharistic elements, whereas the Reformed stressed that his humanity is localized in heaven, not in the sacrament, and that his finite human nature is incapable of containing the infinite divine Word. But both confessions remained firmly attached to the Christological orthodoxy articulated at the Council of Chalcedon: in the one person Jesus Christ fullness of deity and fullness of humanity are united, the union of the natures being such that they can neither be divided nor confused. Within this primary consensus, Lutherans characteristically stressed the union of the two natures ("without division") such that properties of one can be attributed to the other ("communication of attributes"); the Reformed characteristically stressed that the union is at the level of the singular person Jesus Christ (and so is a "hypostatic union"), and not the confusion of finite and infinite. A minority tradition, sometimes traced to Melanchthon, and strongly present in the Pietist and revivalist theologies of the eighteenth and nineteenth centuries, gave priority to the saving benefits of Christ, eschewing what it regarded as Christological speculation, and so privileging Christ's work over his person. Nevertheless, mainstream Protestantism, within which evangelicalism emerged, was broadly committed to orthodox Christology in its exegesis, confessional statements, and didactic and polemical theology.

From its beginnings, the Protestant consensus was not immune to external critique or internal dissent. An important early factor was the rise of theologies which recast Christianity into the idiom of nonsalvific natural religion, abandoning the apparatus of incarnational metaphysics and soteriology and presenting Jesus as sublime moral teacher. Such accounts of Jesus, which later found a home in, for example, Kant's *Religion within the Limits of Reason Alone*, were instinctively, and sometimes explicitly, Arian, since the moral superiority of Jesus required no assertions of his ontological unity with God. They also proved companionable to nineteenth-century historical-critical readings of the rise of Christian faith in Jesus such as those offered by F. C. Baur and D. F. Strauss. Protestant dogmaticians adopted a variety of strategies from accommodation to principled opposition. Those treasured in the evangelical tradition (such as Charles Hodge or W. G. T. Shedd) retained confidence in the norms, methods, and content of Protestant scholasticism, on the basis of which they conducted polemic against the corrosive influence of higher critical investigation of Jesus. Their successors (such as B. B. Warfield and, a little later, J. Gresham Machen) placed greater reliance upon an arsenal of historical arguments to defend orthodox Christian teaching about the deity of Christ. Moreover, as historical criticism acquired greater prestige, early evangelicals (especially in the United States) came to place Protestant doctrines of the authority of Scripture at the center of the defense of the faith. This had the effect of fusing together Christological debates and debates about the reliability of the New Testament evangelists, and so of fostering a preoccupation with historical apologetics which was to continue to characterize evangelical theology well into the twentieth century. It also led to a surprising disinvestment in positive dogmatics: the doctrines restated with such care by the old Princeton theologians were taken as read, and energy was devoted to elaborating their historical-exegetical warrants. Similar work was undertaken by some British evangelical theologians of the same period, such as James Orr; others were less involved in apologetics or the dogmatics of Protestant scholasticism. Both James Denney and P. T. Forsyth, for example, had imbibed Protestant liberalism from studying in Germany, and though they countered its characteristic emphasis on divine immanence by recovering the theology of the reconciliation of sinner through the cross of Christ, they retained some of liberalism's moral concerns, as well as its unease about the ontological categories deployed in classical Christology.

In the middle years of the twentieth century, the revitalization of evangelical Protestantism generated a renewal of its theological self-articulation. Evangelical theology, particularly in the United States, acquired greater self-confidence, supported by a firmer institutional and churchly base, and looked to position itself vis-à-vis mainstream Protestant thought. The timing of the emergence of evangelical theology is important for its subsequent Christological development. In the mid-century, academic theology was dominated by German Protestantism, and in particular by two opposing streams: the blend of skepticism and existentialism of a Lutheran cast which held sway in New Testament studies under the influence of Bultmann; and the commanding presence in dogmatics of the Reformed thinker Barth. Evangelical theologians such as Carl Henry, eager to address themselves to their mainstream setting, judged that their context betrayed "the failure of the Barthian and Bultmannian theology,"[1] and devoted much effort to its critical dissection. One crucial effect of this was that, at the point of its attempt to shake off intellectual isolation, evangelical theology allowed its Christological agenda to be largely set from outside itself. This, in turn, meant that it often operated in reactive or defensive mode: its chief Christological concern was the collision between the dominant conventions of Protestant academia and evangelical teaching about the nature of Scripture and the person of Christ. At the beginning of this most recent phase of its history, that is, evangelical Christology found difficulty in speaking with its own voice.

Why did evangelical theology find it so hard to extricate itself from the mainstream agenda? The difficulty is, of course, familiar to traditions moving from the margins to cautious engagement with the center. But there are a number of factors peculiar to the situation of evangelical theology which should be borne in mind. One – possibly the most important – of these factors is that evangelical theology lacked dogmatic theologians with the degree of intellectual eminence required to steer an independent course aside from their mainline counterparts. Though evangelicalism produced able historians and exegetes of biblical literature, its systematicians were (and, we shall see, remain) very thin on the ground. Some dogmaticians were drafted into the tradition, such as the Dutch Reformed theologian G. C. Berkouwer (though he later became an object of suspicion to some); but the home-produced materials were largely plodding textbooks and controversial literature, none of which seized control of the theological agenda.

This dogmatic mediocrity went hand in hand with a curious lack of interest in historical theology, both patristic and Reformation. Though evangelical Christological literature has made its appeal to some standard sources in the tradition, there has been little evidence of wide and deep study of the Christian past, and instead a tendency to fall back on well-worn readings of the classical materials. This has had the effect of cutting evangelical theology off from a source of renewal which might have enabled it to exercise greater freedom in its immediate setting, providing it with more spacious descriptions of the person and work of Christ than those on which evangelical theologians tended to rely. In the same post-war period that evangelicalism was gathering theological momentum, Roman Catholic theologians such as Congar or von Balthasar were able to shake themselves free from stultifying school theology and stimulate an extraordinary springtime of Christian orthodoxy, in part because they looked to the Christian past as a resource in outthinking the present. Evangelical theology lacked such formidable historical intelligences, how-ever, and was less successful in resisting the pressure of its context.

A third factor which tied evangelical Christology to the trends which it opposed was, paradoxically, the doctrine of Scripture which was its most discriminating mark. For, on the one hand, such was the supremacy of the Scripture principle over all other Christian doctrines that Christological issues could become a subset of questions about biblical authority (as in defenses of the virginal conception of the incarnate Son of God on the grounds that to deny the miracle is to impugn the veracity of the evange-lists' record). And, on the other hand, in a Christological context the Scripture principle was often wedded to a particular commitment to the historical reliability of Bible. This, as we shall see, encouraged interest in historical apologetics, which tended to reinforce rather than diminish attachment to mainline debates, and also to lead to puzzlement about figures like Hans Frei who declined to be drawn into the debate.

The Christological literature produced by evangelical theologians as they tried to map and respond to academic debates has shown general consistency in defending the basic tenets of conciliar orthodoxy by demon-strating their compatibility with the New Testament. Its intellectual level has been varied. In New Testament studies, scholars have produced work of independent academic merit by developing versions of historical meth-ods of inquiry, harnessing them to an evangelical account of the nature of the Bible and using them to generate a historical rationale for orthodox teaching. The doctrinal literature, by contrast, has generally taken one of two forms: textbooks for classroom use, or mid-level surveys of the doctrine of the person of Christ. The former type of material, pedagogical in intent, generally devotes a good deal of space to biblical and historical survey and to outlining what are taken to be the cardinal features of the dogmatic locus.[2] The genre and intended readership of these treatments are such that they survey, rather than reconceive, the topic, and tend to give voice to the consensus without venturing independent or original judgments. None of them possesses the discrimination of earlier orthodox *(reactionary)* Protestant dogmatics such as those of Kähler[3] or Schlatter,[4] or makes any pretence to rival the sheer scale of Herman Bavinck's magisterial treatment (1918); and they are considerably less demanding than the digests of Lutheran or Reformed confessional doctrine by Schmid and Heppe.[5] Perhaps the most able treatment to be found in the textbooks is that by Thomas Oden in the second volume of his *Systematic Theology,*[6] which, more than any other account, thinks the material through afresh on the basis of wide and attentive reading across the range of the Christian tradition. Oden communicates the sheer compelling power of his topic in a way which is rarely achieved in the evangelical literature, though the ecumenical cast of his theology may make him less immediately companionable to some of evangelicalism's dominant strands.

Individual studies of the Christological locus have generally shared many of these restrictions.[7] Most have a common structure: a report on the relevant New Testament materials; an account of the historical career of the doctrine, especially in the patristic and Reformation periods; and an analysis of its fate in the turmoil of modern repudiation of the claims to revelation of the Christian faith. The handling of contemporary theology can be very sharp, even disdainful, as in Runia's hostile account of the main moves in twentieth-century Christology.[8] Modern theologians are presented as trading in accommodations, evasions, and compromises, or as captive to philosophical schemes such as process theism or existential phenomenology which are inimical to the Christian gospel. Not all the literature demonstrates this rancor: MacLeod's *The Person of Christ* is a very well-judged book, full of fine dogmatic description, and generous when engaged in critical appraisal; but it is an exception. The *odium theologicum* which is so often present in the evangelical Christological literature is indicative of some important characteristics of evangelical theology in general: a general (though not always well-articulated) sense that some modern theology defies the instruction of the gospel; a felt distance from the centers of theological prestige and power; and a lack of force in driving forward a program of its own. These characteristics, and the institutional conditions which they reflect, combined with a general lack of dogmatic expertise, have meant that the evangelical tradition has not so far been able to produce the kind of calmly authoritative presentations of Christological orthodoxy that may be found in the work of modern Roman Catholic theologians such as Kasper or O'Collins.[9]

JESUS AND THE NEW TESTAMENT

As evangelical theology gained momentum in the 1950s, its practitioners quickly came to a decision that what were perceived to be the deleterious effects of gospel criticism could only be halted by constructing an alternative account of Christian origins and of the development of early Christology. The school of Bultmann, though more internally varied than is often allowed, combined an account of the New Testament owing much to the early twentieth-century *religionsgeschichtliche Schule*, quasi-Deist reticence about any talk of God's action in the world, and a highly charged theology of Christian existence in which the securities of historical warrants could be jettisoned as mere *fides historica*. Evangelicals mounted their challenge to this primarily by using historical weaponry; only rather slender attention was given to the philosophical underpinnings of historical criticism, or, indeed, to the study of New Testament theology. A common strategy was to demonstrate, first, that a "high" Christology (one in which Jesus is in some sense intrinsic to the identity of God) can already be found in the New Testament, and, second, that such a Christology is not the invention of the early church but can be traced directly to Jesus' own self-understanding and self-proclamation. This had the effect of displacing the Bultmann school's rather abstract existentialist Christology, in which Jesus is presented as an eschatological interruption of history lacking in form and contour, by appealing to historical common sense.

Accordingly, study of the historical Jesus presented itself as a matter of considerable importance, driven by the need to establish the authenticity of the portrayal of Jesus in the Gospels.[10] Both in background studies and in commentaries, evangelicals labored hard to defend the reliability of the canonical record, thereby not only vindicating their doctrine of Scripture but also preparing the way for incarnational teaching. A range of historical arguments was advanced in line with this strategy: early dating of New Testament texts in order as far as possible to close the gap between the history of Jesus and its apostolic interpreters; emphasis upon the dynamics of conservation in early Christian culture and its resistance to external religious influence; and a corresponding de-emphasis upon the creativity of the apostolic authors and their communities. Evangelical historians of the New Testament developed some sophisticated analyses of the tradition history of the Christological titles, and enjoyed success in arguing that earlier history of religions approaches do not emerge unscathed from close scrutiny.[11] Their work found confirmation at the hands of some mainstream scholars often admired by evangelicals, such as Moule[12] or Hengel.[13]

However, increasingly sophisticated use of historical methods of inquiry has made the task of identifying the boundaries of evangelical Christological conviction more difficult. Tension between the "custodial core" of evangelicalism and its "penumbra,"[14] never far from the surface, occasionally flashed into open warfare, as in the furor over Dunn's treatment of the pre-existence of Christ in *Christology in the Making*.[15] Over the last twenty years, however, evangelical scholarship has established itself much more securely in the mainstream, where it often exercises significant leadership, and so has become much less anxious and partisan in tone. The contrast between the earlier evangelical response to mid-century gospel criticism and evangelical engagement with the so-called "third quest for the historical Jesus" is a case in point. Evangelical scholars such as Wright or Witherington have been able to do much to set the terms of the debate rather than simply reacting to a program handed to them, and proved themselves to be capable of meeting Borg or Crossan on the same ground.[16] A more general shift in New Testament studies to understanding Jesus out of the context of Second Temple Judaism has been an important factor here, particularly for those who have suggested that the first Christians viewed Jesus as internal to the identity of the God of Israel, and therefore as an object of worship.[17] Contemporary evangelical historians of Jesus and his early followers are certainly more sophisticated than their forbears, and a good deal more relaxed about the need to defend the viability of confessional orthodoxy or the reliability and authority of the apostolic witnesses. What they have in common with earlier work is the fact that their arguments are historical, not theological, and direct themselves primarily to historical reason rather than the judgment of faith. In this sense, they continue the evangelical tradition of Christology "from below" – not in the sense of proposing a "low" Christology, but in treating Jesus and his human history as apprehensible in relative independence from the dogmatic question of his relation to the divine Logos. This, it should be noted, places them at a considerable distance from one of the primary affirmations of classical Christological teaching, namely that the humanity of Jesus is "enhypostatic" (has its existence in) the second person of the Trinity, and therefore "anhypostatic," that is, possesses no personal center of existence and agency of its own, and so is what it is solely in the Word. If this is so, then Jesus' humanity is not graspable as an historical entity without immediate reference to the Word who assumes it; incarnate humanity is not straightforwardly transparent to historical inquiry. Evangelical New Testament scholars have not so far addressed the adoptionist potential of the methods to which they have committed themselves.

DOGMATIC CHRISTOLOGY

Given the influence which Barth exercised in mid twentieth-century Protestant systematic theology, one of the chief tasks to which evangelical doctrinal theologians set themselves was responding to what was somewhat nebulously labeled "neo-orthodoxy," of which he was taken to be the exemplary instance. Barth's achievement as dogmatician was duly noted, sometimes praised, but rarely pondered at any depth; there is little evidence that those who criticized Barth so severely had much grasp of the details of his Christological thought. His espousal of Nicene and Chalcedonian orthodoxy could scarcely be quarreled with, and his aversion to moralizing renderings of Jesus won him favor. But evangelical systematicians had very little to say about some of the most significant features of his Christology, such as his remarkable reconception of the natures, states, and offices of Christ in *Church Dogmatics* IV, his Christological revision of the doctrine of God, or his distinctly Reformed account of the relation of deity and humanity in the incarnate one. For earlier evangelicals, Barth's Christology was problematic not so much for its material content as for what were taken to be its underlying epistemological flaws, above all its apparent refusal to allow that knowledge of God can be secured from history. "In its substance, Barth's Christology is, to a high degree, 'orthodox'; in its function, however, it is 'neo', constructed out of concessions to Kantianism and reactions to the multiple failures of liberalism."[18] Barth, on this account, remains trapped in Kant's metaphysical skepticism; disallowing that revelation has historical form and that the human mind is ordered toward reception of the objective truth of divine revelation, Barth disconnects Jesus from history, and so simply inverts liberal Christology. This is – to say the least – an odd (though strangely persistent) reading of Barth, inclined to transpose Barth's dogmatic ideas into epistemological mistakes, and heavily philosophical in the alternative it offers.[19] It indicates, moreover, that evangelical theologians have tended to be more exercised about fundamental theology than about material doctrine, as can readily be seen from the characteristic slightness of their treatment of dogmatic themes.

Most of the doctrinal literature from evangelical thinkers has been content to reaffirm Chalcedonian Christology in which fullness of deity and humanity are equally ascribed to the one person Jesus of Nazareth; alongside this, there has been a consistent commitment to the use of ontological categories in Christology.[20] This is naturally linked to an Anselmian soteriology in which the full deity and humanity of the savior are required if humankind is to enjoy divine redemption. Yet, somewhat curiously, there has been no magisterial treatment of these Christological themes, despite their evident centrality. In fact, more evangelical intellectual energy has been devoted to philosophical defenses of the rationality of the doctrine of the incarnation than to its dogmatic depiction.[21] This goes hand in hand with evangelical concern for those topics in Christology which have been subject to a high degree of skepticism, notably the virginal conception of Jesus and his resurrection.

Treatments of the resurrection are a particularly good register of how dogmatic topics have often been assimilated to historical and philosophical apologetics. Some strands of evangelicalism have long had a stake in evidentialist apologetics, and Jesus' resurrection has furnished a test case for the viability of the strategy.[22] In effect, the resurrection assumes a propaedeutic function: as reason surveys the historical evidence, belief in the resurrection acquires plausibility, and with it the Christological claims of Christian faith. The strategy is only effective, it should be noted, on the basis of a relocation of Christian teaching about the resurrection. Moved out of dogmatics proper to foundations, the resurrection becomes faith's ground rather than its object, and its content has more to do with Jesus' resurrection as past event than with his presence and activity as the risen one. The effect of this relocation has rarely been noted by evangelical systematicians, who have been rather swift to subsume the resurrection within the larger project of demonstrating the objectivity and universal validity of the Christian revelation (it is this which explains the warm reception which evangelical theology has accorded to Pannenberg's early Christological work).

On the whole, evangelical systematic theology has not so far been able to shape the direction of theological work. There have, of course, been individual works of great merit, such as a recent Christological treatise of considerable force, Michael Horton's *Lord and Servant*.[23] What is most impressive about this work is the sheer constructive power by which Horton is able to display the intellectual and spiritual structure of Christian teaching about the incarnation, and to draw attention to its interconnections with other parts of Christian doctrine such as Trinity, anthropology, and eschatology. The book reconceives the Reformed tradition of federal theology in terms of the dramatics of divine action. Appeal to this tradition could be stultifying; but here it affords entry into a much more spacious world than that of the lackluster surveys, and enables the book to persuade by descriptive cogency. Yet evangelical work of this range and power is rare; for constructive dogmatic treatments of the person of Christ, it would be more natural to turn to such near neighbors of the evangelical tradition as Otto Weber, T. F. Torrance, Edmund Schlink, or Robert Jenson.

FUTURE DIRECTIONS

The best evangelical theological work emerges from delight in the Christian gospel, for the gospel announces a reality which is in itself luminous, persuasive, and infinitely satisfying. That reality is Jesus Christ as he gives himself to be an object for creaturely knowledge, love, and praise. To think evangelically about this one is to think in his presence, under the instruction of his Word and Spirit, and in the fellowship of the saints. And it is to do so with cheerful confidence that his own witness to himself is unimaginably more potent than any theological attempts to run to his defense. The historical or apologetic anxieties to which evangelical Christology has often succumbed, and the jeremiads against the present age to which it has often given voice, are both overtaken by the sheer splendor of his self-communication. Evangelical Christology is properly doxological in the way it frames and accomplishes its task.

Christology responds to the self-communicative presence of its object in the twofold work of exegesis and dogmatics. Exegesis is not the same as study of the history of biblical literature and religion in their settings. Modern evangelicals have sometimes been bedazzled by the range and sophistication of historical procedures at their disposal, and busied themselves to master them in the hope of outbidding their opponents. But historical studies are the servant of exegesis, not its master. One thing which evangelical doctrines of the sufficiency of Scripture ought to have secured is that the ultimate resource is the text, not what can be reconstructed about what lies behind the text, for the text is an act of God's self-disclosure. The fruits of the immense labors of evangelical New Testament scholars are by no means negligible; but in and of themselves they do not constitute a hearing of the Word, though they may offer much needed preparation for such a hearing. The real test of the utility of historical work is whether it enables exegesis. In a Christological context, this means that there is more to be gained from a potent reading of the Johannine prologue than from the most exquisite dissection of its historical background. Perhaps one of the most significant influences which evangelical theology might bring to bear upon the study of the New Testament would be to recall its practitioners to the task of theological interpretation, that is, reading Scripture as divine address.

Exegesis is served by dogmatics, whose task is to look for systematic connections between the constituent parts of the Christian gospel, and to attempt their orderly and well-proportioned exposition. In particular, dogmatics can help to prevent the distortions of perspective which can be introduced into an account of the faith by, for example, pressure from polemical concerns or excessive regard for extra-theological norms. Modern evangelical Christology has not been well served in this regard, and stands in need of a descriptive dogmatics of real moment. What is required is not an account of the person of Christ with better warrants (historical or philosophical) but a richer, more expansive, and fine-grained portrayal of the doctrine. In fulfilling this task, there is much help in the tradition, both ancient and more modern, and evangelical Christology may need to give its mind to the task of historical theology. As often in intellectual work, the way back may prove to be the way forward.

Further reading

Bloesch, Donald G. *Jesus of Nazareth: Savior and Lord*. Christian Foundations. Downers Grove, IL: InterVarsity, 1997.

Erickson, Millard J. *The Word Became Flesh*. Grand Rapids, MI: Baker, 1991.

Horton, Michael. *Lord and Servant: A Covenant Christology*. Louisville, KY: Westminster John Knox, 2005.

Jacobsen, Douglas, and Frederick W. Schmidt, Jr. "Behind Orthodoxy and Beyond It: Recent Developments in Evangelical Christology." *Scottish Journal of Theology* 45 (1992): 515–41.

Kärkkäinen, Veli-Matti. *Christology: A Global Introduction*. Grand Rapids, MI: Baker, 2003.

MacLeod, Donald. *The Person of Christ*. Leicester: InterVarsity, 1998.

Oden, Thomas. *The Word of Life: Systematic Theology, vol. 2*. San Francisco: Harper, 1989.

Ramm, Bernard. *An Evangelical Christology*. Nashville, TN: Nelson, 1985.

Runia, Klaas. *The Present-day Christological Debate*. Leicester: InterVarsity, 1984.

Wells, David F. *The Person of Christ*. London: Marshall, Morgan and Scott, 1984.

Notes

1. Carl F. H. Henry, "Cross Currents in Contemporary Theology," in Carl F. H. Henry (ed.), *Jesus of Nazareth: Saviour and Lord* (London: Tyndale, 1970), p. 22.

2. See, for example, Millard J. Erickson, *Christian Theology*, vol. II (Grand Rapids, MI: Baker, 1984); James Montgomery Boice, *Foundations of the Christian Faith* (Downers Grove, IL: InterVarsity, 1986); Bruce Demarest and Gordon Lewis, *Integrative Theology*, vol. I (Grand Rapids, MI: Zondervan, 1987); Alister E. McGrath, *Christian Theology* (Oxford: Blackwell, 2001); Veli-Matti Kärkkäinen, *Christology: A Global Introduction* (Grand Rapids, MI: Baker, 2003).

3. M. Kähler, *Die Wissenschaft der christliche Lehre* (Leipzig: Deichert, 1905).

4. Adolph Schlatter, *Das christliche Dogma* (Stuttgart: Calwer, 1911).

5. Bavinck's work is now available in English as *Sin and Salvation in Christ*, vol. III of *Reformed Dogmatics*, 3 vols. (2003–06; Grand Rapids, MI: Baker Academic, 2006). Heinrich Schmid, *The Doctrinal Theology of the Evangelical Lutheran Church*, trans. Henry E. Jacobs and Charles E. Hay (Minneapolis, MN: Augsburg, 1961); Heinrich Heppe, *Reformed Dogmatics*, trans. G. T. Thomson, revised and ed. Ernst Bizer (London: Allen and Unwin, 1950).

6. Thomas Oden, *The Word of Life: Systematic Theology, vol. 2* (San Francisco: Harper, 1989).

7. See, for example, David F. Wells, *The Person of Christ* (London: Marshall, Morgan and Scott, 1984); Bernard Ramm, *An Evangelical Christology* (Nashville, TN: Nelson, 1985); Douglas D. Webster, *A Passion for Christ* (Grand Rapids, MI: Zondervan, 1987); Millard J. Erickson, *The Word Became Flesh* (Grand Rapids, MI: Baker, 1991); Donald Bloesch, *Jesus of Nazareth. Saviour and Lord* (Downers Grove, IL: InterVarsity, 1997); Donald MacLeod, *The Person of Christ* (Leicester: InterVarsity, 1998).

8. Klaas Runia, *The Present-day Christological Debate* (Leicester: InterVarsity, 1984).

9. Walter Kasper, *Jesus the Christ* (New York: Paulist, 1976); Gerald O'Collins, *Christology* (Oxford: Oxford University Press, 1995).

10. For a representative account from this period, see I. Howard Marshall, *I Believe in the Historical Jesus* (Grand Rapids, MI: Eerdmans, 1976).

11. I. Howard Marshall, *The Origins of New Testament Christology* (Leicester: InterVarsity, 1976); *Jesus the Saviour: Studies in New Testament Theology* (Leicester: InterVarsity, 1990), pp. 73–210.

12. C. F. D. Moule, *The Origin of Christology* (Cambridge: Cambridge University Press, 1977).

13. Martin Hengel, *Studies in Early Christology* (Edinburgh: Clark, 1995).

14. Douglas Jacobsen and Frederick W. Schmidt, Jr., "Behind Orthodoxy and Beyond It: Recent Developments in Evangelical Christology," *Scottish Journal of Theology* 45 (1992): 515–41.

15. James D. G. Dunn, *Christology in the Making* (London: SCM, 1980).

16. N. T. Wright, *Jesus and the Victory of God* (London: SPCK, 1996); Ben Witherington, *The Jesus Quest* (Downers Grove, IL: InterVarsity, 1995).

17. Richard Bauckham, *God Crucified: Monotheism and Christology in the New Testament* (Grand Rapids, MI: Eerdmans, 1998); Larry W. Hurtado, *Lord Jesus Christ: Devotion to Jesus in Earliest Christianity* (Grand Rapids, MI: Eerdmans, 2003).

18. Wells, *The Person of Christ*, p. 160.

19. Carl F. H. Henry, *God, Revelation and Authority*, vols. II and III (Waco, TX: Word, 1978, 1980).

20. Runia, *The Present-day Christological Debate*, pp. 101–15.

21. Stephen T. Davis, "Is 'Truly God and Truly Man' Coherent?," *Christian Scholars Review* 9 (1980): 215–24; Thomas V. Morris, *The Logic of God Incarnate* (Ithaca, NY: Cornell University Press, 1986); "The Metaphysics of God Incarnate," in Ronald J. Feenstra and Cornelius Plantinga, Jr. (eds.), *Trinity, Incarnation and Atonement* (Notre Dame, IN: University of Notre Dame Press, 1989), pp. 110–27.

22. Gary Habermas and Antony Flew, *Did Jesus Rise from the Dead?* (San Francisco: Harper, 1987); Stephen T. Davis, *Risen Indeed* (Grand Rapids, MI: Eerdmans, 1993); William Lane Craig, *Jesus' Resurrection: Fact or Figment?* (Downers Grove, IL: InterVarsity, 2000).

23. Michael Horton, *Lord and Servant: A Covenant Christology* (Louisville, KY: Westminster John Knox, 2005).

5   The human person in the Christian story

CHERITH FEE NORDLING

"Who" and "what" is a human person? Depending on which pronoun takes priority, one can answer the "human question" scientifically, philosophically, theologically, morally, socially, or with a combination thereof. These modes of inquiry shape the way a given society negotiates what constitutes human being and personhood. In the process, society arbitrarily engages in "cultural shadow work." It renegotiates the social order through continually redefining the "human being" and ends up shaping a new culture based on a particular set of values.[1]

Although we have forever been asking and defining what it means to be human, the modern-postmodern shift to the human subject as the source and norm for "truth" has ultimately placed humanity (anthropology) at the center of every inquiry. While great strides have been made in understanding human being and personhood, new definitions arise out of new contexts. Present inconsistencies and ambiguities mean that there exist side by side rampant individualism *and* "communal identity," abortion *and* assisted reproductive technologies, genetic engineering *and* euthanasia, without any sense of underlying discontinuity.[2] This generally works to the advantage of those with the greatest amount of influence or the most to gain, often at the expense rather than on behalf of, "the other."

Certain streams of contemporary thought emphasize a theological anthropology "from below," using human experience as the source and criterion to determine divine reality, and encouraging the "construction" of one's own reality as "personal narrative." Christian anthropology, however, does not start with "the phenomenon of human being" as a societal, individual, or even a theological construct. It starts with God. The Christian story assumes that human being and personhood reflect a prior Reality – the triune God – through whom humanity derives its being, personhood, identity, and purpose as divine image-bearers. God has graciously chosen to be made known within the limits of human

experience as Father, Son, and Spirit, in eternally self-giving, loving communion, and freely enters into loving relationship to and with creation,
particularly those who bear the divine image.

In the current climate, it will therefore be helpful to pursue understanding of being human from the biblical narrative and then to emphasize certain doctrinal and ethical considerations for evangelical theology
from the heart of the Christian story.

THE HUMAN *IMAGO DEI* THROUGH CREATION, EXODUS AND NEW CREATION

The Christian story of God's gracious relationship with human beings
is only understandable within the context of God's personal relation to
creation as a whole. The biblical text, in all its richness and variety,
"narrates" the grand story of creation's relation to God: good, fallen,
reconciled, and eschatologically being restored to its final consummation
as creation.[3] The scriptural bookends of Genesis and Revelation describe
the story's beginning and end (as a new beginning) in terms of God's
presence with created reality. "In the beginning God created the heavens
and the earth" and dwelt with his human image-bearers in a garden. The
glorious finale of creation in John's revelation recapitulates this theme:
"Then I saw 'a new heaven and a new earth'" such that once again "the
dwelling of God is with human beings, and he will live with them," this
time in a holy city instead of a garden (Rev. 21:1–22:5).

As participants in the biblical narrative, our experience of the present
and expectations of the future can only be understood from the resources
of the past – the memories, symbols, and metaphors embedded in the
original story of God with his[4] people Israel. They become entry points
into and ways of understanding the lived narrative of divine–human
history. Both the Old and New Testaments are profoundly shaped by
Israel's memory of creation, exodus, and new creation/restoration, particularly pertaining to human beings and their unique place in that creation
as the image-bearers of God.

Israel used known symbols and images to narrate an understanding of
their identity as Yahweh's people over against the myths and ideologies of
the surrounding cultures. In a number of Ancient Near East (ANE) traditions, the act of creation is construed as the building of the deity's temple-
palace. Essential to its completion was to construct and then to place an
image of the god in that setting. First, the image would be formed to depict
attributes and function of the deity. Next, a ritual would be performed to

"enliven" the image, opening its eyes, ears, and mouth and enabling its limbs. Most importantly, the spirit of the deity was invoked to indwell the image in order for it to function in the deity's image, at which point the "enlivened" image was installed in the temple, dependent upon human "sustenance."

Genesis tells a creation narrative of divine–human relation and image-bearing but, in radical contrast to prevailing worldviews, turns the story on its head, completely reversing the pagan order of reality.[5] Humankind does not make a temple-palace for God; God makes *all of creation* his own temple-palace (Isa. 66:1a) and then makes a "garden" for human flourishing. Human beings do not make the divine image; God makes *them* in the divine image ("Let us make human beings in our image, according to our likeness ... So God created humankind in his image, in the image of God he created them; male and female he created them"; Gen. 1:26–27). They do not "open" God's eyes, ears, etc., enlivening or providing for him; instead, he fills them with his breath, giving them life and ongoing sustenance. All human beings, in their embodied maleness and femaleness, are living "pictograms" of Yahweh by his life-giving Spirit, and as such, are subordinate to him as vice-regents to his creation. Divine and human integrity are maintained, such that each maintains an authentic "in itselfness" in relation.

At the Tree of Knowledge of Good and Evil, sin enters as the image-bearers deny Yahweh as creation's ultimate source of wisdom. Failing to live in authenticity to who they are in subordination to whose they are, they usurp God's prerogatives by trusting in their own capacities to perceive and fashion "reality" from a distorted perspective. The resulting falsehood and alienation leads to death and dissolution. Creation suffers as a consequence (Gen. 3:17–18; Rom. 8:20–23), and the temple-palace and the image-bearers both fall into ruin.

Israel's founding moment of salvation/exodus from Egypt as a new people is depicted as a new creation. Israel stands in the darkness before the sea, the fiery pillar brings light, and wind drives back the waters and causes dry land to appear (Exod. 14:19–31; Gen. 1:2–9). These images portray the exodus as a recapitulation of creation (Exod. 14:19–21). Just as Yahweh "rested" in the great pavilion of his cosmos-temple-palace (Ps. 93), so now he once again "tabernacles" with saved/restored humanity, dwelling among them in the glory-cloud over the tabernacle. Ultimately they are brought to a new land where they can flourish in right relation with God, other humans, and the non-human creation. Here "Israel" is established and called Yahweh's "firstborn son." Yahweh recreates a people for his

Name, to bear his image as a holy nation-kingdom of priests (Exod. 19:6). In submitting to Torah, Israel accepts its subordinate status as image-bearer, living out the proper correspondence of humanity in relation to God, others, and the creation.

Truth is again exchanged for a lie, however. Rejecting Yahweh for an idol and divine wisdom for human folly, Israel denies its identity in particular and humanity's in general as true *imago Dei*. Under the "idolater's curse," Israel bears the image of the blind and deaf gods she worships; she has eyes but will not see, ears but will not hear, and staggers naked (Pss. 115, 135; Isa. 6:9–10). Most devastating is the departure of Yahweh's Presence from the temple (Ezek. 10), anticipating Israel's own departure from the sanctuary-land. With the destruction of the false image-bearers, the land falls into chaotic lifelessness and wasteland (Isa. 6:11–12).

Despite the faithlessness of Israel, Yahweh remains faithful to himself and his way of being in loving relation. Hence, as the prophets speak of desolation, they also use the language of new creation to speak of Israel's promised exodus from Babylonian exile. Yahweh will redeem a new humanity as image-bearers; new life will be raised up through the divine Word and the breath of the indwelling Spirit (Isa. 32:15; 44:3; 59:21; Ezek. 37:5–6, 14). In another great reversal of salvation/new creation, God will bring life, health, and wholeness to his people and their land. The blind will see, the lame will walk, the deaf will hear, stone hearts will become "flesh," and the dead will live again (Isa. 35:5–6; 32:15; 45:8, 17; 46:13; 51:3; Ezek. 36:35; Joel 2:3), fully clothed in garments of righteousness, at rest in a restored sanctuary-land (Ps. 132:9, 16, 18; Isa. 23:18; 52:1; 61:10; Zech. 3:3–5; 14:14). Though the remnant returns, full restoration is yet to come. Remnant Israel awaits God's Spirit-filled image-bearer, the divinely "anointed one," to finally restore "true Israel" (Isa. 61). The "new Adam/ new humanity" motif in Daniel 7 extends the eschatological vision of restoration to include not only Israel but all humanity and the cosmos.

As the New Testament describes the fulfillment of Israel's hopes using creation/exodus/new creation motifs, their full meanings are all reordered to Jesus of Nazareth, the human Son of God (Matt. 24:37; Rom. 5:12–18; 2 Cor. 5; 2 Pet. 3:6–7). Jesus Christ, the new "Adam," the firstborn of a newly created humanity, ushers in Israel's new exodus/new creation return from final exile (John 1:1, 4, 14; Rom. 5:12–18; 1 Cor. 15:21–22, 45–49; Luke 1:54–55, 2:4–11; Matt. 1:1–17; Col. 1:15, 18).

Jesus' baptism and temptation recapitulate Israel's exodus experience of being declared God's "Son" who passes through the waters and faces temptation in the desert. This time, however, Yahweh's Spirit-filled Son remains faithful as divine image-bearer. Having relinquished his divine prerogative in order to live out a truly human life in daily obedience by the power of the Holy Spirit, Jesus does only what he sees the Father doing, thus accurately reflecting the divine image (John 5:15–23; 11:38; 14:8–11; Col. 1:15; 2 Cor. 4:4; Heb. 1:4). Bearing the authority of the Lord of creation (Mark 4:14; Matt. 8:27), he preaches the coming of this long-awaited new exodus/new creation and does "signs and wonders" and "mighty deeds" that deliberately echo exodus and creation (Deut. 3:24, 4:34; Ps. 65:6; 107:24).

As God's new "Israel," Jesus keeps the new law of self-giving love (Mark 9:33–10:45). He shows them how to walk in Yahweh's ways "along paths they do not know" – the way of free and loving obedience through the empowering Spirit of God, reflecting the self-giving character of God through cruciform servanthood (Isa. 42:16; Mark 8:14–10:52). As the sinless representative of true human being made sin on our behalf, Jesus offers to the Father the first-fruits of a redeemed creation with his own life. In the ongoing reality of his resurrected human existence as the eternal Son, our humanity is hidden with his humanity in God. From his place of exaltation at the right hand of the Father, Jesus gives the promised Spirit to all whose lives are "crucified" and submitted to him as Lord, who share in his perfect *imago Dei* (Acts 2:14–36). Completely qualified *as one of us* to be the High Priest of the new creation, he leads us to our final, resurrected destiny as true humans in complete Sabbath rest – as sisters and brothers of the New Adam, sons and daughters born into the image of their Father and Creator (Heb. 1–4).

Thus we are "born" of the life-breathing Spirit who stamps the new law on our hearts, marking us as God's dearly loved children with the full privilege of our inheritance – to be truly human in relation to God and all things, imitators of the self-giving God. Already we live by the Spirit in the Kingdom: not yet is the Kingdom fully come, nor is our eschatological hope consummated in full. The Holy Spirit is conforming us to the "likeness of the Son" (Rom. 8:29; 2 Cor. 3:18), restoring us to a new self that is "being renewed in knowledge in the image of its Creator" (Col. 3:10). Eschatologically oriented and empowered by the Spirit, we are "transformed into the same image from one degree of glory to another" in Christ (2 Cor. 3:18), having his same mind (Phil. 2:1–18), already positioned with him in the heavenlies yet still participating in God's restoration of the kingdom of heaven on earth (Eph. 1:18–23; 2:6; Matt. 4:23–6:10).

This eschatological restoration of the image of God is both individual and communal for God's people who belong to Christ and are joined to the fellowship of the triune God through the Spirit. We are both the new temple, the locus of God's Presence, and the royal priesthood in service to God (1 Cor. 3:16–17; 6:19–20; 1 Pet. 2:4–5, 9). As new creatures who together share in the cruciform image of Jesus Christ, we are empowered by the Spirit of Christ and uniquely gifted in love to participate as co-heirs in both suffering and glory (Rom. 8:17). Joined to Christ and to one another as his Body, we are equally re-created, privileged, and empowered as "children of Abraham" to live as image-bearers for one another (Gal. 3:28; 1 Cor. 12–14).

Since creation's fate is inextricably linked to the authenticity of the image-bearer, all creation groans as it awaits our final restoration (Rom. 8:14–35). The climax of the Christian story is not the abandonment of creation but its restoration as the new dwelling of the Lord God Almighty and the Lamb with God's people (Rev. 21–22). As thoroughly eschatological people, from conception through new creation, we are (in Christ) what we are becoming (by the Spirit) and will someday be – fully restored human persons. This vision has nothing to do with simply "going to heaven" as immortal souls. Rather, it has everything to do with being embodied persons whose existence is reconstituted in every way – "spiritually embodied" and relationally restored – to flourish in the life to come as renewed image-bearers in the presence of the triune God. In short, it is becoming who we really are.

THEOLOGICAL AFFIRMATIONS

The biblical witness to the Christian story, telling us that *what* and *who we are*, and *are becoming*, has everything to do with the tri-personal God to *whom* we belong (Eph. 1:3). Human "being" and identity are grounded in the reality of the triune communion of the Father, Son, and Spirit. Bearing the image of God who *is* "being-in-relation," we too are constituted as distinct beings in essential relationality with God and others. Furthermore, the particular human life of Jesus Christ mediates the promise of our final restored humanity as the Spirit transforms us into his likeness.

Evangelicals and orthodox fellow travelers worldwide are retrieving and articulating this essential understanding of human being. These include Ray Anderson, Kevin Vanhoozer, Colin Gunton, C. Stephen Evans, Stanley Hauerwas, Edwin Hui (Xu Zhi-Wei) and Miroslav Volf, among others.[6] In the process, some common assumptions are being challenged and fresh affirmations are being restated in a positive, biblical light. In light of these studies, four essential theological affirmations can be made about human being in the trinitarian Christian story.

First, to be a human being is to be freely loved into being. That is, we are called into created existence by the triune God who exists as a communion of love and thus does not need human fellowship to be in loving relation. Thus, the divine choice to create human beings for personal fellowship is a free act of love, pleasure, and will (Eph. 1:5). We are called into being as gift, not necessity, as beloved ones whose meaning and destiny are given through, and contingent upon, our relation to God.

Second, Genesis speaks of our being made from the "stuff of creation," so that being human means to exist bodily within a given time and space. At the same time, human beings were created to be in relation to God and other human beings. That is, we are created in God's image for fellowship with God, and created male and female to be in relation to one another. Thus, to be human is essentially to be a "who" (a personal, intellectual, moral agent) called forth into existence as a unique, embodied "what" (a biological entity).

Christian history is full of attempts to understand the human person as body, mind, and soul, or body, soul, and spirit, embedding both reason and soul in the definition of humanity in the image of God. The Christian story narrated through Scripture, however, provides a view of human being as "embodied souls"/"ensouled bodies" without division. This means that sexually distinct embodiment, lived as gendered experience, is critical to a balanced Christian theology of human personhood.[7] The doctrines of creation, incarnation, and resurrection, especially grounded in the narrative context of creation/exodus/new creation, hold created human embodiment in highest regard as essential to image-bearing – which is *always both* individual and corporate.

Historically, a variety of forces has undermined this biblical view of humanity. For example, the Augustinian trajectory that runs through evangelical theology has not always affirmed human beings as "very good" creatures. For centuries the church treated the physical world as "bad" (the enemies we fight being "the world, the flesh, and the devil," all bound to sinful humanity and its ruin of the good creation) and human sexuality/embodiment as a curse, a source of depravity from which humans await eternal release. At the other end of the spectrum, post-Enlightenment modernity has also served to undermine a holistic understanding of human personhood in relation in favor of a robust individualism with a bifurcation of human being and personhood. Influenced by such modernity, evangelical pietism in the West has emphasized salvation as an individual reality, while forgetting its corporate dimension. In this individualistic, disembodied view of being human, salvation means getting individual souls into heaven rather than celebrating the resurrection of male and female human beings as new creations who together form an eschatological *people* for and with God.

It is as embodied persons, however, that we have self-consciousness, presence, identity, particularity, sexuality, communication, relation, and action. This basic understanding of being human, central to the biblical witness, is ultimately affirmed in the creaturely, personal, truly human incarnation and resurrection of the Son of God in Jesus of Nazareth, whose raised, and thus ongoing, humanity guarantees the restoration of fallen humankind. This disallows the evangelical tendency to devalue human embodiment and the creation. For just such reasons Paul stresses a "spiritually embodied" view of restored humanity in Jesus Christ, based on Jesus' own life and resurrection (1 Cor. 15). Jesus' life and ongoing High Priesthood further disallow any view of human being in individualistic terms. To be truly human is to be in submission and obedience to God, exercised in the context of community life, for the flourishing of human and non-human creation. It is to be in relation not only *with* but *for* the other as triune image-bearers, in conformity to the cruciform life of Jesus, Yahweh's true child.

Third, the historical reality of our human existence is that we still live in fallenness, resulting in death. With the exception of one particular human being, Jesus Christ, no human has ever been free from the consequential bondage of sin, and thus free to be truly human – to be for another without condition. John Calvin describes the human condition as *incurvatus in se*, turned in on ourselves in our brokenness rather than outwardly toward God and others. Moreover, our naturally birthed fallen human existence is currently limited by death. The one exception, however, changes everything: Jesus of Nazareth, who lived a truly human life in proper relation and obedience to God without sin, who died nevertheless and was subsequently resurrected by God as the "firstborn from among the dead," Lord over the "children of the resurrection" (Col. 1:18; Luke 20:36). Thus, in a mysterious way, human embodiment is de-limited and reconstituted by the resurrected, embodied human Son of God.

This leads to the fourth and final affirmation: To be a human being/person is to be future-oriented. In the New Testament, to be in the image of God is realized corporately in the fellowship of believers as they bear the image of Christ through the agency of the Holy Spirit. This is expressed in a life of love for God, neighbors, and the rest of creation. Paul emphasizes that the renewal of God's image in the Body of Christ is a dynamic and ongoing process of transformation (2 Cor. 3:18; Eph. 4:23, 24). In this process, *being* human is powerfully linked with *becoming* human, so that the endpoint of our renewed image is yet to be reached. Thus, the image of God belongs to time and eternity; it is a dynamic of being and becoming, both of which are held in Jesus Christ (1 Cor. 15:49; 1 John 3:2–3).

Our human identity is eternally grounded in the Son, who continues to be the new Adam at the right hand of the Father, functioning as our High Priest until he comes to bring all things in heaven and earth together when the times will have reached their fulfillment (Eph. 1:9–10). As the perfect image of God, Christ has made it possible for humanity to be renewed and conformed to his image (Rom. 8:29). Since "both the one who makes people holy and those who are made holy are of the same family" (Heb. 2:11), we "become" who we are – holy people – in conformity to him by the power of the Holy Spirit. All that Jesus did and does establishes our identity and vocation as image-bearers of Christ through the indwelling Spirit of God. This means that the future also determines human life in this present age. The character, values, and ethics of the future Kingdom of God are to be lived out "on earth as it is in heaven," even as we await the new creation in its fully restored expression (Matt. 6:10; Rom. 8:19–25).

ETHICAL CONSIDERATIONS

Truly Christian theology is inextricably linked to doxology and ethics. God's revelation to the world as a personal God compels human morality to be personal in lived response, or practical correspondence, to that revelation. To be truly human in Jesus Christ is to live in a particular way with a particular orientation (the "mind of Christ" by the Spirit) toward God, other human beings, and creation as Spirit-filled image-bearers of the triune God. It is to be a particular, eschatologically determined people, living out the reality of the future in the present, empowered to live into the full potential of being human in Christ.

Given this ontological and ethical particularity, Christian (and specifically evangelical) theology is called to address numerous challenges regarding justice and care for the disenfranchised (Amos, Micah, Isaiah); reconciliation regarding race, ethnicity, nationality, and gender (Gal. 3:26–29); eradication of poverty and poor health (Malachi); provision of basic resources for nurture, family, and home (Ps. 68:5–6); and more. This also includes theological clarity regarding diverse issues such as the God–world relation, Christology (challenging views of the Incarnation which fail to take Jesus' humanity or divinity seriously), bioethics (issues of human personhood surrounding assisted reproductive technologies, human cloning, stem cells, the human genome project, abortion, and euthanasia), sexuality and gender, creation care, and cultural/racial contextualization of the Christian story (decentralizing Western categories), to name a few. Entire chapters in this volume are devoted to some of these concerns.

Of key importance are the voices of egalitarian evangelicals or Christian feminists, and evangelicals from Latin America, Africa, and Asia,[8] whose unique insights and fresh articulations are critical among the predominantly white male, Euro-North American voices which have shaped evangelical theology over the past two centuries.[9] One of the great contributions of women in theology in the past century has been the reemphasis on relationality and community as constitutive of human being and lived experience in the image of God. Likewise, contributions from Latin America, Africa, and Asia are forcing evangelical theology to rethink its Western individualistic, consumerist orientation toward human life, relationships, and creation as a whole, calling for justice as an eschatological reality in the present determined by the future.[10]

Creation care and bioethics cannot be given sustained reflection in this volume, but they are nevertheless of critical concern for evangelical theology. As the flourishing of creation is contingent on the flourishing of the divine image-bearer, creation care is a necessary extension of reconstituted human being and personhood.[11] God both named and called human beings to be responsible overseers of creation (Gen. 1:26; 5:1–2) and gave *adam* the privilege of participating in creation through naming all other living creatures. With naming comes recognition and responsibility, exercising "dominion" so that all creation flourishes for God's pleasure and glory. Dominion reordered to the cruciform image of Christ exercises "power on behalf of all things" rather than "power over all things" (e.g., consumerist domination of resources and people).

Debates in bioethics abound, beginning with discussions about what constitutes human being at the atomistic level, describing the "mind" and "soul" in chemical and biological terms. As evolutionary biology and genetics, cognitive sciences and the various neurosciences have brought both human body and mind under scientific investigation, the result is that nearly all of the human capacities once attributed to the soul are considered by certain disciplines to be functions of the brain, which raises a whole host of questions and rigorous debate.[12] Certain evangelicals argue against physical reductionism and traditional body–soul dualisms in favor of "nonreductive physicalism," a view that understands the "soul" to be a functional capacity of the complex physical human organism, rather than a separate spiritual essence inhabiting a human body.[13] This not only challenges traditional dualisms but raises questions beyond present human being to the intermediate state – how do humans exist *as humans* after death and prior to their final bodily resurrection?[14]

Another critical challenge for North American evangelical theology is the need to address the tendency among certain evangelicals to conflate the gospel with a nationalistic ideology that enhances the flourishing of a few at the expense of multiple "others." As happens so often in history, a "local" narrative can subvert the meta-narrative of the universal Christian story of God's grace for the whole world. Though it is not unique, the current divine/earthly "kingdom confusion" in the U.S.A. has enormous ramifications for human personhood and eschatological hope worldwide.[15]

CONCLUSION

A joyful theological event is occurring in the church throughout the world, crossing denominational, confessional, traditional, ethnic, racial, and cultural lines: the affirmation that being human, *human being*, is concomitantly individual and communal "being in relation" based on a robust Trinitarian understanding of God. For evangelical theology, it is causing a helpful shift in the understanding of salvation as essentially bound up with God's restoration of all things. While salvation is singularly personal through the atoning death and resurrection of Jesus Christ, it is *not* primarily about getting a personal pass into heaven. Rather, it is about being reconstituted individually and corporately as an image-bearing people of the Holy Spirit who live the life of the future in the present, becoming who they are as they await their home in the consummation of a new heaven and earth.

In the Christian story, human being means that our lives are not our own. Our humanity is given being and purpose in belonging to an "other." That "other" is first and foremost the triune God to whom we belong and in whom our identity and being are grounded, who is wholly for us in Jesus Christ and the life-giving Holy Spirit. We become as we live for "others," celebrating the sexual, racial, ethnic, cultural, historical distinctions that make us unique in the Kingdom of God without prizing any one over the other, and so reflecting the image, character, and power of the self-giving God in whom we live and move and have our being.

At the center of God's relational self-revelation is what it means to be truly human. Here we meet Jesus Christ, miraculously conceived by the Spirit of God in the womb of a young Galilean woman, born and raised into a particular Jewish family, culture, and history. He lived this fully human life, however, without disobedience to the One who called his life into existence as God for and among us. Thus, to know Jesus as the Son of God is to discover both what God is like and what it means to be a real, unobstructed, perfectly human being – a true bearer of the divine image. God has chosen to speak this narrative into existence and to be its primary Subject for the sake of the world. In so doing, the triune God has chosen in Jesus Christ to be for ever determined by this story, just as our existence as children of the resurrection for ever is determined by our resurrected High Priest and exalted Lord.

The Christian story belongs to every cultural/social/traditional expression of the church and is in fact the organizing meta-narrative which each local community inhabits and rearticulates as the ground of its own narrative. As evangelical theology continues to develop in cultural diversity as well as trans-denominational and trans-confessional unity, the "good news" for human beings remains: in and through Jesus Christ and by the work of the transforming Holy Spirit, we will receive our inheritance in Christ – already to be and finally to become who and what we really are – truly human – to the praise of God's glory.

Further reading

Anderson, Ray S. *On Being Human: Essays in Theological Anthropology.* Grand Rapids, MI: Eerdmans, 1982.

Brown, Warren S., Nancey C. Murphy, and H. Newton Malony (eds.). *Whatever Happened to the Soul: Scientific and Theological Portraits of Human Nature.* Minneapolis, MN: Augsburg Fortress, 1998.

Cooper, John. *Body, Soul and Life Everlasting: Biblical Anthropology and the Monism–Dualism Debate.* Grand Rapids, MI: Eerdmans, 1989.

Grenz, Stanley J. *The Social God and the Relational Self.* Louisville, KY: Westminster John Knox, 2001.

Gunton, Colin E. *Christ and Creation.* Grand Rapids, MI: Eerdmans, 1992.

Hui, Edwin. *At the Beginning of Life: Dilemmas in Theological Bioethics.* Downers Grove, IL: InterVarsity, 2002.

McClay, Wilfred M. *The Masterless: Self and Society in Modern America.* Chapel Hill: University of North Carolina Press, 1994.

Price, Daniel J. *Karl Barth's Anthropology in Light of Modern Thought.* Grand Rapids, MI: Eerdmans, 2002.

Torrance, Alan J. *Persons in Communion: Trinitarian Description and Human Participation.* Edinburgh: T. & T. Clark, 1996.

Volf, Miroslav. *Exclusion and Embrace: A Theological Exploration of Identity, Otherness, and Reconciliation.* Nashville, TN: Abingdon, 1996.

Yu, Carver T. *Being and Relation: A Theological Critique of Western Dualism and Individualism.* Edinburgh: Scottish Academic Press, 1987.

Zizioulas, John. *Being as Communion.* Contemporary Greek Theologians 4. Crestwood, NY: St. Vladimir's Press, 1985.

Notes

1. Bette-Jane Crigger, "At the Center," *Hastings Center Report* 22 (January/
   February 1992), inside front cover and p. 17, cited by Edwin Hui, *At the
   Beginning of Life: Dilemmas in Theological Bioethics* (Downers Grove, IL:
   InterVarsity, 2002), p. 16.
2. Hui, *At the Beginning of Life*, p. 16.
3. Stan Grenz and Kevin Vanhoozer discuss this embeddedness in narrative as
   basic to Christian interpretation and articulation of the gospel in essays found
   in John G. Stackhouse Jr. (ed.), *Evangelical Futures: A Conversation on
   Theological Method* (Grand Rapids: Baker, 2000).
4. The use of male language for Yahweh, the triune God, follows God's personal
   language and action in the Christian narrative. The only authentic "maleness"
   in the triune communion, however, is the male humanity of Jesus Christ, the
   resurrected Son.
5. For an excellent synopsis of this narrative construction, see Rikk Watts, "The
   New Exodus/New Creational Restoration of the Image of God," in John G.
   Stackhouse, Jr. (ed.), *What Does it Mean to be Saved?* (Grand Rapids, MI:
   Baker, 2002), pp. 15–41. I am grateful to Watts's influence in this section of
   the chapter.
6. Since Karl Barth's reemphasis of this patristic understanding of the Trinity,
   the last century has been replete with Protestant, Orthodox, and Roman
   Catholic theologies that interact with Barth, the early fathers, and con-
   temporary rearticulations. See, e.g., Karl Barth, *Church Dogmatics* 3/2,
   ed. G. W. Bromiley and T. F. Torrance (Edinburgh: T. & T. Clark, 1960);
   T. F. Torrance, *The Trinitarian Faith* (Edinburgh: T. & T. Clark, 1988); Alan J.
   Torrance, *Persons in Communion: Trinitarian Description and Human Partici-
   pation* (Edinburgh: T. & T. Clark, 1996); Colin Gunton, *The Triune Creator* (Grand
   Rapids, MI: Eerdmans, 1998); John Zizioulas, *Being as Communion* (Crestwood,
   NY: St. Vladimir's Press, 1985); W. Norris Clarke, S. J., "To Be Is to Be Substance-
   in-Relation," in Paul A. Boggaard and Gordon Treash (eds.), *Metaphysics as
   Foundation* (New York: State University of New York Press, 1993), pp. 164–81;
   Catherine Mowry LaCugna, *God for Us: The Trinity and Christian Life* (New York:
   HarperCollins, 1991); Gary Deddo, *Karl Barth's Theology of Relations, Trinitarian,
   Christological and Human* (Washington, DC: P. Lang, 1999); Miroslav Volf, *After Our
   Likeness: The Church as the Image of the Trinity* (Grand Rapids, MI: Eerdmans,
   1998); Ray Anderson, *On Being Human* (Grand Rapids, MI: Eerdmans, 1982). For a
   general survey of this theological reassertion in the twentieth century, see Stan
   Grenz, *The Social God and the Relational Self* (Louisville, KY: Westminster John
   Knox, 2001).
7. See chapter 11 for a full discussion of human sexuality and gender as an
   essential aspect of lived human personhood.
8. For a particularly insightful theological and scientific critique on individualistic concepts of "being-in-itself" from a non-Western perspective, see Carver
   Yu, *Being and Relation: A Theological Critique of Western Dualism and
   Individualism* (Edinburgh: Scottish Academic Press, 1987). See also Georg
   Vicedom (ed.), *Christ and the Younger Churches: Theological Contributions
   from Asia, Africa and Latin America* (London: SPCK, 1972); John Mbiti,

Concepts of God in Africa (London: 1970); Kwame Bediako, *Theology and Identity: The Impact of Culture upon Christian Thought in the Second Century and Modern Africa* (Oxford, Regnum, 1992).

9. Alister E. McGrath advocates committed evangelical engagement with the whole of Christian tradition without being "mastered" by any prior voice(s). There is specific encouragement of non-Western evangelicals to engage their own historical religious and philosophical traditions and categories without being bound by those of Western Christendom ("Engaging the Great Tradition: Evangelical Theology and the Role of Tradition," in Stackhouse [ed.], *Evangelical Futures*, pp. 139–58).

10. Evangelical commitment to these issues can be found historically in the nineteenth century, particularly in regard to slavery reform and children's/ women's reform. In the twentieth century, strong articulation is prominent from the 1974 International Symposium on the Lausanne Covenant onward. See, e.g., C. René Padilla, "Spiritual Conflict," and Athol Gill, "Christian Social Responsibility," in C. René Padilla (ed.), *The New Face of Evangelicalism: An International Symposium on the Lausanne Covenant* (London: Hodder and Stoughton, 1976), pp. 205–22, and pp. 87–102, respectively.

11. See, e.g., Steven Bouma-Prediger, *For the Beauty of the Earth – A Christian Vision for Creation Care* (Grand Rapids, MI: Baker Academic, 2001); Joseph Sittler, *Evocations of Grace – Writings on Ecology, Theology and Ethics*, ed. Steven Bouma-Prediger and Peter Bakken (Grand Rapids, MI: Eerdmans, 2000); Rolston Holmes, III, *Conserving Natural Value* (New York: Columbia University Press, 1994); Jürgen Moltmann, *Creating a Just Future: The Politics of Peace and the Ethics of Creation in a Threatened World* (Philadelphia, PA: Trinity Press International, 1989).

12. See Malcolm Jeeves (ed.), *From Cells to Souls – and Beyond: Changing Portraits of Human Nature* (Grand Rapids, MI: Eerdmans, 2004).

13. Nancey Murphy explains that " 'Physicalism' signals our agreement with the scientists and philosophers who hold that it is not necessary to postulate a second metaphysical entity, the soul or mind, to account for human capacities and distinctiveness. 'Nonreductive' indicates our rejection of contemporary philosophical views that say that the person is 'nothing but' a body." See "Human Nature: Historical, Scientific, and Religious Issues," in Warren Brown, Nancey Murphy, and H. Newton Moloney (eds.), *Whatever Happened to the Soul?* (Minneapolis, MN: Augsburg Fortress, 1998), pp. 1–29, especially pp. 1–2. In *Whatever Happened to the Soul?*, Brown, Murphy, and Moloney assert that a biological statement made about human being refers to "exactly the same entity" as does a theological statement about the spiritual nature of persons.

14. At the center of this debate is John Cooper, who challenges Nancey Murphy, Joel Green, Kevin Corcoran, and others with his view of "holistic dualism." See *Body, Soul and Life Everlasting: Biblical Anthropology and the Monism–Dualism Debate* (Grand Rapids, MI: Eerdmans, 1989).

15. A sobering examination of a similar moment in German/world history can be found in Eberhard Busch, *Karl Barth and the Pietists* (Downers Grove, IL: InterVarsity, 2004).

6 Justification and atonement

D. STEPHEN LONG

What is "justification" and how is it related to atonement? Justification is being found just or righteous before God. The atonement is how Christ accomplishes our justification through his sacrifice on the cross. The following essay will examine biblical foundations of these doctrines, their historical genesis and controversies, and then in conclusion some pressing questions raised about them in contemporary theology.

BIBLICAL FOUNDATIONS

As Roger Olson rightly notes, for most contemporary evangelicals "justification by grace through faith alone" is the "soul of the Christian Gospel."[1] This is understood to be the heart of the Protestant Reformation, grounded in its emphasis on *sola scriptura*. Martin Luther's reading of Paul's letter to the Romans is the foundation for the doctrine of justification by faith alone, but Protestants claim Paul warrants this doctrine, not Luther. Martin Luther (1483–1546) was originally an Augustinian monk. He read the works of St. Augustine and found them preferable to the theologians of the Middle Ages, who were known as "the Schoolmen." However, not even Augustine offered Luther a satisfactory account of how terms such as "law, sin, grace, faith, righteousness, flesh, spirit and the like" were to be understood.[2] Luther thought the church of his day misunderstood these terms, largely because philosophical categories alien to the Bible led it astray. Luther wrote, "Augustine got nearer to the meaning of Paul than all the Schoolmen but he did not reach Paul. In the beginning I devoured Augustine, but when the door into Paul swung open and I knew what justification by faith really was, then it was out with him."[3] Luther turned from Augustine to Paul to discover how the righteousness of God overcomes our sin.

Paul offered both our problem and its answer. The problem is that the law of God must be fulfilled, not merely externally but internally as well.

The answer is that only faith in Christ fulfills it. Luther's "Preface to Romans" is a central source for the presentation of both. Luther wrote, "[God's] law must be fulfilled in your very heart and cannot be obeyed if you merely perform certain acts."[4] As Paul puts it in Romans 2:13, "For it is not the hearers of the law who are righteous before God, but the doers of the law who will be justified." The keeping of the law makes us "righteous" in God's eyes, but this is impossible for sinful creatures. No one can keep the law, and even those who appear never outwardly to transgress it merely keep it by "works," which are insufficient. In other words, even if you obeyed all the commandments and demonstrated a thorough external obedience, you would still fail to keep the law because the law is not corporeal but "spiritual."[5]

Here is the biblical origin for Luther's doctrine of justification by faith. We are called to obey the law, but this is something more than an external corporeal observance; it is a "spiritual" observance, which only occurs through God's Spirit. How do we receive this Spirit? Luther stated, "But the Holy Spirit is given only in, with, and through, faith in Jesus Christ, as Paul said in his opening paragraph." By this Luther refers to Paul's statement, "Therefore, since we are justified by faith, we have peace with God through our Lord Jesus Christ. Through him we have obtained access to this grace in which we stand, and we rejoice in our hope of sharing the glory of God" (Rom. 5:1–2). Luther concludes with a classical statement of the Protestant understanding of justification:

> We reach the conclusion that faith alone justifies us and fulfills the law; and this because faith brings us the spirit gained by the merits of Christ. The spirit, in turn, gives us the happiness and freedom at which the law aims; and this shows that good works really proceed from faith. That is Paul's meaning in chapter 3[:31] when, after having condemned the works of the law, he sounds as if he had meant to abrogate the law by faith; but says that on the contrary we confirm the law through faith, i.e. we fulfill it by faith.[6]

Luther does not deny that this righteousness becomes truly ours. He goes on to write,

> Faith, however, is something that God effects in us. It changes us and we are reborn from God, John 1 [:13]. Faith puts the old Adam to death and makes us quite different men in heart, in mind, and in all our powers ... O when it comes to faith what a living, creative, active powerful thing it is. It cannot do other than good at all times. It never

waits to ask whether there is some good work to do. Rather, before the question is raised, it has done the deed and keeps on doing it. A man not active in this way is a man without faith.[7]

This raises the question whether justification is only an imputed righteousness, something done for us, or if it is also an inherent righteousness, something done in us.

The doctrine of justification by faith is inextricably linked to how we think about Christ's righteousness and its effects on our relationship with God. As Timothy George put it, "Luther's new insight was that the imputation of Christ's alien righteousness was based, not on the gradual curing of sin, but rather on the complete victory on a cross."[8] This means that we cannot adequately explain the doctrine of justification by faith without also discussing the atonement. How does Christ's sacrifice on the cross atone for our sins and provide for our justification?

The atonement is the doctrine that seeks to show how Christ's life, death, and resurrection reconcile sinful creatures to God; it is inextricably linked to the doctrine of justification. This can be seen in a statement on justification put out by the Overseas Mission Society International:

> Justification is the gracious judicial act of God fully acquitting the repenting and believing sinner (Rom. 3:24–26; 5:1). God grants full pardon of all guilt, release from the penalty of sins committed, and acceptance as righteous, not on the basis of the merits or efforts of the sinner, but upon the basis of the atonement by Jesus Christ and the faith of the sinner (Rom. 3:28; Gal. 2:16; Titus 3:7).[9]

Here the atonement is one of penal substitution. Jesus takes the penalty of God's wrath for us sinners upon himself and acquits us of the judgment we deserve. It is "judicial" and moves us from a state of sin to one of grace.

Although the first seven ecumenical councils of the church laid down the proper teaching for many issues in theology, such as the triune character of God and the relationship between divinity and humanity in the single person of Jesus Christ, they did not set forth a single official teaching (or dogma) on how to explain the atonement. Evangelical theology has tended to go beyond orthodoxy and insist that Holy Scripture does warrant a particular account of the atonement called the substitutionary theory. Such theories tend to fall into two broad categories. One emphasizes objective change in the cosmos that Christ's sacrifice effects. The second emphasizes a subjective change in creatures. Anselm (1033–1109) is usually associated with the former and Abelard (1079–1142) the latter.

Their two respective theories are called "satisfaction" and "moral influence." However, this distinction has more to do with contemporary debates about the atonement than what Anselm and Abelard actually taught. Anselm did not deny a subjective effect from the atonement; nor did Abelard deny its objective consequence. Both Abelard and Anselm agreed that a patristic theme was improper: the devil held no right that God had to honor. Both offered a more sophisticated account of the atonement than that.

Most evangelical institutions and churches affirm a version of Anselm's satisfaction (or, later, the substitutionary) theory. For instance, the eighth affirmation and denial of the "Gospel of Jesus Christ" states,

> We affirm that the atonement of Christ by which, in his obedience, he offered a perfect sacrifice, propitiating the Father by paying for our sins and satisfying divine justice on our behalf according to God's eternal plan, is an essential element of the Gospel. We deny that any view of the Atonement that rejects the substitutionary satisfaction of divine justice, accomplished vicariously for believers, is compatible with the teaching of the Gospel.[10]

The crucial biblical text for this comes from Romans 3:23–25: "since all have sinned and fall short of the glory of God, they are justified by his grace as a gift, through the redemption which is in Christ Jesus, whom God put forward as an expiation by his blood to be received by faith."

This reflects a "penal substitutionary theory of the atonement," which was one of the five fundamentals set forth in the twentieth century to reconcile contending evangelical groups.[11] All have been challenged by mainline liberal Protestant theology, but the penal substitutionary theory has especially been called into question as unworthy of a gracious God.

What is "penal substitutionary atonement" and why is it controversial inside and outside of evangelical circles? Debates in evangelical theology have focused on the Pauline term *hilasterion* in Romans 3:25. Should it be translated as "expiation" or "propitiation"? The latter term emphasizes "appeasement of God's wrath" while the former suggests "covering of sins."[12] What does it mean to say that God's wrath must be appeased? Does this mean that God must change? Does God the Father demand that the Son die? Is this what propitiation means and expiation seeks to avoid? Must there be a "blood sacrifice," and if so what does that say about the nature of God? As we will see below, any suggestion that God is appeased and changed through bloodshedding is a caricature of Anselm's theology. Its point is not to make blood-sacrifice at the heart of God's being, but to show how God takes this suffering upon himself and thus promises to put an end to it as well as make a place for our suffering in God's own impassible life.

The significance of this doctrine can be found in a sermon preached by Samuel Wells, Dean of Duke Chapel, Durham, North Carolina, after the devastation of Hurricane Katrina.

> All God's anger against human depravity . . . all God's anger was experienced by Jesus on the cross. But most importantly death was overcome. The horror of Nature, its death and destruction, does not have the final word. Easter has the final word. So let's never say "how can God do nothing?" for God has already done everything. The one thing he hasn't done is obliterate us. He did that to Jesus instead. Can you believe it?[13]

The statement on justification and its relationship to a penal substitutionary theology of the atonement in the document "The Gospel of Jesus Christ" was controversial because it assumes a staunchly Reformed understanding of justification as primarily "forensic." This means that Christ's righteousness is "imputed" to us, but it is not "inherent" in us. Some evangelical theologians interpreted this statement as a criticism of a document on justification set forth by "Evangelicals and Catholics together," which emphasized holiness and sanctification as much as imputed righteousness. The affirmations and denials in "The Gospel of Jesus Christ" tend to make it difficult for evangelical Wesleyans and Anabaptists to sign on to it, as an examination of the historical issues, and especially the differences among Calvinist, Wesleyan, and Anabaptist evangelicals on the doctrine of justification, makes clear.[14]

HISTORICAL ISSUES

When Luther offered his classical statement of the doctrine of justification, he stated that "faith brings us the spirit gained by the merits of Christ." The term "merits of Christ" is significant. He was reacting against the doctrine of merit in the Roman Catholic Church. Luther opposed John Tetzel, who preached indulgences and evidently stated that "when a coin in the coffer rings, a soul from purgatory springs." Indulgences were acts (such as offering money) that forgive sins. They were based on the Catholic doctrine of merit which assumed that a good work could release a soul from purgatory into heaven. The Catholic doctrine of merit stipulated that a Christian had to accumulate sufficient merit in order to be found righteous in God's eyes. One version of this doctrine of merit, which was taught by Gabriel Biel (1420–95) and grounded in "nominalism," distinguishes two kinds of merit: *meritum de condigno* and *meritum do congruo*. The first form of merit, *de condigno*, or a "merit meeting the standard of God's justice," is based on God's "ordained power" or God's established order. Here God agrees to reward the moral good for those who perform it in a state of grace.[15] The second form of merit, *de congruo*, is "a merit meeting the standard of God's generosity." God accepts this action and grants merit even though it would be performed in a state of sin.[16] Here God's acceptance is based solely on God's "absolute power" to be generous despite how God has so ordered creation.

Luther both was influenced by this theology of merit and reacted against it. When he emphasizes that "faith brings us the spirit gained by the merits of Christ," he is rejecting a doctrine of merit. Justification by faith alone through grace challenges this doctrine. But Luther, and more especially Lutheranism, could so emphasize this justification that it lost the importance of sanctification. In other words, if justification is by faith alone, is it only imputed to us? Are Christians also called to an "inherent" righteousness?

The Council of Trent (1545–63) was the Catholic Response to the Protestant teaching on justification. It both reformed practices in the Catholic Church that Luther exposed, and condemned what the council fathers thought were Protestant heresies in the teaching of justification. This can be seen in the thirty-three canons that were issued on the Council's sixth session, 13 January 1547.[17] Canon 1 rejects Protestant interpretations of Catholic teaching. "If anyone says that man can be justified before God by his own works, whether done by his own natural powers or through the teaching of the law, without divine grace through Jesus Christ let him be anathema." Yet Catholics continued to teach that God's righteousness must not only be imputed, but also inherent (Canon 11), that the human will must cooperate in "disposing and preparing itself to obtain the grace of justification" (Canon 4), and that the Law and Commandments must actually be observed (Canons 19 and 20).[18] Based on these canons, the council fathers also continued to teach a doctrine of merit.

> If anyone says that the good works of the one justified are in such manner the gifts of God that they are not also the good merits of him justified; or that the one justified by the good works that he performs by the grace of God and the merit of Jesus Christ, whose living members he is, does not truly merit an increase of grace, eternal life, and in case he dies in grace, the attainment of eternal life itself, and also an increase of glory, let him be anathema.   (Canon 32)[19]

One of the important questions is how different the Protestant and Catholic positions actually were. Did Catholics caricature Luther and Protestant teaching? Did Luther and Protestants caricature Catholic doctrine? Were they closer than they thought? The "Joint Declaration on the Doctrine of Justification by the Lutheran World Federation and the Catholic Church," affirmed on 31 October 1999, suggests they were. It proclaimed "that on the basis of their dialogue the subscribing Lutheran churches and the Roman Catholic Church are now able to articulate a common understanding of our justification by God's grace through faith in Christ." The heart of that common understanding is found in the statement, "Together we confess: By grace alone, in faith in Christ's saving work and not because of any merit on our part, we are accepted by God and receive the Holy Spirit, who renews our hearts while equipping and calling us to good works." This joint declaration also addresses some of the differences between Catholics and Protestants, clarifying each position. For instance, a Catholic understanding of our cooperation in justification was clarified. "When Catholics say that persons 'cooperate' in preparing for and accepting justification by consenting to God's justifying action, they see such personal consent as itself an effect of grace, not as an action arising from innate human abilities." Likewise, Lutherans affirmed a doctrine of sanctification along with justification. "We confess together that good works – a Christian life lived in faith, hope and love – follow justification and are its fruits." The relationship between a Catholic doctrine of merit and the connection between justification and sanctification was also emphasized.

> When Catholics affirm the 'meritorious' character of good works, they wish to say that, according to the biblical witness, a reward in heaven is promised to these works. Their intention is to emphasize the responsibility of persons for their actions, not to contest the character of those works as gifts, or far less to deny that justification always remains the unmerited gift of grace.[20]

This joint declaration was historically significant, and should have an influence on the doctrine of justification in the evangelical tradition. It has been well received by evangelicals who embrace a strong doctrine of holiness and have a place for the sacraments in the Christian life, but some more staunchly Reformed evangelicals see in this joint declaration a concern that the Reformation's insistence on imputed righteousness is being diminished.

Menno Simons (1496–1561), from whose name the Mennonite Church arose, was a Roman Catholic priest who left the Catholics and joined the

Anabaptists. He wrote against any doctrine of merit. "Notice my dear reader, that we do not believe nor teach that we are to be saved by our merits and words as the envious assert without truth. We are to be saved solely by grace through Christ Jesus ..." But he also opposed any Protestant account of justification that remained satisfied with an appeal to "faith" without holy living; for Menno and the Anabaptists, holiness of life was an essential part of grace.

> All those who disregard this preached grace and do not accept Christ Jesus by faith; who reject His holy Word, will, commandments and ordinances; who hate and persecute; who willfully live according to their lusts, these are all through. It will avail them nothing before the Lord to boast of their faith, new creature, Christ's grace, death and blood; for they do not believe; they remain in their first birth, namely, in their earthly corrupted nature, impenitent, carnally minded, yes, utterly without the Spirit, Word and Christ.[21]

Menno followed the Protestants on justification by faith, but found that they often used it as an excuse for "remaining" content with the old, sinful nature. Here Anabaptists found an ally in the Anglican evangelical, John Wesley, who began the Methodist movement.

One of John Wesley's most important sermons, "the Lord our Righteousness," takes on a theme similar to that noted by Menno. Wesley expresses his concern that many a Christian is using the important Pauline phrase "the Lord our Righteousness" as a "cover for his unrighteousness."[22] Thus while Wesley recognized the Protestant emphasis on justification as an imputed righteousness, he also equally emphasized sanctification as an inherent righteousness. This provoked some Calvinists to accuse him of denying the Protestant faith for that of Catholicism. The Calvinist Hervey asked, "But do not you believe inherent righteousness?" Wesley responded, "Yes, in its proper place; not as the ground of our acceptance with God, but as the fruit of it; not in the place of imputed righteousness, but as consequent upon it. That is I believe God implants righteousness in every one to whom he has imputed it."[23] Calvinist and Wesleyan evangelicals continue to be divided on this issue.

Some Wesleyan evangelicals find in contemporary manifestations of Reformed evangelicals, who reject the significance of the sacraments, emphasize justification by faith in opposition to sanctification, and consistently reject aspects of Christian tradition, more of an influence of a modern (liberal) Protestant doctrine of justification that tends to be iconoclastic. This kind of doctrine of justification can be found in the neo-Protestant teaching of Paul Tillich. He took the doctrine of justification to be the heart of his theology: "Justification brings the element of 'in spite of' into the process of theology. It is the immediate consequence of the doctrine of atonement and it is the heart and center of salvation."[24] The "in spite of" character emphasized that we are always only sinners saved by grace. To assume that we have any inherent righteousness or ability to cooperate in our salvation would be to deny the heart of the Reformation. The only contribution our will makes is that "we must accept that we are accepted" even though our life is not transformed. Much of evangelical theology seems to assume something like Tillich's neo-Protestantism. It bears great similarities to his iconoclastic approach to Christian tradition, where everything that came before needs to be questioned, deconstructed, and removed to make room for a newer, more modern version of the Christian life. Such neo-Protestantism differs markedly from Luther and Calvin, both of whom had a stronger insistence on sanctification. This stronger insistence led both Calvin and Luther to insist on the role of the church, its liturgical life, and the sacraments as necessary means for an ongoing life of holiness. This aspect of Reformed teaching is largely missing in contemporary evangelicalism, although through the work of some contemporary critics it is being recovered.

Calvin developed the doctrine of justification by faith within the context of his Christology, based upon Christ's threefold office as "prophet, priest and King."[25] All three Christological offices mediate Christ's sacrifice to us, and all three offices are intimately related to the life of the church. This means that the whole of Christ's life is redemptive and not just one part of it. As Calvin puts it, "Therefore, we divide the substance of our salvation between Christ's death and resurrection as follows: through his death, sin was wiped out and death extinguished; through his resurrection, righteousness was restored and life raised up, so that – thanks to his resurrection – his death manifested its power and efficacy in us."[26] Calvin too recognized that although "man is justified by faith alone, and simple pardon; nevertheless, actual holiness of life, so to speak, is not separated from free imputation of righteousness."[27] However, he strongly resisted assumptions about the human will's participation in holiness through the liturgical practice of penance. He opposed both the Anabaptists and Jesuits on this point.[28] For Calvin, repentance was a turning from sin out of fear of God, rather than turning to God out of fear of sin. The latter does not seem to be possible given our depravity. Thus Calvin, even more so than Augustine, emphasized that sin always remains in the justified.[29] Because of this, any discussion of inherent righteousness is often viewed by contemporary Reformed evangelicals as incompatible with the imputed righteousness of Christ in the doctrine of justification. This is another essential difference both among and within Reformed, Wesleyan, Anglican, and Anabaptist evangelicals.

CONTEMPORARY THEOLOGY, CRITICISMS, AND THE CURRENT DEBATES

Three contemporary issues challenge the doctrine of justification as often presented by evangelicals. First, does it neglect the importance of deification as taught by the Eastern and Western fathers? Second, does its connection to penal substitutionary theories of the atonement either legitimate violence or posit violence in God's being? Third, is it an adequate reading of Paul and of biblical teaching in general?

Justification and deification

Eastern Orthodox theologians question whether the Christian West's doctrine of justification betrays the church fathers' insistence on deification. Some argue that the West's doctrine is based on a model of "criminal law" whereas the East approaches redemption from the perspective of something more like "civil law."[30] The end result is a different conception of salvation, the Western based on various legal "states" that remove guilt whereas the East emphasizes a more participatory "recapitulation" of our fallen humanity into Christ and the vanquishing of death. Any sharp distinction, however, between the Western and Eastern churches on these matters has been criticized by theologians standing in both traditions.[31]

Protestant theologians have also recognized that a sharp distinction between justification and deification does not necessarily make sense of our tradition. Whatever one's overall assessment of it, the "Finnish" interpretation of Luther[32] shows how Luther, like the Eastern fathers, drew on 2 Peter 1:4, which is essential to both Eastern and Western understandings of the atonement and states that we are to be "partakers of the divine nature."[33] Both Wesley and Thomas Aquinas also placed tremendous emphasis on 2 Peter 1:4.[34]

The Eastern Orthodox theologian David Hart challenges any easy distinction between deification, taking place primarily through the Incarnation, and Western justification, occurring through the cross. He does this by recognizing that Anselm offers us much more than juridical, punitive exchange at the heart of the atonement. Hart finds similarities among Anselm, Athanasius, Gregory of Nyssa, and John of Damascus[35] just as A. N. Williams finds similarities between the "Western" Aquinas and the "Eastern" Gregory Palamas.

Valorizing violence?

While Hart gives a compelling account of Anselm's theology and shows its continuity with the patristic writers, other contemporary theologians find Anselm's proto-substitutionary theory of the atonement dangerous and reject it for valorizing violence. Joanne Carlson Brown and Rebecca Parker find Anselm's "satisfaction" theory of the atonement a sanction for suffering and violence, for God directly wills the Son's death as the means to our salvation, and thus God wills evil that good may come.[36] But whether affirmed or rejected, this is a misreading of Anselm and not the basis for his theory of the atonement. No patristic or early medieval theologians would countenance the possibility that God positively wills evil. Anselm did not teach that God directly desired the Son's death. In fact, he addresses the question, "For what justice is there in giving up the most just man of all to death on behalf of the sinner?" And he responds, "For God did not force him to die or allow him to be slain against his will; on the contrary, he himself readily endured death in order to save men." Why did he die? Not because God directly willed his death, but because of his "obedience." Or as Anselm put it, "Therefore God did not compel Christ to die, when there was no sin in him, but Christ himself freely underwent death, not by yielding up his life as an act of obedience, but on account of his obedience in maintaining justice, because he so steadfastly persevered in it that he brought death on himself."[37]

In other words, Anselm does not locate Christ's obedience in his willingness to die for the sake of sacrifice itself. Anselm understands Christ's death as a consequence of his obedience to God's righteousness in a world where that righteousness is unwelcome. What redeems is Christ's obedience even in the face of death, his unwillingness to turn from God's righteousness. The substitution Christ makes for us is both as the one who fulfills our obedience (the merits of Christ) and as the one who suffers God's judgment against sin, suffering, and death on our behalf. Far from valorizing suffering and death, Anselm's theology proclaims their end.

Is justification by faith a Pauline theme?

A third issue for the Protestant doctrine of justification questions how adequate it is to biblical teaching, Paul's in particular. In his essay "Paul and the Introspective Consciousness of the West," Krister Stendahl first challenged the centrality of a Protestant doctrine drawn from Paul that emphasized justification as the removal of an individual's guilt. Since then some Pauline scholars have questioned whether a Protestant interpretation of Paul should view *dikaiosis* (being found righteous) as referring primarily to individual guilt for sin. Such scholars find this something of a misreading, or at least an incomplete reading. Paul uses this term to explain how Gentiles are brought into union with Jews in Christ's body, which is the new community, the church. So Richard Hays writes, "[T]he church is to *become* the righteousness of God: where the church embodies in its life together the world-reconciling love of Jesus Christ, the new creation is manifest. The church incarnates the righteousness of God."[38] For Hays, then, justification by faith is not primarily a statement in Paul about the removal of an individual's guilt, but about the "being made righteous" Christ effects in his body by bringing Gentiles and Jews together into a new community.[39]

These three issues will need to be addressed as evangelicals continue to offer a sound theological defense of the doctrine of justification by faith, a doctrine upon which the Holy Spirit may be leading all our ecclesial traditions into a holy and unified convergence.

Further reading

Aulen, Gustaf. *Christus Victor: An Historical Study of the Three Main Types of the Idea of Atonement*. Trans. A. G. Hebert. New York: Macmillan, 1969.

Boersma, Hans. *Violence, Hospitality, and the Cross: Reappropriating the Atonement Tradition*. Grand Rapids, MI: Baker Academic, 2004.

Carson, Donald A., Peter T. O'Brien, and Mark A. Seifrid (eds.). *Justification and Variegated Nomism*. 2 vols. Grand Rapids, MI: Baker Academic, 2004.

Green, Joel B., and Mark D. Baker. *Recovering the Scandal of the Cross: Atonement in New Testament and Contemporary Contexts*. Downers Grove, IL: InterVarsity, 2000.

Hill, Charles E., and Frank A. James III (eds.). *The Glory of the Atonement: Biblical, Historical and Practical Perspectives*. Downers Grove, IL: InterVarsity, 2004.

Husbands, Mark, and Daniel J. Treier (eds.). *Justification: What's at Stake in the Current Debates*. Downers Grove, IL: InterVarsity, 2004.

Kärkkäinen, Veli-Matti. *One With God: Salvation as Deification and Justification*. Collegeville, MN: Liturgical, 2004.

Lane, Anothony N. S. *Justification by Faith in Catholic–Protestant Dialogue: An Evangelical Assessment*. New York: T. & T. Clark, 2002.

McGrath, Alister E. *Iustitia Dei: A History of the Christian Doctrine of Justification*. 3rd edition. Cambridge: Cambridge University Press, 2005.

Stott, John R. W. *The Cross of Christ*. Downers Grove, IL: InterVarsity, 1986.

Westerholm, Stephen. *Perspectives Old and New on Paul: The "Lutheran" Paul and His Critics*. Grand Rapids, MI: Eerdmans, 2003.

Notes

1. Roger E. Olson, *A-Z of Evangelical Theology* (London: SCM, 2005), p. 223.
2. John Dillenberger (ed.), *Martin Luther: Selections from His Writings* (Garden City, NY: Doubleday, 1961), p. 20.
3. Timothy George, "Martin Luther," in Jeffrey P. Greenman and Timothy Larsen (eds.), *Reading Romans through the Centuries: From the Early Church to Karl Barth* (Grand Rapids, MI: Brazos, 2005), p. 116.
4. Dillenberger (ed.), *Martin Luther*, p. 20.
5. *Ibid.*, p. 21.
6. *Ibid.*, p. 22.
7. *Ibid.*, p. 24.
8. George, "Martin Luther," p. 116.
9. Thomas C. Oden and J. I. Packer, *One Faith: The Evangelical Consensus* (Downers Grove, IL: InterVarsity, 2004), p. 82.
10. *Ibid.*, p. 7.
11. Brian D. McLaren, *Generous Orthodoxy* (Grand Rapids, MI: Zondervan, 2004), p. 197. (The others were the virgin birth, the verbal plenary inspiration and inerrancy of the Bible, the bodily resurrection of Jesus, and his imminent return.)
12. Olson, *A-Z*, p. 149.
13. Samuel Wells, "Hurricane Katrina: A Sermon Preached in Duke University Chapel on Sept. 4, 2005 by the Rev'd Canon Dr. Sam Wells," www.chapel.duke.edu/documents/sermons/sermon_150.pdf.
14. Olson, *A-Z*, p. 225.
15. Heiko Oberman, *The Harvest of Medieval Theology* (Durham, NC: Labyrinth, 1983), pp. 43, 471.
16. *Ibid.*, p. 471.
17. John H. Leith (ed.), *Creeds of the Churches*, 3rd edition (Atlanta, GA: John Knox, 1982), pp. 408–24.
18. *Ibid.*, p. 420.
19. *Ibid.*, p. 424.
20. The Lutheran World Federation and the Roman Catholic Church, *Joint Declaration on the Doctrine of Justification* (Grand Rapids, MI: Eerdmans, 2000), pp. 10, 15, 17, 24, 25.
21. Menno Simons, *The Complete Writings of Menno Simons*, ed. J. C. Wenger (Scottdale, PA: Herald, 1956), pp. 506–7.
22. John Wesley, *The Works of John Wesley I*, ed. Albert Outler (Nashville, TN: Abingdon, 1984), p. 455.
23. *Ibid.*, p. 458.
24. Paul Tillich, *Systematic Theology*, 3 vols. (Chicago: University of Chicago Press, 1951–63), vol. II, p. 178.
25. John Calvin, *Institutes of the Christian Religion*, ed. John T. McNeill (Philadelphia, PA: Westminster, 1950), p. 494.
26. *Ibid.*, p. 521.
27. *Ibid.*, p. 593.
28. *Ibid.*, p. 595.
29. *Ibid.*, p. 602.

30. David Hart, *The Doors of the Sea: Where Was God in the Tsunami?* (Grand Rapids, MI: Eerdmans, 2005), p. 33.

31. See A. N. Williams, *The Ground of Union: Deification in Aquinas and Palamas* (New York: Oxford University Press, 1999); David Hart, *The Beauty of the Infinite: The Aesthetics of Christian Truth* (Grand Rapids, MI: Eerdmans, 2003).

32. Often associated especially with Tuomo Mannerma, in which Luther's doctrine is interpreted more ontologically and mystically than ethically or juridically.

33. Douglas Harink, "Doing Justice to Justification: Setting it Right," *The Christian Century* (14 June 2005), p. 21; Veli-Matti Kärkkäinen, *One With God: Salvation as Deification and Justification* (Collegeville, MN: Liturgical, 2004).

34. See D. Stephen Long, *John Wesley's Moral Theology: The Quest for God and Goodness* (Nashville, TN: Kingswood, 2005), pp. 196–97.

35. Hart, *Beauty of the Infinite*, p. 366.

36. See Joanne Carlson Brown and Rebecca Parker, "For God So Loved the World," in J. Brown and C. Bohn (eds.), *Christianity, Patriarchy, Abuse* (Cleveland, OH: Pilgrim, 1989), pp. 1–30.

37. Anselm, *Why God Became Man*, in *A Scholastic Miscellany*, Library of Christian Classics (Philadelphia, PA: Westminster, 1956), pp. 111–15.

38. Krister Stendahl, "The Apostle Paul and the Introspective Conscience of the West," *Harvard Theological Review* 56 (1963): 199–215; Richard B. Hays, *The Moral Vision of the New Testament* (San Francisco: Harper, 1996), p. 24.

39. For alternative perspectives in biblical scholarship, see several essays in Mark Husbands and Daniel J. Treier (eds.), *Justification: What's at Stake in the Current Debates* (Downers Grove, IL: InterVarsity, 2004).

7 The Holy Spirit

TERRY L. CROSS

INTRODUCTION

The bane and bog of most evangelical theology for the last century has been the doctrine of the Holy Spirit. Within the evangelical movement it has either bogged down in the sinking quagmire of debate or hovered emptily in the stale air of banality.[1] To be sure, part of this dilemma is shared by all Christian theology in the West, namely, that the Spirit has been portrayed in Scripture without a face or with non-personal characteristics (such as a dove, wind, fire). The result is that theological consideration of the third article of the creed lacks depth and nuance.[2] In some ways, this is fitting since the Holy Spirit points to Jesus Christ (John 15:26) and "will not speak on his own" but only what he hears (John 16:13; TNIV). The Spirit will glorify Christ because it is from Christ that the Spirit receives whatever he makes known to the disciples (John 16:14). Hence, one prominent scriptural image that we receive concerning the Holy Spirit is this manner of deflecting glory and attention to Jesus the Christ. Such a deferential move may be one reason why Christian theology has added very little to the Nicene-Constantinopolitan Creed (AD 381): "And [we believe] in the Holy Spirit, the Lord and life-giver, Who proceeds from the Father and Son, Who is worshipped and glorified together with the Father and Son, Who spoke through the prophets."[3]

Introductions such as the paragraph above have become predictable. In 1956, George Hendry noted this problem: "It has become almost a convention that those who undertake to write about the Holy Spirit should begin by deploring the neglect of this doctrine in the thought and life of the Church today."[4] Yet three perspectives of help and hope will be woven throughout this chapter. Whatever a person's response to Pentecostalism, a surge of interest in the Spirit has been spawned by this movement. While Pentecostalism is in its adolescence, so to speak, in writing discursive theology, it does offer some fresh considerations for the Spirit's role in evangelical thought and life.[5] In addition, Eastern Orthodoxy has provided a persistent focus on the Spirit for two millennia. While evangelicals in the West may not simply borrow Eastern terminology without its entire worldview, the Orthodox do have insight to offer our thinking on the Spirit.[6] Finally, new voices call for a reshaping of the "center" and core identity of evangelicalism itself. These voices are pointing toward renewal of the theological task by the Spirit. Evangelicals are best served by a robust Trinitarian pneumatology that also contains a Christ-centered focus.

In this chapter we will examine specific *loci communes* related to the Spirit. One task will be to provide some expression of evangelical thought on these areas; another will be to engage the new voices mentioned above.

THE SPIRIT AND THE TRINITY

Evangelical thought on the Spirit traces its lineage back to early church discussions on the members of the Trinity. While the biblical discussion regarding the person of the Spirit is limited, there are hints of the divine nature of the Spirit. In a parallel reading of Acts 5:3–4, we discover that Peter describes "lying to the Holy Spirit" and "lying to God" as the same thing. The Trinitarian benediction in 2 Corinthians 13:14 bolsters understanding of the equality and divinity of Father, Son, and Spirit.[7] Beyond this, evangelicals see a particular "logic" of thought in the New Testament regarding the divinity of the Spirit: divine names are given to the Spirit, divine perfections are ascribed to the Spirit, and divine works are performed by the Spirit.[8]

Aligning with Athanasius on the divinity of Christ, evangelicals also follow suit with Athanasius's understanding of the divinity of the Spirit – with some notable differences of emphasis on both. Instead of relying on a metaphysical rationale for Christ's divinity (which remains the focus of some evangelicals), Athanasius seems to argue on the basis of soteriology as found in Scripture.[9] Some thirty years later, Athanasius responds to the attacks of the Pneumatomachians ("enemies of the Spirit") by tracing the scriptural passages concerning the divinity of the Spirit. Athanasius notes that if the Son belongs to the Father, then the Spirit also belongs to the Father since whatever belongs to the Son in turn belongs to the Father.[10] With the same logic, the Spirit cannot be a creature because the Son is not a creature. Since the Spirit is the "seal" of our redemption, the Spirit cannot be a creature. Creatures are "sealed," but something other than a creature is required to do the sealing or to be the seal.[11] Hence, the Spirit is God or else our sanctification (*theosis*) is in peril.[12]

Through various means – but perhaps none as powerful as Augustine – the West adopted a strong focus on the second person of the Trinity (the Eternal Son) and weakened a potentially robust doctrine of the Spirit. With the addition of *"filioque"* ("and the Son") in the Roman version of the creed, the Spirit is viewed by the West as proceeding from both the Father *and the Son*, whereas in the East this phrase is omitted.[13] One result is that the Western church has viewed the Spirit as the reciprocal relation between the Father and Son, with the Spirit's identity being associated primarily with the other two members of the Trinity. The eternal generation of the Son helps to form the identity of the Father and the Son; thus, it is the "primary movement in the eternal God,"[14] while the "secondary movement" is the "eternal spiration" of the Spirit. As Augustine has said, the Spirit is the bond of love (*vinculum amoris* or *communis caritas*) between Father and Son.[15]

Such love language, however, adds weight to the charge that the Western doctrine of the Spirit tends toward the impersonal.[16] Does this mean that the Spirit is not love? Perhaps instead it means that we need to exercise care in how we prescribe the relations of the Trinity. The concepts of circularity of love and *perichoresis* (mutual reciprocity) provide great assistance. Colin Gunton notes that it is the Spirit whose

> function is to make the love of God a love that is opened toward that which is not itself, to perfect it in otherness. Because God is not in himself a closed circle but is essentially the relatedness of community, there is within his eternal being that which freely and in love creates, reconciles and redeems that which is not himself.[17]

Gunton adds that this open circle is radically changed by the addition of an "eschatological note" to the Spirit's endeavor, thereby making the relationships of the inner Trinity part of a community of other-embracing love.[18]

What does all this have to do with evangelicals? One thing is clear: we humans are limited in our understanding of the mystery that is the Trinity. The caution of Sergius Bulgakov is merited: "The human understanding is given the capacity to know these aspects of the being of the Spirit only discursively, by successively passing from one definition to another, for it knows love only as a state or attribute of a hypostasis, not as a hypostasis in itself."[19] We tend to stutter terribly when discussing the inner-Trinitarian relations. Yet, some insight from these relations will assist us in grasping how the Spirit relates to humans, thereby connecting who the Spirit is within the Trinity to what the Spirit does in the human sphere. As Millard Erickson accurately states, "The Holy Spirit is the point at which the Trinity becomes personal to the believer."[20]

What might we learn from the Spirit's relation to the Father and Son? First, the Spirit is "ecstatic," that is, "stands outside of oneself."[21] The Spirit spawns an overflow of God's own rich relationship toward the world. The doctrine of the Trinity is not a portrayal of three Gods, but suggests movement in God. God's being is not solitary, but communal with differentiation.[22] In the persons we find a threefold repetition of God. God's being is a type of self-relatedness whose "being is in becoming."[23]

The immanent relationship within the Trinity comes to fulfillment in its economic movement toward the world.[24] Clark Pinnock describes this well: "God is the ever-expanding circle of loving, and the Spirit is the dynamic at the heart of the circle."[25] Creation and redemption are both the overflow of God's rich Trinitarian fellowship – they are both evidences of God's grace.[26] The Spirit triggers this overflow of love, according to characteristics revealed in Scripture. The Spirit brings humans together in communion or fellowship (2 Cor. 13:14); the Spirit is the love that binds all things in harmony (Gal. 5:22; Col. 3:14); the Spirit works to bring people and things together in God's plan through love, fellowship, unity, and peace (1 Cor. 1:10; 3:3; Eph. 4:2); the Spirit brings humans into the fellowship between the Father and Son (1 John 1:3–4).[27] God's love "has been poured out into our hearts through the Holy Spirit, who has been given to us" (Rom. 5:5). The Spirit operates as the "point person" to open up the Trinity itself to the world.

Second, the Spirit choreographs and participates in the Trinitarian "dance" (*perichoresis*). An ancient notion that was used originally to guard against the division of the Trinity, *perichoresis* refers to the divine persons mutually inhering in one another or drawing "life from one another."[28] While it referred to the inner-Trinitarian relations, it also was expanded to suggest that divinity itself could be communicated – it could "move outside itself, even indwell that which is other and not be thereby diminished."[29] If the joyous dance of God is self-contained – unrelated to creation or humans – then as Catherine Mowry LaCugna intimates, the doctrine of the Trinity is defeated.[30] It spins around itself with no impact on our history or lives. But the rich fellowship of the Trinity is more than a model for our lives. It is a real opportunity for finite humans to experience the transcendent God in ways that are almost palpable. Our mundane lives are for ever transformed (born again?) and being transformed in the life of God, where there is joy in the presence of God for evermore (Ps. 16:11).

Third, the Spirit opens up the "dance of God" for participation by humans and the created order. "It is by the Spirit that we participate in the life of God and God participates in our life together."[31] In this way, the Spirit operates with a mission outward toward the created order. God is a "missionary God," searching the highways and byways to urge people to join God's party. As Daniel Migliore comments,

> The triune God who lives eternally in mutual self-giving love wills to include creatures in that community of love. The welcoming of the other that marks the life of the Trinity in all eternity is extended outward to us. Through the divine missions of Word and Spirit, God welcomes creatures to share the triune life of love and community.[32]

The Spirit provides a bridge or nexus that "relates all creation to the Trinitarian history without succumbing to pantheism or the hierarchical dualism that sharply separates the divine from the creaturely."[33]

Hence, the life of the Trinity *a se* is closely related to the life that God shares with us *ad extra*. The Spirit is the connection between our finite lives and the infinite life of the Trinity. While it is through Christ that we are saved and can join this Trinitarian dance, it is through the Spirit that we are raised up from our deadness to walk in the newness of life – even to dance in the party that is God's life.

THE SPIRIT AND CHRIST

Evangelicals have inherited a tradition that reveres the divinity of Christ while in some cases limiting his humanity. In historical and theological terms, Logos Christology has subsumed Spirit Christology.[34] Perhaps not all evangelicals have this problem, but it is one that seems prevalent. Recent theological scholarship has asked probing questions about the relation of the Spirit to the Christ. To be sure, the Spirit is "there" at Jesus' birth, overshadowing Mary in order to conceive Emmanuel (Luke 1:35); at the "driving" of Jesus into the wilderness to be tempted (Luke 4:1); at the launching of Jesus' official ministry in Nazareth – indeed, he chose a place in the scroll of Isaiah that reads, "The Spirit of the Lord is on me" (Luke 4:18); when Jesus casts out demons and the result is that the kingdom of God has come (Matt. 12:28; Luke 11:20); when Jesus dies as an atoning sacrifice on the cross and "through the eternal Spirit offer[s] himself unblemished to God" (Heb. 9:14; TNIV); and the Spirit is there when Jesus Christ is raised from the dead (Rom. 1:4; 8:11).

Jesus Christ's story has the consistent thread of the Spirit's presence. For evangelicals, this should have some import. For example, while it may be inaccurate to say that Jesus the Christ needed anyone to help him (at least when considering the "divine side" of the God-Human), it does seem appropriate to say that he chose not to enter humanity, history, and ministry alone but with the continual presence of the Spirit (not to mention the Father). In other words, his entire life, death, and resurrection were Trinitarian acts, with the Holy Spirit as the "connector" between the divine and human.

Spirit Christology within an "orthodox" Trinitarian perspective preserves a balance of Christ's divinity and humanity. As Ralph Del Colle suggests, "The primary issue is how to acknowledge the pneumatological dimension of Christology without utilizing it to displace *logos*-Christologies and their Trinitarian outcome. It is a question of complementarity and enrichment rather than wholesale reconstruction and revision of traditional Christology."[35] For evangelicals who naturally prize emphasis on Jesus Christ as the centerpiece of theology, this dimension of the Spirit's relation to Christ could have many positive repercussions.

For example, if the Spirit raised Jesus Christ from the dead, what does it mean to say that Jesus was delivered to death for our sins and was "raised to life for our justification" (Rom. 4:25; TNIV)? In what way is the Spirit joining with Christ in our justification? Is there something of a participatory, subjective side to the classic objective and external understanding of justification?[36]

In 1 Timothy 3:16, a hymn about Christ is sung by the writer: "He appeared in a body, was vindicated [justified] by the Spirit ..." Because it seems odd to say that the Spirit "justified" Jesus, the translators smooth it out to "vindicated". Yet what if the Spirit who raises Christ from the dead has something to do with the justifying event?[37] Viewing redemption "from the perspective of resurrection in the Spirit," we could thereby see salvation in more holistic terms.[38] Through the resurrection, Christ was justified by the Spirit and therefore believers can await the promised assurance of transformed existence. The same Spirit who raised Christ from the dead will raise our mortal bodies (Rom. 8:11). Dabney's comments here are powerful:

> And in raising our mortal body, God will redeem not just that body, the locus of our existence, but the entirety of our embodied life: the whole of our relationships, our experiences and our encounters, all that makes up our identity... What would it mean to have all our broken relationships with God and world and our fellow human beings rectified and made whole?[39]

A final point of consideration relates to the subordinationist tendencies of evangelicals to place the Spirit "under" Christ. In many places, language of rank and hints toward subordination of function *and* essence abound. This is understandable – partly because of the Western propensity to subordinate the Spirit; partly because the cross, atonement, and conversion through Christ's work have been the focus of evangelical worship and theology. However, we do not know how to craft a doctrine of the Spirit that does justice to his behind-the-scenes role in Scripture yet honors him in a way that still allows for equal glory to shine on the Christ. A robust Trinitarian theology of the Spirit would begin to resolve these apparent conflicts. The Spirit points us to Christ, but the Spirit also lives with us, groaning with us to God the Father on our behalf. Why should we purposefully subordinate the Spirit when in fact the entire triune Godhead is at work in our redemption?

If there is hierarchy in God without equality in persons and essence, then there is much greater likelihood to be unhealthy hierarchy among believers. Suggesting that Spirit Christology should balance the polarity of Logos Christology, Donald Bloesch immediately adds: "The challenge today seems to be to rediscover the complementarity of Logos and Spirit while still maintaining the subordination of Spirit to Logos (which is the biblical pattern)."[40] First, we assume subordination of the Spirit is a biblical pattern, but have we examined this adequately? The cursory examination above provides enough evidence that the Spirit is not always behind-the-scenes; at the very least, *subordination* would not be a happy word choice for the Spirit's activity in the New Testament! Second, what does this do to the overall logic of the Trinity as revealed in the Scripture? Is Bloesch referring to subordination of function (as I presume)? Even here, however, such language smacks of subordination of essence. To be sure, the Spirit does not come to humans "as a revelation of independent content, as a new instruction, illumination and stimulation of [humans] that goes beyond Christ, beyond the Word, but in every sense as the instruction, illumination and stimulation of [humans] through the Word and for the Word."[41] Thus, the Spirit is truly the Spirit of Christ.

However, I also wish to push further theological examination of the various functions of the Spirit as supported by Scripture and connected to Jesus the Christ. We can carefully do this without causing a rupture between Christ and the Spirit.[42] For example, the Holy Spirit as the Counselor or Comforter is sent by the Father and the Son (John 14:26; 15:26). Jesus is sending "another counselor" (*allon parakleton*) – which may mean "another who is *similar in kind* to me."[43] In other words, this is a

replacement for Jesus' physical presence. Does this make the Spirit subordinate to the Son? I think not. Yet also the Spirit is not speaking of
himself, but always pointing to Christ. Still, if the Spirit is in some way
"filling in" for Christ until he returns, how can his role or position be
subordinate? Moreover, there are dimensions of the Spirit's work that
expand beyond Christ to the Trinity as a whole.[44] Jürgen Moltmann
reminds us that the "trinitarian Persons do not merely exist and live in
one another; they also bring one another mutually to manifestation in the
divine glory."[45] God the Father is the "Father of glory" (Eph. 1:17); God the
Son is the "reflection of glory" (Heb. 1:3); and God the Spirit is the "Spirit of
glory" (1 Pet. 4:14).

THE SPIRIT AND LIFE

In this final section we shall briefly consider a few ways that we
experience the Spirit in this life, with a hopeful expectation of the life to
come. First we should state that while the Spirit is one bridge of connection between the divine and human lives, the "Holy Spirit is not our
experience. The Holy Spirit is God."[46] Evangelicals cannot afford to mis-
take their experiences and their spirituality for the Holy Spirit. However,
that being said, evangelicals must also not squelch the Spirit's activity – as
if the Spirit only behaves in a way that is tame and bourgeois. As humans
who are asked to dedicate their entire lives to God, believers have a
capacity not just for intellectual understanding but also for emotional,
spiritual, and sensory "understanding." We are whole persons, fragmented
by sin and being pieced back together by God's Spirit through regeneration
and sanctification. Surely we cannot assume that God's Spirit would leave
us just as broken and internally scattered as when he found us!

Understanding the total demand of the Good News requires evangelicals to reconsider their pietistic backgrounds, where the soul is nurtured
and the emotions are free to express love for God and others in a variety of
ways. However, understanding this more holistic dimension of humanity
may also require some deepening of theological talk about sin – about
what splinters our selves. In this regard, some liberation theologies and
feminist theologies provide excellent contextual conversation partners for
evangelical theology, opening the windows of our stuffy rooms to allow
fresh air into the discussion. For example, Serene Jones has provided a
reconsideration of sin that attempts to remain consistent with her tradition (Calvin) while at the same time responsive to the current concerns of
feminist thought. In one place, Jones connects Calvin's view that sin is

unfaithfulness with current conceptual imagery of mistreatment of women. A person in a state of unfaithfulness experiences radical loss, "without both the sanctifying structure of God's love and the ever renewing forgiveness of justification."[47] Hence, humanity produces many different fruits of sin. One of these Calvin describes as "despoilment" – a loss of one's original integrity whereby the "self deteriorates in the absence of its constitutive boundaries, and society is plundered of the justice that gives it integrity."[48] These descriptions provide her with useful ways to reconsider feminist concerns regarding oppression and violence. They also provide evangelicals with a framework to consider re-mapping sin in its many horrid dimensions (especially those we cannot even recognize in ourselves).

Why should evangelicals work at re-mapping sin in today's world? The answer is quite straightforward: how can we speak the Good News to the world without understanding some of sin's permutations in our various contexts?

In addition to experiencing God and our sin in wholeness, evangelicals need to recapture the relational dimension of God's being. As we noted regarding the Spirit and Trinity, God dwells in community – Father, Son, and Spirit. While humans cannot fully recreate that fellowship on earth, there is a sense in which we are taken up into that community by the Spirit. Evangelicals have been wont to announce the Good News with a healthy dose of the bad news. Sin is usually preached about in ways that circulate around behaviors we find abhorrent. We assume that *we* preach people into conviction, neglecting this fundamental role of the Spirit to "convict" or "convince" of sin. The idea of guilt within our evangelical congregations seems much more prevalent than grace. Therefore, the above section on reconsidering sin was *not meant* as new ammunition for the old battery of evangelical guns against sinners. Instead, what if our focus were to switch to the story of God (the Good News!) as one of a lover who has gone searching for his beloved; as one of a woman frantically searching for a choice lost coin; as one of a father who daily stands at the gate, straining to see a wandering son's silhouette in the horizon (Luke 15)? What if union with God were the goal and conversion meant an "awakening to love"?[49] What if the Spirit wants to woo us into God's transforming life? What if the Spirit desires to bring us into intimacy with God and other humans? How would the Good News sound in this language and accent?

Having experienced God's grace through the work of Christ and by the power of the Spirit, believers are established then to share the love of God with fellow human beings. It is the Spirit who stirs in us a responsive love to God and a concomitant love for neighbor (Matt. 22:37–39; Rom. 5:5). The fruit of the Spirit, which resonates almost perfectly with the character of Christ, grows in us by the planting, watering, and sunshine of the Spirit so that we may grow up in all things to be like Christ (Gal. 5:22; Eph. 4:14–16). The fundamental fruit of the Spirit by which we live, by which the Spirit fosters relationality in the Godhead and among humans, is love. As God the Spirit raises us to participation in the very life and fellowship of the triune God, we are transformed from glory to glory so that we may walk in newness of life. It is the Spirit who connects us to the presence of the Infinite God, though we are finite. It is the Spirit who transforms us from death to life. It is the Spirit who propels us to love those who seem unlovable – radically other. This is what it means to be truly evangelical.

Finally, any evangelical talk of the Spirit in a believer's life needs to consider the specter of individualism (especially in the West). God is relational, reaching out to humanity and the created order through the Spirit, so that in some sense we may join in the life of God. However, much evangelical preaching remains focused on the individual – especially, the individual's choice for or against God. This is surely one reason why we may be uncomfortable with talk of a social Trinity and a relational God; it is also certainly *the* reason why evangelicals have not written much about ecclesiology.[50]

While God is clearly concerned for individuals, God's Spirit does not unite us to God for the sake of leaving us alone with our solitary, inner selves. God lifts us into the life of God so that we – transformed and renewed by the Spirit – might enter into the lives of others. This is not just to perform some random acts of kindness, but to assist others in seeing the reality that is God through our lives.

We live in this world as people who are already experiencing new life in Christ through the Spirit but are not yet in the life of the age to come. This tension of "already/not yet" is a well-documented principle in Paul's writings.[51] A fundamental aspect of this tension is the Spirit's role in bringing the new life of the new era into our earthly lives here and now. The Spirit is the seal who marks us in Christ, "a deposit guaranteeing our inheritance until the redemption of those who are God's possession – to the praise of his glory" (Eph. 1:14; TNIV). The Spirit allows us to "taste of the powers of the coming age" (Heb. 6:5; TNIV) without transporting us there *in toto*. This "taste of the heavenly gift" (Heb. 6:4; TNIV) is not merely for gloating with the insight of the world to come or circulating around some super-spiritual realm. It is offered so that we might experience in this world what a full life in union with God will be like one day – in unceasing glory; from this realization, we recognize what a perfect life here on earth would look like and how woefully inadequate our structures, institutions, and lives are by comparison. This vision of God's perfection should propel us into the physical and natural spheres so that we will strive to make all life in this world a better reflection of the life to come.

The perfection of God in the age to come can be described well with the Hebraic concept of *shalom. Shalom* is "peace" or "well being." While it is "intertwined with justice," says Nicholas Wolterstorff, it is more than justice.[52] Cornelius Plantinga suggests further that *shalom* is a "universal flourishing, wholeness, and delight – a rich state of affairs in which natural needs are satisfied and natural gifts fruitfully employed, all under the arch of God's love. Shalom, in other words, is the way things are supposed to be."[53] While I am not necessarily advocating that *we* usher in God's reign of the future in the here and now, at the very least we should reflect the life of that reign in our sinful, broken, and damaged world. It is logically impossible for the love of God poured out in our lives by the Spirit to indwell us as believers and not work for justice and peace in the world. If we have been transformed by participating in the very life of God, then to the best of our human, earthly abilities and with the power of the Spirit, we will love our neighbors by transforming the structures that oppress their very humanity as well as treating them as we would treat ourselves.[54]

It is here that the Spirit works like a buoying force within us. Sin in its various structural and personal forms is ever before us – some days more rampant and sinister than others. How can we strike against something so powerful and inevitable? The Spirit of God brings power and hope in the midst of despair and weakness. The Spirit encourages and stimulates us to resolve conflicts and tear down strongholds of the enemy. The Spirit urges us to work for justice and righteousness here and now as an acknowledgment that things are not supposed to be this way. Therefore, we are pilgrims here, citizens of another home. In the midst of this home, however, the Spirit works for justice. Michael Welker uses a wonderful image to characterize this: "The Spirit of God thus generates a force field of love in which people strive so that all things might 'work for good' for their 'neighbors.'"[55] Hence the Spirit generates genuine hope for the future by engaging God's people to work for righteousness in the present.

In this context we see the Spirit's role in the church. The mission of the church is quite simply the mission of God – to reach out in love as did Christ and invite humanity to join the divinely choreographed dance of the Spirit to the glory of God the Father. Obviously, this dance engages the whole person and indeed the whole of our communal lives on earth. No area of life is untouched by this song and dance because all things are being brought under subjection to Christ. It is the Spirit of God who assists us in completing the purpose for which we have been "apprehended by God" in the first place (Phil. 3:12). The Spirit is heading all things to their intended conclusion in God. The Spirit works in the church to build up a community that reflects the triune life of God as best it can in a sinful world. For evangelicals, then, the Good News is not just preached, but lived in the power of the Spirit. The gifts of the Spirit operate within the community of faith to encourage and strengthen the body of Christ for the fulfillment of its purpose.[56] Therefore, these gifts are signs of hope – signs of the age to come when the Father will place all things under Christ's rule of *shalom* and the reign of God will continue for ever with "justice, joy and peace in the Holy Spirit" (Rom. 14:17).[57] Come, Holy Spirit!

Further reading

Badcock, Gary D. *Light of Truth and Fire of Love: A Theology of the Holy Spirit.* Grand Rapids, MI: Eerdmans, 1997.

Bloesch, Donald G. *The Holy Spirit: Works and Gifts.* Christian Foundations. Downers Grove, IL: InterVarsity, 2000.

Bruner, Frederick Dale. *A Theology of the Holy Spirit: The Pentecostal Experience and the New Testament Witness.* Grand Rapids, MI: Eerdmans, 1970.

Burgess, Stanley M. *The Spirit and the Church: Medieval Roman Catholic and Reformation Traditions (Sixth–Sixteenth Centuries).* Peabody, MA: Hendrickson, 1997.

Fee, Gordon. *God's Empowering Presence: The Holy Spirit in the Letters of Paul.* Peabody, MA: Hendrickson, 1994.

Ferguson, Sinclair B. *The Holy Spirit.* Contours of Christian Theology. Downers Grove, IL: InterVarsity, 1996.

Green, Michael. *I Believe in the Holy Spirit.* Revised edition. Grand Rapids, MI: Eerdmans, 1989.

Kärkkäinen, Veli-Matti. *Pneumatology: The Holy Spirit in Ecumenical, International, and Contextual Perspective.* Grand Rapids, MI: Baker Academic, 2002.

Pinnock, Clark. *Flame of Love: A Theology of the Holy Spirit.* Downers Grove, IL: InterVarsity, 1996.

Smail, Thomas. *Reflected Glory: The Spirit in Christ and Christians.* Grand Rapids, MI: Eerdmans, 1975.

The Giving Gift: The Holy Spirit in Person. London: Hodder and Stoughton, 1988.

Yong, Amos. *The Spirit Poured Out on All Flesh: Pentecostalism and the Possibility of Global Theology.* Grand Rapids, MI: Baker Academic, 2005.

Notes

1. The debate about the Spirit during the last century has frequently focused on issues related to the Pentecostal movement and its connection with evangelicalism. Here I need only raise the specter of one hotly debated experience – speaking in tongues – to remind the reader about the intensity of discussion about the Spirit. As for banality, one need only peruse systematic theology texts of the last century to discover either minimal "nods" to the Spirit in the section on the Trinity or an overall conflation of the doctrine of the Spirit into the "Christian life" (spirituality). Obviously, there are exceptions, but these are more recent developments and it remains open as to whether or not they will become part of "mainstream" evangelical thought.

2. Some writers speak of the Spirit as the "shy" member or the "Cinderella" of the Trinity. See Veli-Matti Kärkkäinen, *Pneumatology: The Holy Spirit in Ecumenical, International, and Contextual Perspective* (Grand Rapids, MI: Baker Academic, 2002), p. 16. Kärkkäinen does not believe this era of silence with respect to the Spirit continues any longer. While more is being written on the Spirit nowadays, I remain unconvinced that it reaches sufficient depth to account for much.

3. "The Constantinopolitan Creed," in John H. Leith (ed.), *Creeds of the Churches: A Reader in Christian Doctrine from the Bible to the Present*, 3rd edition (Atlanta: John Knox, 1982), p. 33.

4. George Hendry, *The Holy Spirit in Christian Theology*, revised edition (Philadelphia: Westminster, 1965), p. 11.

5. The image of "adolescence" comes from Cheryl Bridges Johns, "The Adolescence of Pentecostalism: In Search of a Legitimate Sectarian Identity," *PNEUMA: The Journal of the Society for Pentecostal Studies* 17 (Spring 1995): 3–17, p. 4. See also Terry L. Cross, "A Proposal to Break the Ice: What Can Pentecostal Theology Offer Evangelical Theology?" *Journal of Pentecostal Theology* 10. 2 (2002): 44–73.

6. Intriguing in this regard is Edmund J. Rybarczyk, "Spiritualities Old and New: Similarities between Eastern Orthodoxy and Classical Pentecostalism," *PNEUMA: The Journal of the Society for Pentecostal Studies* 24. 1 (2002): 7–25.

7. Gordon Fee offers a powerful discussion of this in "On Being a Trinitarian Christian," in *Listening to the Spirit in the Text* (Grand Rapids, MI: Eerdmans, 2000), pp. 24–32.

8. L. Berkhof, *Systematic Theology* (Grand Rapids, MI: Eerdmans, 1941), pp. 97–98.

9. Athanasius, "Four Discourses Against the Arians," Discourse 3, section 41, in *Athanasius: Select Works and Letters*, ed. Archibald Robertson, in *Nicene and Post-Nicene Fathers, Second Series*, 14 vols., ed. Philip Schaff and Henry Wace (Peabody, MA: Hendrickson, 2004), vol. IV, pp. 415–16.

10. Athanasius, "Epistles Two-Three," *The Letters of Saint Athanasius Concerning the Holy Spirit*, trans. C. R. B. Shapland (London: Epworth, 1951), p. 170.

11. *Ibid.*, p. 172.

12. Most evangelicals would arrive at the same conclusion as Athanasius, but they would probably not argue for *theosis* in order to get there.

13. I am not wishing to suggest that the Eastern approach is without problems of its own (e.g., a virulent monarchy of the Father), but rather that the *filioque* has inserted a peculiar problem for the West.

14. Stanley Grenz, *Theology for the Community of God* (Grand Rapids, MI: Eerdmans, 2000), p. 373.

15. Augustine, *de trinitate*, 15.27.

16. Gerald Bray, "The Double Procession of the Holy Spirit in Evangelical Theology Today: Do We Still Need it?," *Journal of the Evangelical Theological Society* 41. 3 (September 1998): 415–26, p. 423. Bray suggests there is reason to hold the doctrine of double procession, but mainly to ward off Arian tendencies. He suggests finally that evangelicals may be better off by supporting a concept of *autotheos* – that is, each person of the Godhead is God in himself.

17. Colin Gunton, "God the Holy Spirit: Augustine and His Successors," in *Theology through the Theologians: Selected Essays, 1972–1995* (London: T. & T. Clark, 1996), pp. 105–28, p. 128.

18. *Ibid.*

19. Sergius Bulgakov, *The Comforter*, trans. Boris Jakim (Grand Rapids, MI: Eerdmans, 2004), p. 181.

20. Millard Erickson, *Christian Theology* (Grand Rapids, MI: Baker, 1992), p. 846.

21. Clark Pinnock, *Flame of Love: A Theology of the Holy Spirit* (Downers Grove, IL: InterVarsity, 1996), p. 38.

22. Eberhard Jüngel, *The Doctrine of the Trinity: God's Being is in Becoming*, trans. Horton Harris (Edinburgh: Scottish Academic Press, 1976), p. 30.

23. *Ibid.*, p. 103.

24. Ian A. McFarland, "The Ecstatic God: The Holy Spirit and the Constitution of the Trinity," *Theology Today* 54. 3 (October 1997): 335–46, p. 344.

25. Pinnock, *Flame of Love*, p. 48.

26. Pinnock offers some of the most descriptive prose concerning the Spirit and Creation. See also Colin Gunton: "Wherever the Spirit is, there the true end of creation is anticipated" ("The Spirit Moved Over the Face of the Waters: The Holy Spirit and the Created Order," *International Journal of Systematic Theology* 4. 2 [July 2002]: 190–204, p. 198).

27. See Pinnock, *Flame of Love*, p. 37.

28. Catherine Mowry LaCugna, *God for Us: The Trinity and Christian Life* (San Francisco: Harper Collins, 1991), p. 270. LaCugna notes that *perichoresis* was used as a defense against both tritheism and subordinationism. The root ideas behind *perichoresis* are to make room for another (*chorein*) and to be among or round about (*peri*). One can see the root of the English word "choreography" – hence, the dance of God.

29. Molly Truman Marshall, "Participating in the Life of God: A Trinitarian Pneumatology," *Perspectives in Religious Studies* 30. 2 (Summer 2003): 139–50, p. 146.

30. LaCugna, *God for Us*, p. 198.

31. Marshall, "Participating in the Life of God," p. 150.

32. Daniel Migliore, "The Missionary God and the Missionary Church," *The Princeton Seminary Bulletin* 19. 1, ns (1998): 14–25, p. 18.

33. Marshall, "Participating in the Life of God," p. 147.

34. I am not supporting an Ebionite style of Spirit Christology where Jesus is merely human and somehow the Spirit anoints him to do wondrous things, or

even more recent attempts at Spirit Christology that deny the divinity of the persons of the Trinity altogether.

35. Ralph Del Colle, "Spirit-Christology: Dogmatic Foundations for Pentecostal-Charismatic Spirituality," *Journal of Pentecostal Theology* 3 (1993): 91–112, p. 98. Also, see his *Christ and the Spirit: Spirit-Christology in Trinitarian Perspective* (Oxford: Oxford University Press, 1994).

36. Clark Pinnock urges us to enrich this doctrine with the Eastern model of *theosis* in *Flame of Love*, pp. 149–50. Also see Frank Macchia, "Justification and the Spirit: A Pentecostal Reflection on the Doctrine by Which the Church Stands or Falls," *PNEUMA: The Journal of the Society for Pentecostal Studies* 22. 1 (Spring 2000): 3–21; Veli-Matti Kärkkäinen, "The Holy Spirit and Justification: The Ecumenical Significance of Luther's Doctrine of Salvation," *PNEUMA: The Journal of the Society for Pentecostal Studies* 24. 1 (Spring 2002): 26–39; D. Lyle Dabney, " 'Justified by the Spirit': Soteriological Reflections on the Resurrection," *International Journal of Systematic Theology* 3. 1 (March 2001): 46–68.

37. This is basically Dabney's question in " 'Justified by the Spirit'," pp. 47–48.

38. *Ibid.*, p. 63.

39. *Ibid.*, pp. 61–62.

40. Donald Bloesch, *The Holy Spirit: Works and Gifts*, Christian Foundations (Downers Grove, IL: InterVarsity, 2000), p. 223.

41. Karl Barth, *Church Dogmatics*, trans. and ed. G. W. Bromiley and T. F. Torrance (Edinburgh: T. & T. Clark, 1975), I/1: 452–53.

42. Without supporting some kind of pneumatic abstraction of Christianity by directing our thoughts away from the Son, one can ask penetrating questions of the Spirit of truth, as my friend Amos Yong does in approaching religious pluralism from a pneumatic and phenomenological perspective. See his *Beyond the Impasse: Toward a Pneumatological Theology of Religions* (Grand Rapids, MI: Baker Academic, 2003), and *The Spirit Poured Out on All Flesh: Pentecostalism and the Possibility of Global Theology* (Grand Rapids, MI: Baker Academic, 2005).

43. The Greek word *allon* may have this force with it as opposed to *heteros*, "another of a different kind."

44. For this reason "subordination" language with respect to the Spirit seems inappropriate, yet Bruce Ware even posits that in the age to come the "Spirit will take the backseat to the Son and the Father" (*Father, Son, and Holy Spirit: Relationships, Roles, and Relevance* [Wheaton, IL: Crossway, 2005], p. 125). However, Trinitarian pneumatology would find no one member of the Trinity the undue focus of attention, not allowing hierarchy but instead lively equality. This, too, would help the church in its understanding of humans' equal worth to God (and each other) in thought *and* practice. Peter Hodgson reminds us that "Subordination of the Spirit, marginalization of women, and exploitation of nature have gone hand in hand in the history of the church," as quoted in Marshall, "Participating in the Life of God," p. 142, fn. 21, from his book, *Winds of the Spirit: A Constructive Christian Theology* (London: SCM, 1994), p. 276. This may be an overstatement, but it should jar our senses.

45. Jürgen Moltmann, *The Trinity and the Kingdom: The Doctrine of God* (San Francisco: Harper and Row, 1981), p. 176.

46. David Willis, *Clues to the Nicene Faith: A Brief Outline of the Faith* (Grand Rapids, MI: Eerdmans, 2005), p. 105.

47. Serene Jones, *Feminist Theory and Christian Theology: Cartographies of Grace*, Guides to Theological Inquiry (Minneapolis, MN: Fortress, 2000), p. 107.

48. *Ibid.*

49. Pinnock, *Flame of Love*, p. 157.

50. See Bruce Hindmarsh, "Is Evangelical Ecclesiology an Oxymoron? A Historical Perspective," in John Stackhouse, Jr. (ed.), *Evangelical Ecclesiology: Reality or Illusion?* (Grand Rapids, MI: Baker Academic, 2003), pp. 15–37.

51. The details of Pauline thought on the Spirit are best seen through Gordon Fee, *God's Empowering Presence: The Holy Spirit in the Letters of Paul* (Peabody, MA: Hendrickson, 1994).

52. Nicholas Wolterstorff, *Until Justice and Peace Embrace: The Kuyper Lectures for 1981 Delivered at the Free University of Amsterdam* (Grand Rapids, MI: Eerdmans, 1983), p. 69.

53. Cornelius Plantinga, Jr., *Engaging God's World: A Christian Vision of Faith, Learning, and Living* (Grand Rapids, MI: Eerdmans, 2002), p. 15.

54. See Ron Sider, *Good News and Good Works: A Theology for the Whole Gospel* (Grand Rapids, MI: Baker, 1993); also *The Scandal of the Evangelical Conscience: Why Are Christians Living Just Like the Rest of the World?* (Grand Rapids, MI: Baker, 2005).

55. Michael Welker, *God the Spirit*, trans. John Hoffmeyer (Minneapolis, MN: Fortress, 1994), p. 227. Wolfhart Pannenberg also uses this force field analogy with similar effect. See Pannenberg, *Systematic Theology*, 3 vols., trans. Geoffrey Bromiley (Grand Rapids, MI: Eerdmans, 1994), vol. II, pp. 80–84; 99; 110.

56. Although I am an evangelical-Pentecostal, I have purposefully refrained from returning to debates about speaking in tongues and the gifts of the Spirit. Rather than center on cessationism or non-cessationism, I chose to write about issues that I find more important for the Reign of God in the long run. Hence, comments regarding the gifts of the Spirit come at the end in the section that discusses the community of faith and its responsibility to the world. The Spirit's gifts are meant as God's encouragement for us, not as divisive marks that distinguish us from each other.

57. This is my translation.

8 Conversion and sanctification

MIYON CHUNG

Biblical teaching discloses the reality of the comprehensive saving work through which sinful humans are reconciled to the triune God's eternally gracious presence. The divine love for humanity, first expressed through the grace of creation and election, culminates eschatologically in the death of Jesus Christ (John 19:30; Rom. 5:6–8; 1 Pet. 3:18). The resurrection and ascension of Jesus Christ successively attest to the finality of God's salvific work, thus ushering in the empowering ministry of the Holy Spirit through which the gift of salvation is offered to Jews and Gentiles alike (Acts 1; Rom 8:11). Placed within this eschatologically oriented construal, conversion and sanctification are essentially the Holy Spirit's work of applying Christ's atoning work to us.

THE GRACE OF CONVERSION FROM THE TEXTURES OF SIN

A hallmark of evangelical church life is insistence on a personal conversion experience. Indeed, the gospel message can be summed up as a divine call to conversion of sinners. From the divine side, conversion points to God's electing and transforming grace. From the side of human experience, conversion involves repentance and faith that mark a decisive inauguration of the Christian life. Accordingly, a discussion of conversion calls for phenomenological consideration of the interchange between God and human.

Perhaps, the course and content of Christian conversion are more tangible when written into auto/biographies such as St. Augustine's *Confessions* or Paul's story in Acts. Evangelical thoughts on conversion, however, must arise from careful, integrative scriptural exegesis, rather than simply psychological or phenomenological analyses. Although diverse and vital experiences of conversion may illuminate the Christian community's reading of the Bible, experience alone cannot be constitutive of evangelical theological content.[1]

Here conversion is analyzed as the Spirit's work of applying the paradoxical wisdom of the cross and resurrection to produce repentance and faith. The first part of this section traces the trajectory of saving grace in biblical narratives. Especially important is uncovering the plot of conversion narratives in the Old Testament. The operative hypothesis is that Israel's fiducial journey will be paradigmatic for the shackling reality of sin and the unfailing divine will to save sinful human beings.

The second part, then, highlights New Testament teaching about conversion as an eschatological call. The third part of this section will offer a brief analysis of the *ordo salutis* (order of salvation) to prepare for understanding divine–human dynamics in conversion. Finally, we will use these insights to delineate conversion as the Holy Spirit's work of witnessing to Jesus Christ.

Conversion in Israel's fiducial journey

The Hebraic conceptual equivalent for the Latin word "conversion" is expressed in various forms of *šûb*, which connote an act of "turning" or "returning."[2] Occurring over a thousand times, the root *šûb* does not always carry religious nuances (Gen. 18:22; Lev. 22:13). When used for conversion, however, it is set in a relational construct to signify an unambiguous turn away from sin to a conscious, wholehearted re/turn to God.[3] The term refers to both individuals and nations turning to God in repentance,[4] but the overall thrust of the Old Testament's conversion narratives portrays Yahweh's address toward Israel as his covenanted congregation.

First of all, repentance as an explicit act of re/turning to Yahweh is a requisite for Israel's sustenance as his people, presupposing his covenantal love for them.[5] Repentance begins with a profound acknowledgment and confession of sin (Ps. 32:3–5; Prov. 28:13). As early as Genesis 3, Scripture shows that sin gives birth to a vicious cycle of blame, fear, shame, objectification, paralysis, and alienation.[6] God, however, graciously addresses the first couple, penetrating through their self-imposed alienation and eliciting confession of their disobedience. The theological implication of this narrative is that sin is not a thing but a broken relationship produced by voluntarily yielding to the Tempter. In this predicament, confession of sin becomes divinely instituted provision for reconciliation. Confessing sin empowers sinners to identify and reorder the fundamental chaos ushered in by the primordial attempt to live outside of the divine command.

Secondly, the ultimate goal of the divine summons to conversion is not to punish but to bless. The inchoate event of confession portrayed in Genesis 3 matures into a fully operative legal system through which Israel is to make true repentance and experience pardon. To perpetually wayward Israel, Yahweh faithfully sends his prophets. Since idolatry at heart is apostasy and perfunctory renderings of rituals reduce God to an object, God demands categorical repudiation of Israel's offensive acts and a radical change of their motives and conduct. He wants their devotion (Hos. 6:6). Yahweh insists upon voluntary, genuine, and thorough repentance (Josh. 24:33; 1 Sam. 7:3; 2 Chron. 7:14; Ezk. 33:8–11; Jer. 4:4).

The problem, however, is that Yahweh's holiness makes hyper-ethical demands upon the incorrigibly defiant Israel (Lev. 19:2). His law assiduously accuses Israel of erring, but it is powerless to lift them out of the seductive, gripping power of sin, particularly idolatry. Although Yahweh's love is loyal and his mercy endures for ever, Israel must not remain disloyal because Yahweh loves them exclusively (Deut. 4:24). Consequently, transgression incurs the wrath of the infinitely holy Yahweh. In this relationally tensive context Yahweh's sovereignty, first expressed in electing grace, continually summons Israel to turn to him in repentance.

The basis for this injunction is Deuteronomy 30.[7] After establishing the Sinaitic covenant, God forewarns Israel about their unremitting propensity toward rebellion and thereby commands them to turn to him with a contrite heart. Deuteronomic testimony, furthermore, conveys that repentance is the basis for experiencing Yahweh's goodness, peace, and assurance.[8] Yahweh's injunction to convert/repent as it comes in a three-fold movement – Israel's violation of the covenant, Israel's crying out in misery, and Yahweh's turning to Israel for deliverance – always accompanies a robust message of blessing.[9] In the disclosive power of prophetic indictment against sin, admonition and condemnation move to a grace-filled language of promise. In this way, Israel's requirement to confess their transgression for peaceful dwelling in their promised land (Lev. 26:40–42) demonstrates that the injunction to repent properly belongs to the economy of gift.

Thirdly, because Yahweh's summons comes with a message of blessing, it simultaneously presupposes and propels conscious faith. For Israel, turning away from sin and confessing Yahweh's name reinforce each other (1 Kgs. 8:33, 35). Repentance assumes having knowledge of God and placing unwavering trust in his willingness and power to grant pardon. As Hosea 6:1–6 illustrates, Israel's proclivity toward mercilessness and superficial cultic activities exposes the lamentable fact that they do not know

Yahweh. Because conversion presupposes commitment to a vital relationship with God, no ritualistic observance *per se* can earn pardon.

The prophetic messages also relate returning to Yahweh to trusting him, obeying his word, and turning away from all ungodliness.[10] Perhaps one of the most dramatic demonstrations of faith and repentance comes when the Israelites are ordered to look upon the bronze serpent (Num. 21:4–9). The act of looking up at this provisional Christological symbol recapitulates an inner dynamic which consists of remorseful acknowledgment of apostasy and of decisive resolve to believe in Yahweh's efficacious word for deliverance.

Fourthly, the course of Israel's fiducial journey unveils that conversion must not only be propelled by Yahweh's summons, but also it can only be accomplished by his will to redeem.[11] Israel's recalcitrant pursuit of sin reaches a point of no return, and Yahweh's deliverance on the basis of their conversion is no longer an option (Amos 7:8–8:2; Hos. 5:4–14; Isa. 6:10; Jer. 13:23). At this darkest moment, the exchanges between Yahweh and his prophets elucidate a strikingly strange logic. When Israel is completely bankrupt, Yahweh will first return to them. Only then will Israel seek Yahweh's face (Hos. 5:15; Isa. 44:22).

Furthermore, Yahweh's prophets make extraordinary speeches for a people facing annihilation. They cry out to Yahweh in an audacious summons for him to return and restore them (Isa. 63–64, esp. 63:17; Lam. 5:21).[12] Oddly, the prophets' appeals reveal that the height of Israel's commitment to trust is rendered when Israel is politically, morally, and spiritually depleted. Even more striking, however, is Yahweh's own un/timely response. When his beloved is taken into exile, he promises that a time will come when he will cancel all their sins and regenerate their spirit through the indwelling work of his own Spirit (Jer. 31:31–34; Ezk. 36:24–27; Zech. 12:10). Here, grace is extravagantly beyond the measure of Israel's depravity. Conversion, therefore, is fundamentally "the consequence, not the presupposition, of deliverance."[13]

Finally, the later prophets increasingly anticipate New Testament teachings regarding conversion.[14] Yahweh promises to work redemption through a remnant who will escape the destruction of Israel and turn in trust to him (Isa. 6:11–13; 10:20–21). This remnant, of course, converges into messianic prophecies (Deut. 4:30; Hos. 3:5; Isa. 11:1–5, 10; 28:16; 53:2–12; Jer. 33:3–16; Dan. 9:25; Mal. 4:5–6). Also, although the historical narratives generally address Israel as a nation, Ezekiel implies the conversion of the individual. Through Jeremiah God had already promised a new endowment of a radically internal source of conversion (Jer. 31:31). In Ezekiel, this promise expresses more explicitly the regenerating work of the Holy Spirit in individual persons (11:19; 18:31; 36:24–26; 37:14).

Conversion as an eschatological summons

In harmony with the Old Testament's conversion theme of turning away from evil and to God, the New Testament also presents repentance and faith as the indispensable twin calls of the gospel. Conversion is also depicted as both God's gift and human responsibility, requiring radical reorientation of life.[15] The initiator of the call to repentance in the new era is John the Baptist. The sole purpose of his stirring ministry is summoning the Israelites to repent because remission of sins is the inescapable preparation due for God's reign (Mark 1:4; Matt. 3:2).[16] Even the atypical quality of the Baptist's conception and life already prescribes conversion's radical source and content (Luke 1:5–25, 41, 57–80). John uniquely fulfills Isaiah's messianic promise, preparing for Jesus' ministry of converting sinners to God.

The Baptist's message emphatically announces that Israel is under certain, imminent eschatological judgment and demands that all Israel offer authentic repentance transcending the Jewish religiosity of their time (Matt. 3:1–12; Mark 1:4–8; Luke 3:1–18). Moreover, his terse and graphic critique of the religious establishment exposes the hubris of Jewish presumption regarding the kingdom of God and the application of divine grace. He declares that only repentance leading to a complete abandonment of a sinful life and to generosity would satisfy the eschatological demand. In this way, the Baptist's work of preaching and administering water baptism for the remission of sins actively anticipates the Spirit baptism by Jesus Christ.

Therefore, the call to conversion is indissolubly bound up with the dawning of God's kingdom and the fulfillment of the messianic prophecies.[17] The Baptist's message is eschatologically intensified in the ministry of Jesus Christ precisely because he decisively brings God's eschatological rule in his own person, once and for all (Matt. 4:17; 11:28–30; Mark 1:15; Luke 11:20).[18] He is sent to convert people to God, and he proclaims that repentance is a fundamental requirement for the all-encompassing, present reality of God's kingdom (Luke 5:32; Rom. 2:4). Even his miracles are directed to evoke repentance (Matt. 11:20–24).

In fact, conversion talk in the New Testament inevitably occurs in the context of faith in Jesus Christ, the *eschaton*. This is easily noticeable in the way *epistrephō*, the Septuagint's designation for *šûb*, always includes the gift of faith, *pisteuō*, in Jesus Christ.[19] The book of Acts is replete with reiterations of the *šûb* teachings from the vantage point of faith in Jesus Christ. In Paul's writings and Acts conversion is "a fundamentally new turning of the human will to God, a returning from blindness and error to the Savior of all" by making a decisive movement of faith in and toward Jesus Christ.[20] Conversion must bear concrete fruits of repentance. The emphasis, therefore, lies on the positive aspect of leading a "new life" in Christ, rather than just the negative movement of forsaking the "old life."[21]

Furthermore, Jesus' subversive speeches against the Pharisees not only divulge their filthy conscience and obtuse spirituality, but also declare emphatically that self-righteousness is perversely inadequate (Matt. 5:20). The kind of conversion worthy of God's eschatological rule cannot be achieved by humans, no matter how deeply steeped in religion (John 3:3–8). Conversion can only be received from trusting in God's sovereign freedom to offer it, precisely because repentance is not of the law but of the gospel (Matt. 18:3; Mark 10:27; John 3:16). The impulse to repent, therefore, is a gift that comes interwoven with the gift of faith.

Finally, whereas the Baptist's message about the kingdom is an acute call to repentance, Jesus' ministry highlights the positive aspect of conversion. He comes to lavish divine favor upon people and to give them an abundant life (Luke 4:16–21; John 10:10). In Matthew, Jesus' call to conversion is juxtaposed with ethical renewal that transcends and critiques all human efforts of self-righteousness.[22] Here, the indictment against sin is accompanied by a call to follow Jesus and enter into a close relationship with him as disciples. For Matthew, this life necessitates the impossible possibility of living according to Jesus' Sermon on the Mount. Jesus does not issue this unprecedented, seemingly impossible call as an option but as a requirement for experiencing God's rule precisely because he already is an embodiment of his teachings and as such is also the means for practicing them (Matt. 5:1–7:29).

The dynamics of conversion in divine–human relationship

The above treatment of the biblical conversion narratives shows that conversion is completely the work of God and also completely human. Viewed from the other side of eternity, conversion actually begins from the triune God's sovereign will to redeem fallen humanity (Eph. 1:4–5; Rom. 8:29–30), because no one is capable of righteousness before God (Eccl. 7:20; Rom. 3:23). But Scripture also speaks tellingly about the human responsibility to respond to God's initiating grace. The fact that God is calling sinners to repentance and faith assumes that humans are endowed with genuine freedom (Matt. 9:12–13). In what manner, then, is conversion wrought by the Spirit's work of bearing the fruit of Christ in us? Evangelicals treat this question by placing conversion within a temporal scheme of the *ordo salutis*.

A first classification is the view of Reformed theology, firmly established on the total depravity of humans after the fall: while not absolutely bad as can be, people are affected by sin in all aspects of life and do not seek God. Thus Reformed theologians hold to a monergistic understanding of conversion and locate conversion after regeneration.[23] They distinguish between a general call and a special or effectual call to faith in which the latter is bestowed only upon the predestined; without it all are spiritually dead.[24]

The Holy Spirit must first regenerate sinners in order for them to respond positively to the gospel (Rom. 1:6–7; 1 Cor. 1:9, 26; 1 Pet. 2:9). Repentance and faith, therefore, are the product of irresistible grace working through the Holy Spirit's regenerating work upon those who are effectually called. Accordingly, Reformed theology also holds to the perseverance of the saints – those who are converted cannot finally fail in faith but persist in saving grace. Although Reformed theologians explicitly maintain the voluntary nature of human response to the gospel, they are often criticized for a rather passive depiction of this element in conversion.

The second view involves the various kinds of synergism held by the Radical Reformers, Arminians, and Wesleyans. Like monergism, this view also begins with the priority of divine grace. But emphasis falls on human response to God's call. For the Radical Reformers, a theology of salvation involved rigorous analysis of the inner experience of conversion.[25] Having rejected the external, sacramental means of salvation, they saw conversion as "the quest for a sense of divine immediacy" experienced here and now. Moreover, they understood conversion to be inseparably connected with a call to discipleship. Conversion entailed uncompromising surrender to Christ's Lordship in radical identification with his suffering and death. In final analysis, in the life of the Radicals, conversion was nothing short of a call to martyrdom.

Arminians generally contend that conversion is the result of human obedience to God's universal call (Matt. 23:37; John 1:9; 3:16; Luke 14:16–17).[26] For Arminius, a concept of conversion must safeguard the sanctity of human free will.[27] Though more clearly so by Wesleyans, conversion is attributed to the prevenient grace of God conferred upon sinners by the Holy Spirit, creating a possibility of responding affirmatively when the gospel is preached.[28] Grace here is not necessarily effectual but only enabling and therefore resistible. Regeneration happens as a consequence of repentance and faith, not as a prior condition through which they are born. Arminians typically reject the perseverance of saints.

John Wesley construed conversion from the vantage point of ethical interests.[29] Faced with a morally depraved nation claiming Christianity as its national religion, Wesley's main mission was to re-instill holy life among his people. He believed that true conversion would lead to visible signs of sanctification, even to the degree of perfect love for God (with no voluntary sin, appealing e.g. to 1 John 4:18). In agreement with Calvinists, Wesley denied Pelagian anthropology and subscribed to the doctrines of original sin and total depravity. He also held to a strong theology of the Holy Spirit's witnessing work upon sinners to bring about repentance. Without the "quickening" work of the Holy Spirit, no one can know Christ.[30] Wesley, however, understood conversion within the parameters of God's prevenient grace as that which creates desire for God and faith in Jesus Christ.[31] Like Arminians, Wesley held that this grace is resistible and denied the perseverance of the saints. Some synergists interpret biblical texts that speak of predestination (e.g., Rom. 9) conditionally, in terms of God knowing ahead of time who will exercise faith. Others interpret them corporately, regarding God's choice of the church as his servant people.

A final view, espoused by moderate Calvinists such as Millard Erickson, maintains a partly synergistic understanding of conversion, while retaining the total depravity of humanity, effectual calling, and perseverance of the saints.[32] God's effectual calling ensures conversion, which occurs before regeneration. Regeneration is God's work upon those who respond to the gospel with repentance and faith.

Conversion in the matrix of grace
The conclusion of Israel's conversion testimony discloses that its source is exclusively Yahweh, who not only gives the impulse to repent but also promises to provide a radical means of liberation from the enslaving power of sin. The New Testament makes known that Israel's conversion testimonies culminate with the definitive inauguration of the eschatological ministries of the Messiah and the Holy Spirit. The call to conversion, therefore, finally comes with force to both Jews and Gentiles (1 Cor. 12:13).[33]

In this way, tracing Israel's bleak fiducial journey culminates in the task of plotting out the trajectory of God's superabundant grace and hope-filled promises lavished upon humans in the Son through the Holy Spirit. The overarching thesis is that the impulse and content of the Christian experience of conversion and all their invigorating implications are essentially summed up as the experience of the Holy Spirit.[34]

First, the grace of freedom performs maximally when human sin reaches its fatal apex and the sinner's conscience is completely shut in by a viciously paralyzing cycle of self-righteousness, shame and guilt, and self-condemnation (Rom. 5:20; 7:1–8:4). St. Augustine's *Confessions* illustrates graphically this odd work of grace.[35] He confesses that unregenerate freedom is a confounding conundrum because it expresses itself as a vehemently willful desire to sin against one's own conscience. Freedom is fundamental to being human, but it is a damaged, enslaving freedom. In the event of proclamation, the Spirit opens us up to hear the gospel and "makes the Word effective in us."[36] Indeed, faith comes from hearing the gospel (Rom. 10:14–15), but this seemingly mundane business of "hearing" becomes a grace-filled moment of encountering Jesus Christ as the living Lord in the eschatological activity of the Spirit. If sin is what breaks up relationship and creates alienation, then true freedom is what reopens that broken relationship.[37] Therefore, it is not that the sinner is free to respond to the gospel but that the Spirit's work frees him when to respond. In the event of conversion, the Spirit further effects union with Christ, justification, and adoption (1 Cor. 12:13; Rom. 8:9–17). In my view, Arminian synergism is not confirmed by conversion teachings indigenous to Scripture.

Secondly, conversion and regeneration are intimately related constructs in the working of the Spirit. The blight of sin is invincible, leaving humans in total depravity, but God unilaterally bestows rebirth in Christ through the Spirit (Rom. 8:9; John 1:12–13; 3:6). The New Testament's use of "regeneration" in the context of conversion occurs only once in Titus 3:5. In this verse, "the washing of regeneration and the renewing of the Holy Spirit" indicate together one experience of salvation.[38] The gift of the indwelling Spirit becomes a reality to the one who accepts the gospel by faith, not as a result of water baptism (1 Cor. 1:13–2:5).[39] Water baptism is a reenactment of what has already happened in and through the Spirit. On this view baptismal regeneration is to be rejected because the agent of cleansing is the Spirit, not the ceremony.

Gordon Fee's fruitful study of Pauline pneumatology suggests that "washing/rebirth/life-giving" all together signify the same reality experienced at conversion.[40] The three metaphors indicate the dramatic outcome of the two "turnings" performed by the Spirit and his setting into motion the present experience of blessings anticipatory of the coming age. Therefore, regeneration is emphatically not metaphysical or mystical. Rather, it is the Spirit's relational presence. Regeneration is closely associated with the metaphors of rebirth and renewal promised in the Old

Testament and proleptically actualized by the coming of Christ (Ezek. 11:19–20; Rom. 8:9; John 1:12–13; 3:6).

Furthermore, Paul's use of "sanctification" does not always refer to the work of grace after conversion. Rather, he uses the term as one of the metaphors for conversion.⁴¹ In Romans 15:16, sanctification is used synonymously with conversion. In 1 Corinthians 6:11, washing, sanctification, and justification in Jesus by the Spirit are listed in sequence. In 2 Thessalonians 2:13, he says that "God from the beginning chose you for salvation through sanctification by the Spirit and belief in the truth." Therefore, Paul's fluid and diverse use of conversion metaphors indicates that the dynamics cannot be adequately represented by a single metaphor. It also means that the precise timing or relationships in conversion are not his central concern. Against programmatic interests regarding the operation of grace, the message is that the Spirit is the only "constant" feature in the Christian experience of conversion.

Thirdly, in my view the New Testament church's emphasis on the definitive work of the Spirit in the event of proclamation seems to favor a punctilious view of conversion. Influenced also by the great revival movements, evangelicals generally see conversion as a thoroughly eschatological event that imposes drastic, sometimes also dramatic, beginnings on those who are predestined for the Christian life (Acts 9; 10).⁴² Conversion indicates a power encounter, a change from one dominion to another (Luke 11:17–20; Rom. 5:14–21; Heb. 2:14). The event can evoke profound emotional responses from the converts (Acts 2:37). According to Paul Ricoeur, a phenomenological analysis of religious feelings unveils the theological content inhering in them. The human experiences "absolute feelings" over which s/he cannot declare mastery.⁴³ Religious feelings bear fundamental ontological longings and, therefore, escape intelligibility, even for the one experiencing them. The powerful emotions that some people experience at conversion, therefore, fittingly correlate with the genuine interchange that occurs between the divine and human as free, relationally open beings.

Finally, conversion creates a life that has both centrifugal and centripetal directions. Conversion marks the inauguration of a life in the community of the saints (Acts 2:40–47). This communal reality is not a mere aggregate of autonomous individuals, nor is it an enmeshed clog of a community in which individuality is absorbed or objectified. Rather, it is a community that celebrates the diversities expressed in individuality and thereby becomes enriched as the body of Christ (Rom. 12:3–8; 1 Cor. 12:4–7). The Spirit, as the promised eschatological gift of the Father, gathers converts into the body of

Christ and, at the same time, unleashes the church's preaching ministry for the sake of the world (John 14:16–26; Acts 1:8; 2:1–12).

THE GRACE OF SANCTIFICATION IN THE VICISSITUDES OF LIFE

If conversion is the starting point of the Christian life, sanctification is a process of maturing in Christian freedom to love. In this way, justification provides the basis for sanctification and sanctification works out the content of justification.[44] The Spirit's work of setting us free from the fetters of sin further invites the convert to ever-thriving participation in the triune God's life of reconciliation. Specifically, sanctification has three interpenetrating or intersecting directions: Christological, ecclesial, and eschatological spheres in the Christian life effected and spurred on by the Holy Spirit. Much debate exists about the mechanisms or extent of sanctification, features of which will be demarcated here.

"Sanctification" means to "make holy." The Old Testament employs various forms of קָדַשׁ to connote holiness in the sense of being set apart or separate.[45] Most references occur in cultic and ceremonial contexts. Above all, God alone is holy whereas people and things are holy only by designation or derivation (Lev. 19:2; 20:26; Ps. 99:5). Also, the Old Testament occasionally reflects an ethical dimension of holiness as being inwardly set apart from evil (Ezek. 18:15–17). The New Testament use of the term is applied to all Three Persons in the Godhead. Jesus as the "Holy one of God" taught that God's name is to be "hallowed" (Mark 1:24; Matt. 6:9). Above all, the New Testament letters are replete with references to the Holy Spirit of God. The predominant occurrence of New Testament sanctification language occurs in the context of a lifelong process of ethical transformation effected by the Holy Spirit (Acts 20:32; Eph. 5:27; 1 Pet. 1:15).[46]

First, the Spirit's indwelling presence in the life of the Christian confers a permanent, positional reality of sainthood. The Christian grows in holiness precisely because s/he is already made holy by the work of Christ effected through the Spirit of God (Heb. 10:10, 29). Against perceptions of Roman Catholic theology, each Christian is already a saint (Rom. 8:27; Eph. 1:18). Here the Spirit's work is more closely modeled by a Lutheran emphasis upon the Christian life as becoming what we already are in Christ Jesus by faith.[47]

Secondly, the Holy Spirit is the agent of sanctification (1 Pet. 1:2). Sanctification entails maturing in faith in the word of God and being transformed to do good (Eph. 5:26; Titus 2:14; Heb. 13:20–21); the two are inseparably related (James 2:26). In John's terms, to be spiritual is always referenced by knowing Jesus as God's own embodiment of truth (1 John 4:2; John 17:17). To be sanctified means learning to live by the strength of God's word in the Spirit.

Thirdly, sanctification requires us continually to offer ourselves completely to God and the believing community for edification (Rom. 12:1–21). Against ever lurking idol-creating tendencies, Jesus Christ is the only lasting ground of Christian personhood and identity. Here, proper worship encompasses proper knowledge of God and practicing cruciform, reconciling love. Sanctification, therefore, is embarking on a journey of growing in worshiping God and practicing godly love (Eph. 1:5).

To this eschatological end, I favor an "Augustinian" or "Reformed" emphasis on sanctification as progressive growth through the means of grace we have in union with Christ, and believe Wesleyan/holiness perfectionism must be cautiously critiqued. Talk of "the second blessing" after conversion, also found in Pentecostal or charismatic views of baptism in the Holy Spirit, seems to have been derived from powerful experience of the indwelling Spirit more than biblical study.[48] Grace always and necessarily retains its enigmatic quality proper to the triune God's character and work. Grace cannot be unpacked in totality, nor is it possible to schematize definitively its operation. Perfection, even spoken of in terms of love instead of moralism, goes beyond the ambitious and all-encompassing quality of sanctification by the Spirit in this life.[49] Biblical teachings clearly point to quality of sanctification with tangible manifestations. Perfection, however, should be reserved for a radically new way of Christian life to be experienced in glorification.

Fourthly, sanctification requires sharing intimate fellowship with the Spirit and relying only upon the Spirit's empowerment for life. Jesus came to give life and definitively conquered death (John 3:16–17; 4:14; 10:10; 15:13; 1 Cor. 15:54–55).[50] The activity of the Spirit is behind this very life-giving power of Jesus. After the ascension of Christ, the Spirit brings the force of life that had been unique to the crucified and risen Lord upon converts. He is "the Spirit of life" or the "life-giving" Spirit of God in Jesus Christ (Rom. 8:2, 6; 2 Cor. 3:6).[51] To have the Spirit does not mean to have access to power that can be manipulated. Instead, the believer is to live by the Spirit over against all signs and practices of ungodliness (Rom. 8:4–5, 9–14; Gal. 5:16, 25). Sanctification is not to be considered in objectifying, moralistic terms but relationally.

Fifthly, to enjoy the fellowship of the Spirit is to surrender to an inevitably cruciform life (Phil. 2:1–18), bearing witness to the humble, obedient, and self-giving life of Jesus Christ. Ultimately, having faith in Jesus cannot bypass concrete sharing in "the fellowship of his sufferings, being conformed to his death" (Phil. 3:8–10). This means the Christian must accept a fundamentally different conception of power. Paradoxically, self-denial is the only means of experiencing the impossible possibility of living by Jesus' resurrection power against all life's threatening fragilities. In fact, the logic of Jesus' cross demonstrates that life's weakness is to be embraced with suffering love, not shunned with contempt.

To have faith in Jesus' resurrection means to believe in the hidden operation of divine grace amidst terribly and obviously diminished human capacities for love, righteousness, and hope. In this sobering, unmistakably eschatological context, the believer is to "work out [his] salvation with fear and trembling" (Phil. 2:12), for such is the life God wills and enables. Although God remains always as the supplier of all life's resources, the Christian must not presume upon grace by being slothful or legalistic.

Sanctification engrafts believers into a priestly community for the sake of the world still hostile to God's reconciling presence (1 Pet. 2:9; Rom. 12:1). The believers can be for the world precisely because they are set apart, sanctified against worldliness (John 17).

In conclusion, conversion and sanctification can be summed up as learning to trust in the implications of God *in* us and appropriating God's freedom. In conversion, the sinner is turned and surrendered to God for a radically different way of life. Through sanctification, the Christian learns that living by faith means embarking on a pilgrimage of growing trust in God's power of grace amidst ever encroaching legalism and apostasy. As long as the cross and resurrection stand as "the already and not yet" critique against human conceptualizations about love and righteousness, the Christian must live by prayer with a view toward the return of Christ, knowing that to pray is to unfold God's grace at work in the crevices of human trust. This paradoxical "certainty" that escapes ordinary human reflection involves the Christian life in surprising grace. Therefore, conversion and sanctification involve a process with a definitive beginning, to be achieved gloriously on the other side of the resurrection.

Further reading

Abraham, William J. *The Logic of Evangelism*. Grand Rapids, MI: Eerdmans, 1989.
Alexander, Donald L. (ed.). *Christian Spirituality: Five Views of Sanctification*. Downers Grove, IL: InterVarsity, 1988.
Berkouwer, G. C. *Faith and Sanctification*. Studies in Dogmatics. Trans. John Vriend. Grand Rapids, MI: Eerdmans, 1952.

Chan, Simon. *Spiritual Theology: A Systematic Study of the Christian Life.* Downers Grove, IL: InterVarsity, 1998.

Collins, Kenneth J. (ed.). *Exploring Christian Spirituality: An Ecumenical Reader.* Grand Rapids, MI: Baker, 2000.

Oden, Thomas C. *The Transforming Power of Grace.* Nashville, TN: Abingdon, 1993.

Packer, James I. *Keep in Step with the Spirit.* Tarrytown, NY: Revell, 1984.

Peace, Richard V. *Conversion in the New Testament: Paul and the Twelve.* Grand Rapids, MI: Eerdmans, 1999.

Peterson, David. *Possessed by God: A New Testament Theology of Sanctification.* New Studies in Biblical Theology. Downers Grove, IL: InterVarsity Press, 2001.

Webster, John. *Holiness.* Grand Rapids, MI: Eerdmans, 2003.

Notes

1. For analysis of religious autobiographies that deal with conversion from the vantage point of the struggling human will, see Anne Hunsaker Hawkins, *Archetypes of Conversion: The Autobiographies of Augustine, Bunyan, and Merton* (Toronto: Bucknell University Press, 1985).

2. Willem A. Van Gemeren (ed.), *The New International Dictionary of Old Testament Theology and Exegesis* (hereafter *NIDOTTE*), 5 vols. (Grand Rapids, MI: Zondervan, 1997), vol. IV., s.v. "בוש" by J. A. Thompson and Elmer A. Martens.

3. Gordon R. Lewis and Bruce Demarest, *Integrative Theology: Historical, Biblical, Systematic, Apologetic, Practical* (Grand Rapids, MI: Zondervan, 1996), pp. 85–89.

4. See, for instance, 2 Kings 23:25; Jonah 3:10.

5. Walter Kaiser, Jr., *Toward an Old Testament Theology* (Grand Rapids, MI: Zondervan, 1978), p. 137.

6. Paul Ricoeur, *Symbolism of Evil*, trans. Emerson Buchanan (New York: Harper and Row, 1967), pp. 70–99.

7. Kaiser, *Toward an Old Testament Theology*, p. 137.

8. Walter Brueggemann, "The Kerygma of the Deuteronomic Historian," *Interpretation* 22 (1968): 387–402.

9. Kaiser, *Toward an Old Testament Theology*, pp. 138–39. For a summarized illustration of this pattern, see Psalm 107 and Nehemiah 9.

10. See Jeremiah 26:3–4; 34:5; Isaiah 30:15. See also Gerhard Kittel (ed.), *Theological Dictionary of the New Testament* (hereafter *TDNT*), 10 vols. (Grand Rapids, MI: Eerdmans, 1964), vol. IV, pp. 980–89, s. v. "μετανοέω, μετάνοια" by E. Würthwein.

11. *Ibid.*, pp. 987–89.

12. See also Amos 9:14; Psalm 80:14. For an insightful and comprehensive analysis of Israel's covenantal privilege/responsibility to summon Yahweh in times of trouble, see Walter Brueggemann, *Theology of the Old Testament: Testimony, Dispute, Advocacy* (Minneapolis, MN: Fortress, 1997), Part III, esp. pp. 413–527.

13. Würthwein, *TDNT*, vol. IV, p. 987.

14. *Ibid.*, p. 988.

15. See Acts 8:22; 20:21; 26:20; Hebrews 6:1; Revelation 2:22, 16:9; Acts 2:38; 3:19; 5:31; 11:18; Revelation 2:21.

16. *TDNT*, s. v. "μετανοέω, μετάνοια" by J. Behm.

17. *Ibid.*, vol. IV, pp. 999–1006. See also George Raymond Beasley-Murray, *Jesus and the Kingdom of God* (Grand Rapids, MI: Eerdmans, 1994), pp. 71–75.

18. Behm, *TDNT*, vol. IV, pp. 1001–03.
19. Colin Brown (ed.), *New International Dictionary of New Testament Theology* (hereafter *NIDNTT*) 3 vols. (Grand Rapids, MI: Zondervan, 1975), vol. I, pp. 354–57, s. v. "εριστρέφω, μεταμέλομαι," in "Conversion, Penitence, Repentance, Proselyte," by F. Laubach.
20. *Ibid.*, vol. I, p. 355.
21. On such change see esp. Anthony A. Hoekema, *Saved by Grace* (Grand Rapids, MI: Eerdmans, 1989), pp. 123–27, plus how *metanoeō* and *epistrephō* are used together in the same discourse (Acts 3:19, 26:20).
22. Adolf Schlatter, *The Theology of the Apostles: The Development of New Testament Theology*, trans. Andreas J. Köstenberger (Grand Rapids, MI: Baker, 1999).
23. Hoekema, *Saved by Grace*, pp. 80–131.
24. *Ibid.*, pp. 93–112.
25. Timothy George, "The Spirituality of the Radical Reformation," *Southwestern Journal of Theology* 45 (Spring 2003): 23–32.
26. Roger E. Olson, *Westminster Handbook to Evangelical Theology* (Louisville, KY: Westminster John Knox, 2004), p. 162.
27. James Arminius, *Works of Arminius*, trans. James Nichols (Grand Rapids, MI: Baker, 1986), pp. 189–94.
28. See Thomas C. Oden, *The Transforming Power of Grace* (Nashville, TN: Abingdon, 1993).
29. Timothy L. Smith, "George Whitefield and the Wesleyan Witness," in Timothy L. Smith (ed.), *Whitefield and Wesley on the New Birth* (Grand Rapids, MI: Francis Asbury, 1986), pp. 11–38.
30. John Wesley, "The Circumcision of the Heart," in Kenneth Cain Kinghorn (ed.), *John Wesley on Christian Practice* (Nashville, TN: Abingdon, 2002), 3:24–27. See also "The Witness of the Spirit," p. 190.
31. *Ibid.*, "The Scripture Way of Salvation," p. 191.
32. Millard J. Erickson, *Christian Theology*, 2nd edition (Grand Rapids, MI: Baker, 1998), pp. 943–59.
33. Gordon Fee, *God's Empowering Presence: The Holy Spirit in the Letters of Paul* (Peabody, MA: Hendrickson, 1994), pp. 846–47.
34. *Ibid.*, pp. 848–49.
35. St. Augustine, *Confessions*, trans. R. K. Ryan (New York: Doubleday, 1960), Book 8. See also Miyon Chung, "The Textuality of Grace in St. Augustine's Confessions," Ph.D. diss. (Southwestern Baptist Theological School, 2003), pp. 58–69.
36. Otto Weber, *Foundations of Dogmatics*, trans. Darrell L. Guder, 10 vols. (Grand Rapids, MI: Eerdmans, 1981), vol. II, p. 254.
37. *Ibid.*
38. *TDNT*, s. v. "Παλιγγενεσια," in "γενεά, παλιγγενεσια" by F. Büchsel. See also Fee, *God's Empowering Presence*, pp. 855, 857.
39. Fee, *God's Empowering Presence*, p. 862.
40. *Ibid.*, pp. 855–59. See also his *Gospel and Spirit: Issues in New Testament Hermeneutics* (Peabody, MA: Hendrickson, 1991), p. 117. In this work, he arranges the elements of conversion in the order of repentance and forgiveness of sins, the regenerating work of the Holy Spirit, empowerment for life and obedience to mission, and baptism in water.

41. Fee, *God's Empowering Presence*, p. 859.

42. Olson, *Westminster Handbook*, p. 161. Richard Peace's study about the patterns of conversion from Paul and Jesus' twelve disciples argues that conversion is a process. The fact of their special status with reference to the dawning of eschatological times and the textualized content of the early church's preaching, however, favors to posit conversion as a punctilious beginning for Christian life. See Richard V. Peace, *Conversion in the New Testament: Paul and the Twelve* (Grand Rapids, MI: Eerdmans, 1999).

43. Paul Ricoeur, "Naming God," in *Figuring the Sacred: Religion, Narrative, and Imagination*, ed. Mark I. Wallace, trans. David Pellauer (Minneapolis, MN: Fortress, 1995), pp. 217–35. See also "The Power of Speech: Science and Poetry," *Philosophy Today* 29 (Spring 1985): 68–69.

44. Karl Barth, *Church Dogmatics*, trans. and ed. G. W. Bromiley and T. F. Torrance (Edinburgh: T. & T. Clark, 1975), 4/2:508.

45. *NIDOTTE*, s. v. "קָדַשׁ" by Jackie A. Naudé.

46. *NIDNTT*, s. v. "Holy, Consecrate, Sanctify, Saints, Devout," by H. Seebass and C. Brown.

47. Gerhard O. Forde, "The Lutheran View," in Donald L. Alexander (ed.), *Christian Spirituality: Five Views of Sanctification* (Downers Grove, IL: InterVarsity, 1988), p. 14.

48. Max Turner, *The Holy Spirit and Spiritual Gifts in the New Testament*, 2nd edition (Peabody, MA: Hendrickson, 1998), pp. 44–56, 113. (Though the books of Acts and 1 Corinthians are often used to support the Pentecostal view.)

49. Laurence W. Wood, "The Wesleyan View," in Alexander (ed.), *Christian Spirituality*, pp. 97–102. (The holiness teaching more influential for other Anglo-American evangelicals, the Keswick movement, may not reach for perfection but still sharply divides Christian lives into two phases or states based on being "filled with the Spirit.")

50. Eberhard Jüngel, *God as the Mystery of the World: On the Foundation of the Theology of the Crucified One in the Dispute between Theism and Atheism*, trans. Darrell L. Guder (Edinburgh: T. & T. Clark, 1983), pp. 184–225, 281.

51. Fee, *God's Empowering Presence*, p. 858.

The church in evangelical theology
and practice

LEANNE VAN DYK

When Christmas Day fell on a Sunday in 2005, a minor religious and cultural furor erupted, as reported by American news organizations, when several leading evangelical churches decided to cancel their Sunday morning worship services. This was because Christmas was a "family day," said church spokespersons. One leader observed that it would not be "convenient" for parents to have to deal with excitable children, have Christmas breakfast, and then change clothes and come to church. After all, people could go to one of the scheduled Christmas Eve services – there was nothing *special* about Sunday.

What aroused the most comment on this story was the fact that these were *evangelical* churches–accustomed to bearing the torch of conserving cultural and religious traditions, not discarding them. So, this event was a particular shock to cultural observers. But what was also interesting, yet unacknowledged by editorialists on the front pages of newspapers, was the ecclesiology that such an action revealed, at least among American evangelicals.

This chapter will explore this broad question via historical, descriptive, and constructive approaches. I will propose a version of a renewed evangelical ecclesiology that has continuity with evangelical history and articulates both a broad theological vision and practical fruitfulness.

HISTORICAL ROOTS AND MARKERS

It has often been said that evangelicalism lacks an ecclesiology, or at least a coherent ecclesiology. Stan Grenz believes this is because of the historical foundations of evangelicalism.[1] "Evangelicalism's parachurch ethos works against the ability of the movement to develop a deeply rooted ecclesiological base from which to understand its own identity and upon which to ground its mission";[2] thus a brief survey of the historical roots of evangelicalism will help clarify the contours and the challenges of evangelical ecclesiology.

In the aftermath of the catastrophic religious wars of the sixteenth and seventeenth centuries, there was widespread disillusionment with established church structures. As a result, some sought to find the "true" faith behind or within all the confessional hostilities that had so devastated Europe for over one hundred years. This longing for "purity" is one of the historical seeds of the evangelical tradition and it has momentous implications for evangelical ecclesiology. If the church is deemed the problem, then the solution, clearly, is a deep anti-church attitude. Accompanying this profound suspicion of established ecclesial structures that arose from enormous social upheaval were two streams of seventeenth-century religious development, pietism and religious awakening, both of which eventually flowed into contemporary British and North American evangelicalism.

A common feature both of early Methodism in England and the Great Awakening in America in the seventeenth century was an emphasis on personal experience and testimony. The community of believers, then, was the community of those who had personally experienced the grace of God and who could relate it to others.[3] The intensely personal and individual nature of these experiences was captured in sermons, narratives, and hymns, as well as by untiring preachers like George Whitefield and John Wesley. It is an often observed, yet astounding fact, that Wesley traveled more than a quarter million miles in his lifetime, mostly on horseback.[4] The spread of evangelical fervor that is associated with the Great Awakenings also found a ready home in the free-church movements with their antipathy toward hierarchical ecclesial structures and liturgical forms. Individualism and experientialism were two early markers of the evangelical ethos that have persisted to the present day.

Experiences of inner religious awakening naturally led to an anti-institutional, anti-ecclesial bias.[5] In the place of ecclesial structures and institutions, the model of the church that emerged was that of a voluntary society, a model that has had momentous implications for the subsequent tradition of evangelicalism. Anti-institutional bias is not limited to ecclesial structures but political structures as well. Although the factors are surely complex, it is at least worth noting that the same century that witnessed the two Awakenings in America also witnessed the colonial Revolution. Believers guided by the Holy Spirit, prayer, and Scripture no longer felt bound either by the traditions of the church's teaching office or the authority of the king, when he was deemed unjust.

In addition to the pietist and revivalist traditions that represent the primary historical roots of evangelicalism, Howard Snyder has identified additional historical sources as well.[6] These have influenced evangelical ecclesiology in complex ways. First, the Anglo-Catholic and Reformed/ Lutheran traditions contributed to the evangelical tradition, in spite of evangelicalism's tendency to reject creeds, forms, and hierarchies. An often noted feature of the history of evangelicalism is that it has never replaced denominational structures. In fact, a 1996 poll by the Angus Reid Group in Toronto discovered self-identified evangelicals across a wide variety of denominations in the United States and Canada.[7] Denominational distinctives, then, continue within the diverse evangelical tradition. This is so much the case that some observers of the contemporary evangelical scene conclude that the term is too imprecise to mean anything at all. D. G. Hart states, "Instead of trying to fix evangelicalism, born-again Protestants would be better off if they abandoned the category altogether ... Evangelicalism needs to be relinquished as a religious identity because it does not exist."[8] Nathan O. Hatch agrees: "In truth, there is no such thing as evangelicalism."[9] At the very least, the continuity of the historic denominational structures and the wide diversity of evangelical forms give force to this critique.

A second historical source of the evangelical tradition noted by Snyder is the radical Reformation and the free-church tradition, often carrying on a vigorous ecclesiological critique of the established churches. It is ironic that an original denial of ecclesial traditions is the establishment of a certain tradition of denial. This character of evangelicalism has been noted by George Marsden: "Little seems to hold it together other than common traditions, a central one of which is the denial of the authority of traditions."[10] The "tradition" of denying traditions has had an impact on evangelicalism's ecclesiology, giving it a certain *ad hoc* character. Some contemporary impulses within evangelicalism are moving against this deep suspicion of historic traditions, however.[11]

Third, the revivalist traditions, distinct from the historical period of the Great Awakening, have influenced the evangelical ecclesial ethos. The names of Charles Finney, Dwight Moody, Aimee Semple McPherson, and Billy Graham are included in the long list of influential revivalist preachers that have marked the character of American evangelicalism. The influence and reach of Billy Graham on American evangelical congregations is impossible to overstate.[12]

Fourth, according to Snyder, democracy has been a powerful and unique shaper of the evangelical reality, especially in America. Certainly, strong attitudes of individual choice and voluntarism have entered into the evangelical character through the American experiment. An example of the assumption of personal choice can be seen in an article by Bruce Barron. Surveying the ongoing controversy surrounding women's ordination in some evangelical communities, Barron proposes a solution to the problem, drawing on the principle of individual ecclesial choice: "But Protestants can easily move, if they wish, to a denomination whose view on women's ministerial roles matches their own."[13] Individual choice is the proposed solution to an ecclesial problem; this is uniquely suited to an American democratic, individualistic, modern, and market-driven mentality.

Finally, and related to democracy, is entrepreneurship. In a "can-do" context, easy accommodation has occurred between market values and the identity of the church. In such a pragmatic and utilitarian culture the church is expected to enhance its "clients," to distribute information, goods, and services to Christians, who are related to God as lone individuals.

EVANGELICAL ECCLESIOLOGY: A DIAGNOSIS

An overview of the multiple historical roots and sources just observed perhaps makes it no surprise that scholars of the evangelical tradition often comment on its sheer variety and complexity.[14] Such variety makes accurate description a difficult task for historians, sociologists, and theologians. Confusion over the word "evangelical" is not new. Both B. B. Warfield, the stalwart old-school Princeton theologian and Shailer Mathews, the social-gospel theologian, self-identified as "evangelical," the first in 1920, the second in 1924.[15] Although the word received fresh clarification after the fundamentalist–Modernist controversy and as it became distinguished from fundamentalism in the 1940s, it continues to the present day to cover a dauntingly wide array of religious, cultural, and intellectual opinion, style, ethos, and nuance.

Yet a discernible profile has emerged. According to David Bebbington, four key characteristics mark evangelical belief: crucicentrism, biblicism, conversionism, and activism.[16] These characteristics emphasize salvation through the death and resurrection of Jesus Christ, the literal truth and authority of Scripture, conversion as a life-changing experience of commitment and relationship, and the necessity of active missionary efforts. These characteristics were identified by the 1996 Angus Reid survey given to three thousand Americans and are similar to other lists of evangelical markers.[17] Noticeably absent in these common lists of evangelical characteristics are references to the church, including liturgy, worship, tradition, sacraments, ordination, or church government.

Ecclesiology, it would seem, is not an explicit part of evangelical identity. Some evangelical writers have noticed this apparent disregard for ecclesiology and have issued a call for renewal. In a feisty and prophetic book, David Fitch surveys the evangelical scene and concludes: "we must pursue the tasks of being the church again ... we must receive back from Christ the practices of being the people of God he has called us to be."[18] Fitch believes that evangelicals have sold out to secular culture, have lost their distinctive Christian voice, and have taken up the tools of the marketplace without thought for the cost of Christian witness: "For it is our own modernism that has allowed us to individualize, commodify, and package Christianity so much that the evangelical church is often barely distinguishable from other goods and services providers, self-help groups, and social organizations that make up the landscape of modern American life."[19]

David Wells joins Fitch in his critique. He, too, decries contemporary evangelicals for their wholesale evacuation of the church and its doctrines and tradition in favor of the idioms of secular modernity. "The evangelical world has lost its radicalism through a long process of accommodation to modernity."[20] Other evangelical thinkers as well, including Robert Webber and Simon Chan, join in the call for evangelical transformation, much of it centered on a renewed sense of the church. If a keen and coherent ecclesiology has not been part of evangelicalism's past, there is a growing conviction that it is desperately needed for evangelicalism's future.

The focus of doctrinal energy in evangelicalism has long been on Jesus Christ and Scripture. Other doctrinal issues have also occupied attention, such as charismatic gifts, the extent of salvation, and the last days. But ecclesiology has not aroused much interest or energy. A recent book on issues in evangelical theology includes eighteen doctrinal topics that have interested evangelicals but does not include ecclesiology at all.[21] When issues of ecclesiology have emerged, they have tended to focus on controversies of women's ordination, crises of leadership abuse or scandal, or innovations in worship style that push the boundaries of the community's identity. Ecclesiology, in other words, has tended to be marginalized to matters of polity, governance, finances, and leadership.

Some evangelicals criticize the lack of ecclesiology in the evangelical tradition.[22] Of course, not all communities of faith explicitly state the ecclesiologies that shape them, but all do, in fact, have an implicit ecclesiology. It has often been noted, in parallel fashion, that "noncreedal" churches indeed have implicit creeds and "nonliturgical" churches have implicit liturgies that shape worship. So, it is helpful to observe what evangelical theologians say explicitly about what evangelical ecclesiology is, in what respects they lament its shortcomings, and in what ways an ecclesiology is shaped by the practices and patterns that are often implicit and unarticulated.

Often a discussion of ecclesiology begins with the Nicene marks, identifying what the church *ought* to be. The church is one, holy, catholic, and apostolic. The marks are then analyzed for their necessity and sufficiency for a true church. Some evangelicals have revisited the Nicene marks as a way of claiming continuity with the tradition. Although tradition has not always been a valued concept with evangelicals, the Nicene marks have been a point of reference for some.

They can also be a standard against which the evangelical tradition can measure its own practices. "We consider the four 'marks' . . . and compare these to what we see," says Edith Humphrey, who then proceeds to hold the broad evangelical tradition to the marks as contextual correctives.[23] Unity and holiness are reflected characteristics from God's own self. They are as much a confession of faith as a call to obedience. For example, these marks may well judge and correct certain innovations or self-absorptions in worship. Catholicity or universality, in an evangelical context, is a call "to orient ourselves so that we consider and participate in the entire church – past, present, and future; east, west, north, and south – and to recognize our place there."[24] This mark corrects an ahistorical evangelical tendency. It also corrects a persistent individualistic evangelical tendency. When the church is confessed to be "catholic" or "universal," it is far bigger in God's purposes than the perimeters of individuals or families.

The apostolicity of the church has perhaps been the Nicene mark most embraced by evangelical instincts, but perhaps also most open to reductionism. It is far more than a term of mission and outreach; the apostolic character of the church refers as well to the deposit of the faith, the historic and normative origin of the church's teaching and formation by the guidance of the Holy Spirit. Furthermore, it refers to the structures of the church's organization and authority. Protestant and evangelical communities that deny formal notions of apostolic succession can affirm a spiritual, yet embodied, sense of the church as the temporal location of Christ's teaching ministry.

Although the Nicene marks of the church can perhaps be a useful rubric of reflection and correction, and although they may receive broad acceptance as a necessary ecclesial identifier, they certainly do not mark off a sufficient evangelical ecclesiology, either in a normative or descriptive sense. The task of constructing an evangelical ecclesiology needs to be more attentive to the unique characteristics of the evangelical ethos. Yet, some of the most important descriptors of evangelicalism itself, including individualism, voluntarism, emotionalism often paired with anti-intellectualism, and charismatic leadership, may resist an explicitly formed ecclesiology. This cluster of characteristics suggests that evangelical ecclesiology will find greater resonance with the free-church tradition rather than the classic Nicene marks of the church and the normative ecclesiologies in continuity with them. Drawing on the unique character of the evangelical tradition, Grenz suggests that evangelicalism has no explicit ecclesiology because of its roots as a voluntary society.[25]

The limitations of the Nicene marks with respect to a full and adequate ecclesiology have long been recognized, however. A common response has been to add to the Nicene marks in normative ecclesiologies. The Protestant Reformers further specified the characteristics of a true, visible church: the preaching of the Word and administration of the sacraments as well as proper church discipline. Twentieth-century thinkers have extended the list even more: Ecumenist Willem Visser't Hooft identified three key functions of the church, including witness, service, and fellowship.[26] Dutch Reformed theologian Hendrikus Berkhof included nine elements of the church: instruction, baptism, sermon, discussion, Lord's Supper, diaconate, worship, office, and church order.[27] John Howard Yoder identifies five practices of the Christian community which mark its life as a believing community, including binding and loosing, breaking bread together, baptism, charismatic body ministry, and congregational dialogue as the means of decision making.[28]

Some evangelical thinkers are relatively uninterested in ecclesiology, judging it to be a peripheral concern. "When it comes to evangelical identity, I believe that ecclesiology and especially polity are secondary to the gospel itself," or "Ecclesiology is important, yes. It is certainly interesting. But it is not saving."[29] Yet many evangelical theologians are keenly interested in retrieving a full-scale ecclesiology for the health of evangelical theology as a whole. For these theologians, the ecclesiological deficit in evangelicalism has not gone unnoticed.[30] David Wells argues that modernity has weakened and eroded evangelical congregations and that only a reclaiming of right doctrine and a re-orientation to God as sovereign, holy, and other can give evangelical congregations the kind of identity they need to understand who they really are. Much of contemporary evangelicalism has taken on board a therapeutic understanding of the church and even a therapeutic theology. This is so utterly foreign to an authentic biblical understanding of God, people, and their relation, says Wells, that a complete reorientation is required.[31] Although Wells does not draw out the implications of his critique into a constructive evangelical ecclesiology, others have drawn on such critiques and focused particularly on the church.

The ecclesiological imagination among evangelicals must expand, deepen, and grow more textured. But this ecclesiological deficit can only be overcome if the theological exploration is thorough and integrative. John Webster makes this observation: "A doctrine of the church is only as good as the doctrine of God which underlies it."[32] If ecclesiology were understood to be an articulation of the character, acts, will, and purposes of God for the people of God, that would be a much broader and grander scope of discourse than the rather limited range of topics that often occupy what is assumed to be ecclesiology.

Several vigorous proposals concerning a constructive ecclesiology have recently arisen from those who identify with, or are sympathetic to, evangelical theology. These proposals have some potential to shape evangelical ecclesiology primarily because of their basic congruity with the doctrinal emphasis already present in evangelicalism's traditions. The practical effect of these nascent movements on evangelicalism itself, especially in its broadest sense, has yet to be measured and assessed.

The emergent church movement is one such movement that has potential to re-shape evangelicalism's ecclesiology. The emergent church is consciously associated with evangelicalism, although it has its own unique character. It is a relatively new movement with young leaders who are highly independent. Although loose relationships exist between emergent churches, there is no hierarchy, structure, donor base, or web of supporting organizations such as marks established evangelicalism. This gives the movement an independent, even idiosyncratic atmosphere. In addition, emergent churches are often deliberately postmodern, urban, hip, and eclectic. Yet there are some affinities between the emergent church and broad evangelicalism with definite efforts at communication and affiliation. These affinities make the emergent church conversation worth careful consideration among those interested in evangelical ecclesiology. For one thing, emergent church participants are keenly interested in classic Christian belief and practices. In addition, emergent church instincts run toward renewal, commitment, and activism.

Key differences between emergent conversations regarding the church and more broadly based evangelicalism include emergent's emphasis on the sacraments and liturgy, although both areas of church life find an increasing hearing among evangelicals as well. In fact, the focus of some evangelical leaders matches the concerns of some emergent church leaders, namely, a recovery of worship, liturgy, and sacraments.[33]

Robert Webber, the author of several well-known books on the emergent church, posts a website in which he makes explicit connections to evangelical principles and statements.[34] Webber expands, in an emergent church direction, the 1977 Chicago Call, a statement which evangelical leaders signed affirming the basic doctrinal positions of historical evangelicalism and calling for a recommitment to those basics.[35] On the website he invites those "younger academic evangelicals" who are interested to email their support and blog their comments. The thirty-six affirmations that will, at this writing, eventually be an "emergent church call" include some that are related to ecclesiology: calls to be the people of God, to creedal identity, to narrative worship, to sacramental life, to catechetical teaching, to servant leadership, and to Christian community. A profile takes shape of an emergent evangelical ecclesiology that is focused on sacramental worship grounded in the classic Christian tradition and faithful, aware, and active Christian living that is an organic fruit of that worship.

Another important evangelical conversation that focuses on the church is the missional church movement. The missional church conversation includes a wide network of pastors, theologians, and laypersons, including many evangelicals. Those who are conversant with missional themes and supportive of them also include mainline and Roman Catholic participants. Missional theology has the potential to have a major impact on evangelical ecclesiology because it articulates a vision of the Christian faith that reaches into every doctrine and every aspect of Christian living. The theological themes that find a coherent voice in missional theology are creation and eschatology – or God's "first and final ends," Trinity and Incarnation, community and ethics, Spirit and life, all in an integrative vision. These are theological emphases that find strong affirmation, as well, in the broad evangelical tradition. For the most part, missional theology, networks, publications, and initiatives have been embraced by evangelicals. Although some have offered critiques, these have the tone of friendly insiders.[36]

According to this vision, the church is the people of God, called by God to embody "a particular way of life that exemplifies the ontological reality of the eschatological future brought into the present by the incarnational reality of Jesus Christ."[37] This dense phrase is a fundamental challenge to "business as usual" in many evangelical congregations where "church" is understood to be a purveyor of religious goods and services for the enhancement of the individual's spiritual self.[38] Missional theologians are convinced that the church is the people of God who are summoned to participate, in their particular context, in God's purposes and goals for the world. Those divine purposes and goals have been made known through Jesus Christ and will be fulfilled in God's future. But God's future breaks into our present in ways that can be seen and heard and felt concretely. These particular ways are the embodied gospel in the community of faith. In this way, missional theology is

> a prophetic vision concerning the call of the church in contemporary society. Convinced that the church is now in a cultural setting radically different from old paradigms of Christian cultural hegemony, [missional theology] wishes to articulate a vision of the church that challenges those old assumptions and summons the church to be an alternative community, a gospel community, an authentic witness to contemporary cultures.[39]

The vision of missional ecclesiology means that the church, contrary to much evangelical tradition, in a certain sense is not a voluntary society; it is the people of God, the body of Christ. It has, in other words, divine origin. The church is not a service organization whose purpose is to meet the spiritual needs of its "customers." Rather, the church is a *people* that have been shaped by Jesus – a people who are moving with him toward the consummation of God's work of salvation.[40] Being "in Christ" more accurately and fully describes the reality of the Christian believer rather than having a "personal relationship with Jesus."[41] The "success" of the church is not measured by membership numbers or dollars but by faithfulness, which may well mean suffering by taking up the cross of Christ. The "purpose" of the church has already been revealed by God; the "purpose-driven" church is to participate in God's mission for the world. These affirmations are the heart of a missional/evangelical ecclesiology.

EVANGELICAL ECCLESIOLOGY: A PROPOSAL

Both the emergent church movement, with its emphases on worship, liturgy, sacraments, and a return to the classic Christian tradition, and the missional theology conversation, with its critique of the church's enmeshment within secular modernity and its call for the church to take up the vocation of participating in God's own mission for the world, are encouraging initiatives within the fold of evangelical theology for a renewal of ecclesiology. Questions lurk at the edges, however: will an improved evangelical ecclesiology get to the heart of evangelicalism's ethos and practices? How can a clearly articulated theology reform hearts and minds, perhaps especially of young evangelicals who have been so thoroughly shaped by media and market? The 30 December 2005 *New York Times* reported on the culture of young adult evangelicals who "shop" for worship experiences with their friends, sometimes going to several gatherings for highly scripted, emotionally charged worship events.[42] Crafting a coherent evangelical ecclesiology that articulates the divine origin and *telos* of the people of God is an important evangelical task, but overcoming the "clergy-lay" divide and the "intellectual-lay" divide in order to bring the entire tradition into this comprehensive and fruitful vision is a critical challenge.

A uniquely *evangelical* ecclesiology ought not only to overcome the deficits often noted in the evangelical tradition, but also celebrate the unique strengths of that tradition. The implicit suggestion in the title of a recent book on evangelical ecclesiology is that the Word of God is the organizing principle of an evangelical ecclesiology.[43] This will be an ecclesiology much expanded from issues of polity and governance, an exposition of the classical marks, or urgent calls for renewals in worship. These are all matters of importance, to be sure, but a comprehensive evangelical ecclesiology must present a bolder and more ambitious theological and social vision.

The Word of God as a unifying motif has the potential for just such a theological and social vision. The referent of "Word of God," a wonderfully multivalent biblical and theological term, is primarily weighted here in its Christological meaning, but including, as well, the full expansion of meanings, including Scripture and sacrament.

Such an evangelical ecclesiology would be, first, an *incarnational ecclesiology* because the Word of God took up human flesh for us and for our salvation in Jesus Christ. This basic Christian datum has rich implications for the life of the church. Jesus not only died and was risen; he also ascended and now lives. The church confesses an incarnate Christ who is present to the community of faith in Scripture, preaching, worship, sacrament, and service. John Webster says, "Jesus Christ is alive, gloriously and resplendently alive, because alive with the life of God. He is risen from the dead, and so he is neither inert nor absent, neither a piece of the past nor one who possesses himself in solitude and remoteness; he is majestically and spontaneously present."[44] So, evangelical ecclesiology confesses that Christ is present to the church, sometimes in comfort, sometimes in judgment, always in promise and hope.

The practices of an evangelical congregation that lives out an incarnational ecclesiology of the Word of God would include ministries of justice and mercy in the name of Jesus Christ. These ministries would address the fleshly concerns of people – food, shelter, clothing, employment, health care, and access to legal protections. Practices would include, as well, prophetic resistance to deeply entrenched racism and sexism in church and society, and a call to repentance and reconciliation when these sins have marred the community.

Second, such an evangelical ecclesiology would be a *Trinitarian ecclesiology*, because the Word of God exists within a Trinitarian context in the divine economy. An adequate ecclesiology does not focus only on one or another divine person. Although a certain Trinitarian reductionism is often displayed in evangelical worship practices, sometimes tilted toward Jesus, sometimes tilted toward the Father, sometimes tilted toward the Spirit, evangelical ecclesiology will understand the Word of God to exist in full Trinitarian mutuality and unity. For this reason, the church exists as a people of the triune God and participates in the ultimate plans and purposes of the triune God.

The practices of an evangelical congregation that lives out a Trinitarian ecclesiology would include a wide range of worship commitments. Such a congregation will pay close attention to worship structures and music, keenly interested in how worship reflects and honors the richness of the divine community. Music will be selected not for its emotive power but its congruence to convey the story of the faith and reflect the community's union with the Father through the Son by the Spirit. Furthermore, the authority and inspiration of Scripture will be understood in a much richer context. In continuity with the evangelical tradition, a strong emphasis on the Bible will be valued, but it will be understood within the whole divine economy of salvation. The Bible will no longer be a litmus test of orthodoxy or an object to be guarded but the dynamic means of God's presence and activity in the community of faith, the means by which the Spirit of God forms the people of God.[45]

Third, such an evangelical ecclesiology would be a *sacramental ecclesiology*, because in the community of faith sacraments as well as Scripture present Christ. Evangelicals have often not embraced the sacraments, with notable exceptions, including the emergent church in recent years. Yet, as John Calvin points out, the "office" of the sacraments and the "office" of Scripture are one and the same – both set forth Christ and the grace that comes to us through Christ.[46] Some evidence of a renewal of sacramental identity and practices is a hopeful sign for a whole and healthy evangelical ecclesiology.

The practices of an evangelical congregation that lives out a sacramental ecclesiology would include frequent references within worship and congregational life to our identity-shaping baptismal promises to each other. Practices also include frequent celebration of the Lord's Supper, which is a gift of God to the people of God not to be spurned or lightly regarded. Because God is pleased in the sacraments to nourish and support us through the Spirit by means of common, earthy elements – water, wine, bread – evangelical ecclesial practices shaped by the Word of God in a sacramental sense will also include tender attention to the common and the earthy. Children will not only be nurtured in the faith, but will also be provided safe environments and trained care givers. Good policies will be written and implemented to protect youth from any who might harm them in the community, a place that should be safe, but too often is not. Seniors will be respected and their particular needs carefully considered. These practices reflect a deep sacramental awareness.

Fourth, such an evangelical ecclesiology would be a *proclamatory ecclesiology*, because the Word of God, Jesus Christ, is present in the event of preaching through the power of the Holy Spirit. Here is a mark of an evangelical ecclesiology that is already well attested in evangelical theology and practice. The word is preached. Yet the connection in the divine economy between the written word in Scripture, the preached word in the sermon, and the incarnate Word, Jesus Christ, needs to be clearer so as to avoid a mechanistic biblicism or idolatrous charismatic focus on the preacher. Although a constructive evangelical ecclesiology can be organized by the motif of "Word of God," the persistent, gracious action of the Holy Spirit must also be recognized and integrated at every level in an evangelical theology.

The practices of an evangelical congregation that lives out a proclamatory ecclesiology would include a tangible commitment to Scripture, preaching, and communicating the gospel. This can be seen in many ways in congregational life: by the care and skill with which the Scripture is read in worship, by prayers for illumination before the reading of the Word, by sermons which are attentive to Scripture and how Scripture interprets us, by a willingness to be corrected by the broader Christian community of interpreters, and by eagerness to give witness to Jesus Christ as revealed in Scripture.

Fifth, such an evangelical ecclesiology would be an *eschatological ecclesiology* because the church is sent by God to embody and proclaim the Word of God to a world that will be brought into "life in the world to come," as the Nicene Creed says. So, God's future has already illuminated the church's present through Jesus Christ. The church need not live in fear and anxiety; rather, the church has every reason to be confident in God's promises for the restoration of shalom. There will be times that the church will be sorely tested. But, because Jesus Christ is risen and ascended, the people of God live in hope.

The practices of an evangelical congregation that lives out an eschatological ecclesiology would include worship and ministries that express trust in God. Even in the language of lament, the congregation voices its security in being created, redeemed, and called by God. In its witness, the church expresses hope for the world. Witness, then, ought to be grounded in the promises of God rather than the fear that has sometimes seemed to characterize evangelism in certain sectors of evangelicalism. Witness that is grounded in God does not deny the "no" of God that has been revealed in the cross of Jesus Christ, but it does emphasize the "yes" of God that is proclaimed in the cross. In this witness, the standard for "success" is not solely or even predominantly quantitative growth or expansion. Rather, the standard for the church's self-evaluation is faithfulness to the patterns of the kingdom of God, patterns that have been revealed to the church in Jesus Christ.

The characteristics of an evangelical ecclesiology of the Word of God that have been proposed: incarnational, Trinitarian, sacramental, proclamatory, and eschatological, give contours to an ecclesiology that has continuity with an identifiable evangelical tradition yet seeks to address the deficits so often noted by evangelical observers. It is an ecclesiology that is theologically rich, worshipfully coherent, and practically fruitful.

Further reading

Bloesch, Donald G. *The Church: Sacraments, Worship, Ministry, Mission.* Christian Foundations. Downers Grove, IL: InterVarsity, 2002.

Clowney, Edmund P. *The Church.* Contours of Christian Theology. Downers Grove, IL: InterVarsity, 1995.

Guder, Darrell L. (ed.). *Missional Church: A Vision for the Sending of the Church in North America.* The Gospel and Our Culture. Grand Rapids, MI: Eerdmans, 1998.

Gunton, Colin E., and Daniel W. Hardy (eds.). *On Being the Church: Essays in Christian Community.* Edinburgh: T. & T. Clark, 1989.

Husbands, Mark, and Daniel J. Treier (eds.). *The Community of the Word: Toward an Evangelical Ecclesiology.* Downers Grove, IL: InterVarsity, 2005.

Kärkkäinen, Veli-Matti. *An Introduction to Ecclesiology: Ecumenical, Historical and Global Perspectives.* Downers Grove, IL: InterVarsity, 2002.

Stackhouse, John G., Jr. (ed.). *Evangelical Ecclesiology: Reality or Illusion?*. Grand Rapids, MI: Baker Academic, 2003.

Volf, Miroslav. *After Our Likeness: The Church as the Image of the Trinity*. Sacra Doctrina. Grand Rapids, MI: Eerdmans, 1997.

Notes

1. Stanley J. Grenz, *Renewing the Center: Evangelical Theology in a Post-Theological Era* (Grand Rapids, MI: Baker Academic, 2000), pp. 288, 289.
2. *Ibid.*, p. 290.
3. *Ibid.*, p. 291.
4. Bruce Hindmarsh, "Is Evangelical Ecclesiology an Oxymoron?: A Historical Perspective," in John G. Stackhouse, Jr. (ed.), *Evangelical Ecclesiology: Reality or Illusion?* (Grand Rapids, MI: Baker Academic, 2003), p. 28.
5. D. G. Hart, "The Church in Evangelical Theologies, Past and Future," in Mark Husbands and Daniel J. Treier (eds.), *The Community of the Word: Toward an Evangelical Ecclesiology* (Downers Grove, IL: InterVarsity, 2005), p. 40. Social scientists observe this anti-institutional bias as well in evangelicalism and posit it not only as a result of inner religious feeling but also as a result of social upheaval. Cf. R. C. Gordon-McCutchan, "The Irony of Evangelical History," *Journal for the Scientific Study of Religion* 20. 4 (December 1981): 309–26.
6. Howard A. Snyder, "The Marks of Evangelical Ecclesiology," in Stackhouse (ed.), *Evangelical Ecclesiology*, pp. 93–96.
7. Mark A. Noll, *American Evangelical Christianity: An Introduction* (Oxford: Blackwell, 2001), p. 31.
8. D. G. Hart, *Deconstructing Evangelicalism: Conservative Protestantism in the Age of Billy Graham* (Grand Rapids, MI: Baker Academic, 2004), p. 16.
9. Hart refers to this quote on p. 31 of *Deconstructing Evangelicalism* with reference to Nathan O. Hatch, "Response to Carl F. H. Henry," in Kenneth S. Kantzer and Carl F. H. Henry (eds.), *Evangelical Affirmations* (Grand Rapids, MI: Academie, 1990), pp. 97–98.
10. George Marsden, *Understanding Fundamentalism and Evangelicalism* (Grand Rapids, MI: Eerdmans, 1991), p. 81.
11. The "emergent church" is one example, which will be discussed later.
12. Graham's enormous importance makes the evolution of his views on inter-faith dialogue, political and social justice engagement, and hospitality toward persons with different views than the "orthodox" evangelical line all the more important.
13. Bruce Barron, "Putting Women in Their Place: I Timothy 2 and Evangelical Views of Women in Church Leadership," *Journal of the Evangelical Theological Society* 33. 4 (December 1990): 451–59, p. 459.
14. Mark Noll describes evangelicalism as "diverse, flexible, adaptible, and multi-form" (*American Evangelical Christianity*, p. 14).
15. Hart, *Deconstructing Evangelicalism*, pp. 22, 23, referring to B. B. Warfield's essay "In Behalf of Evangelical Religion" and Shailer Mathews's book *The Faith of the Modernists*.
16. David Bebbington, *Evangelicalism in Modern Britain: A History from the 1730s to the 1980s* (Grand Rapids, MI: Baker, 1989), p. 3.

17. Noll, *American Evangelical Christianity*, p. 31. The poll was also given to the same number of Canadians, with similar results.
18. David E. Fitch, *The Great Giveaway: Reclaiming The Mission of the Church from Big Business, Parachurch Organizations, Psychotherapy, Consumer Capitalism, and Other Modern Maladies* (Grand Rapids, MI: Baker, 2005), p. 18.
19. *Ibid.*, p. 13.
20. David F. Wells, *No Place for Truth or Whatever Happened to Evangelical Theology?* (Grand Rapids, MI: Eerdmans, 1993), pp. 295, 296.
21. Gregory A. Boyd and Paul R. Eddy, *Across the Spectrum: Understanding Issues in Evangelical Theology* (Grand Rapids, MI: Baker Academic, 2002).
22. Thomas Howard, *Evangelical is Not Enough* (Nashville, TN: Thomas Nelson, 1984) and D. H. Williams, *Retrieving the Tradition and Renewing Evangelicalism* (Grand Rapids, MI: Eerdmans, 1999) are two authors, in addition to D. G. Hart, *Deconstructing Evangelicalism*, and several of the contributors to John Stackhouse's book, *Evangelical Ecclesiology*, who regret the absence of an evangelical ecclesiology.
23. Edith M. Humphrey, "One, Holy, Catholic, and Apostolic," in Stackhouse (ed.), *Evangelical Ecclesiology* p. 137.
24. *Ibid.*, p. 145.
25. Grenz, *Renewing the Center*, p. 288.
26. Craig A. Carter, "Beyond Theocracy and Individualism: The Significance of John Howard Yoder's Ecclesiology for Evangelicalism," in Husbands and Treier (eds.), *The Community of the Word*, p. 180.
27. Hendrikus Berkhof, *Christian Faith: An Introduction to the Study of the Faith*, revised edition, trans. Sierd Woudstra (Grand Rapids, MI: Eerdmans, 1986), pp. 350, 351.
28. Carter, "Beyond Theocracy and Individualism," p. 182.
29. Roger E. Olson, "Free Church Ecclesiology and Evangelical Spirituality," in Stackhouse (ed.), *Evangelical Ecclesiology*, p. 162, and Paul F. M. Zahl, "Low Church and Proud," in *ibid.*, p. 215.
30. Both Mark Noll's 1994 book, *The Scandal of the Evangelical Mind* (Grand Rapids, MI: Eerdmans) and David Wells's 1993 book *No Place for Truth* lamented what they observed to be a decline in the state of evangelical theological commitment.
31. Wells, *No Place for Truth*, pp. 300, 301.
32. John Webster, "The Church and the Perfection of God," in Husbands and Treier (eds.), *The Community of the Word*, p. 78.
33. Simon Chan, *Liturgical Theology* (Downers Grove, IL: InterVarsity, forthcoming) is an evangelical writer whose interests are congruent with the emergent church interests.
34. www.churchmart.com/webber/.
35. Some of Robert Webber's recent books, published by a stalwart publisher of evangelicalism, include: *Ancient–Future Faith: Rethinking Evangelicalism for a Postmodern World* (1999); *Ancient–Future Time: Forming Spirituality through the Christian Year* (2004); and *Ancient–Future Evangelism: Making Your Church a Faith-Forming Community* (2003); all published Grand Rapids, MI: Baker.

36. For example, John Bolt's review essay of George Hunsberger's chapter in Stackhouse (ed.), *Evangelical Ecclesiology* suggests that missional theology has a flawed cultural analysis. Cf. John Bolt, "Evangelical Ecclesiology: No Longer an Oxymoron?: A Review Essay," *Calvin Theological Journal* 39. 2 (November 2004): 400–11.

37. Alan Roxburgh, "The Church in a Post-Modern Context," in *Confident Witness – Changing World: Rediscovering the Gospel in North America* (Grand Rapids, MI: Eerdmans, 1999), p. 258.

38. An influential force in American evangelicalism in recent years is Rick Warren and his books *The Purpose-Driven Life* (2002) and *The Purpose-Driven Church* (1995; both Grand Rapids, MI: Zondervan). The ecclesiology of these books can be said to be instrumental: the church exists to fulfill individuals. This is the evangelical ecclesiology that missional ecclesiology challenges at its foundations.

39. Leanne Van Dyk, "The Formation of Vocation – Institutional and Individual," in L. Gregory Jones and Stephanie Paulsell (eds.), *The Scope of Our Art: The Vocation of the Theological Teacher* (Grand Rapids, MI: Eerdmans, 2002), p. 230.

40. Darrell Guder, *Missional Church: A Vision for the Sending of the Church in North America* (Grand Rapids, MI: Eerdmans, 1998), p. 129.

41. For an insightful critique of this evangelical phrase, see John Suk, "A Personal Relationship with Jesus?" *Perspectives: A Journal of Reformed Thought* 20. 5 (November 2005): 5–9.

42. Neela Banerjee, "Going to Church to Find a Faith that Fits," *New York Times*, 30 December 2005.

43. Husbands and Treier (eds.), *The Community of the Word: Toward an Evangelical Ecclesiology*.

44. John Webster, "The Visible Attests the Invisible," in *ibid.*, pp. 96–113 (p. 108).

45. Telford Work, *Living and Active: Scripture in the Economy of Salvation* (Grand Rapids, MI: Eerdmans, 2002), p. 216.

46. John Calvin, *Institutes of the Christian Religion*, ed. John T. McNeill, trans. Ford Lewis Battles (Philadelphia: Westminster, 1960), IV.xiv.17.

Part II

The contexts of evangelical theology

10 Evangelical theology and culture

WILLIAM A. DYRNESS

Though the evangelical movement has become a diverse, worldwide movement, there has been consistency in attitudes toward culture. Throughout their history evangelicals have displayed ambivalence toward their cultural context. The world was either something to be won over in the name of Christ, or to be avoided as a source of temptation, but it could also represent a resource to be exploited in pursuit of their evangelical calling. As a result, their relationship with culture has been ambiguous, marked more often by vigorous campaigns against particular evils believed to threaten Christian living – whether liquor, polygamy or slavery, or, more recently, abortion and gay marriage – than by thoughtful engagement with the complexities of culture. In this respect views of culture reflect the unique historical and theological character of the movement, with its roots in the Reformation, and the revival and missionary movements emanating from Europe and North America.[1] In this article we will use "culture" to refer to artifacts, practices, and institutions by which a people expresses its identity; in theological terms, what humans make of God's good creation.

HISTORICAL SOURCES: REFORMATION AND REVIVALS

Two historical sources in particular have shaped evangelical views of culture: the Reformation and the major revivals. The watchwords of the Reformation – faith alone, the Bible alone, and Christ alone – became central to evangelical theology. But the roots of ambiguity toward culture lay, in part, in the diversity of the views of the major Reformers. John Calvin believed that true worship of God should lead to transformation of cultural structures; Martin Luther taught that the word of God would do its work in the human heart and life, and involvement in political or cultural processes was a matter of relative indifference; Anabaptists felt that radical discipleship involved a more complete break with secular power structures. Each of these attitudes would have influence on evangelical views of culture. But there was one common element that became decisive in all subsequent evangelical theologies of culture: the iconoclastic temperament of the Reformation. Despite their varying emphases, all Reformers rejected the medieval view that particular places and objects conveyed spiritual reality, and, in particular, they denied that these symbolic entities might orient and illuminate social and political life. For the Reformers only the response of personal and informed faith was capable of constituting the people of God. The unintended consequence of this inward turn was, eventually, to cut the theological ground from under any public or social understanding of Christian truth. Little by little what had been widely understood to be the two books of God, revelation in Scripture and in nature, was reduced to God's voice in Scripture alone. And it was in the evangelical movement in particular where this reduction became most evident. In America this led many to believe that the Bible in the hands of the common Christian was a sufficient theological education for anyone. Ironically the very Reformation movements of personal faith and voluntary association most responsible for influencing modern ideas of democracy, tended by their very nature to impede the development of theological perspectives that could support or critique these notions.

The second source for evangelical attitudes toward culture was the revivals of the Anglo-Saxon world, and the missionary movements these influenced. Continuing the emphases of the Reformation, evangelicals have come to believe that God works mostly by way of periodic and intermittent interventions in the lives of individuals and communities. Thus general and broad-based efforts of reform and influence, most evangelicals believe, will be ineffectual apart from the direct working of God in the individual and the larger society. This has led not only to viewing revivals, or personal conversion, as the means to social renewal, but also, curiously, to viewing the pursuit of social causes in revivalist terms – organized by local chapters and culminating in large stadium rallies. While the activism inherent in the promotion of revivals has proved an important engine for social reform, it has also hampered the development of theological resources by which to evaluate these events. As Mark Noll argues, "The very character of the revival that made evangelical religion into a potent force in North America weakened its intellectual power."[2]

NINETEENTH-CENTURY MOVEMENTS: COMMON SENSE REALISM AND ROMANTICISM

In both Britain and America during the early nineteenth century, evangelicalism played an important social and political role; in America it became the dominant religious force. Consistent with the influences that we have traced, there was a widespread assumption that the American form of democracy was essentially Christian. Moreover, the free liberal economy that was developing, dependent as it was on the free choice of the individual, was also felt to be essentially Christian. These views were not so much argued as assumed, and were felt to be so expressive of the gospel that missionaries did not hesitate to make them part of their instruction on the mission field. Their focus on voluntarism and freedom of choice had a large impact on culture in many parts of the world. In part these views flourished because of the support they received from the intellectual system known as common sense realism, which evangelicals came to espouse during the first half of the nineteenth century. Based on the empiricism of Francis Bacon and philosophers of the Scottish Enlightenment, this view assumed that God had so arranged the world that the human mind could know and order it, and indeed come to correct knowledge of the world and God. A famous instance of this thinking is evident in the opening pages of Charles Hodge's influential *Systematic Theology*, written in the middle of the century. There the most influential American theologian argued that as nature contains facts that the scientist arranges, "so the Bible contains the truths which the theologian has to collect, authenticate, arrange, and exhibit in their internal relation to each other."[3] These attitudes reinforced an American pragmatic temperament and helped to fuel the industrial advances of the century, but they did little to encourage a systematic reflection on societal problems.

An even more important influence on American evangelical confidence in the spread of democracy and the free market was theological: evangelicals believed that God had a special role for America to play in bringing about the kingdom. These ideas were related to the eschatological view called postmillennialism, which holds that the kingdom of God is already present in history and is extended through the preaching of the gospel and the work of the Holy Spirit. At the end of this age, Christ would return to judge the world and set up his millennial reign. The Reformers believed that the Fall of Babylon had begun with the Reformation, and this view was elaborated during the Puritan Revolution in England. But it was in New England especially where Christians saw themselves setting up a godly commonwealth. Jonathan Edwards believed that through the revivals God was establishing an earthly kingdom. These views were influential among evangelicals into the nineteenth century – at least until these hopes were dashed during the Civil War and the urban and industrial unrest that followed. Charles Finney sought to Christianize the nation both through his revivals and the social reform they stimulated. In England similar motivations were behind the reforms of William Wilberforce and his friends.

Romanticism with its emphasis on feeling and individual expression arose in Europe as a reaction against the rationalism of the Enlightenment. This movement, with its roots in earlier Pietist movements and the inward turn of the Reformation, was to be particularly influential on evangelicalism. Friedrich Schleiermacher's view of faith as an expression of the feeling of dependence on God – deriving in part from his own Moravian background – was an important example of thinkers who sought a deeper faith that was not confined by the strictures of reason. Evangelicals, while resisting some implications of this emphasis, were drawn to the inward and personal emphases of this religion of feeling. In Britain and America this religion of the heart was largely mediated by the deeper life conferences at the end of the century. The last half of the nineteenth century saw proliferation of perfectionist and deeper life movements that picked up on the emphases of Romanticism and responded to the cultural traumas of that period. By 1875 these formed into a regular series of Keswick conferences, first in England then America. These conferences, and the books and literature they stimulated, encouraged Christians to move from a carnal life to a higher state of consecration by a complete yielding of self to the Holy Spirit. The influence of this movement on social and cultural involvement was ambiguous. On the one hand, at least until the 1890s, the filling of the Holy Spirit was considered "power for service" which led to various programs of social involvement. On the other hand the inward, feeling-based emphases of the movement tended to discourage vigorous involvement in the social arena, especially as more liberal Christians began to champion social causes later in the century.[4]

Attitudes shaped by the revivals and Romanticism came to influence, among other things, evangelical attitudes toward the arts.[5] A dominant and enduring characteristic of American evangelicalism, resulting from both revivalism and Romanticism, has been a focus on immediate experience and conversion. These and other streams converged to discourage any emphasis on discipline and developmentalism. Revivalism stressed a "fresh start"; spirituality growing out of Romanticism stressed "let go and let God." Both of these led to a focus on the ravished individual as agent of change and a locus of creativity. Roger Lundin points out that this complex of ideas led evangelicals to view artists as liberated individuals who create new worlds, like God himself.[6] Ironically these views corresponded almost exactly to secular views of art that would triumph in the twentieth century, though absent a superintending God or a sense of sin.

FUNDAMENTALISM, PREMILLENNIALISM, AND THE GREAT REVERSAL

The revivals of the early nineteenth century stimulated many evangelicals to become involved in social causes. Their efforts against slavery, child labor, and other injustices left a lasting mark on American culture. Later in the century the question of the Christian's relation to culture was contested, and in the first quarter of the twentieth century social and cultural concerns disappeared almost entirely from evangelical consideration. In a few generations evangelical Christians in America went from being a dominant (and constructive) force, both in religion and politics, to being an often despised and culturally invisible minority. There were important historical reasons for this. Believing Christians were placed on the defensive by the challenges presented by Darwin, industrial unrest, immigration and the progressive social gospel this stimulated, and, especially, by the challenge to the authority of Scripture represented by the rise of higher criticism. But arguably the major reasons for the fundamentalist withdrawal from cultural engagement during this period were theological.

The early Puritans brought with them a keen sense of God's interest in the larger culture and the importance of just structures and laws. This Reformed heritage clearly played a role in the revolutionary movements of the eighteenth century. It also played a role in the revivals and reforms of the early nineteenth century, at least among the heirs of this tradition more open to the working of the Holy Spirit. But the spiritual movements later in the century, while not without Reformed influence, tended to focus on individual spirituality and personal efforts to submit to God. All of this encouraged what might be called a lay-level, and unreflective, Arminianism. Since Edwards, revivalism had gradually moved from an emphasis on the working of God, to a focus on human response that came to assume the "free and decisive character of the human free will."[7] The Keswick tradition went even further in this direction by adding an emotional dimension to this free decision of faith. The call to personal spirituality eclipsed any wider responsibility to public life, beyond evangelization, though it did stimulate the development of a rich hymnody and other forms of popular religious art.

A further theological motive for a retreat from culture was the rise of premillennial eschatology, especially in the context of dispensational theology. The predominant view of the end times was postmillennial well into the nineteenth century – reflecting the belief that the world would gradually improve before Christ returned. Later in the century John Nelson Darby and English Plymouth Brethren brought his dispensational system of biblical interpretation to America, where it was warmly embraced by leaders of the Bible conference movement and popularized by C. I. Scofield's annotated 1909 edition of the King James Bible. This view divided history into particular periods according to differing ways God deals with the human race. On this view the present period of Grace would culminate in the premillennial rapture of the saints, preceding a time of troubles known as the tribulation, followed by a thousand-year earthly reign of Christ.

The comfort provided by the "blessed hope" of the rapture of the saints proved attractive to Christians increasingly discouraged by the religious and social events around them. The neat structures of dispensationalist views of history and the belief that the rapture would be preceded by a worsening of the world situation and, especially, by a falling away from the truth by Christians, helped to explain many of the disturbing things they saw around them. While providing comfort and explanation, these views did little to encourage any constructive involvement in the larger culture.

But while they disdained involvement in the larger culture, evangelicals, or fundamentalists as they were called, turned their energies to creating a significant subculture of institutions, which prepared the way for a mid-century revival.[8] Beginning in the 1920s, fundamentalists began to form an impressive array of cultural institutions. Since many of the colleges founded by evangelicals in the nineteenth century had lost their spiritual orientation, many new Bible colleges were founded, which later in the century developed into liberal arts colleges. A variety of publications were set up and new initiatives were taken in missions and evangelism – many making use of the latest technology. To counter secularizing trends in public behavior, fundamentalist institutions began to institute codes of conduct during the 1930s, something that the largely Christian cultural consensus had previously made unnecessary.

By the 1940s fundamentalism had developed into a large and diverse movement with its own institutions and international connections. Theologically, however, the attitudes toward culture formed by dispensationalism and premillennialism prevailed. In general Christians looked around them and saw a largely secular culture, and apart from making various evangelistic forays, they followed the biblical admonition to come out from among them and be separate. A comparison with the first half of the nineteenth century is instructive. Earlier, during the Second Great Awakening, evangelicals in Britain and America were busy forming organizations to address a wide variety of social ills. There was hardly any vice one could think of that did not have a corresponding group seeking its extinction. A century later, evangelical efforts were addressed in quite different directions. Beginning in the 1940s, evangelicals were busy founding an equally impressive range of institutions. But rather than addressing its social needs, fundamentalists addressed the world as an object of mission and evangelism.[9] There were new national evangelistic enterprises – Billy Graham, Young Life, Youth for Christ, Boys' Brigade, and any number of mission organizations. Compassion-based ministries would come later, but during this period only World Vision represented any larger social sense of evangelical responsibility. There was a positive side to these efforts; indeed they would together stimulate a renewal of American Christianity. Many of these ministries made creative use of modern technology and cultural forms in the service of their mission. All of this would eventually have an important cultural impact, but at this early stage any larger cultural impact was missing. In 1947, theologian Carl Henry underlined both the weakness of this tradition, and its potential. In his book *Uneasy Conscience of Modern Fundamentalism* he calls fundamentalists to task for their withdrawal from the public arena and challenges them to take their larger responsibilities more seriously.

FRANCIS SCHAEFFER, LAUSANNE, AND THE RECOVERY OF A CULTURAL VISION

By mid-century evangelicals were once again emerging as a visible presence in American life, but their influence on culture was minimal. The postwar revival did not, immediately, produce political or social reformers. After withdrawing from culture, evangelicals should not have been surprised to look around and see Christian values absent from their schools, movies, and art museums. By this time the increasing secularism in Europe coupled with the cultural retreat represented by fundamentalism had resulted in a situation in which the deep structures of modern thought and culture had been formed by thinkers radically opposed to Christianity – Karl Marx, Friedrich Nietzsche, Sigmund Freud.[10] Little wonder that Christians avoided involvement in the resulting secular culture, sending their children to Christian colleges and their money to missions.

But things were about to change – the renewal of evangelicalism and a longstanding Christian presence in the American South would gradually make its presence felt. The 1960s represent a transformational era not only for American culture generally, but for evangelicalism in particular. When Martin Luther King articulated his call for justice and equal rights at the very center of American public life, his speeches were filled with themes that would have been familiar to evangelical Christians. In that decade Christians from the South, both black and white, schooled in evangelical values, fueled America's struggle over civil rights, even if many northern evangelicals still avoided direct involvement.[11]

The person who did much to awaken evangelicals to reflection on culture was Francis Schaeffer, whose Swiss-based ministry involved a creative ministry to modern intellectuals. Through his lecture tours in America and Britain, and later through his books and videos, Schaeffer influenced evangelicals to think through, often for the first time, their relationship to culture. In a way that recalls Pope John XXIII's intent at the Second Vatican Council to open up the windows of the church to the modern world, Schaeffer brought contemporary philosophical and literary issues into the center of evangelical conversation. For many he provided a window, even a doorway out, into the larger culture. His early books, *Escape from Reason* (1968) and *The God who is There* (1968), became immediate bestsellers. In the latter he describes his program of bearing witness to historic Christianity into the twentieth century. While many of his historical and philosophical claims may be disputed, his purpose of thinking holistically about philosophy, the arts, and culture, in a recovery of a Reformed vision of reality, was striking. His reflections on culture were given credibility by his friendship with Dutch art historian H. R. Rookmaaker, who applied a Reformed analysis of culture to modern art. Schaeffer declared a turning point had been crossed sometime toward the end of the nineteenth century, when existential experience claimed precedence over rational thought, and any final meaning to human life. Only the historic truth of God's reality and Christ's work of salvation, Schaeffer argued, shows "the truth of the external world and truth of what man himself is."[12]

Schaeffer's influence was widespread both in Britain and America. For many at the time the strong critique of modern culture was less significant than the fact that culture was being surveyed and taken seriously at all. Many who ventured out of the evangelical subculture to look more closely where Schaeffer was pointing did not agree with his wholly negative views about culture, but his stimulus was critical.

Evangelicals' continuing commitment to missions and evangelism led to an event that was to shape profoundly their attitudes toward culture: the Lausanne Congress on Evangelism, called by Billy Graham in July 1974.[13] Though growing out of evangelicalism's central commitment to evangelism, the conference heralded an important advance in reflection on culture. For one thing it was broadly evangelical and included Christians from around the world. The leadership of John Stott and Jack Dain was significant in including British (and Australian) evangelicals in the conversation. While there had been much exchange between Britain and America, as we have noted, American evangelicalism up to this point was often insular in its thinking. John Stott opened American Christians to a new and broader interpretation of Christianity (as earlier his fellow countryman C. S. Lewis had done). He and other British evangelicals represented an Anglican Christianity that had not been influenced by the fundamentalism that had troubled American Christianity. Though committed to strong Christian witness and orthodox faith, these represented a version of Christianity and evangelism rooted and trained in England's major universities, rather than in Bible schools as in America. Stott's leadership was particularly important in preparing the Lausanne Covenant, which resulted from the consultation. In addition to sections on Christian social responsibility and on education, the statement included a section on "Evangelism in Culture," which said in part: "Because man is God's creature, some of his culture is rich in beauty and goodness ... The Gospel does not presuppose the superiority of any culture to another, but evaluated all cultures according to its own criteria of truth and righteousness."[14]

Prominent voices at the congress included Latin, African, and Asian theologians, and reports were heard about ministry in all sectors of society and from all parts of the globe. The exposure to the multicultural reality of missions was to have a lasting influence on evangelicalism's self-identity. This decade marks the point at which evangelicals began to recognize their kinship and mutual accountability with Christians from around the world. Interestingly, this included an awakening to their affinity with the movement of the Spirit represented by Pentecostalism. Though its American origins dated back to 1907, Pentecostals had not considered themselves a part of the evangelical movement until well after World War II. In the

1970s this changed when a charismatic awakening took place in many Protestant denominations (and even in many Catholic parishes). These groups immediately recognized their "evangelical" character and often joined with traditional evangelicals in evangelistic and social outreach. Pentecostals had early been involved in international missions, and their presence at Lausanne underlined the spiritual and cultural diversity of evangelicalism. Pentecostalism itself had roots in Black as well as Anglo culture, and so in many ways marked a unique multicultural form of Christianity – a fact that may account for its popularity in Africa and Latin America. Theologically, Pentecostalism's emphasis on the work of the Holy Spirit sparked new reflection (and sometimes controversy) with respect to the Third Person of the Trinity, though, interestingly, it did not lead evangelicals to reflect on the work of the Spirit in the broader culture.

The growing multicultural identity of evangelicalism is arguably the most significant development in evangelicalism's recent history, even if this is not widely recognized. Lausanne was followed by a consultation on Gospel and Culture in Willowbank, Bermuda, in January 1978.[15] There participants recognized that culture includes issues of tribalism, polygamy, and caste unfamiliar to Western Christians. The final report dealt not only with issues of conversion but also with communication and cultural change. The conversation this encouraged, which focused on what was called contextualization or inculturation of the gospel in culture, has proven important not only for missions and missionaries but also for all who are seeking to be faithful disciples in a changing world. While this discussion is only gradually being integrated into evangelical's reflection on culture, it offers the prospect of enlarging that conversation by raising issues of justice, poverty, development, and inter-religious dialogue.

CONTEMPORARY EVANGELICALISM AND CULTURE

Contemporary evangelicalism represents what might be called a divided personality. On the one hand a growing and sophisticated conversation about culture has taken root among evangelicals, especially among those who see themselves as part of a larger Christian community. At the same time continued parochialism marks the efforts of many evangelicals in America. We noted earlier the resources for theological reflection that are part of the evangelical heritage. Early in the last century J. Gresham Machen, articulating a strong Reformation theme, called Christians to transform their culture by the word of God and more recently John Stott followed up Carl Henry's call for Christian reflection and involvement in culture.[16]

During the 1970s and 1980s, in a move expressive of the broadening of the evangelical identity we noted above, there was an important revival of a longstanding conversation between Anabaptist and Reformed theologians regarding Christian attitudes toward culture. In 1972 John Howard Yoder, in his book *The Politics of Jesus*, eloquently described his Mennonite view that Christians are called not to redeem and reform secular culture but to form an alternative culture as disciples of Jesus in community. Reformed voices in the tradition of Abraham Kuyper and J. Gresham Machen, Richard Mouw and Nicholas Wolterstorff responded that the Christian's responsibility extended beyond the walls of the church, laying out a larger view of the Christian mission.[17] These thinkers drew inspiration from Kuyper's notion of "common grace," which held that in addition to God's special saving grace evident in the work of Christ, there is a general sense that God is at work in the larger culture to draw people toward faith. Through books, conferences, and periodical exchange this proved to be a fruitful conversation that offered constructive proposals for both church renewal and cultural engagement. Encouraged by thinkers such as these, recently evangelicals have undertaken to reflect seriously on various aspects of culture. The influence of Yoder continues among younger evangelicals who are discouraged by unreflective activism, and who prefer to follow the call of Yoder, and more recently of Stanley Hauerwas, to seek cultural renewal by being the church. Others more positively want to see Christian presence and thinking more visible in the arts, including the popular media. Here, however, the activism of evangelicalism still rules, as the practice of these arts has outstripped serious theological reflection thereon.[18]

In spite of these encouraging signs, large segments of evangelicalism remain untouched by these conversations. The continuing failure to integrate expanding multicultural experience into a consistent understanding of culture and cultural engagement still bedevils the evangelical movement. This has become increasingly evident with the growing political (and social) visibility of evangelicalism over the last generation. What Mark Noll describes as the activist, biblicist, and populist character of evangelicalism continues to hamper systematic reflection on culture.[19] While these same characteristics could fund a more constructive approach to culture, too often, rather than a nuanced call to engagement, more popular evangelical voices lament the loss of Christian values and simplistically urge Christians to take back culture. Bob Briner, for example, describes his cultural project in these terms: "It is about retaking lost territory, about winning, about conquest."[20] Similarly, Pat Robertson calls evangelicals to take back culture. In terms that recall the older postmillennialism he notes that God has shed his grace on America, but now the nation is at risk. "Either we decide to serve God and obey his commandments and . . . reassert our historical values and beliefs, or we can witness the immanent collapse of our culture."[21] These more popular voices tend to frame their discussion by casting culture in a negative light, as needing rescue rather than sensitive and discerning involvement. Culture is something to be "taken back," and involvement something like a revival campaign.

When one considers the major contemporary influences on evangelicalism and culture, two names come to mind which illustrate the current ambiguity. On the one hand, C. S. Lewis continues to be one of the most important influences in broadening the evangelical culture. Both his thoughtful defense of Christianity and his fictional work have proven immensely stimulating to many evangelicals. But, oddly, when Lewis himself searches for reasons that Christians should value culture he comes up empty, concluding "on the whole, the New Testament seemed, if not hostile, yet unmistakably cold to culture . . . I cannot see that we are encouraged to think it important."[22] The other continuing influence is surely Francis Schaeffer, who is experiencing a renewed popularity, although ironically Schaeffer's influence has migrated from being an avant-garde voice for cultural awareness and Christian engagement in the 1960s, to a conservative defender of now-lost Christian values today.[23] Meanwhile, his teachings on co-belligerency, Christian love, and responsibility for the environment have been overlooked.

In surveying evangelical involvement in culture, various theological themes – or, better, theological practices – have emerged that have often encouraged, and sometimes impeded, constructive engagement with culture. We conclude with a brief discussion of four of these. First, the biblical orientation of evangelicals has proven both an asset and a liability. On the one hand, Scripture has provided a language and framework in terms of which believers can address the issues of the day. Small group Bible studies and home groups have become not only an evangelistic strategy but also a kind of evangelical civic culture. Families, neighborhoods, and church congregations are often revitalized by these intimate groups and the study they encourage. At the same time dependence on Scripture has sometimes led to proof-texting and an unrealistic expectation that complex contemporary cultural issues can be resolved by the study of Scripture alone.

Secondly, the evangelical call for personal faith and conversion has had important cultural influence. This individualist emphasis has sometimes discouraged larger cooperative efforts of cultural renewal – partly because they are impersonal but also because, to evangelicals, they entail compromise of their biblical standards. But the need for personal response has also stimulated a lively and creative volunteerism, by which Christians band together to address social and spiritual issues. The emphasis on personal faith in Christ has also led to a rich tradition of hymnody and gospel singing that has characterized the evangelical movement since the Reformation.

Thirdly, we have noted a strong sense of God's sovereign direction of history and, especially, the sense that God is interested in cultural and political events. The wildly popular "Left Behind" series of novels, which focus on end-time events, whatever their literary value, reflect the lively evangelical sense that God is working in human history and that world events relate in important ways to this providence. Ironically, this sense of history and its ending has both encouraged social and cultural renewal, as during the Second Great Awakening, and discouraged it, as during the period of fundamentalism. But both cases reflect the mysterious relevance of God's purposes for human culture and for faithful discipleship.

Finally, because of their robust sense of God's working in history, evangelicals have consistently displayed a strong commitment to mission. Their personal faith, based on biblical teaching, has led them to commit vast resources and personnel for reaching out to the world in the name of Christ, first in evangelism but increasingly in social and cultural activities as well – from the Salvation Army to World Vision and the Lausanne Movement. This sense of mission has led them to appropriate, especially, popular culture and the latest technology to assure the relevance and efficacy of their mission.

Evangelical attitudes toward culture, at least in America, continue to respond to the deep-seated desire to convert sinners, or more recently, society, according to what evangelicals believe to be biblical principles. This calling represents their strength and their weakness. Evangelicals care deeply about the state of culture: they seek its redemption. But overall evangelicals address culture; they do not listen to it. While these efforts are often admirable and well-intentioned, in general the evangelical relation to culture has been strategically rather than theologically motivated. Indeed, the activism and populism have largely precluded discerning involvement in culture, and, sadly, the wisdom of culture has not been allowed to move the church toward greater maturity.

Further reading

Carpenter, Joel. *Revive Us Again: The Reawakening of American Fundamentalism.* New York: Oxford University Press, 1997.

Carson, D. A., and John D. Woodbridge (eds.). *God and Culture: Essays in Honor of Carl F. H. Henry.* Grand Rapids, MI: Eerdmans, 1993.

Coote, Robert T., and John R. W. Stott (eds.). *Down to Earth: Studies in Christianity and Culture, The Papers of the Lausanne Consultation on Gospel and Culture.* Grand Rapids, MI: Eerdmans, 1980.

Henry, Carl F. H. *The Uneasy Conscience of Modern Fundamentalism.* Foreword by Richard J. Mouw. Grand Rapids, MI: Eerdmans, 2003.

Marsden, George. *Fundamentalism and American Culture: The Shaping of Twentieth Century Evangelicalism.* Revised edition. New York: Oxford University Press, 2006.

Mouw, Richard J. *When the King Comes Marching In: Isaiah and the New Jerusalem.* Revised edition. Grand Rapids, MI: Eerdmans, 2002.

Newbigin, Lesslie. *The Gospel in a Pluralist Society.* Grand Rapids, MI: Eerdmans, 1989.

Noll, Mark A. *The Scandal of the Evangelical Mind.* Grand Rapids, MI: Eerdmans, 1994.

Schaeffer, Francis A. *The Complete Works of Francis A. Schaeffer.* 5 volumes. Wheaton, IL: Crossway, 1985.

Stott, John R. W. *The Contemporary Christian: Applying God's Word to Today's World.* Downers Grove, IL: InterVarsity, 1995.

Yoder, John Howard. *The Politics of Jesus.* Grand Rapids, MI: Eerdmans, 1973.

Notes

1. While it is recognized that evangelicalism is now a worldwide phenomenon, this article focuses largely on developments in North America and, to a lesser extent, Britain.
2. Mark A. Noll, *The Scandal of the Evangelical Mind* (Grand Rapids, MI: Eerdmans, 1994), p. 24. This also contributed, he notes, to making evangelicalism into an "affectional and organizational movement."
3. Charles Hodge, *Systematic Theology*, 3 vols. (Grand Rapids, MI: Eerdmans, 1952 [1871]), vol. 1, p. 1.
4. The complexities of the period both theologically and socially are described in George Marsden, *Fundamentalism and American Culture: The Shaping of Twentieth Century Evangelicalism* (New York: Oxford University Press, 1980, 2nd edn. 2006), pp. 72–93. The best argument that a socially progressive evangelism was seriously privatized by century's end in America is Kathryn T. Long, *The Revival of 1857–1958: Interpreting an American Awakening* (New York: Oxford University Press, 1998).
5. I am dependent here on Roger Lundin, "Offspring of an Odd Union: Evangelical Attitudes Toward the Arts," in George Marsden (ed.), *Evangelicalism and Modern America* (Grand Rapids, MI: Eerdmans, 1984), pp. 135–47.
6. *Ibid.*, pp. 140, 141.
7. Marsden, *Fundamentalism*, p. 99. And for what follows see p. 100.
8. On this period see Joel Carpenter, *Revive Us Again: The Reawakening of American Fundamentalism* (New York: Oxford University Press, 1997).

9. David O. Moberg has taught us to think of the evangelical withdrawal from social action and engagement in the first half of the twentieth century as the "Great Reversal." See Moberg, *The Great Reversal: Evangelism Versus Social Action* (London: Scripture Union, 1972).

10. See Noll, *Scandal*, p. 17. He refers to Robert Wuthnow's discussion of this situation.

11. See Charles Marsh, *God's Long Summer: Stories of Faith and Civil Rights* (Princeton, NJ: Princeton University Press, 1997).

12. Francis Schaeffer, *The God who is There* (Downers Grove, IL: InterVarsity, 1968), p. 129.

13. See J. D. Douglas (ed.), *Let the Earth Hear His Voice: International Congress on Evangelism: Official Reference Volume* (Minneapolis, MN: World Wide Publications, 1975). Schaeffer led an important track at this conference.

14. *Ibid.*, pp. 6, 7.

15. See *Down to Earth: Studies in Christianity and Culture, The Papers of the Lausanne Consultation on Gospel and Culture* (Grand Rapids, MI: Eerdmans, 1980).

16. See John Stott's *Christian Mission in the Modern World* (Downers Grove, IL: InterVarsity, 1985); *Human Rights and Human Wrongs* (Grand Rapids, MI: Baker, 1999).

17. John Howard Yoder, *Politics of Jesus* (1972); Richard J. Mouw, *Political Evangelism* (1973); *When the Kings Come Marching in* (1984); and Nicholas Wolterstorff, *Until Peace and Justice Embrace* (1984), all published by Eerdmans, Grand Rapids, MI.

18. Though this is changing; see Jeremy Begbie, *Voicing Creation's Praise* (Edinburgh: T. & T. Clark, 1991); W. Dyrness, *Visual Faith: Art, Theology and Worship in Dialogue* (Grand Rapids, MI: Baker, 2001); and Robert Johnston, *Reel Spirituality: Theology and Film in Dialogue* (Grand Rapids, MI: Baker, 2000).

19. Noll, *Scandal*, p. 173.

20. Bob Briner, *Roaring Lambs: A Gentle Plan to Radically Change Your World* (Grand Rapids, MI: Zondervan, 1993), p. 23.

21. Pat Robertson, *The Turning Tide* (Dallas, TX: Word, 1993), p. 303.

22. C. S. Lewis, "Christianity and Culture," in Walter Hooper (ed.), *Christian Reflections* (Grand Rapids, MI: Eerdmans, 1967), p. 15. Hooper argues in the introduction that this is an early work of Lewis which does not reflect his mature thinking, but it certainly reflects (and probably influenced) the thinking of many evangelicals! See p. xii.

23. For an earlier assessment of Schaeffer's influence see Ronald Ruegsegger (ed.), *Reflections on Francis Schaeffer* (Grand Rapids, MI: Zondervan, 1986). Garry Wills underlines Schaeffer's role in the religious right in *Under God: Religion and American Politics* (New York: Simon and Schuster, 1990), pp. 318–28.

11 Evangelical theology and gender

ELAINE STORKEY

WHAT IS GENDER?

"Gender" is not an indigenous theological concept but a sociological one. And on its journey into theology it checked in a large amount of baggage which needs to be reclaimed, unpacked, and examined before the concept can be accorded new citizenship. Where this has not happened, the concept's culture and background have been incorporated into new territory, its debates and assumptions unwittingly absorbed, without being fully understood. So our first task is to look at what the concept of "gender" has brought with it from the social sciences and the implications this has for theology.

Sociology's concern with social institutions and processes means the areas of work and family have been significant in the development of the discipline. Inevitably these have involved discussions of the varied societal roles of men and women, including the division of labor. Yet for decades such discussions were somewhat clichéd, based on uncontested stereotypes masquerading as empirical sociological data. The functionalist Talcott Parsons, for example, offered categories which he felt adequately described role differences within the family. He presented the "feminine role" as *expressive*, fulfilling functions "internal" to the family (strengthening family bonds, socializing children), whilst the "masculine role" was *instrumental*, performing the "external" functions of a family (provision of monetary support).[1] There was little acknowledgment that such descriptions were, in fact, heavily theoretically loaded and embraced many assumptions waiting to be contested.

Huge volumes had been written on the family[2] before writers in the late 1960s and 1970s began to challenge the assumptions beneath much previous research. A new generation of sociologists argued that such role analyses were not neutral descriptions of how things were in society (and thereby implicitly how things should be) but, more accurately, a way of actually endorsing the *status quo* by embracing uncritically the power mechanisms which kept them in place. These sociologists exposed the biological essentialism on which many of the male–female roles were predicated. Sexuality had been biologically defined, and the analysis of social roles built on an assumed biological basis of behavior. Now it became evident that work or family roles were not simply correlated to our biology but related to power structures which operated through conventions, legal statutes, and educational expectations. Women did not spend most of their time in housework and child-care because they were hard-wired through chromosomes or hormones to find these pursuits satisfying and fulfilling, but because children needed to be cared for, homes needed to be cleaned, and the lot fell to them. Moreover, the structure of employment and the education system were constructed in such a way as to make it difficult for them to gain access to the sorts of jobs open to men.

So sociologists stopped writing about the *sexual* division of labor, and the concept of *gender* forced its way, self-consciously, into the vocabulary of the social sciences.[3] Whereas "sex" related to what was biological, natural, predetermined, continuous, and the same in all cultures, "gender" referred to what was cultural, socially constructed, assigned, bound up with expectations, and constantly changing. Being a biological male or female may be the same the world over. But being a man or a woman (or "masculine" or "feminine") is shaped by the prevailing culture, for that is where we learn the conventions and attitudes, behavior, and communication patterns which form gender identity. And cultures vary: "feminine" behavior in much of Africa, for example (women carrying huge loads on their heads and backs whilst their men remained unburdened), would be regarded as quite inappropriate in North America or Northern Europe. So, "gender" provided a concept more fluid and varied for understanding social interaction and institutions than the oppositional binary of "sex."

GENDER IN THEOLOGY

In traveling from the social sciences to theology, therefore, "gender" brings some radical challenges to older ways of thinking, challenges not always appreciated by those who annex the concept. It marks a departure from a single, fixed way of understanding relationships between men and women, and rejects essentialism. It implicitly confronts any hermeneutic model which smuggles a biological reductionism into the interpretation of biblical texts. It raises new questions in the areas of doctrine, liturgy, spirituality, ethics, and pastoralia. It recognizes the inescapable significance of the cultural context, and interrogates the interaction of gender in the way we understand and relate to God.

Evangelical theology has produced its own body of work in the area over the last quarter of a century, as it has increasingly been drawn into debate about gender. Yet there are enormous variations in how the debate has been perceived. At one end of the spectrum there has been a desire not to force the concept into some ghetto of "women's issues," but to investigate how gender engages with the full breadth of theological curricula. And whole symposia on gender have been dedicated to examining questions of Trinity, Christology, soteriology, personhood, or eschatology. Scholars have looked at theology and language, especially at the way in which gender has been read into the Godhead and reinforced in the understanding of the church through male images in doctrine and liturgy. There have been attempts to explore how one can present a non-gendered view of God which yet remains personal. There have also been studies on how reflections on the Trinity can help to understand the construction of gender identity. In some academic circles, evangelical theologians have entered into dialogue with feminist theology, being willing to examine the charges brought against them by women who have rejected the biblical canon on the grounds of its alleged irredeemable patriarchalism. Much writing has been sociologically aware and fruitful, offering a creative dynamic between faithfulness to evangelical orthodoxy and openness to theological exploration on God and gender. I shall be looking at the results of some of these initiatives later.

At the other end of the spectrum, however, and particularly amongst some evangelical writers in North America and Australia, the debate has become stuck within an obsession with male–female roles, reflecting a similar old essentialism to that which dominated the Modernist mind-set in the social sciences. This has been characteristic of the many articles and books defending what the authors call "biblical manhood and womanhood,"[4] which have demonstrated a marked reluctance to move beyond a fixed and static view of male and female, or to engage at all with the issues implicit in the concept of gender. Even the concept of "role" is handled as though it were unproblematic. From this perspective the debate has been presented largely as a contest between two opposing positions, in effect reflecting the very binary view of male and female which begs to be examined. Although it has been highly productive in terms of written output, much of the space and energy has been dedicated to repeating the same points to the same critics. Inevitably the result lacks the imaginative and creative engagement which subjects its own assumptions to examination and wrestles with bigger issues, and the arguments become predictable. Nevertheless, what has been useful for theology is that this debate has raised key questions in hermeneutics and language, and it is to these I now turn.

GENDER AND THE BIBLICAL TEXT

One of the defining features of evangelical theology has been its commitment to the canon of Scripture, believing the Bible to be the inspired Word-revelation of God, through which God addresses us with truths of eternal significance. In the task of knowing God, the Bible is indispensable, as well as in the task of knowing ourselves. For the Bible tells the story of our humanity, our identity derived from our relationship with God; it unearths for us our meaning and value as human creatures, reveals to us something of the nature of our struggle with sin, and calls us into redemption through Jesus Christ. As both the shaper of a worldview, and as a moral and spiritual guide for personal and communal life, the Bible unites evangelicals and remains the key source of understanding for their faith.

Most evangelical theologians do not have a fundamentalist or absolutist view of the Bible, recognizing that God chose to give this Word, not as a series of timeless and infallible theological imperatives, but through human authors writing over thousands of years in an amazing diversity of literary genres. These human authors wrote in specific cultures and periods, and the cultural context is inevitably woven into the shape and structure of its content. So the Bible is both divine and human; it has eternal relevance and historical particularity; it embodies the unity of the Spirit of God in the diversity of human writings. Evangelical theologians generally agree that since God spoke an eternal Word through time-bound authors we read it to discern the intent of the Holy Spirit as expressed by those authors, and apply it today. This is of course a contested view, challenged by the postmodern deconstruction of the text, but evangelicals have always utilized a kind of deconstruction of their own. As Gordon Fee puts it, "Our task is to discover and hear that Word in terms of God's original intent and then hear that same Word again in our own historical setting, even when our particulars are quite different from those of the original setting."[5]

Agreement amongst evangelicals as to the essential truth and unity of the Bible, does not, however, safeguard against disagreements which arise when we look at the actual text. We might disagree about what we believe to be the intent of the author, or how it should be applied today, which texts should have primacy in providing a more general framework of interpretation, or whether all texts have equal interpretative value. We might disagree about whether the cultural context of the text should be reproduced today (e.g., patriarchy) or about what differentiates a "timeless truth" from a "historical particular" (male leadership). Hermeneutics involves choice, and in making decisions on what a particular text might mean, choice operates at a number of stages, some of which lie beyond the subject in question. All of this comes to a head on the issue of gender, and has produced sharp divisions with implications beyond exegetical concerns. For the text itself presents us with complex choices. This important point is not always acknowledged by some exegetes who argue that theirs is the only proper (that is "unbiased") interpretation. Nevertheless, if we are to understand the Bible at all, we need to recognize that we all come to it as fallible creatures making hermeneutical decisions under the guidance of the Holy Spirit.

The debate between evangelicals, predominantly in North America, over gender and textual interpretation, has become polarized between "complementarians" and "egalitarians," each claiming biblical justification for their position ("biblical manhood and womanhood" versus "biblical equality"). At one level the disagreement involves arguments over very specific verses, especially in the New Testament epistles; whether these verses allow or forbid women from exercising leadership in the church, whether they establish a universal principle of "male headship" or mutual submission, whether they are definitive for doctrine and practice today or are culturally nuanced. The contest often involves scrutinizing the specific identity and roles of people in the New Testament. For example, was Junia really an "apostle" and what did Paul mean when he used that term of her (Rom. 16)? What kind of *authority* did Priscilla have as Paul's co-worker and why was her ministry an acknowledged teaching one (*didaskō*) (Acts 15) when women are told they may not teach (*didaskō*) (1 Tim. 2)?[6] Who was Phoebe and why does Paul commend her to the Romans in a way similar to the way he commends Timothy to the Corinthians (Rom. 16; 1 Cor. 4)? The debate also involves disputes over the translation of individual words, *kephalē, authentein, hypotassomai, exousia, didaskō*, where different writers cite usages which generally concur with their own interpretations (H. Scott Baldwin lists eighty-two examples of *authenteō* in ancient Greek literature with the aim of showing that they all involve the concept of authority[7]). The limitations of this kind of debate are recognized by many who are involved in it. Marianne Meye Thomson admits: "Both those who favor women in ministry and those who oppose women in ministry can find suitable proof texts and suitable rationalizations to explain those texts. But if our discussion is ever to move beyond proof texting we must integrate those texts into a theology of ministry."[8] This has not won over the complementarians and the focus of much of their work remains that of proving the egalitarians wrong. Wayne Grudem, for example, has published a book of 850 pages which he devotes entirely to 118 points of disagreement he has with Christians for Biblical Equality.[9]

We need to learn from the biblical text how we should relate to God and each other, not least from the letters of Paul to the New Testament communities. But there are serious problems with both the methodology and the exegetical assumptions behind the urge to find the true characteristics of "biblical manhood and womanhood" and replicate these in our Christian communities today. To start with, it involves complex hermeneutical decisions about what to include or exclude, given the diversity of male and female roles in the Bible. Second, it is trying to get from the biblical text something which the text is not trying to give; for example, nowhere are there listed the necessary ingredients for gender identity – nothing is said about "masculinity" or "femininity," but a great deal about preferring one another, and showing the fruit of the Spirit (love, joy, peace, kindness, gentleness, faithfulness, self-control) which should characterize every Christian. Third, even if there were such a list, we would need reasons for lifting it out of context and relocating it into our current setting; we would need to be convinced of its time-transcendent universality. Yet, any sociological awareness shows that the very cultural-laden nature of gender characteristics makes this extremely difficult. That is why Volf concludes: "Biblical 'womanhood' and 'manhood' – if there are such things at all ... are not divinely sanctioned models but culturally situated examples; they are accounts of the successes and failures of men and women to live out the demands of God on their lives within specific settings."[10]

Disagreements on gender between evangelicals are thus not fundamentally about what may legitimately be included in the range of meanings of a Greek word, or whether '*ezer* in Hebrew implies subordination,[11] but about issues which lie beneath the exegetical process and enter the hermeneutic at the level of assumption. Crucial among these are ideas about the nature of human personhood. If we come to the text with what Alan Torrance calls a "supposition of a *reified fixity of innate, polarized sex*

roles with their attendant character-traits or personality definitions,"[12] our
interpretation of the text will be quite different from that of someone who
approaches with a supposition of human mutuality. Similarly, assumptions about creation, the meaning of *imago Dei*, the characteristics of sin,
the nature of redemption, and the shape of the redeemed community in
Christ all feed into our exegetical understanding, as do ideas about power,
hierarchy, and authority. An evangelical theology of gender can only be
developed by unearthing presuppositions in all these areas, for we will
read the text in the light (or blur) of them. At the most crucial level we need
to be sure that the view of God which undergirds both theology and life in
community is itself compatible with the triune God revealed to us in Jesus
Christ, the incarnate Word.

HUMAN PERSONHOOD – PERSONS IN RELATIONSHIP

Theology has long wrestled with what it means to be a human person.
Whatever the prevailing view in philosophy, theology has picked up and
reflected some of that view in its own formulations. And the history of
ideas has been shaped by concepts of the self as a substance, having a
nature, an essence, according primacy to thought over activity, individual
autonomy over relationality. Aristotle's link between biology and hierarchy, Boethius's definition of the person as an individual substance in a
rational nature, and Descartes' mind–body dualism all provided the back-
cloth against which theology has had to articulate its own view of the
person.

Human identity is derived, given to us in relation to the Creator in
whom we live and move and have our being. So to understand the nature
of the person, theology wanted to know what constituted the *imago dei*, for
once we knew that, we would better understand our humanness. Early
theological anthropology, with its soul–body dualism, located the *imago
dei* in the soul – the intellectual faculty of the person.[13] The Reformation
writers saw the divine image more relationally; Torrance asserts: "Calvin
always thinks of the *imago* in terms of a mirror."[14] Yet even in the nineteenth century there were those in the evangelical tradition who had not
shaken off the link between the image of God and reason. Cited most often
in this respect is Charles Hodge. Under the heading "Man Created in the
Image of God," Hodge suggests, "God is a Spirit, the human soul is a spirit.
The essential attributes of a spirit are reason, conscience and will. A spirit
is a rational, moral, and therefore also, a free agent." He then goes on to

claim scriptural authority for a dubious idea: "The Scriptures . . . teach us that we are partakers of [God's] nature as a spiritual being, and that an essential element of that likeness to God in which man was originally created consists in our rational or spiritual nature."[15] (Hodge's implicit rationalism at this point helped shape his view of subordination within the Godhead, which his successor at Princeton, Benjamin B. Warfield, had later to refute.[16])

Our understanding of gender is inevitably influenced by our ideas of human identity. If human beings are seen as individual, separate opposites with natures, then it is easy to deduce that male humans have one kind of nature and females another, even to the extent that "[t]he image of God is in man directly, but in woman indirectly."[17] This polarized view of gender identity indeed has its roots within the dualisms of Greek, medieval and Enlightenment thinking, with "reason" identified with maleness, and "body" or "emotion" with femaleness. So wherever "reason" has been allowed to define the essential kernel of humanness, it inevitably reinforces inequality and buttresses the idea of the male as the natural bridge between humankind and God, and the locus for authority and decision making.

What has been striking over the last half century is the way evangelical theology has become both wary and weary of this old dualistic way of thinking about the person. The influences of both Martin Buber and Jürgen Moltmann acted as a catalyst in the shift away from the idea that "everyone is a self-possessing, self-disposing centre of action which sets itself apart from other persons."[18] Buber's notion of the "I"–"Thou" relation took the focus off the person as individualistic. The location of our humanness in some "nature" or "rational essence" began to give way to an understanding of personhood which is relational, where interdependence marks our identity. Rather than posit the "separateness" bequeathed by the Enlightenment or the *angst* of the existentialists, it gave a different answer to some of the problems of our existence; the reason why isolation or alienation is so debilitating is not because it is the reality of our human predicament, but because it is the very denial of who we are. Since we are created in relation to God, to each other and to the rest of creation, relationships are not extrinsic to our being, but constitutive of it. This means "without the social relation there can be no personality."[19] To exist at all is to exist in relation to others. To be and to be in relationship are the same thing,[20] for we are persons-in-relationship.

This recovery of human identity as relational rather than some substance with an essence or nature changes the focus of the gender debate.

It mounts yet another challenge to the assumptions undergirding the attempt to find some definitive biblical gender characteristics. For it does not presume that the defining characteristic of the man–woman polarity is difference, reflected at the very center of our spiritual being; it does not see men and women as having distinct natures, brought together under the principle of complementarity. It does not posit some hierarchy of relationship, or call upon an authority structure within which men and women live with separate and distinct roles of rule and submission. It holds that the reifying of human nature or essence, and its distillation into the polarized concepts of "manhood" and "womanhood," are fundamentally flawed. Ontologically, our very identity lies in who we are in relationship.

THE RELATIONAL TRINITY

This rethinking of the person owes much to the revival of Trinitarian theology which has provided the context for our human anthropology to be reshaped. The Trinity presents us with God, Father, Son, and Spirit, as three persons in the full analogical sense of the term, distinct from each other, centers of love, truth, and will, but in an eternal relationship of union. It is an understanding which has been part of Christian theology from the beginning, yet relevant in new ways for each time and era. It can now be seen to have significant implications in the search for human personhood in our postmodern condition; Stanley Grenz even goes so far as to suggest that its retrieval has enabled us to develop a fully theological anthropology to claim back what had been abdicated to the human sciences.[21] As Grenz also points out, the renewal of Trinitarian theology has not occurred simply amongst scholars of the Cappadocians. It has swept through evangelical, Catholic, reformed, liberation, charismatic, and feminist circles. Whatever the disagreements, and many remain, there is now widespread agreement that the concept of "person" has more to do with relationality than substantiality, and with community than abstracted individualism.

The union of the Trinity is seen as a union of *being*, where the personal identity of each member of the Trinity reflects the indwelling of the other persons in them. There is no oppositional separation; the identity of one cannot be thought without the other: "the Father is the Father in no other way but in the dynamism of his relationship to the Son and the Spirit."[22] This does not, however, collapse the identity of the Father into that of the Son or Spirit. If that is what was meant by identity-in-relationship, then ultimately all persons would disappear into a common undifferentiated nature. But as James Houston explains, the members of the Trinity are "always particularized. The Father is always the Father, and the Son is always the Son, and the Holy Spirit is neither Father nor Son."[23] Openness to "the presence of other in the self"[24] is quite different from the obliteration of the self. For Moltmann, the example of the Trinity reminds us that persons must not be dissolved into relations. Though persons are interdependent and identity is shaped in relationship, there is still a need to differentiate between "person" and "relation." We must see them in a reciprocal relationship: "there are no persons without relations; but there are no relations without persons."[25]

This helps to unlock the issues of our gender interrelatedness. It means that "the identity of one gender cannot be thought 'without' the other. Men cannot be defined simply as what 'women are not'; women cannot be defined simply as 'what men are not.'"[26] Instead each, in its own way, already contains the other. The identity of each grows out of connectedness. It is Paul's picture in I Corinthians II where woman is "from" man, and man is "through" woman. But we retain our particularity. The identity of the woman is not to be absorbed into that of the man, as happens in patriarchal contexts. Nor is the one subordinated to the other.

Made in the image of the Trinity, our human relatedness is given its real goal and direction as persons-in-communion. In his much-used analogy of the body, St. Paul pictures women and men in Christ as intrinsically and organically connected as members together, our identity disclosed as part of the body, sharing, even suffering, together as pain affects us all.[27] This is the real biblical vision for our gendered humanness. Alan Torrance says, "It is only when we operate with an ontology of communion that we are liberated from the monist/dualist dilemma, for dynamic and relational ways of conceiving of selfhood."[28] This ontology does not negate difference, individuation, or particularity. It is neither an androgynous vision, nor one of fusion into others. We remain personal and sexed bodies. But it does give us room to breathe in communion as women and men, removing the crippling stereotypes of seeing the other as the "opposite" sex and experiencing our gendered selves through connectedness. It also places our identity where it belongs, in our relationship with each other.

SUBORDINATION IN THE TRINITY?

Not all evangelical writers have seen in the Trinity the vision for gender interrelatedness and equality. There are those who have insisted that there is eternal subordination within the Trinity – that of the Son to the Father – on which they base the rationale for the subordination of women to men. Some have argued that the eternal subordination of the Son is ontological, embedded in the very being of the triune God,[29] others that it is functional – related to the roles within the Trinity. These writers insist that just as God the Son can be eternally subordinate to the Father in function or role, whilst equal in Being, so women can be permanently subordinate to men in role, but retain "equality." Since this latter view is unknown in church history, and seems newly devised over the last few decades by those who have a strong view of male authority, it sounds to Kevin Giles like "an attempt to make an acceptable-sounding case for the permanent subordination of women."[30]

Christians have long understood that in his incarnate life Jesus was subject to the Father. The gospels teach it and the epistle writers affirm it. Jesus prayed to the Father, spoke of obedience to the Father, and did the will of the Father. But Paul also says (Phil. 2:5–11) that the Son had equality with the Father before he voluntarily emptied himself to become a servant and die on the cross for our salvation, and that afterwards he was exalted as Lord. Christ's submission to the Father was, like his humanity, part of his earthly life.

The idea of subordination in the Godhead (and in human relations) rests on a view of power and authority which is radically challenged by the New Testament, for it is one of autocracy and command, not of mutual self-giving. This is extrinsic, not intrinsic, to the gospel and is antagonistic to any notion of equality. Yet, throughout its history the church has held that the members of the triune God are co-equal, one in being, authority, divinity, power, and majesty. No case can be made, either, for splitting the role of God, the Father or Son, from God's Being. Christ forgives, saves, judges, reigns – he fulfills the "role" of God because he is God.

The eternal subordinationist view has reappeared as heresy from Arius onwards. But Athanasius (296–373) "vanquished subordinationism"[31] and cogently articulated the Trinitarian doctrine which has been held by the church, its creeds, and councils through the centuries as key to the Christian faith.[32] It would be a tragedy for evangelical theology if historic Trinitarian orthodoxy were hijacked and Christ eternally emptied of his co-equality with God so that the hierarchy of men over women could be maintained.

THE GENDER OF GOD?

The revival of Trinitarian theology does not resolve the question of the gender of God. Feminist theologians insist that to describe God as "Father" and "Son" inevitably reinforces a sense of maleness, especially when reinforced by so many other masculine images. Even if one attributes "feminine attributes" to the Holy Spirit, that still leaves a two-thirds male Godhead! Feminist alternatives have variously re-presented God as androgynous, the community of women, wind or power, Sophia,[33] the Verb,[34] or as the Primal Matrix or great womb.[35] Not attracted by any of these reformulations, and resisting the plea to "assert the femininity of God in order to connect with women" on the grounds that neither femininity nor masculinity has any concrete content in the Godhead,[36] evangelical theology has responded in a number of other ways. The first is to argue that, given the history of linguistic usage, along with the patriarchal culture of Israel, the predominance of male terms and masculine imagery for God is unremarkable. More surprising are the many feminine images which occur in the Scriptures, and warrant attention.[37] The second is to recognize that we speak of God in language which is a human and social construction. We use gendered metaphors for God, not because God is male and/or female, but because God is personal and we have no other language to use for persons. The third is to deny that gendered terms for God imply anything about the masculinity of God. Sexual distinctions are what that God has breathed into our temporal world and do not define the Godhead. Fourth is to reject the idea that God offers us models of masculinity which should direct human (male) action, including actions toward women. "For God to be the model of masculinity one must first project maleness on to God and then use the projection to legitimize certain allegedly specifically male characteristics and activities."[38] In this respect, even God's fatherhood is not a model for human fathering, for in the creaturely realm, fathers are male.

James Torrance is instructive: "In theology, we listen to and seek to interpret God's self-interpretation to us in Christ (John 1.12) and do not simply project on to God, for example, our preconceived images of 'father,' 'son,' 'begetting,' and 'generating' derived from our 'experience' in patriarchal, hierarchical, male-dominated culture (Matthew 23. 9–11)."[39] And in seeking to interpret God's "self-interpretation" we cannot then focus on Christ's maleness, any more than on his Jewishness, his trade as a carpenter, or any other temporal human characteristics which Jesus possessed. The focus has to be on what Christ discloses about the reality of God, that God is creative, powerful, wise, interpersonal, sacrificial, forgiving, and redeeming Love, who calls us into reconciliation and communion. If language about God does not ultimately point away from gender and to the fundamental truth of divine love, then we have overwhelmingly missed the point.

It is when this love becomes the focus that, paradoxically, we can most fully appreciate the significance of Jesus' gendered life. For, as a male rabbi in a patriarchal culture he points over and over again beyond that culture to a radical new vision for women and men.[40] In his life, teaching, relationships, encounters, and even language Jesus cuts through patriarchy. Women's daily lives are reflected in his parables: baking bread, sweeping rooms, looking for lost coins. He affirms women throughout the gospels: the menstruating woman who breaks Jewish hygiene laws to touch him, the prostitute who pours perfume over his feet, Mary who listens and learns instead of doing housework, the Syro-Phoenecian woman who argues about her own inclusion in his ministry, the much-married Samaritan woman at the well who discovers he is the Messiah. It is women who support him financially, women who stay with him in his last agonizing moments on the Cross, women who come to anoint his body, and to women he gives the message of resurrection.

The evangelical theology which comes to the concept of gender with openness to the Word of the Trinity and the Spirit of God recovers nuggets of faith and affirms the mutuality and reciprocal gifting of the people of God. And when the church lives out that theology, captured by the radical vision of a new humanity, we see again in our own era the first fruits of a redeemed community.

Further reading

Beck, James R., and Craig L. Blomberg (eds.). *Two Views on Women in Ministry.* Grand Rapids, MI: Zondervan, 2001.

Campbell, Douglas (ed.). *Gospel and Gender: A Trinitarian Engagement with Being Male and Female in Christ.* Studies in Theology and Sexuality. London: T.&T. Clark, 2003.

Giles, Kevin. *The Trinity and Subordinationism: The Doctrine of God and the Contemporary Gender Debate.* Downers Grove, IL: InterVarsity, 2002.

Graham, Elaine. *Making the Difference: Gender, Personhood and Theology.* London: Mowbray, 1995.

Grudem, Wayne. *Evangelical Feminism and Biblical Truth: An Analysis of 118 Disputed Questions.* Leicester: InterVarsity, 2005.

Mickelson, Alvera (ed.). *Women, Authority and the Bible.* Downers Grove, IL: InterVarsity, 1986.

Pierce, Ronald W., and Rebecca Merrill Groothuis (eds.). *Discovering Biblical Equality: Complementarity without Hierarchy.* Leicester: InterVarsity, 2004.

Piper, John, and Wayne Grudem (eds.). *Recovering Biblical Manhood and Womanhood: A Response to Evangelical Feminism.* Wheaton, IL: Crossway, 1991.

Storkey, Elaine. *Origins of Difference: The Gender Debate Revisited.* Grand Rapids, MI: Baker Academic, 2001.

Sumner, Sarah. *Men and Women in the Church: Building Consensus on Christian Leadership.* Downers Grove, IL: InterVarsity, 2003.

Notes

1. Talcott Parsons and Robert F. Bales, *Family Socialization and Interaction Process* (Glencoe, IL: Free Press, 1955).

2. See, e.g., Ruth Nanda Ashen (ed.), *The Family: Its Function and Destiny* (New York: Harper and Brothers, 1949); Robert Flinell, Robert McGinnis, and Herbert R. Barringer, *Selected Studies in Marriage and the Family* (New York: Holt, Rinehart and Winston, 1962); F. Ivan Nye and Felix M. Berado, *The Family, its Structure and Interaction* (New York: Macmillan, 1973).

3. Robert J. Stoller, *Sex and Gender* (New York: Science House, 1968).

4. John Piper and Wayne Grudem (eds.), *Recovering Biblical Manhood and Womanhood: A Response to Evangelical Feminism* (Wheaton, IL: Crossway, 1991).

5. Gordon D. Fee, "Hermeneutics and the Gender Debate," in Ronald W. Pierce and Rebecca Merrill Groothuis (eds.), *Discovering Biblical Equality: Complementarity without Hierarchy* (Leicester: InterVarsity, 2004).

6. Thomas Schreiner, "Women in Ministry," in James R. Beck and Craig L. Blomberg (eds.), *Two Views of Women in Ministry* (Grand Rapids, MI: Zondervan, 2001); Michael Burer and Daniel B. Wallace, "Was Junia Really an Apostle? An Examination of Romans 16:7," *NTS* 47 (2001): 76–91; Linda L. Bellville, "Women Leaders in the Bible," in Pierce and Groothuis (eds.), *Discovering Biblical Equality*, pp. 110–25; see also Richard Clark Kroeger and Catherine Clark Kroeger, *I Suffer not a Woman: Rethinking 1 Timothy 2 in Light of Ancient Evidence* (Grand Rapids, MI: Baker, 1992).

7. H. Scott Baldwin, "A Difficult Word: *Authenteo* in 1 Timothy 2:12," in Andreas J. Kostenberger, Thomas R. Schreiner, and H. Scott Baldwin (eds.), *Women in the Church: A Fresh Analysis of 1 Timothy 2:9–15* (Grand Rapids, MI: Baker, 1995), pp. 65–80.

8. Marianne Meye Thompson, "Response to Richard Longenecker," in Alvera Mickelson (ed.), *Women, Authority and the Bible* (Downers Grove, IL: InterVarsity, 1986), p. 94.

9. Wayne Grudem, *Evangelical Feminism and Biblical Truth: an Analysis of 118 Disputed Questions* (Leicester: InterVarsity, 2005).

10. Miroslav Volf, "The Trinity and Gender Identity," in Douglas A. Campbell (ed.), *Gospel and Gender: A Trinitarian Engagement with Being Male and Female in Christ* (London: T. & T. Clark, 2003), p. 170.

11. See a very useful discussion of '*ezer* in Stanley J. Grenz, *The Social God and the Relational Self: A Trinitarian Theology of the Imago Dei* (Louisville, KY: Westminster John Knox, 2001), p. 276.

12. Alan Torrance, "Personhood and Particularity," in Campbell (ed.), *Gospel and Gender*, p. 139.

13. Thomas Aquinas, *Summa Theologiae*, 1a.76.1.

14. T. F. Torrance, *Calvin's Doctrine of Man* (London: Lutterworth, 1949).

15. Charles Hodge, *Systematic Theology*, 3 vols. (Grand Rapids, MI: Eerdmans, 1965), vol. 11, pp. 96–97.

16. Benjamin B. Warfield, "The Biblical Doctrine of the Trinity," in *Biblical Foundations* (London: Tyndale, 1958).

17. Roger Beckwith, "The Bearing of Holy Scripture," in Peter Moore (ed.), *Man, Woman and Priesthood* (London: SPCK, 1978), p. 57.

18. Jürgen Moltmann, *The Trinity and the Kingdom: The Doctrine of God*, trans. Margaret Kohl (San Francisco: Harper and Row, 1981), p. 145.

19. *Ibid.*

20. See Elaine Graham, *Making the Difference: Gender, Personhood and Theology* (London: Mowbray, 1995), p. 38.

21. Grenz, *The Social God and the Relational Self*, p. 16.

22. Ibid., p. 175.

23. Aram Haroutunian, "No-one Closer: A Conversation with James Houston," *Mars Hill Review* 6 (Fall 1996): 58 (www.leaderu.com/marshill/).

24. Volf, "The Trinity and Gender Identity," p. 166.

25. Moltmann, *The Trinity and the Kingdom*, p. 172. See also Miroslav Volf's analysis of Moltmann in "The Trinity and Gender Identity," pp. 167–69.

26. Volf, "The Trinity and Gender Identity," p. 174.

27. Rom. 12; 1 Cor. 12; Eph. 4.

28. Alan Torrance, "Personhood and Particularity," p. 149.

29. By "ontological" I mean subordination in "essence or being" as in the 1999 Sydney Anglican Diocesan Doctrine Commission report, "The Doctrine of the Trinity and its Bearing on the Relationship of Men and Women," which refers to the "differences of being" (para. 25) within the Godhead and state that the subordination of the Spirit and Son "belongs to the very persons themselves in their eternal natures" (para. 33). The document is printed as an appendix in Kevin Giles, *The Trinity and Subordinationism: The Doctrine of God and the Contemporary Gender Debate* (Downers Grove, IL: Intervarsity, 2002).

30. Kevin Giles, "The Subordination of Christ and the Subordination of Women," in Piper and Grudem (eds.), *Discovering Biblical Equality*, p. 338. Giles cites the debate where the Son's role subordination was first used to support the role subordination of women. See also Giles, *The Trinity and Subordinationism*.

31. Wolfhart Pannenberg, *Systematic Theology*, trans. G. W. Bromiley (Grand Rapids, MI: Eerdmans, 1991), vol. 1, p. 275. Quoted by Giles, "The Subordination of Christ and the Subordination of Women," p. 340.

32. Giles, *The Trinity and Subordinationism*; Thomas Torrance, *The Christian Doctrine of God: One Being, Three Persons* (Edinburgh: T. & T. Clark, 1991).

33. See Elisabeth Schussler Fiorenza, *Jesus, Mirian's Child, Sophia's Prophet: Critical Issues in Feminist Christology* (London: SCM, 1994).

34. Mary Daly, *Beyond God the Father* (Boston: Beacon, 1982).

35. Rosemary Radford Ruether, *Sexism and God-Talk: Towards a Feminist Theology* (London: SCM, 1983), p. 45.

36. Volf, "The Trinity and Gender Identity," p. 141.

37. Exod. 19:4; Deut. 32:18; Job 38:28–39; Ps. 22:9–10; 131:2; Prov. 1:20–21; 4:5–9; 8:1–11; 9:1–6; Isa. 42:14; 49:14–15; 46:3; 66:13; and Hos. 13:8 are amongst the most oft-quoted in the Old Testament.

38. Volf, "The Trinity and Gender Identity," p. 159.

39. James B. Torrance, "The Doctrine of the Trinity in Our Contemporary Situation," in Alasdair I. C. Heron (ed.), *The Forgotten Trinity* (London: BCC/CCBI Inter-Church House, 1989), p. 5.

40. Aida Besancon Spencer, "Jesus' Treatment of Women in the Gospels," in Piper and Grudem (eds.), *Discovering Biblical Equality*, pp. 126–42, is one of the latest in a large number of studies. See also Alan Storkey, *Jesus and Politics: Confronting the Powers* (Grand Rapids, MI: Baker, 2005).

12 Race and the experience of death: theologically reappraising American evangelicalism

J. KAMERON CARTER

... the politics of race is ultimately linked to the politics of death.

Achille Mbembé[1]

Some boards were laid across the joists at the top [of the house], and between these boards and the roof was a very small garret, never occupied by any thing but rats and mice ... To this hole I was conveyed ... [and it] was to be my home for a long, long time. *Harriet A. Jacobs*[2]

AMERICAN EVANGELICALISM: TOWARD A THEOLOGICAL MODE OF STORYTELLING

Once upon a time not too long ago, religious historians told the story of American evangelical Protestantism – that staple of American religion and bedrock of American identity[3] – as if, at best, black people were not central actors; as if, Ralph Ellison might say, they were "invisible."[4] At worst, the tale was told as if black folks existed not at all; as if black folks were not historical subjects; as if, both as a group and as distinct persons, they were *persone non gratae*.

But a new breed of religious historian eventually arose, and new questions dawned. The new breed recognized the incompleteness of their inherited story of American religion, generally, and American evangelicalism, particularly. The saga had to clarify the signal importance of black folks, account for chattel slavery, and foreground the rise of black evangelicalism.[5]

So the new breed of historian set for their guild a more critical and nuanced scholarly agenda, to provide a more "promiscuous" narrative. For, while evangelical religion in America may have started out essentially as a white phenomenon – as a movement that was also a social process of middle and lower-middle class white social uplift – the slaves' reception in large numbers of their masters' evangelical religion for ever changed American evangelicalism.

American evangelicalism became a movement with a crisis in its very heart, racially at odds – indeed, at war – with itself. This split in religious sensibility was a reflection of the moral crisis of the nation itself as it centered on race. The split, however, within the religious sphere created a space of critical leverage by which black Christianity, which was principally evangelical in orientation, would exert evaluative judgment back upon American evangelicalism itself and, finally, upon the nation.

Yet, if the new historiography has made strides in beginning to correct the failure of attending to black folks as *historical* agents, there has been much less success in attending to black folks as *theological* agents, indeed, as persons whose *historical* agency was performative of a particular *theological* orientation. As a matter both of historical clarification and contemporary religious concern, there has been virtually no critical attention paid to what was *theologically* unique about the decision made by many blacks "to make Jesus their choice."[6] Nor have scholars asked how black evangelicalism reconfigures our understanding of American evangelicalism as a social process, as a vantage point from which to view sociopolitical identity formation. The lacuna may finally be posed in the form of a question: how did the many black folks who chose the evangelical religion of their masters alter it in the very process of *their* receiving it, and what historical difference does this observation make for understanding American evangelicalism as a political economy?

To appreciate the force of such questions, I suggest understanding them on two, interrelated levels. At the first level, the question may be posed thus: if American evangelicalism is understood not merely as oriented around a set of disembodied, doctrinal claims, but rather, following a contemporary critical theorist like Judith Butler, as "performative,"[7] that is, as a socio-cultural process that came to be tied to the enterprise of building the nation, of constituting "We the People . . .," and thus as tied to the processes of determining what constitutes American identity – if American evangelicalism is understood in these performative terms, then we must ask how black folks' reception of the religion of their masters represents a counter-performance of American evangelicalism itself. How was it socially and politically dislocated and relocated?

A second question – which may appear, prima facie, to abandon the level of politics, but in fact only burrows more deeply into the socio-political meanings of American evangelicalism – asks how black folks theologically reoriented Christianity in America, generally, and evangelicalism, particularly.

How, in other words, did black Christians' political counter-performance of American evangelicalism constitute a *theological* or *theo*-political counter-performance of and within it? The aim of this essay is to develop an answer to this two-tiered set of questions and in the process suggest a theological reappraisal of American evangelicalism.

Black folks' appropriation of their masters' religion entailed a subtle theo-political engagement with what one theorist has called modern "necropolitics."[8] Black folks theo-politically engaged the politics of death animating modernity, generally, which lay at the heart of the American political economy, more specifically. This politics of death was one in which persons of African descent were racialized so as to be bounded on all sides by death, either actual physical death or the commuted death sentence of cultural and "social death,"[9] which could be revoked at any instant. Thus, in being raced as black within the framework of the politics of death, black folks were made to be what another theorist has called "death-bound-subjects."[10] In countering the necropolitics of modernity with Christianity's politics of the sacrificial cross, black folks came to inhabit American evangelicalism in a distinct way and to infuse it with new, theological meaning. A new trajectory replete with a new mode of socio-political identity and agency was opened up. In short, reading black folks' appropriation of American evangelicalism through the experience of death and – importantly – its transformation is key to the reappraisal sketched here.

MAPPING THE ARGUMENT

This essay develops in three parts. I begin with a section that theorizes the death-bound-subjectivity of persons of African descent in the New World. In inhabiting the death-world, the slave became the modern embodiment of the figure of ancient Roman law, *homo sacer* or "sacred man." I make particular reference to the work of philosopher Giorgio Agamben and literary theorist Adbul M. JanMohamed to develop this point.

Next, I consider the reception by many antebellum blacks of American evangelical religion and its "simple message of conversion" secured in the death and resurrection of Jesus Christ, despite the ways in which this "simple message" was socially deployed to keep blacks in their place of social death.[11] Fundamental to my claim here is that the appeal of American evangelicalism for many blacks lay in the fact that they saw in its discourse of the sacrifice of Christ, at the point of his death and resurrection, a different political economy and thus a different locus of agency and identity. Because life and freedom were the twin modes of existence marking Christ's divine economy of sacrifice or death, it opened up a new subject position for blacks, one that could challenge, at the site of evangelicalism itself, the American political economy. I briefly illustrate this social and theological dislocation and relocation of evangelical belief effected by black folks through considering a poem by the novelist Richard Wright and Harriet Jacobs's 1861 autobiographical slave narrative. Both suggest a link between the Christian *triduum mortis* and the killed paschal Jewish flesh of Jesus Christ and the liberation of black flesh from death-bound-subjectivity. Were there more space, I would have established in a thicker way the links, on the one hand, between Jacobs's account of her Easter release from the political economy of death-bound-subjectivity and, on the other hand, St. Augustine's account in *City of God* of Christ's sacrificial death and the overcoming of the ancient Roman *imperium*, or perhaps St. Anselm's account in *Cur Deus Homo?* of the gift-economy of Christ's sacrificial flesh that overcomes the feudal economy of debt/death. Such a constructive evangelical theology, with moorings in the iconic status of killable black flesh as linked to Jesus' killable Jewish flesh, can only remain implied here. It is enough simply to establish the theological subjectivity of black folks as rooted in their dislocating and relocating of evangelical belief through their racialized experience of death.

HOMO SACER; OR, THE DEATH-BOUND-SUBJECT[12]

Grasping the peculiar existence into which persons of African descent, through enslavement, were conscripted requires sober reflection on how the slave ship was more than just a ship,[13] the slave auction block was more than just a podium,[14] and the slave plantation was more than just a farm.[15] These, in fact, were icons of how the world was ordered, veritable emblems of the socio-political space now broadly known as modernity. Moreover, grasping the perverse meaning of the economy of slavery requires coming to terms with the slave as a figure whose humanity was made to be "the perfect figure of a shadow."[16] In this section, I consider the "inhuman bondage,"[17] the form of "life" into which the slave was conscripted. ("Life" is in scare quotes because what life and death mean is precisely the issue.) That form of life was a modernized version of the ancient figure *homo sacer* or "sacred man."

The Italian critical theorist Giorgio Agamben, in his research into the foundations of modern political economy, has developed an insightful analysis of the central role of *homo sacer* for how sovereignty has come to work in Western political life. The links he makes between *homo sacer,* the sphere of "the religious," and finally death, are quite to the point here. For in detailing the central role of "sacred man," Agamben makes a powerful case for understanding death itself, from antiquity to modernity, as the foundation of the political. Thus, he makes a case for understanding Western political life from its inception as being a "thanatopolitics" or what Mbembe has called a "necropolitics." Of particular interest for this study of race and American evangelicalism is Agamben's important, but in the end insufficiently developed, suggestion about how religion as a social phenomenon can often aid and abet the socio-political processes of death.

As Agamben has pointed out, it was first in archaic Roman law that "sacredness" became tied to the very definition of humanity, or more accurately, to the socio-political project of forging human life together. Seeing "sacredness" as tied to such an enterprise, he tells us, was not always so. When the ties were eventually made, however, sacredness took on a peculiar character. The peculiarity of the link between "sacredness" and what it means to be a human being who is not merely alive (as is the case with non-rational animals) is captured by the ancient rhetor Pompeius Festus. In his treatise *On the Significance of Words,* Festus observes the following about the strange character of sacredness as it came to be linked to the human:

> The sacred man (*homo sacer*) is the one whom the people have judged on account of a crime. It is not permitted to sacrifice this man, yet he who kills him will not be condemned for homicide; in the first tribunitian law, in fact, is noted that "if someone kills the one who is sacred according to the plebiscite, it will not be considered homicide." This is why it is customary for a bad or impure man to be called sacred.[18]

The sacred person is enigmatic, a figure marked by a double exception. This double exception indicates how the sacred person is pressed by the isomorphic forces of a dual, social exclusion, the forces of religion or divine law and order and the forces of politics or human law and order. For his crime, *homo sacer* may be executed, and the executioner has committed no jurisprudential infraction. The executioner has violated no human law (*ius humana*). Thus, the notion of "killing" is inadequate, for this is precisely what, according to the "law," has not occurred. As Festus notes, the executioner "will not be condemned for homicide." But more precisely, the reason no "killing" has taken place is that *homo sacer's* punishment occurs outside the precincts of human right (not to be confused with human rights) and therefore outside all jurisprudence, indeed, outside the total sphere of politics. *Homo sacer,* simply put, is not a "citizen subject."[19]

This notwithstanding, it cannot be said, either, that the punishment is strictly sacrificial in nature. At the same time that *homo sacer*'s condemnation falls outside the scope of *ius humana,* it also falls outside the scope of divine law or the rules of religious order (*ius divinum*). For just this reason *homo sacer*'s execution does not come under the prerogatives of ritual or sacrifice.[20]

Such is *homo sacer*'s strange predicament, which went against a norm of ancient Roman socio-political life. What would probably be viewed by contemporary observers as an act of capital punishment was for the ancient Romans a religious rite of purification, a ritual killing. In these ancient rites, the criminal was excluded from the human domain, the sphere of human law and right. But unlike *homo sacer,* the criminal as criminal was made the object of another sphere, the religious (*ius divinum*). Thus, not unlike many modern Western societies, ancient Roman socio-political life functioned under a tacit separation of the "church" or religion from the state inasmuch as these were distinct, non-overlapping spheres of the human.

Now, as the norm would have it, because the criminal before his condemnation was a citizen within the *polis,* and thus more than bare life (*zoē*), he had the status of always being socially locatable. Stated differently, the criminal by virtue of his humanity was always "somewhere" and never "nowhere." Employing terms drawn from my Duke University colleague, the crítical theorist and philosopher Kenneth Surin, one can say that while under normal conditions the criminal was not a *subjectum* ("the thing that serves as the bearer *of* something, be it consciousness or some other property of the individual"), the criminal nevertheless was always a *subjectus* ("the thing that is subjected *to* something else," the thing that submits to some other authority).[21] That before which the criminal was subjected was sovereign power itself in its task to determine and uphold the field of the human as mapped across the independent subfields constitutive of our existence. These subfields, according to Agamben, are the political and the religious. All else, we can infer, functions between these poles. The criminal in the normal, rather than the suspended, order is never banished from the general field of human existence, though due to his crime his central subfield shifts from the political sphere to the religious. The important point is that the criminal never loses normal status as human, not even when condemned for violating *ius humana.*

What this finally meant, then, was that in bringing divine, rather than human, retribution to bear, sacrifice, rather than murder or killing, was accomplished. The criminal was made the *subjectus* of the sovereign gods, and thus his death was carried out with purification rites. In regular, ancient "capital punishment" the one condemned to death by the political body was handed over to the gods. Therefore, the one put to the scorn of humiliating public death was not merely a "victim"; he was a *consecrated* victim, a religious figure.

There is a marked difference between the ordinary criminal's condition and that of *homo sacer*. For *homo sacer* is not simply "ex-cepted," or cast out, from the human sphere of politics and law. In contrast to the "victim" of a ritual killing, *homo sacer*'s sacrality consists precisely in his being excepted from the religious sphere, the sphere of divine law and right, too. *Homo sacer* exists in a death-void. The double exception that marks *homo sacer*'s odd and ambivalent status as "sacred" is the insignia of his or her existence in the death-void – outside the polis and the cult. But the point to emphasize is that the cult, or religion, performs the political by declaring the criminal a "political" sacrifice. Through the religious the criminal is incorporated back into the political at the same time that this fact is masked. Sacrality, by contrast, unmasks this fact by articulating the subhuman and the inhuman exterior that can never be incorporated into the binary structure of the human. Yet it is this unincorporated third term, this exterior death-void, that enables the dialectical encoding of the political and the religious, and thus, the human. Sacrality, therefore, is that which *bios* declares by sovereign fiat to be politically and religiously unredeemable *zoē*.

Homo sacer's deathly existence is savage (what Aristotle in proto-Rousseauean fashion calls "sweet naturalness"), the zone of the sub-political and the sub-religious, the zone of bare life. Something like this is precisely what marked the slaves (and their progeny) in the New World. Their existence was that of the death-bound-subject (not just in the sense of *subjectus*, but also *subjectum*) inasmuch as they, like *homo sacer*, were neither political subjects nor, at least early on, were they considered capable of being Christian, religious subjects. Abdul JanMohamed's comments on Richard Wright's literary corpus are apposite. JanMohamed reads Wright's literary remains as functioning between archaeology and biology. Archaeologically speaking, Wright's oeuvre, through such characters as *Native Son*'s "Bigger Thomas" (1940), excavates the site of the death-bound-subject position. As Wright asks in the essay "How 'Bigger' was Born":

why should I not try to work out on paper the problem of what will happen to Bigger? Why should I not, like a scientist in a laboratory, use my imagination and invent test-tube situations, place Bigger in them, and follow the guidance of my own hopes and fears, what I had learned and remembered, work out in fictional form an emotional statement and resolution of this problem?[22]

"Bigger" was for Wright a symbolic character, through whom he could exhume and then examine the remains of the death-bound-subject of social death in Jim Crow society, as those remains remained buried in Wright's own psyche – in his own hopes and fears to which he sought to give voice on paper. Wright's fiction explored how the threat of death penetrated the psyche of the victims of social death, and how the death-threat socially subjected the death-bound-subject to the political economy's various techniques or, as Foucault would say, to its varied "technologies of the self."[23] These are the technologies of a socio-political order structured according to class distinctions and ultimately upon the dictates of white supremacy.

JanMohamed notes that the metaphor of archaeology alone, however, is not enough to capture the situation of *homo sacer*, the socially dead person ever poised on the precipice of being physically killed. For this metaphor suggests merely a dead subject, one "sedimented and calcified in place by the prevailing forces of social-death."[24] To capture more fully what is going on, Wright, according to JanMohamed, turns to another metaphor: biology. Wright's project explores how, with the death-bound-subject, death circulates like blood, so to speak, to "nourish" the subject. Wright recognizes that, to revert back to Agamben's language, *homo sacer* or "bare life," life that is readily killable, is not merely dead. Rather, he is "alive" in his very death. Moreover, this is, to speak paradoxically, a "deathly aliveness" that inheres in the very "flesh" of the readily killable one. Death "nourishes" the "life" of *homo sacer*'s dead, but alive flesh. To clarify what this means JanMohamed extends the work of literary critic Hortense Spillers, in which she distinguishes between "body" and "flesh" in order to distinguish between captive and liberated subject-positions.[25] JanMohamed pushes this further into a distinction between "flesh" and "meat."

"Flesh," I would contend, is not *quite* the zero degree of "social conceptualization" or subjectivity, for, though denuded almost entirely of its subjectivity, flesh is still *alive*. Bare life/flesh is close to the zero degree of subjectivity in that it is defined as readily killable. However, we must remember that, when one kills flesh, it is transformed, it dies and becomes *meat*; meat, one can say, is insensate flesh. And, to the extent that meat rather than flesh is the absolute zero degree of subjectivity, my extension of Spillers's formulation allows us to define the zone inhabited by "bare life" or the death-bound-subject as that between flesh and meat. Viewed from within the subjectivity trapped in this zone, one needs to stress that bare life always exists as "flesh" that is readily and easily convertible to "meat" and that it is precisely this convertibility, what we might call "negative latency," between the two that constitutes "bare life."[26]

Wright himself, however, goes further still. He grasps, in a way that Agamben (or even Wright's brilliant interpreter JanMohamed) only partly does, how religion performs the political in all this. Wright's biological archaeology of death grasps that what dark flesh and dark meat disclose about modernity is the interconnection between religion and politics in constituting the zone that bare life occupies. These two spheres function isomophorically within a politics of death; within necropolitics religion and politics actually parody and perform each other. An essential claim that I want to make in this essay is that American evangelicalism has functioned in this way. It has religiously performed the necropolitical and has done so on the back of black flesh. Wright's genius, over against Agamben, is that he grasps that it is only from *within* the subject position of *homo sacer* himself, that of the death-bound-subject, that the overlap between religion and governmentality in the necropolitics of death can be seen and – this is important – possibly overcome. The task, therefore, is not the evasion of death; rather, it is entry into it, into the position of the death-bound-subject so as to rewrite the "death contract" that founds Western politics and life. The result of rewriting the death contract would be the realization of a new material reality.[27]

However, such a move is not utterly new with Wright. He is the inheritor of a tradition of black writing and black intellectual reflection that gets this fundamental point. The experience of death, indeed, its inner dimensions, cannot be circumvented, if a counter-reality is to be articulated. A significant part of Wright's insight comes from black Christianity's distinctive appropriation of American evangelicalism. That appropriation dislocated and then relocated American evangelical belief and practice within the horizon of the death-experience. The result, for black folks, was the metamorphosis of the death-bound-subject-position into a new kind of theological subject-position.

It will be necessary to consider briefly the harmonics or the cadence of this theological subject-position. For the dominant white evangelicalism, the result of this black alteration was the possibility that American evangelicalism, should its adherents choose, would cease to ventriloquize the politics of death, which was the inner core of political economy in modernity, generally, and in America, specifically. The next two sections take up these matters. The next, in particular, briefly considers Richard Wright's 1935 poem "Between the World and Me," for (Wright's own Marxist critique of black Christianity notwithstanding) it will take us into the core of how evangelical belief came to be *socially* dislocated as a result of its passage through the death-experience of those raced as black. We will then be poised in the concluding section to consider how evangelical belief came to be *doctrinally* relocated so as to open up a new political economy, the economy of the cross and more specifically the economy of Holy Saturday.

BLACK CHRISTIANITY AND THE SOCIAL DISLOCATION OF EVANGELICAL BELIEF

In "Between the World and Me," Wright recounts in four stanzas the story of a lynching. Important here is that Wright narrates the story of this lynching from "the persona's *subjective* experience of being lynched," that is, from the subjective experience of death itself.[28] It is the lynched subject, the living dead person, who has been resurrected to tell the story of what it means to be *homo sacer*, killable flesh. This becomes clear as one follows throughout the poem the shifts in narrative voice. In the first stanza, the narrative voice is more distanced and "objective." Speaking in the third-person, the narrator looks out at the "stony skull" of a lynched man lying upon the ground, into whose empty eye sockets "the sun poured yellow/surprise."[29] But in the final stanza the lifeless, dead man, which had been gazed upon from the distanced, objective stance of an observing outsider, is shown to be, in fact, the lyrical reportage of a subjective, first-person witness: "Now *I* am dry bones and *my face* a stony skull staring in yellow at the sun."[30] What the movement from the first through the final stanzas tracks is the evolution of consciousness and transformation of narrative voice needed to give voice, not just to a corpse, but to the living experience of being a corpse. Wright's move is amenable to theological translation: this is the subject-position of the Paschal Christ on Holy Saturday, that interstitial zone between crucifixion and resurrection, existing in the state of being non-existent.[31] I will return to this below when considering the theological significance of Harriet Jacobs's slave narrative for Black Christianity's doctrinal relocation of evangelical belief.

For now it can simply be said that Wright's verse registers this doctrinal relocation of American evangelical belief on the social plane of the death-bound-subject's mode of existence. This mode of existence is always caught betwixt-and-between the lynch-crucifixion of actual physical death and the commutation of this death sentence, which can at any point be revoked.

A reading of Wright in terms of an endless cycle of death and resurrection has textual merit. From the third, penultimate stanza of the poem we learn that "the dry bones" of the first stanza "stirred, rattled, lifted, [melted] themselves/into my bones."[32] They became alive again, but only as they "formed flesh firm and black, entering into/my flesh."[33] Thus, the dead one comes back to life by taking on the flesh of another black person, the third-person observer. But as the stanza continues, we discover that having been resurrected, the lynched man of the first stanza, who again takes on black flesh, would soon be lynched again in his resurrected body later in the third stanza. The final stanza comments on the re-lynching: "My skin clung to the bubbling hot tar falling from/me in limp patches. . . Then my blood was cooled mercifully, cooled by a/baptism of gasoline./ And in a blaze of red I leaped to the sky . . . /Panting, begging I clutched childlike, clutched to the hot sides of death."[34] So, what is finally disclosed in this fourth and final stanza is that the condition of those raced as black in modernity, those raced to be *homo sacer*, "sacred man," is one in which death circulates endlessly. Their existence is a perpetual cycle of lynchings and resurrections and subsequent re-lynchings. Wright seeks to allow the experience of perpetual death as the mode of "life" to speak. He is poetically experimenting with what it would mean to hear this experience and thus, while "clutching to the hot sides of death," grope toward the overturning of the death contract that founds the Western socio-political imagination.

The allusions to Christianity are unmistakable. However, the question is: what and where is the social location of this Christianity? How does it seek to dislocate and then relocate persons in social space? At the heart of the poem is Wright's own poetic exegesis of Ezekiel 37:1-14 in which YHWH questions the prophet as to whether the dry bones, which YHWH says are the whole house of Israel, could live again and have flesh come upon them. The poem connects its allusive reference to the prophecy of Ezekiel about Israel's dry bones with the theme of resurrection from the dead.[35] The subtle invocation of Israel as a nation calls to mind the notion in early American Puritan Christianity, the taproot of American evangelicalism, of America as "God's New Israel" on its errand in the wilderness.[36] Wright seems to be suggesting that America's founding vision is predicated on death – first of the native Americans and also of those raced as black and enslaved. It is founded on a triumphalist vision of Christianity, which is predicated on a nationalism that is but a variant on the theme of Christian supersessionism against Jewish covenantal flesh. The subtler move buried in this, which Wright is archaeologically exhuming in a desperate attempt to resuscitate it, is the effort to reimagine the connection between Jewish flesh, or the readily killable life of the people Israel, and black flesh, or the readily killable life of people of African descent in modernity. Wright attempts to reimagine the "birth of a nation" and reconstitute national identity.[37] I am not claiming that Wright was some sort of astute "theologian," but rather that he is drawing on a tradition of "reversal" in black Christianity involving sustained critique of America's triumphalist appropriation of Israel's story by which it framed itself as "city on a hill," with black faith as living into the trope of the Suffering Servant.[38]

How do these phenomena, Jewish flesh and black flesh, come together as the twin sides of *homo sacer*'s existence in modernity? And, how does the modern political economy racialize all non-white flesh between these bell-curved polarities?[39] Key for now, in relationship to these questions, is Wright's insight that the link binding the phenomenon of Jewish flesh and black flesh together is race as a socially constituted death-phenomenon. Thus, race as a construct of death functions between these fleshly poles, and all races are "raced" between these extremities.[40] Moreover, Wright's poetry implies that the racial denigration of black and Jewish flesh is in fact a theological problem, not a result of the failure of democracy. Rather, linked to the twinned phenomena of democracy and totalitarianism,[41] it results from the failure of a theological or covenantal vision of human identity and of its politics. In the American context, this was a failure of evangelical theological imagination at the moment of the nation's founding. Therefore, rectifying this problematic binding together of all non-white flesh as inferior to white flesh requires a feat of theological imagination. Such imagination would need to refigure the connection between Jewish and non-Jewish flesh, between Jews and Gentiles (to employ scriptural language) in YHWH's covenant with creation, seeing that refigurement as nourishing and thus sustaining the body politic of Christ in its resistance to the necropolitics of white supremacy.[42]

Wright's discourse – perhaps against its own intentions – suggests that already within American evangelicalism is a starting point for the new theological imagination, a place in which it has, in an embryonic way, already been socially performed. For, if American evangelicalism aided and abetted the necropolitical social processes of the nation's founding (as John Patrick Daly's research into the emergence of Southern evangelicalism suggests),[43] then Wright's poem bears the traces of a black Christian evangelicalism that moves toward a theological (rather than racialized) linking of the Jewish body and the black body.[44] This new linkage occurs at the site of Christ's socio-political body, that is, at the site of his body's excess beyond (but only by means of passing through) the "necropolitics" of Holy Saturday. This is the day of the Paschal mystery in which Christ exists in the state of death. Resurrection does not overcome this, in the sense of leaving it behind. Rather, resurrection converts Holy Saturday into Christ's and the believer's mode of new life.

Wright has unwittingly tapped into this. This connection, in which black flesh is articulated within a different space – Jesus' killed flesh, which in being the flesh of Israel concentrates in itself YHWH's covenant – lay at the ground of black Christianity's inhabitation of early American evangelicalism. In displacing American evangelical belief into the liminally tight and eerily dark space of the death-bound-subject, now made iconic of the death-experience of Christ the Jew on Holy Saturday, the path of American (and Western) triumphalism (the path that rushes quickly to deploy politically Christ's resurrection as the guarantee of white male hegemony over the world) gets converted by means of black flesh into the *via crucis*, the *sacrficium Christi*. Thus, there arose a new theo-political possibility of and materiality for, a new social embodiment of American evangelicalism – a new way of ordering the world, the way of Christ's wounded Jewish flesh. In this new theological materiality, reality is no longer to be orchestrated from the colonialist subject-position of white male flesh – from *bios* as Aristotle put it – outward toward the rest of the world, but rather from the subject-position that is most opposite the subject-position of the white male, Christian triumphalism on which modernity is founded and in which American evangelicalism has participated.

BLACK CHRISTIANITY AND THE THEOLOGICAL RELOCATION OF EVANGELICAL BELIEF

In the short space of this essay I have labored to capture something of the theological subjectivity of black folks, historically articulated mostly in American evangelical terms. What was the nature of the subject-position blacks were made to occupy, and then importantly, how did they receive evangelical belief in such a way as to articulate a subject-position beyond the necropolitics of America? I have sketched an answer saying, in effect, that evangelical belief was dislocated from the necropolitical order and made to pass through *homo sacer*'s, that is, through black folks' experience of racialized social death. Evangelical belief was received by persons of African descent "who made Jesus their choice" so as to bear witness to a different, non-triumphalist Christian reality. If the prior section spoke to the social dislocation of evangelical belief into black Christianity, I conclude by speaking to how the social dislocation was, in fact, a crafty and theologically astute doctrinal relocation. For this I briefly consider the theological contours of a scene in Harriet Jacobs's (who wrote under the penname Linda Brent) 1861 slave narrative *Incidents in the Life of a Slave Girl*.

In *Incidents* Jacobs reconstructs her life as a slave and her eventual escape to freedom. However, what distinguishes her slave narrative from those of her black male counterparts (probably the most celebrated example of which would be Frederick Douglass's famous 1845 *Narrative*) is that her account disclosed not only such atrocities as the breakup of families through the selling of slaves, the brutal treatment and whippings of slaves, and other heinous acts. Jacobs's narrative also establishes the distinctly gendered contours of all this. Her narrative sought to lift slavery's veil to reveal the peculiar place – or, non-place – of the black female body in the economy of the nation. In disturbing detail she takes her mainly abolitionist readership through the journey of homelessness that marks black flesh in the New World. But even more, *Incidents* dramatizes how in black female flesh, perhaps more than any other, the abjectness of black folk's social death is fully displayed. In her body we learn what it means to be *homo sacer*, and thus to live in the state of being killable flesh that is convertible into raw meat.

To live in that condition is social death. That Jacobs writes in the genre of autobiography, and thus in first-person, means that *Incidents* is Jacobs's attempt, as Wright will attempt generations later, to give voice to death-bound-subjectivity and thus to transform the subject-position of death, utter entrapment, and radical aloneness. Indeed, *Incidents* is the story of Jacobs's effort to overcome this condition, which displayed itself most forcefully in her master's, Dr. Norcom's (whose penname was Flint), persistence in trying to rape her. Rape itself presupposes the conversion of the body into killable meat. What is important is that Jacobs represents the moment in which social death in some sense was overcome and freedom commenced as a supremely Christian theological moment. More specifically, she represents it as a deeply Christological and Paschal, or Easter, moment. In this moment we see the theological relocation of evangelical belief as it passed through the racial-gendered axis of death-bound-subjectivity. This moment occurs approximately in the middle of *Incidents*, in chapter 21, which she entitled "The Loophole of Retreat."

In order to evade Norcom's sexual advances but nevertheless stay close enough to ensure that her children are sold away toward the North and thus to freedom, Jacobs hid in an airless, mice-infested, nine-feet long, seven-feet wide, and three-feet high attic-like garret, which was part of the roof of her grandmother's house.[45] About this garret into which she was spirited away, Jacobs says, "The air was stifling; the darkness total." With a bounty on her head, she was confined to this "wretched hiding place" for seven years, during which time she was visited only by a few relatives and had no more movement and exercise than this coffin-like crawl space would allow. Suffering the extremes of cold and heat, to say nothing of the psychological and physical anguish she endured, Jacobs only had contact with the outside world through a small hole, a "loophole of retreat," in one of the roof boards. This dismal place with its mere peephole onto the outside world was her home.[46]

Though Jacobs at the end of her seven-year period of self-imposed incarceration made her way North, she actually dates her freedom to the beginning of her seven-year entombment! This was the moment in which her "lot as a slave" improved. Note the Christological terms in which she represents this improvement:

> I suffered much more during the second winter than I did during the first. My limbs were benumbed by inaction, and the cold filled them with cramp. I had a very painful sensation of coldness in my head; even my face and tongue stiffened, and I lost the power of speech. Of course it was impossible, under the circumstances, to summon any physician. My brother William came and did all he could for me. Uncle Phillip also watched tenderly over me; and poor grandmother crept up and down to inquire whether there were any signs of returning life. I was restored to consciousness by the dashing of cold water in my face, and found myself leaning against my brother's arm, while he bent over me with streaming eyes. He afterwards told me he thought I was dying, for I had been in an unconscious state sixteen hours.[47]

Jacobs presents herself as undergoing death in a tomb. Indeed, later in the same paragraph she says that this is all "part of the price that I had to pay for the *redemption* of my children."[48] Jacobs articulates her freedom in soteriological terms. Her incarceration was in service of securing the freedom of her children. Part of the power of Jacobs's discourse is that it evokes Christ's Pasch to give voice to all this. More specifically, it evokes

Holy Saturday as the Christological moment she herself inhabits. What Jacobs presents us with, then, is a theological poetics of Christ's Passion, which in somewhat unevangelical fashion presumes a kind of icon theology centered on the uniqueness of Christ's flesh. His flesh, though Jewish, is not racial flesh, for racialized flesh functions out of a logic of purity. It is this logic that calls for miscegenation laws. But Christ's flesh is most itself as it brings other flesh, even Gentile flesh, to participate in it. Just in this way, non-Jewish flesh can be grafted onto the flesh of Israel (cf. Rom. 9–11) and thereby be an icon of Christ's way of being in the world.

Jacobs is only deepening the evangelical Christianity already at work in the *Interesting Narrative of the Life of Olaudah Equiano, or Gustavus Vassa, the African, Written by Himself* (1792). In his narrative, Equiano reports after a time of "deep consternation" over the question of how salvation occurred, whether it was a gift of God or else earned by work, that

> the Lord was pleased to break in upon my soul with his bright beams of heavenly light; and in an instant as it were, removing the veil, and letting light into a dark place (Isa. xxv.7). I saw clearly, with the eye of faith, the crucified Saviour bleeding on the cross on Mount Calvary: the Scriptures became an unsealed book; I saw myself a condemned criminal under the law which came with its force to my conscience . . . I saw the Lord Jesus Christ in his humiliation . . .[49]

Read intertextually, Jacobs takes this moment on only to push it a step further, for it is not just the crucified Christ of Good Friday in light of which she articulates her existence, nor for that matter is it Douglass's Christ of Easter Sunday by whose power he defeats the "nigger-breaker" Edward Covey in the 1845 *Narrative*. Rather, the site in which freedom is given voice is the dead Christ of Holy Saturday, who exists in the state of being dead in the tomb, of suffering-Godforsakenness. Herein lay the heart of Jacobs's poetics of black theological subjectivity, a center that theologically relocates evangelical belief from a resurrection schema that too quickly rushes past suffering flesh in order, on the one hand, to mount the heights of the theoretical and the speculative so as, on the other, to get to salvation (on a personal level) and to realize white nationalist triumph (on the cultural and socio-political levels). Equiano was closer to the mark in seeing salvation as inhering in the despised and killed Jewish flesh of Christ. He "saw the Lord Jesus Christ in his humiliation." He saw "the Crucified Saviour bleeding on the cross on Mount Calvary." Jacobs's discourse, however, envisions a subject-position that inhabits Jesus' state of being dead as the counter-politic to death-bound-subjectivity.[50] To live in the resurrection means not moving past the reality of living in Christ in his state of enduring being dead. The resurrection witnesses to the transformation of this sinful death-void into a mode of life, a mode of life that alters the social reality precisely by inaugurating a new theological one. To dramatize this point, Jacobs does what even Equiano does not do. Echoing Paul's assertion that he bore in his body the marks, the stigmata, of Christ (Gal. 6:17), she too presents her body as the iconic repetition of Christ's body in his state of being dead.

It is important that Jacobs's gesture not be simply interpreted as a strategic, literary deployment of the symbol of the cross. Were this the case, nothing would be accomplished; her discourse would be more like Wright's, which in the end comes to reenact the rape of black female flesh rather than imagine a new political economy. It is better to understand Jacobs's as a poetics of "recapitulation" (as in Irenaeus's *Adversus Haeresis*),[51] of "repetition" (as in Kiekegaard's *Repetition*),[52] or of *l'état Christ* or the states of Christ (as in Bérulle).[53] Each of these terms indicates the ways, according to classical theologians, by which in the mystery of the divine economy of redemption events can be over as regards their historical execution, yet present and perpetual as regards their power. Against this backdrop, we can say that Holy Saturday, in Jacobs's discourse, is similarly effectual.

Black flesh is an iteration within the perpetuity of Christ's flesh, the wounded, Jewish flesh of the Holy Pasch. Jacobs herself had a sense of this mystery and, indeed, the consequent questions of theodicy: "These things took the shape of mystery, which is to this day not so clear to my soul as I trust it will be hereafter."[54] But this "hereafter" is the "here"-"after" of the new time and new place of YHWH's, the triune God's, presence. It is the "now" that socio-politically transforms the politics of death, the "now" that makes the slave ship an icon. Here is American evangelicalism's theological alternative to modernity's necropolitics, indeed, its alternative to the American necropolitics.

The crucial point is that Jacobs represents her body as being not simply at a metaphoric remove from Christ's. Rather, Christ's body articulates her body and her body his, thus making black flesh an icon, an analogical repetition, of the very body of Christ. The force of Jacobs's poetics is to say that in entering the socio-political reality most opposite white male supremacy – the reality of black (female) flesh insofar as it is iconic of the wounded flesh of Christ – one enters a new, redemptive theopolitics. The rush to the resurrection in evangelical belief, and perhaps in theological orientations that are not of American evangelical vintage though they too claim Christian orthodoxy, is often not "radically orthodox" at all. Rather, it betrays a triumphalist passage beyond, and thus a violent overcoming of, the world's wounded flesh. It is, in short, to rape once again. For Jacobs, by contrast, the resurrection is a resurrection of the ever-scarred body of Christ; only in his scarred flesh is necropolitics overcome.

What we see in Jacobs's evangelical faith is emblematic of the dislocation and relocation of evangelical belief as a result of its passage through race and the experience of death. She displays the theologically profound counter-tradition that is tucked within the tradition of American evangelicalism. This is the tradition of black Christianity, which in fact retrieves crucial aspects of the broader catholic Christian traditions that were lost with the dawning of the modern world as we know it. One sees this to be the case particularly as one comes to understand the connection between the European conquest of the Americas (and indeed, much of the globe) as the signal on-the-ground moment of the dawning of modernity and the way in which theology did the intellectual work of justifying the conquests and thus legitimating a reign of suffering for those on modernity's dark underside. The question black Christianity poses to persons black, white, and all shades in between who, at present, want the name "evangelical" is this: what would it mean to receive the Jewish Saviour, but at the site of dark despised flesh? Indeed, what would it mean to enter into the body politic of the wounded, not triumphalist, flesh of Christ, but as given in the bodies of the Harriet Jacobses of our racialized world, and so be saved?

Further reading

Agamben, Giorgio. *Homo Sacer: Sovereign Power and Bare Life*. Translated by Daniel Heller-Roazen. Stanford, CA: Stanford University Press, 1995.

Bassard, Katherine Clay. *Spiritual Interrogations: Culture, Gender, and Community in Early African American Women's Writing*. Princeton, NJ: Princeton University Press, 1999.

Carter, J. Kameron. *Race: A Theological Account*. New York: Oxford University Press, forthcoming.

Daly, John Patrick. *When Slavery Was Called Freedom: Evangelicalism, Proslavery, and the Causes of the Civil War*. Lexington: University Press of Kentucky, 2002.

Davis, David Brion. *Inhuman Bondage: The Rise and Fall of Slavery in the New World*. New York: Oxford University Press, 2006.

Emerson, Michael O., and Christian Smith. *Divided by Faith: Evangelical Religion and the Problem of Race in America*. New York: Oxford University Press, 2000.

Harris, Leonard (ed.). *Racism: Key Concepts in Critical Theory*. Amherst, NY: Humanity Books, 1999.

JanMohamed, Abdul R. *The Death-Bound-Subject: Richard Wright's Archaeology of Death*. Durham, NC: Duke University Press, 2005.

Mathews, Donald G. *Religion in the Old South*. Chicago: University of Chicago Press, 1977.

Patterson, Orlando. *Slavery and Social Death: A Comparative Study*. Cambridge, MA: Harvard University Press, 1982.

Raboteau, Albert J. *Slave Religion: The "Invisible Institution" in the Antebellum South*. New York: Oxford University Press, 1978.
    Canaan Land: A Religious History of African Americans. New York: Oxford University Press, 1999.
Turley, David. *Slavery*. Oxford: Blackwell, 2000.

Notes

I would like to thank the following persons for their comments on this essay: Tammy Williams, Curtis Freeman, Willie James Jennings, Dan Rhodes, Amy Laura Hall, Ken Surin, Lauren Winner, and Jonathan Wilson-Hartgrove.

1. Achille Mbembé, "Necropolitics," *Public Culture* 15. 1 (2003): 17.
2. Harriet A. Jacobs, *Incidents in the Life of a Slave Girl*, ed. Jean Fagan Yellin (Cambridge, MA: Harvard University Press, 1987), pp. 114, 13. *Incidents*, the earliest slave narrative we know to have been authored by a black woman, was first published in 1861.
3. This is the claim of Harold Bloom, *The American Religion: The Emergence of the Post-Christian Nation* (New York: Simon and Schuster, 1992). The issue I take with Bloom's otherwise insightful account of why American religion, including most of its Christianity, is "Gnostic," is that his account of African American Christianity has no sense of what theologically drives it.
4. I allude to Ralph Ellison, *Invisible Man* (New York: Vintage, 1995), originally published in 1952. While recognizing how race is a theological issue across the "Black Atlantic" and across the world, and therefore for global evangelicalism, for the sake of concreteness I focus on the American story of race. The other reason, however, for focusing attention here is that I seek to provide a paradigm for how other racially denigrated groups might *theologically* reimagine their identity.
5. See A. G. Miller, "The Rise of African-American Evangelicalism in American Culture," ch. 18 in Peter W. Williams (ed.), *Perspectives on American Religion and Culture* (Malden, MA: Blackwell, 1999). Since then, there has been a groundswell of studies into the importance of blacks in the historical unfolding of American religion in the South, generally, and American evangelicalism, specifically. See writers such as Donald G. Mathews; Jon F. Sensbach; Jon Butler; and Christine Leigh Heyrman.
6. Those familiar with "black theology" may take issue with this claim. For, does not black theology purport to account *theologically* for black folks' decision for Christianity? I cannot here make the case for why, black theology's own claims notwithstanding, a *theological* attempt to interrogate black existence, generally, and black Christian existence, more specifically, is not to be found there. See J. Kameron Carter, "Contemporary Black Theology: A Review Essay," *Modern Theology* 19. 1 (2003): 117–38; "Race, Religion, and the Contradictions of Identity: A Theological Engagement with Douglass's 1845 *Narrative*," *Modern Theology* 21. 1 (2005): 37–66; and the three chapters comprising Part II of *Race: A Theological Account* (New York: Oxford University Press, forthcoming).
7. Judith Butler and Sara Salih, *The Judith Butler Reader* (Malden, MA: Blackwell, 2004), pp. 90–118.
8. Mbembé, "Necropolitics."
9. Orlando Patterson, *Slavery and Social Death: A Comparative Study* (Cambridge, MA: Harvard University Press, 1982).

10. Abdul R. JanMohamed, *The Death-Bound-Subject: Richard Wright's Archaeology of Death* (Durham, NC: Duke University Press, 2005).

11. John Patrick Daly, *When Slavery Was Called Freedom: Evangelicalism, Proslavery, and the Causes of the Civil War* (Lexington: University Press of Kentucky, 2002), p. 7.

12. I depend on, but also theologically qualify, recent work in philosophy and critical theory addressing the political and metaphysical condition of modernity. Here I engage mainly Giorgio Agamben and Abdul R. JanMohamed. Behind these figures, though, looms Michel Foucault, whom I engage in chapter 1 of the forthcoming *Race: A Theological Account*.

13. Cheryl Finley, "Committed to Memory: The Slave-Ship Icon and the Black Atlantic Imagination," *Chicago Art Journal* 9 (1999): 2–21.

14. Walter Johnson, *Soul by Soul: Life inside the Antebellum Slave Market* (Cambridge, MA: Harvard University Press, 1999).

15. Mbembé, "Necropolitics," p. 21.

16. *Ibid.*

17. See David Brion Davis, *Inhuman Bondage: The Rise and Fall of Slavery in the New World* (New York: Oxford University Press, 2006).

18. Quoted in Giorgio Agamben, *Homo Sacer: Sovereign Power and Bare Life*, trans. Daniel Heller-Roazan (Stanford, CA: Stanford University Press, 1995), p. 71.

19. Etienne Balibar, "Citizen Subject," in Eduardo Cadava, Peter Connor, and Jean-Luc Nancy (eds.), *Who Comes after the Subject?* (New York: Routledge, 1991), pp. 33–57.

20. It is worth noting that John Milbank has taken issue with Agamben on the point that *homo sacer*'s execution is non-sacrificial. For him, it is quite sacrificial, even if it does not take the form of ritual. See *Being Reconciled: Ontology and Pardon*, Radical Orthodoxy (New York: Routledge, 2003).

21. Kenneth Surin, "Rewriting the Ontological Script of Liberation: On the Question of Finding a New Kind of Political Subject," in Creston Davis, John Milbank, and Slavoj Zizek (eds.), *Theology and the Political: The New Debate* (Durham, NC: Duke University Press, 2005), pp. 240–66. Surin's distinction between *subjectum* and *subjectus* draws on Balibar's notion of "citizen subject."

22. Quoted in JanMohamed, *The Death-Bound-Subject*, p. 35.

23. Michel Foucault, *Technologies of the Self: A Seminar with Michel Foucault*, ed. Luther H. Martin, Huck Gutman, and Patrick H. Hutton (Amherst: University of Massachusetts Press, 1988).

24. JanMohamed, *The Death-Bound-Subject*, p. 35.

25. Spillers makes this distinction in a justly celebrated essay, "MaMa's Baby, PaPa's Maybe: An American Grammar Book," in Hortense J. Spillers, *Black, White, and in Color: Essays on American Literature and Culture* (Chicago: University of Chicago Press, 2003), pp. 656–72.

26. JanMohamed, *The Death-Bound-Subject*, p. 10.

27. Central to the death contract, as is clear from Hegel's master–slave dialectic of *Phenomenology of Spirit*, is the commodification of the slave's fear of death, which gets transformed into labor-value. Cf. JanMohamed, *The Death-Bound-Subject*, p. 280.

28. JanMohamed, *The Death-Bound-Subject*, p. 29 (italics original).

29. Wright's "Between the World and Me" is collected in Ellen Wright and Michel Fabre (eds.), *Richard Wright Reader*, 1st edition (New York: Harper and Row, 1978), pp. 246–47. This quote is from p. 246.

30. *Ibid.*, p. 247; italics mine.

31. Hans Urs von Balthasar, perhaps more than any other modern theologian, has devoted much attention to the significance of Holy Saturday. See Hans Urs von Balthasar, *Mysterium Paschale*, ed. David L. Schindler, trans. Aidan Nichols, O. P., (Grand Rapids, MI: Eerdmans, 1990) and, most deeply, *Theo-Drama: Theological Dramatic Theory*, 5 vols. (San Francisco: Ignatius, 1988–98).

32. *Wright Reader*, p. 247.

33. *Ibid.*

34. *Ibid.*

35. On resurrection as a Jewish theme see Jon D. Levenson, *The Death and Resurrection of the Beloved Son: The Transformation of Child Sacrifice in Judaism and Christianity* (New Haven, CT: Yale University Press, 1993) and Michael Wyschogrod, "Resurrection," *Pro Ecclesia* 1. 1 (1992): 104–12.

36. See the rich compilation of texts in Conrad Cherry (ed.), *God's New Israel: Religious Interpretations of American History*, revised and updated edition (Chapel Hill: University of North Carolina Press, 1998).

37. The problem with Wright's own alternative is its articulation of a black nationalism rooted in the coming of age of black male consciousness – at the expense of black woman. A frontal critique of this appears in chapter 3 of Houston A. Baker's *Workings of the Spirit: The Poetics of Afro-American Women's Writing* (Chicago: University of Chicago Press, 1991).

38. See Eddie S. Glaude, Jr.'s in the end non-theological, and thus limited, account of this in *Exodus! Religion, Race, and Nation in Early Nineteenth-Century Black America* (Chicago: University of Chicago Press, 2000).

39. My invocation of the bell-curve follows upon the masterful work by Sander L. Gilman, *Smart Jews: The Construction of the Image of Jewish Superior Intelligence* (Lincoln: University of Nebraska Press, 1996). Gilman analyzes the discourse of the bell-curve not so much from the lower end where persons of color and, particularly, blacks get situated as from the upper end of the curve where "smart Jews" are situated. He brilliantly shows how the ends of the curve are linked so as to parody each other.

40. The burgeoning literature on critical race theory has no consideration of this *theological* point. See my forthcoming *Race: A Theological Account*. On critical race theory the interested reader can start with Kimberle Crenshaw; Ivan Hannaford; and Leonard Harris (ed.), *Racism: Key Concepts in Critical Theory* (Amherst, NY: Humanity Books, 1999).

41. In addition to Agamben's *Homo Sacer*, on this point see Hannah Arendt, *The Origins of Totalitarianism* (New York: Harcourt Brace, 1951).

42. For more on the linkage of covenant and creation, see Jon D. Levenson, *Creation and the Persistence of Evil: The Jewish Drama of Divine Omnipotence* (Princeton, NJ: Princeton University Press, 1994). My claims here draw on insights from Foucault, Balthasar, and Karl Barth. But more immediately, they are the result of vibrant conversations with a fellow theologian and friend, Willie James Jennings.

43. Daly, *When Slavery Was Called Freedom*. Donald E. Mathews's *Religion in the Old South* (Chicago: University of Chicago Press, 1977), in its own way, makes this point as well.

44. Wright's poem bears the marks of the relationship between blacks and Jews when both remained outsiders to full American citizenship and its benefits. See further Eric J. Sundquist, *Strangers in the Land: Blacks, Jews, Post-Holocaust America* (Cambridge, MA: Belknap; Harvard University Press, 2005).

45. For a full corroboration of this event, see Jean Fagan Yellin, *Harriet Jacobs: A Life* (New York: Basic Civitas, 2004).

46. Jacobs, *Incidents*, pp. 114, 121–22.

47. *Ibid.*, pp. 114, 122.

48. *Ibid.*, p. 123; italics mine.

49. The edition of Equiano's narrative as contained in Henry Louis Gates (ed.), *The Classic Slave Narratives: The Life of Olaudah Equiano; the History of Mary Prince; Narrative of the Life of Frederick Douglass; Incidents in the Life of a Slave Girl* (New York: Penguin, 1987), pp. 142–43.

50. I should also say that Jacobs's gesture to inhabit Christ's Holy Saturday existence in its perpetuity constitutes a different and, in the end, more theologically fruitful and faithful emphasis from what one finds in John Milbank's account of Christ as *homo sacer* in *Being Reconciled*, esp. chapters 4–6. While Milbank is theologically correct that Christ's resurrected body does not disband hierarchy, his refusal to think within the horizon of Christ's wounded and killed flesh means he has no way to ensure that hierarchy will not become a deadly, socio-political repetition of colonialist, white male, Christian oppression. In short, why should the once colonized be satisfied with Milbank's proposal? By contrast, Jacobs's discourse suggests the "minor-7," blues-inflected chord of Christ's wounded, Jewish flesh (and the subsequent chord progressions in relationship to this minor chord) as the harmonics or melody of redemption and as the buffer against distorted, oppressive hierarchy. The sufferings of Holy Saturday, which are the sufferings of Godforsakenness that perdure in the resurrection, indicate a Christian spirituality, the blues-note of the mystical counter-body politic of Christ (Gregory of Nyssa).

51. For a critical engagement with the hermeneutics of Irenaeus's recapitulatory Christology, see the chapters on Irenaeus in John Behr, *The Way to Nicaea*, Formation of Christian Theology, vol. 1 (Crestwood, NY: St. Vladimir's Seminary Press, 2001).

52. For a critical, theological engagement with the Kierkegaardian notion of repetition, see Arnold B. Come, *Kierkegaard as Theologian: Recovering My Self* (Montreal and Kingston: McGill-Queen's University Press, 1997). But also see the profound use of the Kierkegaardian notion of repetition in Ferdinand Ulrich, "Das Problem Einer 'Metaphysik in Der Wiederholung'," *Salzburger Jahrbuch für Philosophie* 5/6 (1961/62).

53. Pierre de Bérulle was a sixteenth-century theologian and eventual cardinal at the French oratory. A selection of his writings appears in Pierre de Bérulle and William M. Thompson, *Bérulle and the French School: Selected Writings*, Classics of Western Spirituality (New York: Paulist, 1989).

54. Jacobs, *Incidents*, p. 123.

13 Evangelical theology and the religions
VELI-MATTI KÄRKKÄINEN

INTRODUCTION: EVANGELICALS ENTER THE THEOLOGY OF RELIGIONS

The question of the theology of religions[1] – the relation of Christian faith to other living faiths – is an urgent issue for evangelicals for several reasons.[2] First of all, evangelicalism, unlike any other contemporary Christian movement except for the Roman Catholic Church, finds itself embedded within all major religions and cultures of our shrinking globe. Second, evangelicals in general are the most mission-minded believers of all; their encounter with Muslims, Buddhists, Hindus, and followers of other religions is an everyday experience. Third, evangelicals' entrance into the mainstream theological academy during the past decades has exposed them to a fruitful dialogue with views different from their own.

With sweeping generalizations, one can say that there have been three main stages in the development of evangelical theologies of religions during the twentieth century. The first phase, lasting until the mid-century, continued the typical Protestant particularist attitude according to which not only is salvation found in Christ, but also a person has to make a personal response of faith in order to be saved. The second phase in my chronology started when a few influential evangelicals such as the British scholar of religions Sir Norman Anderson[3] and another Englishman, the literary critic C. S. Lewis, started questioning the particularist viewpoint in the mid-twentieth century.

In the third phase, beginning from the late 1980s, a proliferation of views and approaches has come to characterize the evangelical camp when it comes to other religions. I discern three overlapping subcategories: the majority of theologians and pastors still adhere to a more or less particularist paradigm. A rapidly growing minority, however, is coming closer to the view most often called "inclusivism," which by any account is the dominant view across the ecumenical spectrum. The Roman Catholic

Church's inclusivism is the most well-known: Jesus is the (ontological) basis of salvation, yet salvation is available to people of other faiths (under certain conditions, such as by following the light given to them within their own religion) even apart from hearing the gospel. Evangelical inclusivism finds itself between this full-blown inclusivism and evangelical particularism: some evangelicals entertain the possibility of attaining salvation apart from hearing the gospel, but do not make it a doctrine (as the post-conciliar Catholic church has done). Yet another wing of evangelical scholars, those trained in other religions, has recently started explorations into finding potential common ground between religions. Titles such as *Can Evangelicals Learn from World Religions?* (2000), *A Tapestry of Faiths: The Common Threads Between Christianity and World Religions* (2002), and *Christianity at the Religious Roundtable: Evangelicalism in Conversation with Hinduism, Buddhism, and Islam* (2002)[4] pointedly illustrate this new trend, which had already become quite common among more liberal Christians. Pluralistic views have not gained much support among evangelicals.

To make the following discussion more specific, I will first survey evangelical views on religions both in terms of collective statements and representative theologians. Following that, I will assess what will be the main themes and what would be a fruitful way into the future.

EVANGELICALS ON OTHER RELIGIONS: AN INVESTIGATION OF VIEWS

Statements on other religions by international evangelical bodies

We are fortunate to have several international statements made by the evangelical movement.[5] We will look briefly at the three most significant, namely the Frankfurt Declaration (1970), the Lausanne Covenant (1974), and the Manila Manifesto (1992).

Frankfurt Declaration

The "Frankfurt Declaration" in 1970 offered a stern rebuttal of the liberal positions' "fundamental crisis" and "insidious falsification" as perceived by evangelicals. The declaration stated that only the Bible is the proper frame of reference and criterion for Christianity's relation to other religions. Salvation can be found only through the cross of Christ and is available only through "participation in faith." Therefore, evangelicals "reject the false teaching that the nonChristian religions and worldviews are also ways of salvation similar to belief in Christ." This means that there is "an essential difference in nature" between Christianity and other religions and that dialogue with other religions may not be seen as a substitute for proclamation.[6]

Lausanne Covenant

The highly influential International Congress on World Evangelization in Lausanne, Switzerland, in 1974, which included a significant number of non-Western representatives, basically affirmed the Frankfurt statement but in a more conciliatory way. The main concerns had to do with issues such as syncretism, universalism, and lack of evangelistic zeal.[7] Paragraph 3, entitled "The Uniqueness and Universality of Christ," affirmed "only one Saviour and only one gospel." "There is no other name by which we must be saved." While acknowledging the existence of some knowledge of God through general revelation, it also emphasized the effects of the fall and sin. Universalism and syncretism were strongly opposed and two human destinies outlined. Unlike Frankfurt, however, Lausanne acknowledged the importance of dialogue; yet unlike more liberal approaches, Lausanne did not view dialogue as an end but as a means of building contacts (para. 5).

Manila Manifesto

In 1992, under the title "The Unique Christ in Our Pluralistic World," an international team of evangelicals again wanted to combat the challenge of pluralism and respond theologically to the question of the possibility of salvation in other religions. Manila's standpoint was that religions are not salvific: "Only God saves ... all salvation stems solely from the person and atoning work of Jesus Christ..."[8] What is noteworthy about Manila is that it made a distinction between two kinds of "particularisms" with regard to other religions. Manila firmly agreed that Christ is indispensable to salvation. Yet the Assembly debated the possibility of salvation for those who never heard. The issue was left open; no consensus was reached.[9]

The defense of particularism

Traditionally, evangelicals have approached other religions with either suspicion or outright denial of their value. The reasons have been many: belief in the singular authority of Scripture, insistence on the uniqueness of Christ, and conviction regarding only two destinies for men and women, to mention the most obvious ones.[10] For the majority of evangelicals, evangelicalism is probably synonymous with particularism.[11] The major issue of debate has been the destiny of those who have never heard (and those, like infants or the handicapped, who are not in any position to hear).[12] The earlier generation of evangelicals was influenced by the dialectical theology of Karl Barth,[13] yet differing from him in many important issues such as the doctrine of Scripture's inspiration. To elucidate the current state of evangelical exclusivism, three theologians' contributions will be briefly introduced: Millard Erickson, Harold Netland, and Vinoth Ramachandra.[14]

In his *How Shall They Be Saved?*,[15] Erickson maintains that for evangelicals critical questions in relation to pluralism and religions concern the person of Christ, Scripture, and a propositional/cognitive view of Christian doctrine (as opposed to "mythical" or "experiential").[16] In other words, there is "a strong emphasis on the need of understanding, belief, acceptance, and commitment on the basis of the facts of Christ's life."[17] Furthermore, as the subtitle of the book illustrates (*The Destiny of Those Who Do Not Hear of Jesus*) the focus of discussion has to do with the question of salvation.[18] He insists on the necessity of repentance as the condition for salvation. Nevertheless, the "amount" of salvific knowledge necessary is proportionate to the amount given by God.

Harold Netland, with first-hand knowledge of Asian culture (Japan), illustrates another current concern among evangelicals, namely, the importance of encountering religious pluralism. He engages in a sustained philosophical and theological analysis of John Hick's pluralism, which posits a "rough parity" between religions. He argues that the "culture of modernity" is the bedrock of Western pluralism. For Netland, pluralism is more than a matter of worldview; it is "a form of unbelief," and it "emerges from and serves humankind's sinful tendencies."[19]

What, then, is the pluralistic religion of modernity? Netland responds: "In particular the ethos of pluralism is supported by the cumulative effects of skepticism about traditional Christianity; sustained exposure to religious diversity, and the emphasis upon pragmatism and personal experience reflected in the privatization of religion."[20] The question of the truth of the gospel, thus, becomes a key issue. Netland continues, yet with more caution, the program he started with his earlier book, *Dissonant Voices: Religious Pluralism and the Question of the Truth*,[21] to develop some criteria for judging the truthfulness of worldviews (or lack thereof). While well aware of the critique posed against "propositional" epistemology, he is not willing to lay it aside.

In the last chapter of his *Encountering Religious Pluralism*, Netland sets forth some principles of an evangelical theology of religions mainly based on key biblical principles dear to evangelicals, such as the holiness and righteousness of God; the creation of human beings in God's image; the definitive revelation in the Bible and the incarnation; the pervasive influence of sin; and God's provision of atonement for reconciliation. Furthermore, Netland proposes the importance of accuracy in portraying other religions. This kind of careful scrutiny helps evangelical theologians to determine both the continuity and discontinuity between Christianity and other religions.[22]

Vinoth Ramachandra of Sri Lanka, in his *The Recovery of Mission*,[23] enters into dialogue with some leading Asian pluralists.[24] The focus is on Christology, yet another key term for evangelicals in relation to religions. Like Netland, Ramachandra strongly opposes what he calls "normative and programmatic" pluralism.

Ramachandra is also critical of the attempts of his more liberal Asian colleagues such as Stanley J. Samartha to accommodate to the perceived Hindu, non-dualistic *advaita* tendency to assimilate all other religious traditions and figures. For Ramachandra, such assimilation not only means denying the self-understanding and self-perception of the religious adherents themselves, but also creates a path to relativism, which hardly is a synonym for tolerance.[25] While by no means ignorant of the limits of doctrinal formulations, Ramachandra is concerned about the tendency of some Asian theologians to minimize or eliminate the cognitive content from the notion of "faith." He wonders if Samartha's indifference to matters of religious doctrine is more a product of post-Enlightenment secular consciousness than of a heightened religious sensibility. And he notes that even in the Indian religious tradition salvation/enlightenment is bound up with right belief.[26]

For Ramachandra, the Christian message is radically historical in its orientation. Therefore, evangelical theology cannot avoid the perennial problem of negotiating the particularity of Jesus and universality of the gospel. In contrast to pluralistic Christologies of Asia and the liberal agenda of the West, Ramachandra argues: "The normativeness and ultimacy of Jesus Christ in God's salvific dealings with his world . . . far from being an arbitrary and repressive doctrine, is *intrinsic to Christian praxis and self-understanding*, then and now."[27]

The normativeness of Jesus, however, rather than being something foreign imposed on Asian religions, in fact, "safeguards some of the legitimate concerns of contemporary Asian theologians."[28] Unlike the major Asian religions, Christianity, for example, takes seriously the cause of the poor, fully endorses the equality of all persons created in the image of God, and celebrates humility and self-sacrificial life and service, among other things. The "gospel of humanity" results in the creation of a new human community that celebrates plurality under one God. Furthermore, differently from many of his more conservative Western counterparts, Ramachandra argues that the problem of particularity should not be confused with the problem of the ultimate status of those who are not Christians.[29]

The challenge of inclusivist evangelicalism

A decade after the appearance of Norman Anderson's work, the leading North American senior evangelical scholar Clark Pinnock published his widely debated book with a title that conveys its basic dynamic, *A Wideness in God's Mercy: The Finality of Jesus Christ in a World of Religions* (1992).[30] In this and subsequent writings,[31] he has wanted to find a third option between relativism and "restrictivism" (Pinnock's word for exclusivism/particularism). The two poles of the Christian message, the universal will of God to save all and the finality of salvation only in Christ, are to be handled in a way that does not discourage evangelism, but on the other hand does not make salvation unavailable to most people. An evangelical theology of religions for Pinnock is governed by two foundational parameters. First is the biblical and theological basis for an optimism of salvation grounded in the love of God for all humanity. This opposes the "fewness doctrine" according to which only a small number of people will be saved. The second foundational concern is Christological. He calls for a high Christology, necessary for any evangelical theology of religions that takes the uniqueness of Jesus Christ for granted. But he does not understand it in a way that closes the door of salvation to the majority of people. While resisting attempts to conceive of incarnation as mythical (J. Hick and others) or truncate the orthodox doctrine of the Trinity, Pinnock "will insist just as emphatically that a high Christology does not entail either a pessimism of salvation or an exclusivist attitude toward people of other faiths."[32] He argues that God's redemptive work in Jesus Christ was intended to benefit the whole world.[33]

More recently known as the pioneer of "Open Theism," Pinnock champions a view of God that is of "unbounded generosity," which leads into a hermeneutic of hopefulness, a characteristic that was lost by the Augustinian doctrine of double predestination.[34] In his hermeneutic of hopefulness, Pinnock makes much of the example of "pagan saints" in the Bible, those from outside the elected community, yet included.[35] The key to hope for the unevangelized lies in Pinnock's idea of the faith principle:

according to the Bible, people are saved by faith, not by the content of their theology. Since God has not left anyone without witness, people are judged on the basis of the light they have received and how they have responded to that light. Obviously, people cannot be held responsible for not responding to revelation they never received.[36]

The later work *Flame of Love: A Theology of the Holy Spirit*[37] continues the inclusivist program and argues for a pneumatological theology of religions. In that outlook, counting against restrictivism is not only God's nature as Father and the universality of the atonement of Christ but also the ever-present Spirit, "who can foster transforming friendship with God anywhere and everywhere."[38] The gateway for Pinnock to an appreciation of a more unlimited ministry of the Spirit is the "cosmic range to the operations of the Spirit."[39] Emphasis on the Spirit's work in salvation should not be read as a denial of his work in creation on which it is based, as too often has been the case.[40]

The leading younger-generation evangelical theologian of religions, Amos Yong, has also worked hard in the area of an inclusivist theology. Reflecting his heritage as a Pentecostal (Assemblies of God) and coming from a Chinese-Malaysian background, he first produced a major work entitled *Discerning the Spirit(s)*,[41] in which he started searching for criteria to distinguish the work of God's Spirit from that of other spirits. In his recent *Beyond the Impasse* (2003), the move "toward a pneumatological theology of religions"[42] came to full fruition. While Trinitarian in his approach, Yong attempts to build a more inclusivist, yet Christologically orthodox approach to religions. It is significant that unlike Yong, most Pentecostals have tended to be quite particularist and aligned themselves with the more fundamentalist wing of evangelicalism in their theology of religions. Many charismatic evangelicals, however, have tended to be more open to the work of the Spirit outside the sphere of the church.[43]

Continuing dialogue within the evangelical camp

As has become clear above, there are two camps (with variations) within evangelicalism when it comes to other religions: particularist and inclusivist. Both camps share a lot in common, indeed, all the basic tenets of traditional orthodoxy from the divine inspiration of Scripture to the uniqueness of Christ to two religious ends, heaven or hell. The basic debate is about whether hope for eternal life can be extended beyond the borders of (confessing) Christians. This debate continues and is unlikely to reach any kind of conclusion.

John Sanders, himself an inclusivist, sets forth the following guide-lines to challenge his particularistic colleagues to open up for more hope:[44]

1. While for Christians salvation comes through faith in Jesus Christ, to others it may come by faithfully responding to God within the light given to them apart from hearing the gospel.
2. General revelation is more than just preparation for the gospel; it can also have salvific effects.
3. It is not unwarranted to believe that God is able to bring about salvation even for those who never heard.
4. To affirm the uniqueness of Christ and his incarnation does not have to mean necessarily the complete denial of all other divine manifestations among religions.
5. God is at work redemptively among all cultures and religions of the world in various times.

The particularist critique of this kind of challenge is predictable:[45] that the inclusivist argument fails exegetically; that the authority of Scripture has been compromised; that the historic Christian stance of Augustine, Calvin, and others in the Reformed tradition has been betrayed; that natural revelation is damning rather than salvific; that the missionary mandate of the church is jeopardized; that moderate evangelicals have conceded far too much to modernity.

WHITHER AN EVANGELICAL THEOLOGY OF RELIGIONS?

Defining the key issues

The foregoing discussion has revealed some key topics that seem to govern evangelical approaches to religions. Evangelical theologians seem to find the following topics the most critical:

1. The question of salvation: while there is a division in the evangelical camp as to the extent of God's salvific offer when it comes to those who have never heard, clearly soteriological issues have dominated discussions. This in turn reflects the earlier approach to the Christian theology of religions in general.
2. The status of Christ: again, echoing the earlier focus of the theology of religions discourse, much of evangelical reflection has focused on defending and elucidating the uniqueness of Christ. Both particularist and inclusivist evangelicals agree here.

3. The challenge of pluralism: to a growing degree, evangelicals both in the West and outside have taken a critical look at pluralistic ideology that posits a "rough parity" between religions.

4. The question of revelation: intertwined with all these issues is the role of Scripture. While there are some differences among evangelicals as to the extent and value of "natural" knowledge of God, they all place Scripture as the norming norm.

5. The epistemological challenge: the question of the criteria for establishing the truthfulness of the Christian message among religions has occupied a lot of evangelical thinking.

6. The urgency of mission and evangelism: all evangelicals agree on the biblical mandate of carrying on mission to all people. Even those evangelicals here named as inclusivists such as Anderson and Pinnock work hard not to give an impression of neglecting mission in light of their more open-minded approach.

The two newer approaches to the theology of religions among evangelicals as investigated above are the turn to pneumatology on the one hand and a new focus on studying living faiths to be able to speak specifically to some concrete issues in interfaith dialogue, on the other hand.

Toward a Trinitarian theology of religions

What are some of the ways evangelicals in the beginning of a new millennium may advance the theology of religions quest? In my recent *Trinity and Religious Pluralism: The Doctrine of the Trinity in Christian Theology of Religions* (2004),[46] I have taken my point of departure from the turn to pneumatology but expanded that movement toward building a genuinely Trinitarian approach to religions. I have attempted to offer a critical analysis of several existing theologies of religions from a Trinitarian perspective, such as those of some leading pluralists, Roman Catholics, and mainstream evangelicals as well.

In the development of a Trinitarian theology of religions I find the following themes critical.[47] First, I emphasize the criteriological role of the Trinity in helping distinguish the Christian God among other gods. The Christian God exists only as Father, Son, and Spirit. This approach resists the typical flaws of the theologies of religions in which either (as most often) the Spirit is divorced from the Son to be an itinerant deputy or Christology is cut off from its role as the Way to the Father. Thus, second, there is the critical relation of the Trinity to Christology.

While one does not need to be exclusivist in the question of the extent of salvation, only a "high" Christology makes the view of God as Trinity possible. This in turn, third, relates the Trinity to history (incarnation, cross, resurrection) and resists the kinds of approaches in which Jesus Christ is divorced from historical contours (such as Raimundo Panikkar's "Christic principle" according to which "Jesus is Christ but Christ is not Jesus").

Fourth, the Trinity safeguards an integral relationship between the Spirit, church, and kingdom of God. The presence of God through his Spirit in the world is Trinitarian. Thus, the Spirit's work is always related – even if not subordinated – to the Paschal mystery of Christ, and the goal of the Spirit's invitation is to form a community, the body of Christ. The church, while in no way identical to the kingdom of the triune God, the coming of which Jesus Christ serves in the power of the Spirit, is in the service of the kingdom and subservient to it.

Fifth, the triune God as communion represents both unity and diversity, thus making possible a genuine encounter with the Other. Christians, while commissioned to invite people of all religions to turn to everlasting communion with the triune God, are both enriched and challenged by the encounter with the Other, thus making them humble disciples. The Holy Spirit not only calls people to place their trust in God; the Spirit also calls Christians for a "relational engagement"[48] with the Other.

Further reading
Corduan, Winfried. *A Tapestry of Faiths: The Common Threads Between Christianity and World Religions.* Downers Grove, IL: InterVarsity, 2002.

Kärkkäinen, Veli-Matti. *An Introduction to the Theology of Religions: Biblical, Historical and Contemporary Perspectives.* Downers Grove, IL: InterVarsity, 2003.

Trinity and Religious Pluralism: The Doctrine of the Trinity in Christian Theology of Religions. Aldershot: Ashgate, 2004.

McDermott, Gerald R. *Can Evangelicals Learn from World Religions? Jesus, Revelation and Religious Traditions.* Downers Grove, IL: InterVarsity, 2000.

Netland, Harold. *Encountering Religious Pluralism: The Challenge to Christian Faith and Mission.* Downers Grove, IL: InterVarsity/Leicester: Apollos, 2001.

Okholm, Dennis L., and Timothy R. Phillips (eds.). *More Than One Way? Four Views on Salvation in a Pluralistic World.* Grand Rapids, MI: Zondervan, 1995.

Pinnock, Clark H. *A Wideness in God's Mercy: The Finality of Jesus Christ in a World of Religions.* Grand Rapids, MI: Zondervan, 1992.

Ramachandra, Vinoth. *The Recovery of Mission: Beyond the Pluralist Paradigm.* Carlisle: Paternoster, 1996.

Sanders, John. *No Other Name: An Investigation into the Destiny of the Unevangelized.* Downers Grove, IL: InterVarsity, 1995.

Tennent, Timothy C. *Christianity at the Religious Roundtable: Evangelicalism in Conversation with Hinduism, Buddhism, and Islam.* Grand Rapids, MI: Baker Academic, 2002.

Tiessen, Terrance L. *Who Can Be Saved? Reassessing Salvation in Christ and World Religions.* Downers Grove, IL/Leicester: InterVarsity, 2004.

Yong, Amos. *Beyond the Impasse: Toward a Pneumatological Theology of Religions.* Grand Rapids, MI: Baker Academic, 2003.

Notes

1. For basic concepts and issues, see Veli-Matti Kärkkäinen, *An Introduction to the Theology of Religions: Biblical, Historical and Contemporary Perspectives* (Downers Grove, IL: InterVarsity, 2003). Typologies are still in the making; the most widely used is that of exclusivism (to be saved, one needs to respond to the gospel offered by Christian proclamation), inclusivism (while Christ is the only Savior, in order to be saved one does not need necessarily to have an explicitly Christian faith response when that is not possible), and pluralism (all religions are basically equal ways of salvation). With all the critique against its limitations, for a general survey like this one, this typology still is useful at least heuristically and pedagogically. In my own book (following the Catholic Jacques Dupuis), I name these ecclesiocentrism, Christocentrism, and Theocentrism. Instead of using the term *exclusivism*, which easily becomes a pejorative term, here I prefer the term *particularism*, denoting the traditional Christian view according to which salvation entails a (personal) response of faith to the gospel offered by the proclamation of the church.

2. For current evangelical surveys and assessments, see Gerald R. McDermott, *Can Evangelicals Learn from World Religions? Jesus, Revelation and Religious Traditions* (Downers Grove, IL: InterVarsity, 2000), pp. 21–44; Winfried Corduan, *A Tapestry of Faiths: The Common Threads Between Christianity and World Religions* (Downers Grove, IL: InterVarsity, 2002), pp. 221–39; Harold Netland, *Encountering Religious Pluralism: The Challenge to Christian Faith and Mission* (Downers Grove, IL: InterVarsity, and Leicester: Apollos, 2001), pp. 48–51, 308–10; Timothy C. Tennent, *Christianity at the Religious Roundtable: Evangelicalism in Conversation with Hinduism, Buddhism, and Islam* (Grand Rapids, MI: Baker Academic, 2002), pp. 9–16. See also Ralph Covell, "Jesus Christ and the World Religions: Current Evangelical Viewpoints," in Charles van Engen, Dean S. Gilliland, and Paul Pierson (eds.), *The Good News of the Kingdom: Mission Theology for the Third Millennium* (Maryknoll, NY: Orbis, 1993), pp. 162–71; Terry C. Muck, "Evangelicals and the Interreligious Dialogue," *Journal of the Evangelical Theological Society* 36. 4 (1993): 517–29; "Is There Common Ground among Religions?" *Journal of the Evangelical Theological Society* 40. 1 (1997): 99–112; Stanley Grenz, "Toward an Evangelical Theology of the Religions," *Journal of Ecumenical Studies* 31 (1994): 49–65.

3. Sir Norman Anderson, *Christianity and World Religions: The Challenge of Pluralism* (Downers Grove, IL: InterVarsity, 1984).

4. See note 2 for bibliographical details.

5. For a detailed discussion, see Kärkkäinen, *Introduction to the Theology of Religions*, pp. 144–50.

6. The full text, from which the present citations come, can be found in *Christianity Today*, 19 June 1970, 844–46.

7. The text can be found, e.g., in "Lausanne Congress, 1974," in Gerald A. Anderson and Thomas F. Stransky (eds.), *Mission Trends No. 2: Evangelization* (New York: Paulist, 1975), pp. 239–48.

8. "The WEF Manila Declaration," in Bruce J. Nicholls (ed.), *The Unique Christ in Our Pluralistic World* (Grand Rapids, MI: Baker, 1994), p. 14.

9. *Ibid.*, p. 15.

10. For a succinct treatment, see McDermott, *Can Evangelicals Learn from World Religions?* pp. 28–34.

11. For representative voices, see Arthur Glasser, "A Paradigm Shift? Evangelicals and Interreligious Dialogue," *Missiology* 9 (1981): 392–408; John Piper, *Let the Nations Be Glad!* (Grand Rapids, MI: Baker, 1993); Ronald Nash, *Is Jesus the Only Savior?* (Grand Rapids, MI: Zondervan, 1994); Douglas R. Geivett and W. Gary Phillips, "A Particularist View: An Evidentialist Approach," in D. L. Okholm and T. R. Phillips (eds.), *More Than One Way? Four Views on Salvation in a Pluralistic World* (Grand Rapids, MI: Zondervan, 1995), pp. 211–45, 259–70; D. A. Carson, *The Gagging of God: Christianity Confronts Pluralism* (Grand Rapids, MI: Zondervan, 1996).

12. For evangelicals who are particularists yet more open to the question of the eternal destiny of those who have never heard, see, e.g., John Stott, *The Authentic Jesus* (London: Marshall Morgan and Scott, 1985); Klaas Runia, "The Gospel and Religious Pluralism," *Evangelical Review of Theology* 14 (October 1990): 341–79; Alister McGrath, "A Particularist View: A Post-Enlightenment Approach," in Okholm and Phillips (eds.), *More Than One Way?* pp. 149–80; Gordon T. Smith, "Religions and the Bible: An Agenda for Evangelicals," in Edward Rommen and Harold Netland (eds.), *Christianity and the Religions: A Biblical Theology of World Religions*, Evangelical Missiological Society Series 2 (Pasadena, CA: William Carey, 1995), pp. 9–29.

13. For a helpful discussion of Barth's influence on evangelicals in terms of the theology of religions, see Paul F. Knitter, *Introducing Theologies of Religions* (Maryknoll, NY: Orbis, 2002), pp. 23–31.

14. For a fuller account of each these theologians, see Kärkkäinen, *An Introduction to the Theology of Religions*, pp. 36–38.

15. Millard Erickson, *How Shall They Be Saved?* (Grand Rapids, MI: Eerdmans, 1996).

16. *Ibid.*, pp. 14–20.

17. *Ibid.*, p. 192.

18. A massive study (over 500 pages!) has recently come out by Terrance L. Tiessen, *Who Can Be Saved? Reassessing Salvation in Christ and World Religions* (Downers Grove, IL, and Leicester: InterVarsity, 2004) advocating a Reformed evangelical position, yet open to the limited possibility of salvation for those who have never heard.

19. Netland, *Encountering Religious Pluralism*, p. 18.

20. *Ibid.*, p. 125. Netland quotes from Wade Clark Roof, who speaks of "quest culture," in *Spiritual Marketplace: Baby Boomers and the Remaking of American Religion* (Princeton, NJ: Princeton University Press, 1999).

21. Harold Netland, *Dissonant Voices: Religious Pluralism and the Question of the Truth* (Grand Rapids, MI: Eerdmans, 1991). That book set forth ten criteria – such as logical principles, non-contradiction, coherence, and internal consistency – for assessing worldviews. Yet the proposal received quite a lot of critique from both evangelicals and others.

22. Netland, *Encountering Religious Pluralism*, pp. 325–27.

23. Vinoth Ramachandra, *The Recovery of Mission: Beyond the Pluralist Paradigm* (Carlisle: Paternoster, 1996).

24. His other titles include *Gods That Fail: Modern Idolatry and Christian Mission* (Downers Grove, IL: InterVarsity, 1996) and *Faiths in Conflict? Christian Integrity in a Multicultural World* (Downers Grove, IL: InterVarsity, 1999).

25. Ramachandra, *Recovery of Mission*, p. 17.

26. *Ibid.*, p. 20.

27. For the argumentation, see ch. 6 in *ibid.*, quotation on p. 216 (italics added).

28. *Ibid.*, p. 216.

29. *Ibid.*, p. 130.

30. Clark H. Pinnock, *A Wideness in God's Mercy: The Finality of Jesus Christ in a World of Religions* (Grand Rapids, MI: Zondervan, 1992).

31. Clark H. Pinnock, "The Finality of Jesus Christ in a World of Religions," in M. Noll and D. F. Wells (eds.), *Christian Faith and Practice in the Modern World: Theology from an Evangelical Point of View* (Grand Rapids, MI: Eerdmans, 1988), pp. 152–68; "Toward an Evangelical Theology of Religions," *Journal of the Evangelical Theological Society* 33 (1990): 359–68; "Evangelism and Other Living Faiths: An Evangelical Charismatic Perspective," in P. Hocken and H. D. Hunter (eds.), *All Together in One Place: Theological Papers from the Brighton Conference on World Evangelism* (Sheffield: Sheffield Academic Press, 1992), pp. 208–18; "An Inclusivist View," in Okholm and Phillips (eds.), *More Than One Way?* pp. 93–148.

32. Pinnock, *A Wideness in God's Mercy*, pp. 13–14.

33. *Ibid.*, p. 17.

34. *Ibid.*, pp. 18–20.

35. See *ibid.*, pp. 25–29 especially.

36. *Ibid.*, pp. 157–58 especially; the rest of ch. 5 is an elaboration of this principle.

37. Clark Pinnock, *Flame of Love: A Theology of the Holy Spirit* (Downers Grove, IL: InterVarsity, 1996), pp. 185–215.

38. *Ibid.*, pp. 186–87.

39. *Ibid.*, p. 49. In an ecumenical spirit, Pinnock quotes here with approval from Pope John Paul II who speaks of "the breath of life which causes all creation, all history, to flow together to its ultimate end, in the infinite ocean of God."

40. Pinnock, *Flame of Love*, p. 51. A case in point is evangelical theologian W. H. Griffith Thomas (*The Holy Spirit of God* [Grand Rapids, MI: Eerdmans, 1964], pp. 187, 196, 201) who preferred to bypass the cosmic activities of the Spirit as he saw them threatening the uniqueness of the gospel.

41. Amos Yong, *Discerning the Spirit(s): A Pentecostal-Charismatic Contribution to Christian Theology of Religions* (Sheffield: Sheffield Academic Press, 2000).

42. Amos Yong, *Beyond the Impasse: Toward a Pneumatological Theology of Religions* (Grand Rapids, MI: Baker Academic, 2003).

43. See further my "Toward a Pneumatological Theology of Religion: Pentecostal-Charismatic Contributions," *International Review of Mission* 91. 361 (April 2002): 187–98; "A Pneumatological Theology of Religion?" in Amos Yong (ed.), *Toward a Pneumatological Theology: Pentecostal and Ecumenical Perspectives on Ecclesiology, Soteriology, and Theology of Mission* (Lanham, MD: University Press of America, 2002), pp. 229–40.

44. John Sanders, *No Other Name: An Investigation into the Destiny of the Unevangelized* (Downers Grove, IL: InterVarsity, 1995), pp. 239–40.

45. As listed by Yong, *Discerning the Spirit(s)*, pp. 55–56.

46. Kärkkäinen, *Trinity and Religious Pluralism: The Doctrine of the Trinity in Christian Theology of Religions* (Aldershot: Ashgate, 2004).

47. *Ibid.*, pp. 164–84 especially.

48. Here I am indebted to the Catholic Trinitarian theology of religions of Gavin D'Costa, *The Meeting of Religions and the Trinity* (Maryknoll, NY: Orbis, 2000), pp. 109–17 especially.

14 Evangelical theology in African contexts

TITE TIÉNOU

This chapter examines the conscious and academic theologizing done by evangelicals on the African continent. The purpose thus stated seeks to specify the nature of the present study on one hand and, on the other hand, it acknowledges the fact that conscious academic theology is not necessarily the same as the theology lived and practiced by Christians on a daily basis, whether in Africa or elsewhere in the world. As we will see in the following pages, one needs to keep in mind the distinction between academic and lived theology as one explores evangelical theology in an African context. In light of the foregoing, then, I will first make some brief remarks on the words *evangelicalism, theology*, and *African*. Secondly, I will describe the background of contemporary Christian conscious theologizing in Africa. Thirdly, I will review the role of Byang Kato in determining the specificity of evangelical theology in Africa. This will bring us to the concluding section where the status of current concerns in evangelical theologizing in the continent will be examined.

PRELIMINARY CONSIDERATIONS

I begin this exploration of evangelical theology in an African context with preliminary considerations of the words *evangelicalism, theology*, and *African* in order to establish the broader context of the present task and also to minimize misunderstanding. The intention is to offer perspectives guiding the present endeavor. It is neither to define these words authoritatively and finally nor to deal with the voluminous literature on each one of them. These preliminary considerations will help establish the broader contextual factors of evangelical theology in Africa. It is appropriate that we begin with *evangelicalism*.

For our purposes here *evangelicalism* is used as Timothy George defines it. For him "Evangelicalism ... is a renewal movement within historic Christian orthodoxy with deep roots in the early Church, the

Reformation of the sixteenth century, and the great awakenings of the eighteenth century (and it includes puritanism, pietism, and pentecostalism as well as fundamentalism)."[1]

If one accepts George's definition, as I do, then evangelicalism would be viewed as a movement focused on fidelity to God's gospel. It is not located in specific organizations or ecclesiastical bodies. For the African continent this means that every effort must be made not to restrict evangelicalism to the Association of Evangelicals of Africa or to churches and schools castigated for what is presented as their defining characteristic, namely their "refusal of ecumenical dialogue."[2] In this regard it is worth noting that Tokunboh Adeyemo, third General Secretary of the Association, then known as the Association of Evangelicals of Africa and Madagascar, states that "an evangelical is one who believes in [the] good news, who has experienced ... redemption, who is committed to its propagation; and who lives steadfastly in obedience to the authority of the Book – the Word of God – as his rule of faith and practice."[3] Based on this, the label *evangelical* can and should be applied to millions of Christians in Africa, regardless of their church or denominational affiliation. Consequently, instead of seeing Christianity in Africa through the unhelpful and distorting contrast between evangelicals and ecumenicals, observers should recognize the fact that on the continent "[t]he mainline churches are increasingly evangelical in their worldview."[4] This reality of the complex nature of evangelicalism in ecclesiastical life raises a number of significant questions for understanding the scope of evangelical theology in an African context. For example, should one's inquiry be limited to self-identified evangelical persons and materials? Or should one include all materials and persons having an evangelical ethos? Moreover, has not the time come for a re-evaluation of some of the familiar groupings and typologies of the theological discourse in Africa? This is not the place to pursue an examination of these and similar questions. We will revisit them later. We now need to turn our attention to *theology*.

For Christians, theology is essentially an enterprise for facilitating the knowledge of, and obedience to, the self-revealed God.[5] Knowing God is expressed in a multifaceted way. It must be verbalized in words about God and religious matters but it must also be made visible in rituals and in the Christian's social interactions, whether these have to do with culture, economics, or politics. In that sense the existence of Christian life without theology is inconceivable.[6]

Christian theologizing in Africa did not have to await the publication of articles and monographs or the convening of symposia devoted to

"African Theology" because it existed, and continues to exist, in the prayers of African Christians, in their daily conversations, their songs, and in the sermons preached and heard, for these are some of the indicators of relating Scripture to various aspects of human life.[7] Can Christian theologians anywhere afford to neglect these other dimensions of theology? What are the consequences of the apparent distance between academic theology and what Millard Erickson calls "the issues of life"? In 1983 an editorial of *The East Africa Journal of Evangelical Theology* entitled "What is African Evangelical Theology?" warned that "African evangelical theology can never be merely academic. Its aim is intensely personal."[8] Evangelicals are not alone in the call to relate academic theology to the lives of ordinary Christians in Africa. It is noteworthy that in 2003 at least two theologians, one Catholic and the other Protestant, made pleas similar to the one found in the 1983 editorial. For Catholic Jean-Marc Ela, "African theology must make major changes in order for it to regain credibility in church and society."[9] Protestant Tharcisse Gatwa argues that "[a] link needs to be established between academic rigour and the requirements of the churches" because of what he calls "the lack of dialogue between theologians and the people of God in the churches."[10] It is ironic that African theology, an endeavor based on the necessity of taking the needs of the churches in Africa seriously, should be viewed as too preoccupied with academic concerns. There are, no doubt, many reasons for the present predicament of African theology. But, perhaps, none is more basic than defining what is Africa and what is meant by *African*. It is for this reason that I include here a brief scrutiny of *African*.

We have, thus far, used *Africa* and *African* without any indication that these words can be polemical in any way. Continuing on this path would be an error because "[t]rying to define, describe or explain 'Who is an African' is an issue that has often generated controversy. This may apply for the question 'What is Africa'."[11] Moreover, according to Efoé Julien Pénoukou, one needs to aware of the pitfall of "unscientific generalization" when speaking of "Africans" or "African tradition."[12] Yet many people, in the general public and in the academy, seem to pay little attention to the views expressed by Getui, Pénoukou, and others. The 1983 editorial of *The East Africa Journal of Evangelical Theology* illustrates the generalizing tendency. In it the editorialist asks "What makes evangelical faith African?" and suggests that "[t]he key is the area of application. African evangelical theology is simply evangelical theology applied to the African context."[13] The singular, "the African context," is surprising (even when the date of 1983 is taken into account) given the obvious diversity one finds in the continent. Is it possible that the notion of a single Africa and a single African context contributed to the distance between academic discussions of African theology and the regular pastoral concerns of Christians in the continent? While further analysis of this question cannot be undertaken here, one cannot hastily dismiss Bénézet Bujo's observation that "African theology, on the whole, remains elitist" and fails "to focus on the basic questions which Africans are raising."[14] What if this failure is due to what Pénoukou calls "unscientific generalization" about Africa and Africans? The history of the study of indigenous religions in Africa illustrates the problem of generalization.[15]

What can one do in light of the fact that generalization about Africa and Africans will likely continue for the foreseeable future? Recognition of its limited usefulness and acknowledgment of its potential perils seem to be wiser. After all, generalizations are unavoidable. But, if specificity is required, as is the case for theology, then generalizations have to be understood for what they are. So, it is important to keep in mind that this chapter is only about general issues of evangelical theology in Africa. No specificity is possible or attempted. Consequently, for our purposes here *Africa* refers to the continent. *African* is used as an adjective without the usual cultural, racial, or ethnic connotations. *Africa* and *African* are therefore more useful when making comparisons and contrasts with other continents.

ROOTS OF CONTEMPORARY CHRISTIAN THEOLOGY IN AFRICA

After establishing the broader context of evangelical theology in Africa, we now turn our attention to some of the historical events which marked the beginning of contemporary Christian theology in the continent. This is necessary because academic disciplines and movements of ideas are historically grounded. Understanding the history of a movement can often shed light on some of its present particularities. In the case of contemporary Christian theology in Africa, neglecting its history can have serious consequences.

The beginning of contemporary Christian theology in Africa can be dated with some accuracy since it is generally agreed that the publication of the book *Des prêtres noirs s'interrogent* in 1956 marks the birth of the quest for conscious self-theologizing by Africans. This book is a collection of essays by various Catholic authors and not all of them were priests or from Africa (for example the preface was written by Frenchman Marcel

Lefebvre, then Archbishop of Dakar and Apostolic Delegate for French West Africa and there were contributions by Caribbean authors such as Haitian J. C. Bajeux). The book was essentially a call for the recognition of the legitimacy of black and/or African voices in all aspects of the universal church, theology included.[16] These can be called cautious steps toward ecclesial and theological emancipation.[17]

Mention should be made of similar developments in Protestant circles. A specific example is Paul D. Fueter's article "Theological Education in Africa" published the same year in *The International Review of Missions*. Although Fueter, like the "black priests," did not articulate an African Christian theology, he did venture the suggestion that "the study of Biblical mythology ... give[s] us a background for an African theology, which will express in a language understandable to Africans those truths which we believe to be fundamental to our faith."[18]

What made 1956 such a significant year for African Christian theology? The answer to this question must be sought in the cultural and political changes that were taking place in the continent. In politics, ideologies of national self-determination and rule, which gained momentum after the Second World War, would lead to the independence of entities that were heretofore European colonies. So, in 1957 British Gold Coast became the independent and sovereign country of Ghana and in 1958 French Guinea became the Republic of Guinea. Thus began the decolonization of the many African territories held by European nations. This process would last about two decades. In most cases the claim to the right to political autonomy also included calls for religious and cultural emancipation and rehabilitation. Rosino Gibellini has ascertained correctly that "[i]t is against this backdrop of an African cultural rebirth that the problem of an 'African theology' arose in the 1950s and 1960s."[19] No one should therefore be surprised that the question of identity, with ramifications for the value of African cultures and religions, has been, and continues to be, an important issue in African Christian theology.

The question of identity, in one form or another, seemed to surface in the various discussions of African Christian theology from the 1950s and throughout the 1970s. These discussions took place in academic symposia and publications. They happened in ecclesial gatherings and media also. Since evangelical theology is the focus of this chapter, two Protestant ecclesial bodies, the All Africa Conference of Churches and the Association of Evangelicals of Africa, merit attention. 1963 marks the beginning of the All Africa Conference of Churches (AACC) but its history goes back to the Ibadan (Nigeria) conference of 1958. The AACC provided the auspices for many conferences and consultations which led to publications such as *Biblical Revelation and African Beliefs* edited by Kwesi Dickson and Paul Ellingworth (1969). In many ways the agenda for Protestant Christian theology in Africa was set by discussions and people more or less associated with the All Africa Conference of Churches. So, when the Association of Evangelicals of Africa (AEA) held its first General Assembly in 1969,[20] African theology had already received much attention from Catholics and Protestants. Byang Kato called attention to the importance of theology during the AEA's second General Assembly in 1973. It is for this reason that I provide a review of the role of Byang Kato in shaping the specificity of evangelical theology in Africa.

BYANG H. KATO AND EVANGELICAL THEOLOGY IN AFRICA

In his foreword to Sophie de la Haye's *Byang Kato: Ambassador for Christ*, Tokunboh Adeyemo presents Kato as one "whose name has become synonymous with the continent's Evangelical movement" and whose "emphasis was two-fold: the trustworthiness of the Word of God against all theological liberalism and the proper contextualization of theology in African setting without adulterating the Gospel."[21] Byang Henry Kato (1936–1975) was the first African evangelical noted for his participation in the debate on African theology. His publications, especially *Theological Pitfalls in Africa* (1975), cannot be ignored. Many Christians, in Africa and elsewhere, and not just rigid biblicists, would hold the same commitment to the final authority of the Bible. Not a few evangelicals would agree with his sentiment that "[a]lthough the *content* of the Bible remains the same the way of *expressing* it is changeable."[22] Yet, are these necessary and sufficient reasons for regarding Kato as the perennial representative and spokesperson for evangelical theology in Africa?

The continued portrayal of Kato as *the* representative of the evangelical type of theology in Africa is problematic for numerous reasons. Two will be noted here: first, Kato's works were published more than thirty years ago. Even without the complicating factor of his untimely death which prevented further maturation of his thought, is it really plausible to assume that no change happened in African evangelical circles after Kato's death? As we will see below, that assumption is flawed because "Kato's successors in Africa" have moved with the times in their thinking and preoccupations.

Kato is sometimes presented as a critic whose main contribution to African Christian theology is his negative attitude toward African cultures and religions. For instance, in a chapter devoted to Kato in his *Theology and Identity*, Kwame Bediako makes the assertion that "there is little in his [Kato's] outlook which does not stem from his deep roots in the conservative evangelical tradition – particularly the North American variant – of Christianity."[23] Toward the end of the chapter Bediako writes about Kato's "negative and unsympathetic posture towards the African pre-Christian religious heritage." This is the reason why, in Bediako's view, Kato "did not have an integrating framework for rooting the Christian faith in African tradition. In Kato's schema of the relationship between the Christian Gospel and the African heritage in religion, Africans, in practice, come to the Christian faith religiously and spiritually empty."[24] More recently, Bediako characterizes Kato as an extremist because of "the radical discontinuity stoutly championed by Byang Kato, representing the thought of those Christian churches and groups linked with the Association of Evangelicals of Africa."[25] Though he acknowledged, in *Theology and Identity* and in *Jesus and the Gospel in Africa*,[26] that evangelicalism in Africa is no more monolithic than other groups, Bediako's statement only reinforces the notion that African evangelicals are biblicists who see no value in African religions and cultures. Was Kato really a proponent of "radical discontinuity" as Bediako claims?

Given the serious implications of Bediako's claim, it is not surprising that some evangelicals in Africa have offered their own assessment of Kato's approach. Timothy Palmer's article "Byang Kato: A Theological Reappraisal" is one example. Palmer concludes that "Byang Kato is not a representative of 'radical discontinuity'; instead he is a mainline evangelical who sought to defend the faith and to contextualize it in the African culture ... An evaluation of the African church today would put Kato solidly in the mainstream of African Christianity."[27] One need not share Palmer's view that Kato would be "in the mainstream of African Christianity" in order to agree with him that Kato should not be seen as a proponent of "radical discontinuity." Indeed, when Bediako proposes that for the future "the task of African theology, [should] consist, not in 'indigenising' Christianity, or theology as such, but in letting the Christian Gospel encounter, as well as be shaped by, the African experience,"[28] he is not making a statement that Kato would have rejected *in toto*. After all, Kato is also known for these two statements: "Let *African* Christians be *Christian* Africans" and "Every effort should be made to make the gospel indigenous in the local culture where it has been introduced."[29] Unless it can be shown that Kato's intentions are opposed to what his two statements seem to indicate, one must conclude that he did take African contexts seriously. Perhaps he did not give the same positive value to African religions as other African scholars and theologians. But, does Christian identity not require Christians to evaluate their ancestral traditions in light of the gospel? Kato may not have drawn the conclusion some people wished he had, and he may have overstated his case here and there, yet this does not mean that he believed that "Africans . . . come to the Christian faith religiously and spiritually empty." Kato's approach was more in line with the idea that "[t]he context is not the source of theology. It is a starting point":[30] that aspect of Kato's legacy is legitimate and not antithetical to taking all aspects of African life seriously.

CURRENT CONCERNS IN EVANGELICAL THEOLOGY IN AFRICA

Kato's successors in the orbit of the Association of Evangelicals of Africa have continued to build on his legacy by focusing on the ecclesial vocation of Christian theology and by engaging in the intellectual and theoretical discussions related to African theology.

Isaac Zokoué, the former Dean of the Bangui Evangelical School of Theology in the Central African Republic, is an example of a person who is engaged in both tasks. He calls for a focus on "identity and spiritual maturity" in evangelical theology in Africa in the twenty-first century. He also stresses the need to transcend "the conflict between conservative theology and the necessity to evolve with the needs of the times."[31] Zokoué is not alone. Participants in a June 1999 consultation devoted to evangelical theology in Africa, which was convened by the Faculté de Théologie Evangélique de l'Alliance Chrétiennne of Abidjan (Côte d'Ivoire), expressed similar views. In February 2000 a continent-wide consultation, with the theme "Serving the Church: Leadership Development in Africa," was held on the campus of the Nairobi Evangelical School of Theology. Evangelicals in Africa have made significant progress. Such a focus on theology, pastoral concerns, and the multi-dimensional African reality could only be a matter for dreams and speculation in 1973. In this regard, the 1998 publication of *Issues in African Christian Theology* represents a significant indicator of the progress made in evangelical theologizing on the continent. Foundational and methodological concerns as well as the enduring issues of worldview and religions (African "traditional" religions and world religions) are addressed in this edited volume.[32]

There are also encouraging signs of African evangelicals' participation in substantial intellectual and theoretical discussions. Mabiala

Justin-Robert Kenzo is an example of an evangelical who is engaged in significant theoretical work. In his article "Thinking Otherwise about Africa: Postmodernism and the Future of African Theology," Kenzo argues that "postmodernism offers Christianity a unique opportunity to gain a hearing in Africa since it offers the promise of a truly contextual theology."[33] The point here is not that Kenzo's argument will convince everyone; rather it is that Kenzo, an African evangelical, is engaged in one of the most important topics of intellectual discussion of our time, thereby paving the way for future generations of evangelical theologians and scholars in the continent. These theologians and scholars will need to deal with new and complex issues (such as the one tackled by Kenzo) as well as the perennial issue of life and faith in Africa (for example, the burden of being African; poverty; ethnicity; religious pluralism) with intellectual rigor and probity together with a clear focus on the integrity of the gospel.

Conscious evangelical theologizing in Africa has now entered a very promising phase. Time will tell if expectations will become reality or not. The most pressing challenge for evangelical theology in Africa is the requirement to serve fully the needs of Christians and churches in Africa without being an appendix to Western or other theologies and also without being an exotic mixture of Christianity and African cultures or religions. Ultimately, African Christian theology is not about crafting new doctrines; it is rather about stating Christian teaching in language and thought forms understandable to Africans in their contemporary situations. In that sense, evangelical theology in Africa has the same obligations as evangelical theology anywhere; namely, it must contribute to the understanding of the gospel and the Christian message, translating the mystery of divine revelation into wisdom for daily living. When evangelical theology achieves that without denying the importance of Africa, it will be African.

Further reading

Bediako, Kwame. *Jesus and the Gospel in Africa: History and Experience.* Maryknoll, NY: Orbis, 2004.

Theology and Identity. Oxford: Regnum Books, 1992.

Breman, Christina Maria. *The Association of Evangelicals in Africa: Its History, Organization, Members, Projects, External Relations and Message.* Zoetermeer, The Netherlands: Uitgeverij Boekencentrum, 1996.

de la Haye, Sophie. *Byang Kato: Ambassador for Christ.* Achimota, Ghana: Africa Christian Press, 1986.

Gibellini, Rosino. *Paths of African Theology.* Maryknoll, NY: Orbis, 1994.

Kato, Byang H. *African Cultural Revolution and the Christian Faith.* Jos, Nigeria: Challenge Publication, n. d.

Ngewa, Samuel, Mark Shaw, and Tite Tiénou (eds.). *Issues in African Christian Theology.* Nairobi: East African Educational Publishers, 1998.

Schreiter, Robert J. (ed.). *Faces of Jesus in Africa.* Maryknoll, NY: Orbis, 1991.

Stinton, Diane B. *Jesus of Africa: Voices of Contemporary African Christology.* Maryknoll, NY: Orbis, 2004.

Notes

1. Timothy George, "Evangelicals and Others," *First Things* 160 (February 2006): 15. For other definitions of evangelical or evangelicalism, see David W. Bebbington, *Evangelicalism in Modern Britain: A History from the 1730s to the 1980s* (London: Unwin Hyman, 1989); Alister McGrath, *Evangelicalism and the Future of Christianity* (Downers Grove, IL: InterVarsity, 1995); Douglas A. Sweeney, *The American Evangelical Story: A History of the Movement* (Grand Rapids, MI: Baker Academic, 2005); and Timothy Larsen's initial chapter in this volume.

2. Tharcisse Gatwa, "Theological Education in Africa: What Prospects for Sharing Knowledge?" *Exchange* 32. 3 (2003): 203. It is rather telling that an article published on theological education in Africa in 2003 fails to take seriously self-described evangelical theological institutions and also states, without proof or nuance, "These churches represent trends in Christianity which have always kept their distance from those who joined the ecumenical movement. These divisions that were exported by the Europeans to Africa, a past into which Africans should no longer identify with, are being perpetrated today" (pp. 203–204; "perpetrated" should, perhaps, have been "perpetuated"). This is an astonishing statement in light of the complexity of history and of the reality on the ground.

3. Tokunboh Adeyemo, "What and Who is an Evangelical?" *AEAM: Association of Evangelicals of Africa and Madagascar: History and Ministries* (Nairobi: AEAM, n. d.), p. 6.

4. Timothy Palmer, "Byang Kato: A Theological Reappraisal," *Africa Journal of Evangelical Theology* 23. 1 (2004): 16.

5. My understanding of Christian theology is akin to Millard J. Erickson's. He defines theology as "that discipline which strives to give a coherent statement of the doctrines of the Christian faith, based primarily on the Scriptures, placed in the context of culture in general, worded in contemporary idiom, and related to issues of life" (*Christian Theology*, second edition [Grand Rapids, MI: Baker, 1998], p. 23).

6. Tharcisse Tshibangu, *La théologie africaine: manifeste et programme pour le développement des activités théologiques en Afrique* (Kinshasa: Editions Saint Paul Afrique, 1987), p. 7, states emphatically, "Il n'y a pas de vie d'Eglise sans théologie en activité" ("church life cannot exist without active theology").

7. Prayers and songs have been noted as indicators of Christian theology in Africa. See, for example, chapter 1 (pp. 4–19) of Kwame Bediako's *Jesus and the Gospel in Africa: History and Experience* (Maryknoll, NY: Orbis, 2004). This chapter contains excerpts of *Jesus of the Deep Forest*, the prayers of Ghanaian Christian woman Afua Kuma. One can also consult Diane B. Stinton's *Jesus of Africa: Voices of Contemporary African Christology* (Maryknoll, NY: Orbis, 2004). For

songs, see Howard S. Olson, "Singing our Theology," *Africa Theological Journal*, 15. 1 (1986): 16–28; Ezra Chitando, "Jesus Saves! Gospel Music as a Mode of Identity Formation in Zimbabwe," *Swedish Missiological Themes* 90. 2 (2002): 149–62; and Lovemore Togarasei, "African Oral Theology: The Case of Shona Christian Songs," *Swedish Missiological Themes* 91. 1 (2003): 67–80. For the role of orality in African Christian theology see John S. Mbiti, "Cattle are Born with Ears, Their Horns Grow Later: Towards an Appreciation of African Oral Theology," *Africa Theological Journal* 8. 1 (1979): 15–25. Wiel Eggen's remark must always be kept in mind. In his examination of African theological writings for the year 1994 he states: "[I]t must be clear that religous [sic] thought and its communication, especially in Africa, dispense almost entirely with writing" ("African Theological Journals in 1994," *Exchange* 24. 3 [1995]: 259).

8. "Editorial: What is African Evangelical Theology?" *The East Africa Journal of Evangelical Theology* 2. 1 (1983): 1–2. This journal has been renamed *Africa Journal of Evangelical Theology*.

9. Jean-Marc Ela, *Repenser la théologie africaine: Le Dieu qui libère* (Paris: Editions Karthala, 2003), p. 429. My own translation.

10. Gatwa, "Theological Education in Africa," p. 205. Likewise Simon Kofi Appiah contends that [p]eople can only live and practise their religion when that religion can be made anthropologically concrete" ("The Quest of African Identity," *Exchange* 32. 1 [2003]: 65).

11. Mary Getui, "Africa, Church and Theology: Do They Need Each Other?" *Ministerial Formation* 184 (January 1999): 29.

12. Efoé Julien Pénoukou, "Christology in the Village," in Robert J. Schreiter (ed.), *Faces of Jesus in Africa* (Maryknoll, NY: Orbis, 1991), p. 29.

13. "What is African Evangelical Theology?" p. 2.

14. Bénézet Bujo, "Africa: Theological Education and Its Implications in Africa," *Pro Mundi Vita Studies* 4 (1988): 33, 34.

15. For a very helpful examination of the effects of generalizations, in this case about religion in Africa, see Jan Platvoet and Henk van Rinsum, "Is Africa Incurably Religious?: Confessing and Contesting an Invention," *Exchange* 32. 2 (2003): 123–52. The authors contend that two well-known African scholars of religion in Africa, Mbiti and p'Bitek, "were inspired, and constrained, in their interpretation of the indigenous religions of Africa, by particular developments in Western intellectual history . . . Such generalizations seem always to contain more ideology than fact, being extrapolated from very limited historical data in highly selective and biased ways, and declared valid for the whole of 'Africa'." The authors conclude, correctly, that the religious reality in Africa is "much more varied and variable" (p. 153).

16. Note, for example, these statements by Joseph Thiam: "Africa is awaking from its sleep . . . She claims the right to speak. She asks to be heard; she has something to say" (*Des prêtres noirs s'interrogent, deuxième édition* [Paris: Les Editions du Cerf, 1957], p. 41, my own translation from the second edition. The first edition was published in Paris in 1956 by Présence Africaine).

17. Many years after 1956, Meinrad P. Hebga could still write a book calling for the emancipation of the churches of Africa. See his *Emancipation d'Eglises sous tutelle* (Paris: Présence Africaine, 1976). It is worth noting that the subtitle is

"Essay on the post-missionary era." In a 1977 article Sidbe Semporé described the situation of the day as one in which we, African Christians, "inherited a 'missionary' church hastily built for us and without us" ("Les églises d'Afrique entre leur présent et leur avenir," *Concilium* 126 [1977]: 15, my own translation). One should also keep in mind the fact that the need for the emancipation of African churches was stated before the middle of the twentieth century. For example, Mojola Agbebi (1860–1917) stressed the requirement of African agency in bringing about an indigenous African Christianity. See E. A. Ayandele, *A Visionary of the African Church: Mojola Agbebi (1860–1917)* (Nairobi: East African Publishing House, 1971).

18. Paul D. Fueter, "Theological Education in Africa," *The International Review of Missions* 45 (1956): 388.

19. Rosino Gibellini, "Introduction: African Theologians wonder . . . and Make Some Proposals," in Rosino Gibellini (ed.), *Paths of African Theology* (Maryknoll, NY: Orbis, 1994), p. 6.

20. The Association of Evangelicals of Africa was actually formed in 1966. In this regard the AEA has followed a pattern similar to the AACC with the first General Assembly held a few years after the creation of the organization. To date the best single volume study of the AEA is Christina Maria Breman's *The Association of Evangelicals in Africa: Its History, Organization, Members, Projects, External Relations and Message* (Zoetermeer, The Netherlands: Uitgeverij Boekencentrum, 1996).

21. Tokunboh Adeyemo, "Foreword," in Sophie de la Haye, *Byang Kato: Ambassador for Christ* (Achimota, Ghana: Africa Christian Press, 1986), pp. 11, 12.

22. Byang H. Kato, *African Cultural Revolution and the Christian Faith* (Jos, Nigeria: Challenge Publication, n. d.), p. 50 (italics in the original). It should be noted that J. K. Agbeti, whose views are criticized by Kato, wrote a statement very similar to Kato's: "Christianity and its theology will remain essentially the same universally, even though the expression of the faith may differ from place to place" ("African Theology: What It Is," *Presence* 5. 3 [1972]: 7).

23. Kwame Bediako, *Theology and Identity* (Oxford: Regnum Books, 1992), p. 386.

24. *Ibid.*, p. 414.

25. Bediako, *Jesus and the Gospel in Africa*, p. 55.

26. See *Theology and Identity*, p. 416 and *Jesus and the Gospel in Africa*, p. 55.

27. Timothy Palmer, "Byang Kato: A Theological Reappraisal," *Africa Journal of Evangelical Theology* 23. 1 (2004): 20.

28. Bediako, *Jesus and the Gospel in Africa*, p. 55.

29. Byang Kato, *African Cultural Revolution*, pp. 51 and 54. Italics in the original.

30. Michael J. Amaladoss, "Contextual Theology and Integration," *East Asian Pastoral Review* 40. 3 (2003): 266.

31. Isaac Zokoué, "The Crisis of Maturity in Africa," *Evangelical Review of Theology* 20. 4 (1996): 354.

32. Samuel Ngewa, Mark Shaw, and Tite Tiénou (eds.), *Issues in African Christian Theology* (Nairobi: East African Educational Publishers, 1998).

33. Mabiala Justin-Robert Kenzo, "Thinking Otherwise about Africa: Postmodernism and the Future of African Theology," *Exchange* 31. 4 (2002): 341.

15 Evangelical theology in Asian contexts

SIMON CHAN

INTRODUCTION

The approach adopted in this essay is largely descriptive, looking at some distinctive features of Asian evangelicalism. But in order to flesh out these features, some comparison and contrast will be made with its older, Western counterpart on the one hand and with non-evangelical expressions of Protestant Christianity in Asia on the other.

The terms "evangelical" and "theology" in the title as understood in the West cannot be transferred into Asia without further qualifications. This is because, as Paul Freston has pointed out, evangelicalism in the non-Western world cannot be defined in strictly institutional terms and in the way it is understood in the West.[1] One could still use a "working definition" like David Bebbington's which highlights four features: conversionism (the belief that lives can be changed), activism (the expression of the gospel in some form of effort, especially in mission and evangelism), biblicism (a particular regard for the Bible as a source and norm for truth), and crucicentrism (a stress on the sacrifice of Christ on the cross).[2] But these beliefs are much more widespread in Asia. There is, of course, an Asian evangelicalism that corresponds closely to its Western forms, including various national "evangelical fellowships" which maintain links with similar fellowships elsewhere under the umbrella of the World Evangelical Alliance (WEA), and regional theological fraternities affiliated with the WEA Theological Commission. In Asia, the latter is represented by the Asia Theological Association (ATA). Outside this formal grouping, there is a broad spectrum of Christians who could be described as evangelical in orientation. They include many Pentecostal bodies, some of which are not associated with any Western classical Pentecostal denominations, and significant parts of mainline Protestant denominations which over the years have become evangelical and even charismatic.[3] For reasons that we shall be showing later, many mainline

Protestant churches in Asia either did not imbibe the liberal spirit of their Western counterparts or abandoned it soon afterwards. Protestantism in China is a good case in point. The theology represented by the "very top" officials of the China Christian Church (CCC) is probably not shared by most of the members of CCC congregations or even their rank-and-file pastors, the theology of the latter being mostly evangelical and charismatic.[4]

"Theology" also needs to be qualified. What is usually understood by that term are the critical reflections expressed in essays, church confessions, official declarations, and statements by institutionally accredited theologians or theological fraternities whether evangelical or liberal. But this kind of theology belongs to a relatively small group of people, and it is doubtful if it adequately captures what goes on at the grassroots: the vast reservoir of implicit or "primary theology" (theologia prima) found in sermons, hymns, poetry, testimonies, etc. of the practitioners of the faith.[5] The latter type of theology is often placed within the category of "devotion" or "spirituality" but it is no less theological.[6] A study of evangelical theology in Asia cannot afford to ignore this rich theological resource. In short, to deal adequately with evangelical theology in Asia we will have to consider not only the explicit theology done by evangelical theologians, but also the implicit theology that runs through most Protestant denominations. But before we look at these, some explanation is needed for the largely evangelical nature of Asian Christianity.

THE EVANGELICAL CHARACTER OF ASIAN CHRISTIANITY

What we have just noted above about the nature of Christianity in China applies to many parts of Asia as well. There are two major reasons for this, one historical, the other ethnographic. Many churches in Asia, whether independent, Free Church-type or denominational, are either products of or deeply influenced by innumerable evangelical para-church organizations and non-denominational mission agencies. In many urban centers, campus groups like Inter-Varsity Fellowship, Navigators, and Campus Crusade for Christ have been important avenues for channeling converts to churches, regardless of their denominational backgrounds. This process has tended to blur denominational distinctives and strengthen their common evangelical roots.[7]

Perhaps a more basic reason for the essentially evangelical character of Asian Christianity is that evangelicalism has much in common with the spiritual instinct of Asians. It has been noted that most of the conversions in Asia occur among minority groups and tribal peoples where the primal religious instinct is particularly pronounced. But where the core population belongs to one of the "world religions" the impact of Christianity is minimal, except in Korea and Singapore.[8] Even in these countries the situation may not be so exceptional when we consider that the bulk of conversion has come from adherents of shamanistic forms of Buddhism, Daoism, and Confucianism.[9]

The close affinity between Christianity and primal religions has been noted in other contexts, such as Africa.[10] This primal worldview in Asia is often described as "premodern," but this is using the categories derived from the Western intellectual tradition of rationalism. To call it premodern assumes that it represents an earlier stage of human development that needs to be outgrown eventually. Since this is often the operating assumption of many mainline Asian theologians, their Asian version of Christianity turns out to be essentially a Christianity viewed from the constricted perspective of the Enlightenment.[11] In contrast, the primal worldview sees reality in its totality and affirms a spiritual world behind the world of observable reality. Such a world has closer affinities with evangelicalism with its emphasis on spiritual conversion ("born again") than with liberal Protestantism. It resonates even more deeply with the Pentecostal-charismatic world.[12]

The preponderance of evangelical and charismatic elements has resulted in the emergence of a new form of ecumenism where denominational loyalties are transcended and traditional divisions between mainline and non-mainline no longer apply. Although similar patterns are emerging in the West,[13] what is different in some parts of Asia is that evangelicals have found it possible to cooperate with traditional "mainliners" within a broader framework like the National Council of Churches, resulting in a much revitalized NCC.[14] At the international level, exchanges are now occurring between Asian and African churches.[15] It must be noted, however, that pragmatic rather than theological considerations usually underlie these ecumenical impulses, such as the need to cooperate in evangelism and to deal collectively with civil authorities.

EVANGELICAL THEOLOGY AS EXPLICIT THEOLOGY

The explicit theology of Asian evangelicals is perhaps best represented by the ATA. A quick look at the various ATA theological consultations shows that Asian evangelicals have much in common with their counterparts elsewhere. First, there is a serious commitment to the norms of Scripture (Bebbington's "biblicism"). As Ken Gnanakan, former general-secretary of the ATA, puts it, "if there is one thing that holds evangelicals together all over the world it is their commitment to demonstrate this . . . fact that the reliable and authoritative Bible has something essential to say to a world that needs to hear God's message."[16] The concern for scriptural authority was articulated in the sixth ATA consultation in Seoul in 1982 under the theme "The Bible and Theology in Asia Today." The Bible was described as "infallible and inerrant" and syncretism was rejected because it made culture more determinative than Scripture and compromised the integrity of the gospel.[17] For most evangelicals context is always subservient to Scripture. In their theological reflection the general tendency is to use doctrines to elucidate the Asian context rather than vice versa.[18]

"Conversionism" and "crucicentrism" are equally pronounced, as seen in the ninth ATA consultation in Seoul. Whether one is preaching the gospel in the Hindu, Islamic, or Buddhist contexts, the common presupposition for these evangelical theologians is the lostness of fallen humanity and the need of conversion to Christ.[19] The importance of conversion for evangelical theology cannot be underestimated. This is poignantly demonstrated by Vishal Mangalwadi in his work as founder-director of the Association for Comprehensive Rural Assistance in India. Mangalwadi discovered early in his ministry among the poor villagers that legislative changes alone would not fundamentally change the structure of a caste-based society if the oppressed simply accepted their lot assigned them by the iron law of karma. Seeking structural changes (à la liberation theology) is well-nigh impossible where oppressors are not a few people at the top, but number in the hundreds of thousands. The only way to free the victims from "mental and ideological slavery" is the Christian message of conversion. As he puts it, "Oppressive systems survive by propagating falsehood. Evangelism liberates by spreading truth, i.e. by undercutting the intellectual foundations of an exploitative system and by creating an alternative social structure which seeks to live out the truth."[20]

Evangelicalism would lose its essential character without "conversionism." At the same time Asian evangelicals are also acutely conscious of the need to articulate the common evangelical concerns in a distinctively Asian way in order to address distinctively Asian problems. They repeatedly highlight methodological issues, focusing mainly on the non-dualistic, concrete ways of doing theology in Asia using stories, parables, and songs, as opposed to the Cartesian, abstract, or "Greek" way of the West.[21] But so far little has been done that actually *applies* the "Asian way of thinking" to theology. What we do find are the extensive use of stories in sermons[22] and Asian themes in songs.[23] In short, more contextual theology is being done implicitly than explicitly. Underlying the emphasis on methodology is the concern to make the gospel "relevant to the peoples of Asia who seek after God and yet grieve him by creating and worshipping gods of their own making."[24] If the gospel is to have any deep influence on Asia it has to address religious, social, political, and economic issues peculiar to the continent. Thus the "Seoul Declaration" (1982) calls on evangelicals "to grapple with such questions as the resurgence of indigenous religions, the struggle for justice in the face of oppression, totalitarian ideologies and regimes, the tensions between traditional values, corruption, and modern consumerism."[25]

The evangelical commitment to holistic mission has become more evident since the Lausanne Congress on World Evangelization (1974).[26] But what Asian evangelicals understand as holistic differs somewhat from liberal Protestantism. For one thing, their understanding of issues like racism and sexism does not presuppose Western egalitarianism or the feminist rejection of biblical norms.[27] Furthermore, for Asian evangelicals the priorities of the church in Asia lie elsewhere. Of greater concern are the challenges posed by rapid technological changes in many Asian societies, such as the impact of global trends like market capitalism and information technology.[28]

Unlike many mainline Asian Protestants, Asian evangelicals also take seriously their ethnographic contexts and reject their reductionistic interpretations.[29] Principalities and powers are not just descriptions of political and social structures but spiritual realities as well.[30] It is precisely because of this that issues such as ancestral veneration and food offered to deceased ancestors and idols are major concerns for evangelicals in East Asia.[31] But on such questions as when veneration becomes worship and how to distinguish the social from the religious dimensions of ancestor practices, Asian evangelicals have difficulty forging a broad consensus.[32] These intractable questions continue to exercise the church in Asia today as they have in the past.[33]

But it is in the area of mission that Asian evangelicals have expended most of their energies. It would not be an exaggeration to say that much of evangelical Asian theology is mission theology.[34] The reason is not hard to find. Asia is where the challenge of the world's major religions is most acutely felt. How is the church to proclaim the uniqueness of Christ in the concrete world of rival truth claims without being perceived as arrogant and imperialistic? Non-evangelicals have generally adopted some form of pluralist theory that downplays the uniqueness of the gospel, but for evangelicals this would undermine the very essence of mission. As Gnanakan puts it, "Our commitment to God's mission will only be a real commitment if it is based on a conviction of its uniqueness."[35] The pluralists, according to Gnanakan, "are not saying anything different to [sic] what the liberal Hindu has been saying all along [that] all religions are of equal value and lead to the same God."[36] Gnanakan, however, is no "hard line exclusivist," preferring an agnostic view about the salvation of non-Christians, a position similar to the views of Lesslie Newbigin, Clark Pinnock, and John Stott.[37] What the gospel of Jesus Christ requires us to affirm is both "the particularity of salvation through Jesus Christ alongside the universal availability of God's grace."[38]

The challenge that pluralism poses to Christian mission is also taken up by the Sri Lankan, Vinoth Ramachandra, in a carefully nuanced essay criticizing the pluralists Stanley Samartha, Aloysius Pieris, and Raimundo Pannikar. He shows that these writers, while championing Asian contextual theologies, are in fact deeply influenced by post-Enlightenment thought.[39] His critique of Pieris highlights a characteristic we noted earlier of liberal theology in its liberationist form, namely, its reductionist tendency.[40] For example, in Pieris, sin is reduced to the oppression of Mammon, and consequently liberation is understood only in terms of oppressor and oppressed. The nature of the situation, according to Ramachandra, is far more complex: human beings are simultaneously executioner, victim, and spectator. Similarly, Pieris understands the "religious consciousness of the poor" in largely socio-political terms, whereas Ramachandra argues that the "religious consciousness of the poor" in Asia has more to do with shamanism, magic, avoiding evil spirits, and finding good fortunes. These realities are either ignored or reduced to social dynamics in liberal theology.[41] He concludes that "unless we reflect biblically, rather than pragmatically or ideologically, on the diverse forms of human suffering, all our praxis will simply short-circuit."[42] It is evangelical theology in its serious grappling with Scripture and the Christian tradition that provides a wider horizon for evaluating the complex human condition in Asia, whereas a theology reduced to a political ideology often ends up quite blind to the dangers from below. For example, Pieris's hailing the Iranian revolution under the ayatollahs and C. S. Song's singing the praises of the communist revolution under Mao Zedong as liberation movements are both misguided and naive as subsequent histories of these countries have shown.[43]

EVANGELICAL THEOLOGY AS IMPLICIT THEOLOGY

Theology, as noted earlier, should not be confined to critical reflection on the truths of the Christian faith and its results; a larger part of theology is being done in the stories, testimonies, and songs coming from ordinary Christians. This process is no less a theological reflection of their understanding of God, albeit implicitly, and could therefore be called implicit or primary theology, or in William Dyrness's term, "vernacular theology." It is a process of "working on the whole symbolic complex of a community's Christian life so as to distill a vocabulary in which its meaning can be described, shared, and then valued."[44] When implicit theologies are not taken into consideration, it is not surprising that the theological contributions of large segments of the Christian church in Asia often go unrecognized. This is the case with Paul Freston's study of evangelicals and politics in the Third World. When Asian Christianity is evaluated according to theories and practices of political engagement developed in the West (namely, the Niebuhrian or Moltmannian "political theology"), it is no wonder that many Asian evangelicals would be perceived as apolitical. Thus little is said about the socio-political impact of Pentecostals in Korea. Yet, these supposedly apolitical Christians may have done more to influence the politics of their land in other ways, as Allan Anderson has argued.[45] Similarly, Thomas Harvey, in his study of Wang Mingdao, has shown that what is perceived from the political theology viewpoint as apathetic is actually a subtle form of political critique.[46] Given the very different socio-political conditions which set the contexts for churches in Asia, it would appear that the "theological politics" of Wang and the house churches, and the Pentecostals in many parts of Asia, constitutes a far more effective form of social engagement.[47]

Space does not permit us to do more than highlight a few features of this implicit theology and to show how such a theology could further enrich our understanding of evangelical theology in Asia. The house churches of China are a good place to begin. Dyrness describes the "theological framework" of the house churches as Christocentric, with the following features clearly discernible: following Christ in his suffering and testifying to what Jesus has done in day-to-day living. Not uncommonly, they experience healings, conversions, and miraculous interventions in response to prayer. The Bible is assiduously read and taken at face value. Their shared experience of the gospel of Jesus Christ has led to a kind of ecumenical networking among the house churches.[48] While in recent years they have become more theologically articulate,[49] there are still many aspects of their spirituality that have not attracted much theological reflection. Take, for example, their accounts of physical healings and miraculous escapes from prison among many others.[50] How do these experiences affect our traditional doctrine of salvation? For one, they show that salvation is not just about psychological well being (the peace and joy in standard evangelical testimonies of conversion), but is concrete and holistic, affecting the *physical* dimension of existence. The experience of many Asian Christians has shown that the biblical idea of the Holy Spirit as the foretaste of the new creation (2 Cor. 1:22; Eph. 1:13, 14) is more than an idea; it is a present reality.

As noted earlier, evangelicalism, especially its Pentecostal-charismatic version, shares much in common with the primal religions. One of the main characteristics of primal religions is their sacramental worldview, that is, the understanding that "the 'physical' acts as a vehicle for 'spiritual' power."[51] What we find among many Asian evangelicals is that they are more sacramental than they are ready to admit. Practices like prayer with laying-on-of-hands and anointing with oil,[52] and the quasi-magical regard for baptism and the Lord's Supper especially among the illiterate, represent an implicit sacramental theology.[53] Yet, in line with the Free Church tradition, the Eucharist is usually given a "memorialist" interpretation. Perhaps Asian evangelicals should consider bringing their explicit theology in line with their primary theology and with the liturgical tradition of the ancient church.

One of the most interesting, if controversial, features of implicit theology is found in the testimonies of what I would call "the strange works of God," such as this one: a non-Christian woman walked into a Pentecostal church in Singapore one Sunday morning, and went through the motions of worship with the rest of the congregation, standing when they stood, sitting when they sat, raising her hands when they raised theirs. Then she prayed, "Jesus, if you are real, give me a lottery number!" When she opened her eyes she saw four digits projected on the screen. She left the church, betted on the number, and won. The next week she returned to testify that Jesus was indeed real![54] One could ostensibly explain it away as sheer coincidence, except that I have personally encountered similar testimonies (usually involving lotteries). Evangelicals who seem to know beforehand what God's answer is to the ethics of gambling are, quite understandably, uncomfortable. But rather than dismiss them out of hand, the strange ways of God should force us to rethink some of our long-standing assumptions. For one thing, they may force us to rediscover what we have long forgotten. In this case, we learn that a highly respected Puritan theologian Richard Baxter actually had a far more nuanced view about gambling than many today who claim to be his heirs. In his massive work on casuistry, *A Christian Directory*, Baxter argues that wagering is legitimate provided that three conditions are met.

> 1. That the true end of the wager is to be a penalty to him that shall be guilty of a rash and false assertion, and not to gratifie the covetousness of the other. 2. That it be no greater a summ than can be demanded and paid, without breach of charity, or too much hurt to the looser . . . 3. That it be no other but what both parties are truly willing to stand to the loss of. . .

Other types of wager he mentions are cards, dice, and lottery; wagering over sports like bowling, running, and shooting would all be acceptable if "your wager be laid for sport, and not for covetousness."[55] The issue for Baxter was not the act *per se* but the motive. But deeper theological issues are involved besides the ethics of gambling: what do such stories teach about the concept of *praeparatio evangelii*, God's mysterious work in non-Christians, the nature and extent of contextualization (does God accommodate himself even to human foibles, in this case the Chinese penchant for gambling?)? Perhaps a larger question would be, what is the role of non-Christian religions in the salvific plan of God?[56]

It is from such implicit theologies that new possibilities arise. Secondary theologies grow out of the church's living witness to the life, death, and resurrection of Jesus Christ in the power of the Holy Spirit.[57] This is not to state a case for making individual experiences the starting point and norm of theology; rather, it is to recognize that *ecclesial* experience is the substance of primary theology.[58]

CONCLUSION

How should Asian evangelical theology be assessed? In terms of explicit theology, Asian evangelicalism has much in common with evangelicalism in the West. Although Asian evangelicals often contrast the "Asian way of thinking" with the rationalism of the West, it should be noted that this way of thinking is not exclusively Asian as it has much in common with the spiritual exegesis of the church fathers and certain strands of postmodern thought.[59] One hopes, however, that Asian evangelicals would move beyond theological method to showing how it should be applied.

Compared with their Asian mainline counterparts, Asian evangelicals take ethnographic contexts much more seriously by refusing to reduce the spiritual world to sociological categories. Herein lies the strength of evangelical theology. Its serious grappling with "spiritual reality" is what accounts for much of its missionary success especially in tribal societies. But Asian evangelicalism may be a victim of its own success. In places where Christianity has acquired a majority status, evangelicalism has also undergone radical change. In Nagaland, northeast India, where the vast majority of the Christians are Baptist, the Baptist polity of church–state separation no longer applies. Corruption affects both state and church, and tribalism is rampant.[60] Another problem comes from taking the primal religious worldview too seriously. It gives rise to the temptation to manipulate spiritual power, thus reducing Christianity to a form of magic.[61] Coupled with this, the fine balance in biblical eschatology is resolved into an over-realized eschatology that focuses almost exclusively on "blessings" and denies the present reality of suffering.[62]

In their understanding of social engagement, Asian evangelicals have tended to rely rather heavily on the "political theology" model of engagement. It would appear that complex situations such as India's, and the minority status of Christianity in many parts of Asia, require more than political theology. Asian evangelicals will have to consider other options, such as Stanley Hauerwas's "theological politics."[63] The significance of the Hauerwasian approach is that it focuses on ecclesial life and this will inevitably deepen the appreciation of the church's primary theology. Asian evangelicals are only beginning to do this, especially the Pentecostals.[64] It is in the systematic reflection on the ongoing primary theology of the church and making it explicit that Asian evangelicalism is likely to make a distinct contribution to the larger church.

Further reading

Aikman, David. *Jesus in Beijing.* Washington, DC: Regnery, 2003.

Anderson, Allan, and Edmond Tang (eds.). *Asian and Pentecostal: The Charismatic Face of Christianity in Asia.* Oxford and Costa Mesa, CA: Regnum Books, and Baguio, Philippines: APTS Press, 2005.

Bieler, Samuel, and Stacey Bieler (eds.). *Chinese Intellectuals and the Gospel.* Vancouver: China Horizon, 1999.

Freston, Paul. *Evangelicals and Politics in Asia, Africa and Latin America.* Cambridge: Cambridge University Press, 2001.

Gnanakan, Ken (ed.). *Salvation: Some Asian Perspectives.* Bangalore: ATA, 1992.

Biblical Theology in Asia. Bangalore: Theological Book Trust, 1995.

Harvey, Thomas A. *Acquainted with Grief: Wang Mingdao's Stand for the Persecuted Church in China*. Grand Rapids, MI: Brazos, 2002.

Hwa Yung. *Mangoes or Bananas? The Quest for an Authentic Asian Christian Theology*. Oxford: Regnum, 1997.

Kuo, Eddie, Jon S. T. Quah, and Tong Chee Kiong. *Religion and Religious Revivalism in Singapore*. Singapore: Ministry of Community Development, 1988.

Lambert, Tony. *China's Christian Millions: The Costly Revival*. London: Monarch, 1999.

Ma, Wonsuk, William Menzies, and Hyeon-sung Bae (eds.). *David Yonggi Cho: A Close Look at his Theology and Ministry*. Seoul: Hansei University Press, and Baguio City: APTS Press, 2004.

Mangalwadi, Vishal. *Truth and Social Reform*. London: Spire, 1989.

Ro, Bong Rin, and Ruth Eshenaur (eds.). *The Bible and Theology in Asian Contexts: An Evangelical Perspective on Asian Theology*. Bangalore: ATA, 1988.

Ro, Bong Rin (ed.). *Christian Alternatives to Ancestor Practices*. Taichung, Taiwan: ATA, 1985.

Sng, Bobby. *In His Good Time: The Story of the Church in Singapore, 1819–2003*. Singapore: Bible Society of Singapore and Graduates' Christian Fellowship, 2003.

Notes

1. Paul Freston, *Evangelicals and Politics in Asia, Africa and Latin America* (Cambridge: Cambridge University Press, 2001), p. 2.

2. David Bebbington, *Evangelicalism in Modern Britain: A History from the 1730s to the 1980s* (London: Unwin Hyman, 1989), p. 3.

3. In this essay we will leave out Christians who are in some respects evangelical, but whose institutional identity and theology are somewhat ambiguous. The "cultural Christians" among the Chinese intellectuals are a good case in point. (Similar non-institutional forms of Christianity are found in Japan and India.) In terms of their potential influence, cultural Christians could well become a dominant feature of Christianity in China. See Samuel and Stacey Bieler (eds.), *Chinese Intellectuals and the Gospel* (Vancouver: China Horizon, 1999), chs. 7 and 8.

4. This fact has been pointed out by many observers of the church in China. See Tony Lambert, *China's Christian Millions: The Costly Revival* (London: Monarch, 1999), p. 110; David Aikman, *Jesus in Beijing* (Washington, DC: Regnery, 2003), pp. 136–37; Gotthard Oblau, "Pentecostals by Default? Contemporary Christianity in China," in Allan Anderson and Edmond Tang (eds.), *Asian and Pentecostal: The Charismatic Face of Christianity in Asia* (Oxford and Costa Mesa, CA: Regnum Books, and Baguio, Philippines: APTS Press, 2005), pp. 411–36, esp. pp. 418–19.

5. The distinction between primary and secondary theology has been much more clearly explicated in the field of liturgical theology, perhaps because of its central guiding principle: *lex orandi lex credendi* (the rule of praying is the rule of believing). See, e.g., Aidan Cavanagh, *On Liturgical Theology* (New York: Pueblo, 1984).

6. See, e.g., William A. Dyrness, *Invitation to Cross-Cultural Theology: Case Studies in Vernacular Theologies* (Grand Rapids, MI: Zondervan, 1990); Chan Kim-Kwong and Alan Hunter, *Prayers and Thoughts of Chinese Christians* (London: Mowbray, 1991).

7. Singapore is a classic example. See Bobby Sng, *In His Good Time: The Story of the Church in Singapore, 1819–2003* (Singapore: Bible Society of Singapore and Graduates' Christian Fellowship, 2003), pp. 262–68. The United Church of Christ in the Philippines has seen remarkable growth in some of their conferences as a result of greater acceptance of graduates from evangelical seminaries in recent years. In the Lowland Cavite and South Manila Conference (LCSMC) some 70 percent of the 140 ministers are evangelical (Interview with Rev. Carlos de la Cruz, a former conference minister of the LCSMC).

8. Freston, *Evangelicals and Politics*, pp. 59–60.

9. The similarities between Korean Christianity, especially its Pentecostal variety, and shamanism have been noted by Walter Hollenweger, *Pentecostalism: Origins and Developments Worldwide* (Peabody, MA: Hendrickson, 1997), pp. 99–105 and others. But how that relationship is to be understood is a matter of dispute among Pentecostal scholars. See Allan Anderson, "The Contextual Theology of David Yonggi Cho," in Wonsuk Ma, William Menzies, and Hyeonsung Bae (eds.), *David Yonggi Cho: A Close Look at his Theology and Ministry* (Seoul: Hansei University Press, and Baguio City: APTS Press, 2004), pp. 133–59. In Singapore, there are other factors that draw converts to Christianity. The younger, English-educated people find Christianity more intellectually attractive compared to Chinese folk religions and Daoism, which are highly ritualistic and lack an explicit theology. See Eddie Kuo, Jon S. T. Quah, and Tong Chee Kiong, *Religion and Religious Revivalism in Singapore* (Singapore: Ministry of Community Development, 1988).

10. Kwame Bediako, *Jesus in Africa: The Christian Gospel in African History and Experience* (Ghana: Regnum Africa, 2000), ch. 7.

11. See the evangelical Vinoth Ramachandra's trenchant critique of the theologies of Samartha, Pieris, and Pannikar in *The Recovery of Mission: Beyond the Pluralist Paradigm* (Grand Rapids, MI: Eerdmans, 1996).

12. Harold Turner, "The Primal Religions of the World and their Study," in *Australian Essays in World Religions* (Bedford Park: Australian Association of World Religions, 1977), pp. 32, 37.

13. See Cecil M. Robeck, "The New Ecumenism," in Max L. Stackhouse, Tim Dearborn, and Scott Paeth (eds.), *The Local Church in a Global Era: Reflections for a New Century* (Grand Rapids, MI: Eerdmans, 2000), pp. 168–77.

14. Thomas Harvey, "Engagement Reconsidered: The Fall and Rise of a National Council in Singapore," *Trinity Theological Journal* 14 (2006): 48–70. This is in marked contrast to George Lindbeck's observation of the lack of ecumenical interest in the Singapore and Malaysian churches in the late 1960s. See "The Present Ecumenical and Church Situation in West Malaysia and Singapore," *Southeast Asian Journal of Theology* 11 (Autumn 1969): 72–81.

15. Rosalind I. J. Hackett, "New Directions and Connections for African and Asian Charismatics," *Pneuma: The Journal of the Society for Pentecostal Studies* 18. 1 (Spring 1996): 69–77.

16. Ken Gnanakan (ed.), *Biblical Theology in Asia* (Bangalore: Theological Book Trust, 1995), p. v.

17. "The Bible and Theology in Asia Today: Declaration of the Sixth Asia Theological Consultation," in *ibid.*, pp. 261, 266–67. See also Bruce Nicolls, "A Living Theology for Asian Churches: Some Reflections on the Contextualization Syncretism Debate," in *ibid.*, pp. 26–32.

18. E.g., Sunand Sumithra's *Holy Father: A Doxological Approach to Systematic Theology* (Bangalore: Theological Book Trust, 1993), one of a few full-length Asian evangelical systematic theologies, argues for the primacy of Scripture (pp. 80–82). Contrast this with the more liberal Korean theologian Jung Young Lee's *The Trinity in Asian Perspective* (Nashville, TN: Abingdon, 1996) which reinterprets Trinitarian doctrine in terms of Daoist philosophy.

19. Ken Gnanakan (ed.), *Salvation: Some Asian Perspectives* (Bangalore: ATA, 1992).

20. Vishal Mangalwadi, *Truth and Social Reform* (London: Spire, 1989), pp. 36–37.

21. Rodrigo Tano, "Towards an Evangelical Asian Theology"; Saphir P. Athyal, "Towards an Asian Christian Theology" Lorenzo Bautista, Hildalgo B. Garcia, and Sze-Kar Wan, "The Asian Way of Thinking in Theology"; in Bong Rin Ro and Ruth Eshenaur (eds.), *The Bible and Theology in Asian Contexts: An Evangelical Perspective on Asian Theology* (Bangalore: ATA, 1988) pp. 93–118; 49–62; 167–82 respectively. These essays were reprinted in Gnanakan (ed.), *Biblical Theology in Asia*. See also Peter Chang, "Steak, Potato, Peas and Chopsuey: Linear and Non-Linear Thinking in Theological Education," *Evangelical Review* (October 1981): 279–86; Moonjang Lee, "Reconfiguring Western Theology in Asia," *Trinity Theological Journal* 10 (2002): 31–40.

22. E.g., John Sung, *Revival Sermons*, trans. Timothy Tow (Singapore: Alice Doo, 1983).

23. E.g., many songs of Xiaomin, a peasant girl from the house church, celebrate the beauty of creation and victory in the midst of suffering. See *The Cross: Jesus in China*, no. 4 [DVD] (China Soul for Christ Foundation).

24. "Confession of Faith: 9th ATA Theological Cousultation 1990," in Gnanakan (ed.), *Salvation*, p. 185.

25. "Toward an Evangelical Theology for the Third World: the Seoul Declaration," in Gnanakan (ed.), *Biblical Theology in Asia*, p. 283.

26. See René Padilla and Chris Sugden (eds.), *Texts on Evangelical Social Ethics 1974–1983* and *How Evangelicals Endorsed Social Responsibility*, Grove Booklets on Ethics nos. 58 and 59 (Nottingham: Grove, 1985). Cf. Ken Gnanakan, *Kingdom Concerns: A Biblical Exploration Towards a Theology of Mission* (Bangalore: Theological Book Trust, 1989), p. 102.

27. See Nicol MacNicol and Vishal Mangalwadi, *What Liberates a Woman? The Story of Pandita Ramabai, A Builder of Modern India* (New Delhi: Nivedit Good Books, 1996); Joseph Abraham, "Feminist Hermeneutics and Pentecostal Spirituality: The Creation Narrative of Genesis as a Paradigm," *Asian Journal of Pentecostal Studies* 6. 1 (2003): 3–21.

28. See Carver Yu, "Evangelical Theology for the Future" and Ivan M. Satyavrata, "Theological Education towards 2020." Presented at the 2004 ATA consultation in Bangkok "Re-envisioning Theological Education for Ministry."

29. In *minjung* theology, for example, the spirits are reduced to sociological phenomena. See David Suh and Lee Chung Hee, "Liberating Spirituality in the Korean Minjung Tradition," in Virginia Fabella, Peter Lee, and David Suh (eds.), *Asian Christian Spirituality: Reclaiming Traditions* (Maryknoll, NY: Orbis, 1992), pp. 31–43. See also Ramachandra's critique of Pieris below.

30. Gnanakan (ed.), *Salvation*, p. 184.

31. Bong Rin Ro (ed.), *Christian Alternatives to Ancestor Practices* (Taichung, Taiwan: ATA, 1985).

32. The statement that came out of the consultation was called "A Working Document Towards a Christian Approach to Ancestor Practices," rather than a "declaration" (Gnanakan [ed.], *Biblical Theology in Asia*, pp. 287–95).

33. The extreme complexity of the issue is highlighted in a work by Derek Newton, *Deity and Diet: The Dilemma of Sacrificial Food at Corinth* (Sheffield: Sheffield Academic Press, 1998). He concludes that although Paul is generally opposed to the practice of eating food offered to idols, the different responses he gives indicate his sensitivity to the different views in the Corinthian church. Paul's approach shows that the problem cannot be resolved with a single, objective answer applicable to all situations. This is usually how "outsiders" (e.g., missionaries) would look at the problem. The understandings and attitudes of the "insiders" must be taken into consideration as well (pp. 383–99).

34. This is evidenced by a number of book-length works in this area. E.g., Hwa Yung's *Mangoes or Bananas? The Quest for an Authentic Asian Christian Theology* (Oxford: Regnum, 1997) is essentially a theology of mission. Other works are cited below.

35. Gnanakan, *Kingdom Concerns*, p. 199.

36. Ken Gnanakan, *The Pluralist Predicament* (Bangalore: Theological Book Trust, 1992), p. 3.

37. *Ibid.*, pp. 173–89. See Lesslie Newbigin, *The Gospel in a Pluralist Society* (Grand Rapids, MI: Eerdmans, 1989); Clark Pinnock, *A Wideness in God's Mercy: The Finality of Jesus Christ in a World of Religions* (Grand Rapids, MI: Zondervan, 1992); David L. Edwards and John Stott, *Essentials* (London: Hodder and Stoughton, 1988).

38. Gnanakan, *Pluralist Predicament*, p. 178.

39. Ramachandra, *Recovery of Mission*, pp. 24–25, 30.

40. *Ibid.*, p. 51.

41. *Ibid.*, pp. 52–59.

42. *Ibid.*, p. 60.

43. *Ibid.*, pp. 67–68. Apart from critique, Ramachandra offers an apologetic for the gospel as particular and public truth, very similar to Newbigin's. See chs. 7, 8.

44. Dyrness, *Invitation to Cross-Cultural Theology*, p. 33.

45. "Although ... Minjung theology has espoused the concerns of the poor and oppressed, it is to Pentecostal churches like YFGC [Yoido Full Gospel Church] that the poor and oppressed have flocked for relief" (Allan Anderson, "The Pentecostal Theology of David Yonggi Cho," *Asian Journal of Pentecostal Studies* 7. 1 [2004]: 121).

46. Thomas A. Harvey, *Acquainted with Grief: Wang Mingdao's Stand for the Persecuted Church in China* (Grand Rapids, MI: Brazos, 2002).

47. The phrase "theological politics" is applied to the "political" theory of Stanley Hauerwas, but it could well describe Wang's approach as well. See Arne Rasmusson, *The Church as Polis: From Political Theology to Theological Politics as Exemplified by Jürgen Moltmann and Stanley Hauerwas* (Notre Dame, IN: University of Notre Dame Press, 1995).

48. Dyrness, *Invitation to Cross-Cultural Theology*, pp. 51–60.

49. For example, they issued a confession of faith in 1998 to distinguish themselves from cults like the Eastern Lightning on the one side and the China Christian Church on the other. See Aikman, *Jesus in Beijng*, pp. 295–307.

50. Paul Hattaway, *The Heavenly Man: The Remarkable True Story of Chinese Christian Brother Yun* (London: Monarch, 2003). These are not unique to China. Similar accounts can be found in Pentecostal churches elsewhere. See, e.g., David Yonggi Cho, *A Call in the Night*, Sermon series (Seoul: Seoul Logos, 1983, 2002). Cf. Myung Soo Park, "Korean Pentecostal Spirituality as Manifested in the Testimonies of Believers of the Yoido Full Gospel Church," in Wonsuk, Menzies, and Bae (eds.), *David Yonggi Cho*, pp. 43–67; Anderson and Tang (eds.), *Asian and Pentecostal.*

51. Harold Turner, "Primal Religions," pp. 32–33.

52. Park, "Korean Pentecostal Spirituality," p. 50.

53. It is not uncommon to find non-Christians allowing their children to go to church as long as they are not baptized. For them, baptism is what makes one a real Christian; it is the point of no return.

54. As told to me by a colleague from that church.

55. *A Christian Directory* (1673), 4.19.5.

56. I would suggest that concrete instances of the strange ways of God working in non-Christians may provide a better starting point for a theology of religions than general principles like general revelation.

57. Simon Chan, "The Church and the Development of Doctrine," *Journal of Pentecostal Theology* 13. 1 (2004): 57–77.

58. This point has been argued by liturgical theologians like Alexander Schmemann, *Introduction to Liturgical Theology* (Crestwood, NY: St. Vladimir Seminary Press, 1996) and Aidan Cavanagh, *Liturgical Theology*. For the place of ecclesial experience in the formation of doctrine, see my *Liturgical Theology: The Church as Worshipping Community* (Downers Grove, IL: InterVarsity, 2006).

59. See Susan K. Wood, *Spiritual Exegesis and the Church in the Theology of Henri de Lubac* (Grand Rapids, MI: Eerdmans, and Edinburgh: T. & T. Clark, 1998); Michael Polanyi, *Personal Knowledge: Towards a Post-Critical Philosophy* (Chicago: University of Chicago Press, 1962).

60. Freston, *Evangelicals and Politics*, pp. 88–92. Freston's assessment, again, shows the inadequacy of "political theology." It does not account for how the Nagas are politically apathetic and active simultaneously.

61. Jean DeBernardi, "Spiritual Warfare and Territorial Spirits: The Globalization and Localization of a 'Practical Theology,'" *Religious Studies and Theology*, 18. 2 (December 1999): 66–96.

62. Simon Chan, "The Pneumatology of David Yonggi Cho," in Wonsuk, Menzies, and Bae (eds.), *David Yonggi Cho*, pp. 95–119.

63. See, e.g. Stanley Hauerwas, Michael G. Cartwright, and John Berkman (eds.), *The Hauerwas Reader* (Durham, NC: Duke University Press, 2001).

64. As seen in Anderson and Tang's *Asian and Pentecostal*. Similar reflections have been going apace in the West, such as Nathan O. Hatch, *The Democratization of American Christianity* (New Haven, CT, and London: Yale University Press, 1989) and Grant Wacker, *Heaven Below: Early Pentecostalism and American Culture* (Cambridge, MA: Harvard University Press, 2001).

16 British (and European) evangelical theologies

STEPHEN R. HOLMES

It is possible to tell the story of the British evangelical movement as beginning with a *theological* discovery. The tale of John Wesley's quest for assurance, and his discovery of the Reformation doctrine of salvation *sola fide*, remains iconic and, with the heart "strangely warmed" from trusting Christ alone for forgiveness, these experiences remain central to evangelical theology and culture alike. Evangelicalism, at least in its British formulations, however, has never particularly been a movement that is driven by, or even possessed of, a distinctive theology, a point made particularly clear by considering the wider European context. Wesley's evangelical conversion took place at a Moravian meeting, after all, listening to a reading from Luther. Yet Moravians, even Böhler's societies, and Lutherans, even Pietistic ones, are not generally included under the heading "evangelical." Further, if the doctrine of salvation by faith alone is to be the distinctive mark, then there were many teaching that doctrine in England in Wesley's day, often with far more theological sophistication than any evangelical in eighteenth-century Britain, and these were sharply opposed to the new movement.[1]

The two most significant recent historians of evangelicalism, David Bebbington and Mark Noll, have defined the movement in non-theological ways. Noll focuses on social context and contacts: evangelicalism is primarily a network, or a series of networks, with individuals identified as belonging to the movement if they are a part of the network.[2] Bebbington's famous fourfold definition, that evangelicals are cross-centred, conversionist, biblicist, and activist,[3] implies some theological beliefs, but there is no sense in which there is a distinctive theology that is evangelical, and only evangelical. In its early expressions in Britain at least, evangelicalism was a movement defined by relationships and activities at least as much as by theology.

Indeed, with the single exception of the doctrine of Christian perfection, John Wesley believed he was little more than a faithful interpreter of classical Anglican theology. He and Charles were convinced to read and listen to Luther prior to their conversions not least because they began to acknowledge that the Lutheran doctrines were consonant with the doctrines declared in the *Homilies*.[4] Charles Wesley even remained committed to Anglican church order, objecting in vitriolic terms to his brother's assuming the right to ordain although not a bishop. George Whitefield has been painted by his recent (American) biographers as enjoying an "embattled" relationship with his church,[5] but this is only in part true: Whitefield certainly denounced moral and doctrinal laxity in Anglicanism, and pleaded for the rights of Dissenters in the colonies, but I can find no trace of him departing from the Church of England in any matter of defined doctrine (other, perhaps, than a refusal to insist on episcopacy). Indeed, some readers have tested his doctrine against the Anglican standards and found no divergence.[6]

Any attempt to define eighteenth-century British evangelicalism as a theological movement is destined to failure. Its leaders were preachers and hymnwriters, not theologians; its distinctives were practical and experimental, not doctrinal. Whilst maintaining basic doctrinal conservatism and orthodoxy, which set it against broader currents in British church life, it was doctrinally divergent on such then-central issues as church order or predestination. Evangelicals claimed they were doing little more than repeating the historical teaching of the Church of England, or of the Puritans; whilst this was no doubt in part an apologetic strategy, it is difficult to argue they were wrong.

Eighteenth-century British evangelicalism, then, was broadly and fairly unreflectively orthodox in Trinitarian and Christological matters: humanity was sinful and without help, save for the merits won by the substitutionary death of Christ, appropriated by faith, a gift of the Holy Spirit granted in a moment to enliven the heart and enlighten the mind. The Wesleys and others were traditionally Arminian; Whitefield and others classically Calvinist, but these differing positions did not result in new theological arguments being developed. Charles Wesley was a committed episcopalian; John Wesley more moderate; John Erskine a good Presbyterian kirk-man; Ralph and Ebenezer Erskine Presbyterians (but outwith the kirk); Dan Taylor a congregationalist; Whitefield apparently cared little for any particular church order.[7] Again, however, there is no striking defense of these positions: the question of church order is either ignored, or argued along traditional lines. If there is anything that looks like theological innovation, it is a willingness on the part of some – but by no means all – of the evangelical leaders to accept that questions concerning the doctrines of grace or church government were not of first importance; even this, however, is paralleled in Deism and other eighteenth-century movements. It has been suggested that part of the essence of evangelical theology was a de-emphasis on certain traditional positions and this is perhaps partially supported by this observation.

One might argue that there were distinctive practices amongst the evangelicals: field preaching, the gospel invitation and, in some circles (notably under Howel Harris in Wales), genuine "enthusiasm,"[8] including a claimed recovery of the prophetic ministry. In no case of which I am aware, however, is there any serious theological work behind the innovative practice. (We might compare Harris with a figure from a later generation: Edward Irving. Irving, right or wrong, was theologically serious and inventive in defending his recovery of the miraculous gifts; it is difficult to claim the same for Harris.)

It was perhaps among Old Dissent that the first original evangelical theology was done.[9] Two reasons for this might be identified: first, the Dissenters (in common with all strands of Scots Presbyterianism) were generally more doctrinally serious than the Anglicans; and second, certain theological positions common amongst Dissenters needed to be defeated if evangelicalism was to be embraced. Two in particular stand out: the belief that salvation came gradually, and demanded an extended period of conviction of sin before assurance of forgiveness might be known; and the high Calvinism of John Gill and others, under which scheme it was assumed that, since God would infallibly save the elect, and since the reprobate could not respond in faith to God, there was no general duty to believe the gospel, and any invitation to believe was both useless and improper. While such views held sway, evangelical experience would be suspect, and evangelistic preaching necessarily excluded.

Andrew Fuller (1754–1815) may not have been the first to engage these issues in an attempt to support evangelicalism, but one result of his developing evangelical Calvinism, the founding of the Baptist Missionary Society, and with it the evangelical missions movement, is significant. The tale of Fuller's growing dissatisfaction with the inherited doctrines of Gill has often been told; the fact that he was pointed by friends across the Atlantic to Jonathan Edwards for theological works to develop an "evangelical Calvinism" perhaps lends support to my thesis that British evangelicalism had not produced significant theological works to this point.

Mention of Fuller leads to perhaps the most significant recent theological controversy in British evangelicalism. In the course of his arguments,

Fuller denied, or at least redefined, the particular doctrine of the atonement often held to be central to evangelicalism, penal substitution. This doctrine had been deployed, fairly unreflectively,[10] by all previous evangelical leaders. It was not, however, an evangelical distinctive: so moderate a churchman as Bishop Butler could defend it in his great *Analogy of Religion*.

The other great evangelical distinctive, commitment to the truth and authority of the Bible, is similarly placed at the beginning of the nineteenth century. Although biblical criticism had begun in earnest in Germany, and various traditional doctrines and claims concerning miracles had been questioned in Britain by Deists and others, evangelical insistence on a conservative view of Scripture was not yet distinctive. William Paley, after all, was hardly evangelical, but his apologetic efforts were devoted in part to upholding the historical truth of the Bible.

Finally concerning the eighteenth century, there was little or no distinction between British and American evangelical theology. Edwards was the great theologian of the movement, on either side of the Atlantic. There was perhaps some divergence over the propriety of an Established Church (British evangelicals were split on the issue; in America the movement was fairly strongly against), but George Whitefield and John Wesley could cross and re-cross the Atlantic, and even Edwards could ruminate about accepting a (Presbyterian) charge in Scotland, without much apparent need for cultural translation.

Into the nineteenth century this changed. British evangelicalism was decisively affected by the Romantic movement, and this led it down different paths than the American branch. The central figure in this change was no evangelical, but enormously influential upon many who were, and on others who left the fold: Samuel Taylor Coleridge. In such central areas as social engagement, attitude to the Bible, and apologetic strategy, Coleridge represented, and in part determined, what British evangelicalism needed to come to terms with. He was also famous as a conversationalist, influencing others to an astonishing degree by the spoken, rather than the written, word (among evangelicals Edward Irving was the most striking example).

This is not to say that all early nineteenth-century British evangelicalism was Romantic in tone. Coleridge's influence, notwithstanding his friendship with Irving, was perhaps largely confined to England. In Wales, Thomas Charles (1755–1814) continued the work of Calvinistic Methodists without change of doctrine or tone, deploying organizational genius in the founding of Sunday Schools, and, later, the Bible Society. In Scotland Thomas Chalmers (1780–1847) forged a significant evangelical theology building on works of common-sense philosophy and evidentialism not dissimilar to Paley's in ways that perhaps preempt the great Princeton theologians. Chalmers also introduced another key note of early nineteenth-century British evangelical theology: social and political involvement. For Chalmers, early acquaintance with the social commentary of the Scottish Enlightenment, and broad acceptance of the arguments of Malthus in particular, combined with personal experience of urban deprivation in Tron, led first to the "St. John's experiment," where Chalmers sought to create a self-sufficient Christian community in an urban parish in Glasgow, and then to a desire to see such principles spread across the nation, through lecturing at St. Andrews and Edinburgh Universities, the convenorship of the church extension campaign, and even his pan-Protestant appeal of 1844, looking beyond the Free Church to his long-held ideal of a "godly commonwealth." There is little doubt that Chalmers's oratorical style appealed to Romantic tastes, but his philosophy was resolutely Enlightened.

Chalmers influenced a group of brilliant young Scots evangelical theologians who were, to a greater or lesser degree, more Romantic in their expressions of Christianity, and who certainly were prepared to embrace the call to free-thought and authenticity to self that Romanticism offered. John McLeod Campbell, Thomas Erskine of Linlathlen, and Irving all in different ways fell foul of church establishments in pursuing visions of evangelicalism that were tinged by Romantic sensibilities. McLeod Campbell has been most celebrated, but was perhaps the least able theologian of the three; Irving was probably the best. All three objected to accounts of the atonement that reduced (as they saw it) the awesome event of the cross to a logical or pecuniary transaction with no emotional impact (Campbell's call for a "filial" rather than "legal" account of the atonement captures the complaint well).[11] Irving, in addition, found great rhetorical power in his insistence on the fallen human nature of Jesus Christ – enlarging on his heroic struggles and sufferings, and pressing his empathy with us poor sinners.[12] Again, the (remarkable, for an evangelical) stress on ritual and the mystery of the supernatural in his Catholic Apostolic Church could have been designed for a generation raised on Coleridge's *Christabel* and *The Lyrical Ballads*.

If Chalmers represents the most complete evangelical social theology of the early nineteenth century, the most famous example of political campaigning was undoubtedly the abolitionist movement. In legend this was the solitary life-work of William Wilberforce. The anti-slavery movement, however, is but one example of the first great movement amongst evangelicals in Britain into the nineteenth century: the rise of the pan-evangelical campaigns: it was an effective movement because built on a coalition; and Wilberforce was personally involved in dozens of different organizations or campaigns. The first non-denominational missionary society, the London Missionary Society, was founded in 1795; campaigns for Sunday Schools, for the provision of Bibles to the poor of Britain and the world, for "a reformation of manners" (as Wilberforce would put it, seizing a phrase used by the king and others), brought together Anglicans and Dissenters, Calvinists and Arminians, Episcopalians, Presbyterians, and congregationalists. Such cross-denominational unity was an evangelical distinctive, often hard-won.

If in the (slightly earlier) rise of the evangelical missionary movement practice had followed theology, and change in practice had depended on theological innovation, the same could not be said of the great pan-evangelical campaigns. The anti-slavery movement depended far more on the (admittedly remarkable) eloquence of Hannah More than any theological discussion. Two lacunae were to prove troublesome in years to come: the justification for united action across lines of division, with the accompanying question of evangelical attitudes to denominationalism; and the question of the motivation behind social action. Chalmers's social concern unquestionably flowed from evangelical piety; his social theories, however, seem not to have been closely connected to his theology. Wilberforce was committed to evangelical Christianity but did not develop a theological justification of political action beyond a demand that true Christianity demanded morality in every area of life. It was perhaps not until the Lausanne Covenant that the latter question was finally settled to broad satisfaction; the former is still a matter of debate.

Chalmers excepted, the best British theologians of the pre-Victorian era were not evangelicals. Coleridge is one example; another is John Henry Newman. Newman was born into an evangelical family but, under Romantic influence, moved away from the tradition, finally and famously receiving a cardinal's hat from the pope. He claimed never to have read Coleridge, although there are similarities of thought and diction that would be remarkable if this were true. Newman, and the rest of the Oxford Movement, posed theological questions to evangelicalism that chimed with the Romantic tenor of the times: questions concerning tradition; mystery; sacramentality; aesthetics; ecclesiology.

Individual evangelicals provided worthwhile theological accounts of one or another of these subjects. Irving's ecclesiology has already been mentioned, and was perhaps the most theologically interesting offering of the day. In a rather different key, J. N. Darby developed a critique of all traditional ecclesial practice and denominationalism, dispensing with clergy and other "accretions" in an attempt to reconstruct a church order that reflected the New Testament (Robert and James Haldane attempted something similar in Scotland, and Robert later in Geneva). This "restorationism" (to borrow an anachronistic term) has remained an important minority report within British evangelicalism. Because some emphases of the Oxford Movement were precisely what evangelicals had de-emphasized to discover unity, however, the only pan-evangelical response possible seemed to be simple denial. So an evangelical approach to the sacraments developed which simply suggested they were of little importance (at best "enacted sermons"), and evangelical ecclesiology became codified in the (slightly embarrassed) assumption that it did not matter very much.

In all this, of course, there were theological convictions assumed, but it is difficult to argue that they were ever defended. When the London Missionary Society insisted that missionaries should not comment about disputed ecclesial matters, and so invited converts to make their own choices, it was implicitly proclaiming that such issues did not matter. Such a position may be theologically defensible, but it appears to have been reached for pragmatic reasons – *good* pragmatic reasons, undoubtedly – yet enshrined without much theological argument. Evangelicalism in 1840 knew (Irving, Darby, and one or two others excepted) it did not believe that ecclesial questions were important, but not why.

Alongside ecclesiological innovations, Irving and Darby were at the forefront of another shift, to premillennialism, and with it some convictions concerning the Bible. In 1841 Louis Gaussen argued in *Theopneustia* that, since every part of the Bible was the word of God, it must all be equally inspired. Such views became common, if not majority, within Victorian evangelicalism. The turn to premillennialism introduced social pessimism perhaps at odds with the social involvement of evangelicals (I know of no figures to prove the point, but it seems that the most aggressively premillennial denominations were the least socially engaged), and certainly with the progressive spirit of the age.

It may be that the most able evangelical theologian of the mid-nineteenth century was the now almost forgotten but then controversial T. R. Birks. Interestingly, Birks was also one of the relatively few British evangelicals to object to Darwin's ideas, despite his apparent openness to revisionist theology. Most evangelicals seemed serenely untroubled by the thought that Darwinism may affect their faith in any way, and Henry Drummond even incorporated the ideas into an apologetic approach.

Later in the century, a pair of Scottish theologians, T. J. Crawford and George Smeaton, defended a classical Calvinistic evangelicalism. Both took a particular stand on the question of penal substitution,[13] but both were essentially representatives of a conservative, confessional, Calvinistic tradition of evangelical theology. At the same time, writers such as R. W. Dale and James Denney fit more perhaps into the mold cast by Chalmers: passionately pastorally concerned with social questions (particularly Dale), they broadly assumed the correctness of evangelical theology, whilst developing it creatively to meet perceived needs.

By the end of the nineteenth century, then, we may discern four broad streams in British evangelical theology. There was a "mainstream," running from figures like Wilberforce and Chalmers to Denney and Dale, which was theologically serious without any need to be particularly original, and tended to develop its best thought in questions of social engagement and apologetic response. There was what we might call a "left wing," finding its most powerful expression in McLeod Campbell or Erskine of Linlathlen, that remained evangelical but restlessly explored and often modified the inherited traditions; there was a "right wing," finding its most able exponents in Crawford and Smeaton, that, on doctrines concerning salvation at least, refused the pan-evangelical compromise and pressed for the maintenance of Calvinistic orthodoxy; finally there was a "radical" stream, pushing for a restorationist ecclesiology, represented by Darby and others.

Of course, all such schemas are impositions upon a messier reality. Birks hovers somewhere between the mainstream and the left-wing, on this account; Irving between the radicals and the left-wing; and Robert Haldane between the radicals and the right-wing. The great evangelical leaders whose ministries defined the movement tended to be more-or-less within the mainstream: Simeon comfortably so; Spurgeon with a little less willingness to compromise over certain denominational and Calvinistic distinctives; William and Catherine Booth extraordinarily willing to ignore questions of ecclesiology in pursuit of individual salvation and social change.

The nineteenth century also saw the beginnings of evangelicalism as a movement in continental Europe. Robert Haldane had been eager to send missionaries to Germany and Italy in the early years of the London Missionary Society, and his own residence in Geneva (particularly his lectures on Romans) gave rise both to a number of evangelical ministers within the Reformed churches of Europe, and to a small Independent congregation that reflected his slightly restorationist views. At the inaugural meeting of the Evangelical Alliance in 1846, delegates were present from various European countries. For the first significant theology from Europe that might reasonably be classed as evangelical, however, we need to look to the last third of the century, and the extraordinary achievements of Abraham Kuyper. Before he became Dutch Prime Minister in 1901 he had been instrumental in founding a university (the Free University of Amsterdam), a newspaper, a political party, and a denomination claiming a million adherents (the Reformed churches); he had also published works which offered large-scale philosophical engagement with social and cultural issues from a specifically Calvinist perspective. Whilst prime minister he wrote a massive theological account of culture and history, *Die gemeene gratiae* (1902–04). Due to the enormous influence of Karl Barth in the Netherlands, Kuyper's influence is now perhaps stronger in the USA than his own nation, but the scope of his life's work remains astonishing; whether he may properly be denominated "evangelical" must depend on the precise definition of that term, but beyond question his thought has decisively influenced certain wings of the movement.

Back in Britain, several new currents were emerging alongside the four streams mentioned above. Although Charles and Elizabeth Finney made two visits to Britain in the middle of the century (with Elizabeth having arguably the more successful ministry), it was not until Moody's visits in the 1870s that there was any real sense of a native revivalist strand to British evangelicalism. Even then, it is difficult to argue that revivalism[14] became as important in Britain as it was in America, despite the tradition's affinity with classical Wesleyan theology. Which British name, after all, could be placed in a list that ran from Finney via Moody to Billy Graham?

Second, also an American import, although it grew only when grafted onto a native root-stock, a neo-Wesleyan theology seeking holiness in quietude and entire surrender to God found an influential home in the annual Keswick convention, which continues to this day, albeit with less emphasis on this distinctive theology. Pearsall Smith's holiness teaching reached Britain fairly quickly in the 1870s, but the espousal of the tradition by such leaders as Bishop H. C. G. Moule in the new century established it as central – for a time, perhaps *the* central tradition – within British evangelicalism. Bebbington has helpfully traced the emergence of a distinctively Romantic flavor to the British holiness tradition,[15] with the Lake District becoming the spiritual home of both movements. Although the distinctive Keswick theology became de-emphasized into the new century, a blend of an anti-intellectual version of Keswick spirituality, premillennialism, and hostility to higher criticism gave Britain its own fundamentalist movement for a while, but it was never a major influence on British evangelicalism.

The same cannot be said of two other streams. The most able theologian associated with the evangelical movement at the turn of the century was P. T. Forsyth. Although trained in liberal theology, in his thirties he was evangelically converted (from, as he would later put it, being "a lover of love" to being "an object of grace"), but never lost his respect for some central aspects of liberal theology, not least higher criticism. He wrote extensively and persuasively, stressing human sinfulness and God's response in the cross of Christ. His academic credentials were recognized in his appointment as President of the theological faculty of Hackney College, London. Forsyth left some legacy amongst the students he trained for Congregational ministry in Hackney, but was later rediscovered as a native, and evangelical, forerunner of Barth. British evangelicalism's relationship with "neo-orthodoxy" has not been untroubled, but many of its best theologians have been appreciative of Barth, and Forsyth's influence may lie behind that somehow; at least his theology appears prescient. In the second half of the twentieth century, a number of highly gifted and broadly orthodox theologians influenced by Barth were teaching in Britain. Headed perhaps by T. F. Torrance and Colin Gunton, these were not always personally identified with evangelicalism, but broadly sympathetic.[16] They taught many evangelical students, so that the present generation of evangelical theologians in Britain is, if not "Barthian," at least understanding of and sympathetic toward Barth's program, appreciative of the resources he offers. Evangelical theology, or at least evangelical theologians, are also remarkably central to British academic theology: a few years back, three Oxford professors of theology would have owned the label "evangelical"; there are many young evangelicals in leading university departments, and one or two significant centers where evangelicals perhaps make up a majority on the theological faculty.

Before this movement, however, the beginning of the twentieth century saw the rise of the "liberal evangelical" party, which between 1920 and 1940 was greatly influential. An eponymous book of 1923 made the decisive issue between liberal and conservative evangelicals the question of substitutionary atonement. Conservative evangelicalism was at this point stoutly defending its theological heritage, but little more. The beginnings of the student movement that would become the Universities and Colleges Christian Fellowship, an alternative to the liberal Student Christian Movement, in Cambridge before 1920 was, in retrospect, decisive, however. After the 1939–45 war, the liberal evangelicals either drifted into outright liberalism or assimilated into a mainstream evangelicalism that was perhaps broader and more generous than a generation previously. Conservative evangelical scholarship flourished, by contrast, with the founding of the Tyndale Fellowship for Biblical Research uniting a generation of able evangelical biblical scholars, headed by such luminaries as F. F. Bruce and George Beasley-Murray. A doctrinal equivalent would have to wait until 1983, with the opening of Rutherford House in Edinburgh. This reflects accurately the relative strength of different aspects of the theological task: evangelical biblical scholars made the historical-critical method their own, deploying it with skill and brilliance, and reaping the academic rewards;[17] only very recently have evangelical theologians produced work that has won similar recognition.[18]

This is not to say that there was no doctrinal scholarship amongst evangelicals. In the 1950s Martin Lloyd-Jones founded an annual conference devoted to recovering Puritan insights. Alongside J. I. Packer, and the Banner of Truth publishing house, this indicated a return to the confessional and Calvinist expression of evangelicalism championed by Smeaton and Crawford, and Edwards prior to that. In a new twist on the old question of denominationalism, again drawing on the Puritan tradition, Lloyd-Jones argued passionately against John Stott that the future of evangelicalism lay in separatism, in coming out of the historic denominations and looking for churches "fully Reformed." This tradition still continues, finding its natural home in Rutherford House, the Highland Theological College, or (in an Anglican form) the Reform movement. Typically suspicious of Barth's influence and opposed to the ecumenical and charismatic movements, this remains an intellectually serious and vocal strand of the British evangelical tradition.

This is also probably where the weight of European evangelicalism in the twentieth century lay. Beyond Britain, most European evangelical movements have been minority movements, in many cases within nations having Roman Catholic or Eastern Orthodox churches established strongly in law, and intertwined strongly with culture. Such conditions have tended naturally to produce relatively conservative and conformist theological expressions, with anti-Catholic polemic often being a fairly central concern. The work of Frenchman Henri Blocher is a very notable example.

The mainstream of British evangelicalism has been less aggressively Reformed and more open to the influence of the ecumenical and charismatic. Informality in liturgical matters from dress and musical style to the structuring or length of services has become commonplace, and with it a renewal of a tradition, first represented perhaps by Watts or Whitefield, that is impatient with doctrinal dispute, seeing vitality in worship and preaching, and energetic evangelistic and social action, as far more significant markers. Again, denominations are generally seen as less important than spirituality, and distinct softening of classical anti-Roman polemic is observable. Within this movement, theologians influenced positively by Barth, and/or intent on exploring questions that push at the bounds of classical evangelical orthodoxy (for example, divine passibility), find a comfortable home; Irving and McLeod Campbell are recovered as heroes whose questioning faith highlighted real issues which still need airing today.

The charismatic movement has also created a new radical wing of British evangelicals. The 1960s House Churches often grew out of Brethren assemblies, and for a while Restorationism, a Darbyite conscious attempt to reconstruct the pure New Testament church, was a significant influence. This is waning, but in its place have come two other forms of radicalism: what we might call evangelical Anabaptism, and the Emerging Church.

The "post-Christendom" movement is presently influential. It perhaps began with a sense of cultural transition, and questions about adequate modes of evangelism in a culture that no longer respects the church or remembers the gospel. Responses, however, have often drawn on a (perhaps slightly romanticized) recovery of the sixteenth-century Anabaptist movements, and creative reflection on their practices of church and mission. This has been strongest in denominations that have traditionally emphasized a gathered church with defined boundaries – Baptists, and many of the new churches that arose within the charismatic movement – and the key thinkers and leaders have come from these traditions (Nigel Wright;[19] Stuart Murray-Williams;[20] Alan and Eleanor Kreider), but the influence of the movement has been wider.[21]

Alongside this, and arising out of similar questions about cultural change, although with less focus on the church's place in the culture and more on changing cultural modes of expression, is the "Emerging Church" movement. The beginnings might be dated to Dave Tomlinson's book *The Post-Evangelical*,[22] which, although justly criticized for weak analysis, seemed to crystallize a feeling that was relatively widespread within evangelicalism, that modes of expression and cultural trappings were ripe for renewal, if the vital spark of spirituality was not to be lost. The "emerging church" is endlessly imagined and re-theorized, particularly through weblogs; the extent to which it is lived is perhaps more open to question. But in 2006 a mainstream evangelical denomination, the Baptist Union of Great Britain, announced a "liquid" strand to its annual Assembly (picking up the language of Pete Ward's *Liquid Church*,[23] which in turn borrows from Bauman's language of "liquid modernity").[24] This might be no more than a self-conscious attempt on the part of organizers to be up to date, but is nonetheless suggestive of the extent to which the language and thought-forms of "emerging church" theorists have permeated the mainstream.

The collapse of communism across Eastern Europe has framed questions about appropriate expressions of evangelical Christianity there in a very particular way. Whilst individuals in a number of post-communist countries have proved very receptive to the gospel, post-communist societies have tended to become very nationalistic, reasserting the cultural identities that communist regimes sought to downplay. In many or most post-communist countries, such national identity has been bound up with the historically established church. To be Serbian is necessarily to be Orthodox, for example, or so the assumption runs. Indigenous evangelical churches, therefore, are being forced into developing an apologetic that insists on their valid place within the national culture,[25] and foreign missionaries are finding that, while hearts and minds may be open, cultures and societies are increasingly closed. Arguably, the key success of such leaders as Thomas Chalmers, Hannah More, or Abraham Kuyper was to narrate evangelicalism as a significant part of Scots, English, or Dutch culture; even as in Britain significant strands of evangelicalism are redescribing themselves as apart from the dominant culture to reclaim their evangelistic effectiveness, across post-communist Europe (and traditionally Catholic Europe), the earlier task is still needed.

In Britain, the pressing tasks are rather different. If, as I suggested, at the end of the nineteenth century British evangelicalism could be divided into four broad streams, the sense at the beginning of the twenty-first is more of binary polarization. Is evangelicalism properly understood as a fundamentally unitary and conservative movement, strong on a set of doctrinal distinctives, or as a much more amorphous movement, defined by a protean ability to adapt to cultural change in ways that maintain evangelistic effectiveness? Particularly in recent public debates over penal substitutionary atonement,[26] certain representatives of both wings have been willing to excommunicate the others. The urgent task for British evangelical theology would seem to be finding ways to hold the conservative and radical wings of the movement together, perhaps by finding a re-narration which allows both sides to recognize themselves and the others as within the movement.

Alongside this, a major feature of British evangelicalism has been the rise of black majority churches,[27] bringing recognizably African expressions of Christianity to Britain. Theologically, this is a strongly supernaturalist movement, combining classical Pentecostal emphases with a very strong focus on questions of spiritual warfare and deliverance ministry (exorcism), and a strong expectation of God's work in the believer's daily life, including securing her material prosperity. Ecclesiologically, these churches tend to stress congregational independence from any outside body, and the authority of local leadership. Whilst accurate statistics are not easy to come by, there is no question that growth in the size and number of these churches has been astonishing in recent years. Most self-identify as part of the evangelical movement, which has led to some theological controversy, notably around the "prosperity gospel" and theologies of the demonic and practices of exorcism. A successful theological account of British evangelicalism in the twenty-first century will need to make space for this as well.

What continuities run from Wesley's Aldersgate experience to post-communist Europe and postcolonial/postmodern Britain? Bebbington's famous "quadrilateral," already alluded to, lists four historical marks: focus on the Bible, the cross, the experience of conversion, and activism. Theologically, these provide interesting bases for reflection. With the American evangelical movement so strongly focused on a particular account of biblical authority, the doctrine of inerrancy, it might be surprising to discover that this plays almost no role in British evangelical life. This is not to say that accounts of biblical authority are unimportant to British evangelical theology; but "inerrancy" is not a way of expressing the issue that has been found generally helpful. The natural ways for British evangelicals to speak of the Bible have been to affirm its "inspiration" and to confess it as "authoritative" and "trustworthy."

The differing choice of language is theologically suggestive both in origin and consequence. A decisive point for the divergence of British and American evangelicalism was the influence in Britain of the Romantic movement; a word such as "inerrancy," linking truth and authority to factual accuracy, clearly owes much to Enlightenment ways of thinking, somewhere near the heart of the vision of Christianity that Coleridge so mercilessly mocked. "Authority" and, particularly, "trustworthiness," by contrast, suggest a more Romantic focus on meaning over fact, and on the personal over the scientific. As it happens, most such formulations of Scripture logically entail its inerrancy, but the decision not to make this the central claim suggests that rather different understandings of the nature of truth are operating on either side of the Atlantic Ocean.

The consequences of the decision are also significant, in that British evangelical theology has avoided some American debates. While there is certainly a creationist movement in Britain, for example, creationism has never yet been a defining issue, or a significant point of controversy, within evangelicalism. There may be many reasons for this, and sociology plays its part, but it seems that insisting on the word "inerrancy" makes it much more likely that a particular[28] reading of Genesis will hold sway than if we stress the text as trustworthy.

All of which is to say that, perhaps in some contrast to America, there is not a self-consciously definitive position on the Bible within British evangelicalism. Differing theologians might hold to an inerrantist position, or a position derived from Barth that stresses "authority" and "trustworthiness" in almost existential terms, seeming fairly uninterested in the factual, rather than theological, reference of the text (except on the passion and resurrection narratives). The Bible is central to the British evangelical movement, but a particular theology of Scripture is not a defining feature.

The same might be said of focus on the cross. As noted, British evangelical theology has more than once found its most intractable arguments to concern atonement. This of course indicates the centrality of belief in (and experience of) the atonement within evangelical theology and piety: we argue about this because we care deeply and fervently. There is not, however, a unifying belief to be found here either.

Such significant leaders as Stott or Packer have wanted to find such a unifying belief, and to find it in the doctrine of penal substitution. Packer asserted that this was "by and large, a distinguishing mark of the worldwide evangelical fraternity,"[29] a claim which Stott quotes and endorses.[30] Historically, however, this is simply not true; and when Steve Chalke, arguably the most high-profile evangelical leader in Britain today, can be so opposed to penal substitution as to describe it as "cosmic child abuse," the point is beyond argument. Whatever should be the case, British evangelicals can sharply disagree on the question of the atonement.

Emphasis on conversion is again culturally a defining point, but it would be difficult to find a particular theological account that both commanded broad assent amongst evangelicals and distinguished us from other Christian traditions. Finally, again, evangelical activism has not generally been built on sound theological foundations – the pressing needs of working for the Kingdom pushing out, perhaps rightly, the luxury of wondering why they are so pressing.

Mark Noll defines evangelicalism in terms of networks, rather than beliefs. This perhaps recalls Alasdair McIntyre's famous description of traditions of thought as continuities of conversation.[31] There is no British, still less any European, evangelical theology, if by that is meant an identifiable commonly held and distinctive position; instead, there is an ongoing conversation, returning often to central themes, but in different ways, open to other voices, borrowing gratefully sometimes, pausing to denounce stridently at others – or often, different voices within the conversation responding in each of these ways. We are also open, very open, to the influence of culture and society, believing passionately that Jesus Christ is the answer, but often confused and unsure as to what the question might be. "The world is my parish!" declared Wesley at the head of the movement, as he sought to take the good news to all people. The world of twenty-first century British and European evangelicals is a diverse and confused place indeed, rapidly changing and endlessly fragmenting; perhaps, if there is any commonality from Wesley to his evangelical heirs today, it is standing in continuity with an older intention still, in an overwhelming and all-consuming intention to "become all things to all people, that I might by all means save some" (1 Cor. 9:22).

Further reading

Bebbington, David W. *Evangelicalism in Modern Britain: A History from the 1730s to the 1980s.* London: Routledge, 1993.

Dudley-Smith, Timothy. *John Stott, The Making of a Leader: A Biography: The Early Years.* Downers Grove, IL: InterVarsity, 1999.

John Stott, A Global Ministry: A Biography: The Later Years. Downers Grove, IL: InterVarsity, 2001.

McGrath, Alister E. *J. I. Packer: A Biography.* Grand Rapids, MI: Baker, 1997.

Noll, Mark A. *The Rise of Evangelicalism: The Age of Edwards, Whitefield and the Wesleys.* Vol. 1 of *A History of Evangelicalism.* Leicester: InterVarsity, 2004.

Rack, Henry D. *Reasonable Enthusiast: John Wesley and the Rise of Methodism.* London: Epworth, 1992.

Randall, Ian M. *Evangelical Experiences: A Study in the Spirituality of English Evangelicalism 1918–1939.* Carlisle: Paternoster, 1999.

Stott, John R. W. *Evangelical Truth: A Personal Plea for Unity, Integrity and Faithfulness.* Leicester: InterVarsity, 2005.

Stout, Harry S. *The Divine Dramatist: George Whitefield and the Rise of Modern Evangelicalism.* Grand Rapids, MI: Eerdmans, 1991.

Tomlinson, Dave. *The Post-Evangelical.* London: SPCK, 1995.

Ward, Pete. *Liquid Church.* Carlisle: Paternoster, 2002.

Notes

1. The high- or hyper-Calvinists such as John Gill are an obvious example, both in the mainstream of the Scots kirk, and amongst the English Dissenters.

2. Noll developed this perspective in his *Between Faith and Criticism: Evangelicals, Scholarship, and the Bible in America* (New York: Harper & Row, 1986), and deploys it in his recent *The Rise of Evangelicalism: The Age of Edwards, Whitefield and the Wesleys,* vol. 1 of *A History of Evangelicalism* (Leicester: InterVarsity, 2004).

3. David W. Bebbington, *Evangelicalism in Modern Britain: A History from the 1730s to the 1980s* (London: Routledge, 1993), pp. 3–17.

4. So Henry D. Rack, *Reasonable Enthusiast: John Wesley and the Rise of Methodism* (London: Epworth, 1992), pp. 140, 143. The *Homilies* are a series of sermons that stand alongside the *Book of Common Prayer* as foundational documents of Anglicanism.

5. So, e.g., Harry S. Stout, *The Divine Dramatist: George Whitefield and the Rise of Modern Evangelicalism* (Grand Rapids, MI: Eerdmans, 1991), p. 270 (see also pp. 110–12); Frank Lambert, *"Pedlar in Divinity": George Whitefield and the Transatlantic Revivals* (Princeton, NJ: Princeton University Press, 1994), pp. 22–23, 210–18.

6. So Lambert, *"Pedlar in Divinity,"* pp. 157–58.

7. "I saw regenerate souls among the Baptists, among the Presbyterians, among the Independents, and among the Church folks – all children of God, and yet all born again in a different way of worship: and who can tell which is the most evangelical?" (quoted in Noll, *Rise of Evangelicalism*, p. 13).

8. "Enthusiast" in the eighteenth century carried the sense of "fanatic" and was a charge regularly leveled at the evangelicals.

9. "Old Dissent" refers to the non-Anglican Protestant denominations in England and Wales that date from before the evangelical revival, notably Presbyterians, Baptists, and Congregationalists.

10. See my "Ransomed, Healed, Restored, Forgiven: Evangelical Accounts of the Atonement" (forthcoming) for a defense of the claim that these positions were held "unreflectively," and for some exploration of Fuller's views.

11. See, variously, McLeod Campbell, *The Nature of Atonement* (1856); Erskine, *The Brazen Serpent* (1831), *The Unconditional Freeness of the Gospel* (1828), and others; Irving, *Third Sermon on the Incarnation* (1828).

12. See Irving, *Sermons on the Incarnation* throughout.

13. See Crawford, *The Fatherhood of God* (1866) and *The Doctrine of Holy Scripture Respecting the Atonement* (1871) and Smeaton, *The Doctrine of the Atonement* (1868).

14. The language of "revival," and prayer that it might happen, was a common part of British evangelical spirituality, of course; the pursuing of revival through organized mass-meetings and so on has always been something of a transatlantic import, though often a welcome, and at times a necessary, one.

15. Bebbington, *Evangelicalism in Modern Britain*, pp. 167–80; see also Ian M. Randall, *Evangelical Experiences: A Study in the Spirituality of English Evangelicalism 1918–1939* (Carlisle: Paternoster, 1999), pp. 14–39.

16. Colin Gunton commented to the present author a few months before his death in 2003 that he would not object to the label "evangelical."

17. The great heir to this tradition at present is of course N. T. Wright.

18. Ironically, perhaps, they have often done it by repudiating precisely the methods that the biblical scholars of an earlier generation deployed. The rise of theological interpretation of Scripture is one facet of a return to tradition-based theological enquiry that has proved hospitable to evangelicals.

19. See especially Nigel Wright, *Disavowing Constantine: Mission, Church and the Social Order in the Theologies of John Howard Yoder and Jürgen Moltmann* (Carlisle: Paternoster, 2000).

20. See particularly Stuart Murray-Williams, *Post-Christendom: Church and Mission in a Strange New World* (Carlisle: Paternoster, 2004), but also several other of his books.
21. The writings of the Croatian theologian Miroslav Volf have been significant within this movement. I am not sure that Volf can be considered part of any "movement": his theology is bound up with a very particular personal history. He is perhaps an indication that such thinking has been present in evangelicalism in Europe beyond the British Isles, however.
22. Dave Tomlinson, *The Post-Evangelical* (London: SPCK, 1995).
23. Pete Ward, *Liquid Church* (Carlisle: Paternoster, 2002).
24. Zygmunt Bauman, *Liquid Modernity* (Cambridge: Polity, 2000).
25. I was told recently by an Estonian church leader that his church's biggest task was demonstrating that it was possible to be both evangelical and Estonian.
26. The papers from a debate on this subject arising from Steve Chalke and Alan Mann's *The Lost Message of Jesus* (Grand Rapids, MI: Zondervan, 2004), which had criticized penal substitution in the strongest imaginable terms, are at present on the Evangelical Alliance website, and should soon be published. They bear testimony to this point.
27. "Black majority church" is a standard term, although misleading. Many churches whose congregations and leadership happen to be mostly, or entirely, black, fit comfortably within the theologies and practices of traditional denominations. Since about 1985, however, a significant number of new churches have been planted or formed, usually without any denominational allegiance, which have brought a distinctively different tradition of Christianity to the British scene. Of the several terms used to denote this phenomenon, none of which is entirely happy, "black majority churches" seems to be the most common and least misleading.
28. And historically slightly peculiar: when Luther chose to read Genesis 1 as referring to six literal days, he believed he was the first person in the history of the church to do so. He was wrong, but it was very much a minority opinion amongst the church fathers.
29. In his 1973 Tyndale Lecture, "What did the Cross Achieve?" (RTSF Monograph; n.d.), p. 3.
30. See John R. W. Stott, *Evangelical Truth: A Personal Plea for Unity, Integrity and Faithfulness* (Leicester: InterVarsity, 2005), p. x.
31. See especially Alasdair McIntyre, *Whose Justice? Which Rationality?* (London: Duckworth, 1988).

17 Evangelical theology in Latin American contexts

C. RENÉ PADILLA

It is a well-known historical fact that the modern Latin American nations came into existence under the aegis of the Roman Catholic Church. Only a year after the "discovery of America" by Christopher Columbus on 12 October 1492, the cross and the sword were officially joined together to carry out the spiritual and military conquest of the New World for the Roman Pontiff and the Spanish king and queen. More than the Christian faith as such, what the Spanish and later the Portuguese *conquistadores* brought to these lands was the Roman Catholic Church – a hierarchical religious structure closely associated with the state. As John A. Crow has put it,

> While other countries were content to establish themselves under Protestant or mixed Catholic and Protestant regimes which would grow toward religious liberalism, the Iberian countries created the Church–State type of authoritarian absolutism in which government and religious doctrine became inseparable. Other countries made of religion a national expression, but Spain and Portugal maintained unbroken belief in the holy internationalism of the Catholic Church.[1]

There is no exaggeration in saying that this "Church–State type of authoritarian absolutism" became the most decisive factor in the history of Latin America for almost five hundred years, not only politically and religiously, but also socially, culturally, and economically.

There is enough evidence to prove that Protestant Christianity had already arrived on the shores of this continent in the sixteenth century. The two or three Protestant colonies established in Venezuela and Brazil during that century, however, were isolated cases and in no way changed the fact that this was a Roman Catholic continent. For this reason, the International Missionary Conference held in Edinburgh in 1910 did not allow the participation of any Latin American representatives and excluded all reference to this region as "missionary territory."

Under these circumstances, it is not surprising that evangelical theology initially developed in a context of controversy with Roman Catholicism and was clearly marked by the plight of a small (and often persecuted) religious minority. Until approximately the middle of the twentieth century, in Roman Catholicism, with honorable exceptions such as the one represented by Bartolomé de Las Casas,[2] theology played the role of an ideology to justify Constantinianism and the "divine right of kings." In Protestantism, on the other hand, theology was used to defend religious freedom – the right even to *exist* in Latin America as a non-Roman Catholic Christian and to spread the Christian faith as understood from a non-Roman Catholic perspective.

That was, in general terms, the thrust of Protestant theology in Latin America during the first half of the twentieth century. Beginning in the 1960s, however, the emphasis shifted from concern for religious freedom to concern for the meaning of the Christian faith in a revolutionary context. The question that evangelical theologians had to address was no longer, "What is the basis for the existence of non-Roman Catholic churches in a Roman Catholic continent?" The question they now had to address was, "What is the role of evangelical Christians in a continent generally regarded as Christian but deeply affected by increasing poverty and social unrest?"

In the last three decades or so another important factor has been added to the Latin American context, namely, a drastic change in the proportion between the number of Roman Catholics and the number of evangelical Christians. While the Roman Catholic Church has been losing thousands and thousands of members, evangelical churches (as is also the case with many religious sects) have been growing in an amazing way.

Aside from this transformation of the religious map of Latin America, beginning in the 1980s the phenomenon of globalization has become a very important factor that no theology can ignore without the risk of losing all relevance to human life today. Because the present-day economic system is sowing appalling oppression and poverty around the world, the time seems to have arrived for both Roman Catholics and evangelicals to update their theology in order to face this new challenge with Christian integrity.

The present article will briefly describe the basic tenets of evangelical theology in relation to the predominant contextual factor in each of three succeeding stages of its history: Roman Catholicism, a revolutionary situation, and the numerical growth of evangelical churches. It will conclude with a reflection on the challenge that globalization poses today to all

Christians and particularly to "evangelicals" – a term that in Latin America is widely used as a synonym for "Protestants."

ROMAN CATHOLICISM AND EVANGELICAL SELF-IDENTITY

An outstanding example of the sort of apologetics that evangelical theologians felt compelled to articulate in the face of Roman Catholic hegemonic power in Latin America is *The Other Spanish Christ*, originally published in English in 1933 and translated into Spanish in 1952. Written by a Scottish missionary to Peru, John A. Mackay (1889–1983), this book, designed to be "A Study in the Spiritual History of Spain and South America," became a classic and is still regarded as one of the best explanations of the *raison d'entrée* of Protestant Christianity in a Roman Catholic continent.

According to Mackay, the Christ that the Spanish conquerors brought beginning in the sixteenth century was "a Christ known in life as an infant and in death as a corpse, over whose helpless childhood and tragic death the Virgin Mother presides; a Christ who became man in the interests of eschatology, whose permanent reality resides in a magic wafer bestowing immortality."[3]

This Spanish Christ was naturalized in Latin America as the Christ of popular religion, whose earthly life was reduced to two dramatic roles: "the role of the infant in his mother's arms, and the role of a suffering and bleeding victim." "It is," Mackay adds, "the picture of a Christ who was born and died, but who never lived," "an important safety valve" but ethically insignificant.[4]

According to this distinguished Scottish missionary, theologian, and educator who lived in Latin America for sixteen years (1916–32), the Spanish Christ of traditional Roman Catholicism "was not born in Bethlehem but in North Africa," in Tangiers. Strongly influenced by Islam, this Christ was a combination of a sense of tragedy and a passion for immortality, which are "the warp and woof of Spanish popular religion."[5] He came to Latin America, while the other Spanish Christ "wanted to come, but His way was barred."[6]

"The other Spanish Christ," however, says our author, is also very much a part of the Spanish tradition and of present-day life in Spain. It is the Christ of Raymond Lull in the thirteenth century, of the great Spanish mystics and the followers of the Protestant Reformation in the sixteenth century, and of precursors of the new Spain, such as Don

Francisco Giner de los Ríos and Don Miguel de Unamuno in the twentieth century. It is the Christ for whom a number of important intellectuals in Latin America, including some religious thinkers, are groping.

Chapters 1 to 10 of Mackay's literary masterpiece prepare the way for his discussion of evangelical Christianity in Latin America, with which he deals in chapters 11 and 12. It becomes quite clear that his intention is to show the relevance of Reformed Christianity to the spiritual quest in this continent. From his perspective, what people in this region need is not "a replica of Protestant institutions which have grown up in Anglo-Saxon countries, still less a projection into the Latin world of the sins of Protestant denominationalism."[7] What they need is "a personality, One who bears the marks of the Other Spanish Christ."[8] In Mackay's own words,

> It is difficult to conceive anything more necessary in the spiritual life of the Iberian world than the personal religious concern which Protestantism kindles, than the insistence with which it directs the thoughts of men [and women] to the unique revelation of God contained in the Christian Scriptures, than the affirmation that in and through Jesus Christ any and every [person] who so desires can approach and enjoy communion with the Eternal.[9]

Mackay's thesis can only be understood in light of a context in which it was assumed that national identity was equivalent to membership in the Roman Catholic Church. Over against that assumption, he and various other representatives of the first generation of evangelical theologians in Latin America, both before and after him, rejected the hegemonic claims of Roman Catholicism and affirmed their Christian identity on the basis of personal faith in Jesus Christ as the Risen Lord. Outstanding among them were several evangelical intellectuals associated with the Committee on Cooperation in Latin America (CCLA), which was founded at the first Latin American Evangelical Congress held in Panama in 1916: Samuel Guy Inman (a US missionary who lived in Mexico), Juan Orts González (a Spaniard who became the first director of *La Nueva Democracia*, the official CCLA magazine), Alberto Rembao (a Mexican who succeeded Orts González as director of the magazine), Gonzalo Baéz-Camargo (a Mexican in charge of the CCLA Christian education program for the whole continent), and John Ritchie (a Scottish missionary to Peru, where he founded the Peruvian Evangelical Church). Other names that could be added to this list are: Moisés Sáenz of Mexico, Angel M. Mergal of Puerto Rico, Justo González of Cuba, Stanley Rycroft of England, Erasmo Braga of Brazil, Jorge Howard, Juan C. Varetto, and Santiago Canclini of Argentina.

These writers represented a wide variety of nationalities and denominations. They shared, however, a common Protestant theological identity that could be synthesized in the classical Reformation tenets: *sola gratia, sola fide, sola scriptura, solus Christus.* They also shared a common vocation: to spread the gospel and to establish church communities fully committed to making disciples. In the context of a Roman Catholic continent that necessarily involved struggle for a faith centered in the historical Jesus of Nazareth, who was crucified, risen, and made both Lord and Messiah, over against the Spanish Christ of traditional popular religion. It involved, furthermore, a struggle for freedom of conscience and religious freedom, over against an "official" religion imposed by the state. It involved, finally, a struggle for the priesthood of all believers, over against a hierarchical ecclesiastical structure.

CHRISTIANS IN A REVOLUTIONARY SITUATION

The Latin American situation beginning in the 1960s may be described as a revolutionary situation. The growth of poverty, exacerbated by the problems resulting from increasing urbanization and industrialization and closely related to both internal corruption and international exploitation, was fertile soil for the seed of a socialist revolution. Encouraged by the triumph of the Cuban revolution in 1959, labor and student movements considered that the time was ripe to overthrow US imperialism and to change the socio-economic and political structures through a Marxist revolution. With this idea in mind, convinced of the inevitability of violence, many young people, including university students, joined guerrilla groups in several countries.

It was in this context that the First Latin American Consultation on Church and Society (23–27 July 1961) took place in Lima, Peru. This meeting, sponsored by the World Council of Churches (WCC), resulted in the formation of Church and Society in Latin America (ISAL, the acronym in Spanish), which was initially a think-tank made up mainly of Protestant theologians such as Julio de Santa Ana and Julio Barreiro of Uruguay, José Míguez-Bonino of Argentina, and Rubem Alves of Brazil. Eventually, however, ISAL produced greater impact in Roman Catholic circles. Consequently, liberation theology, which started with ISAL, became known largely as progressive Roman Catholic theology, represented by outstanding theologians such as Gustavo Gutiérrez of Peru, Juan Luis Segundo of Uruguay, Pablo Richard of Chile, Enrique Dussel of Argentina, José Miranda of Mexico, Leonardo Boff and

Clodovis Boff of Brazil, and Ignacio Ellacuria and Jon Sobrino of Spain/El Salvador.

The first major work by a liberation theologian, however, was written by Rubem Alves (a Protestant) – *A Theology of Human Hope*,[10] based on his PhD thesis at Princeton Theological Seminary. Gustavo Gutiérrez's *A Theology of Liberation* was originally published in Spanish two years later, in 1971. It was soon translated into several languages, including English, and became much more widely known than Alves's. As a result of this work Gutiérrez came to be known as "the father of liberation theology."

The revolutionary mood, which spread like wildfire all over Latin America, threw into relief the urgent need for both Roman Catholic and Protestant Christians to define the relationship between the church and the revolution which was taking place. Justo L. González,[11] the distinguished Cuban church historian, an evangelical, claimed that in the face of the ongoing revolution – "an intellectual, economic, social, political, and moral revolution"[12] – the church had three alternatives: to try to stop it, to ignore it, or to get into it and do everything possible to conduct it. He discarded the first two alternatives and argued that the only position consistent with the Incarnation – "the basic Christian doctrine" – was the third one: to be involved in the revolution, even as "our Lord participated in our suffering." He warned, however, against the danger of becoming Christian *revolutionaries* instead of revolutionary *Christians* – Christians who seek to worship God not only among believers but also outside the Christian community, "in the factories, classrooms and centers where the life of society is wrought." He was critical of any attempt to identify a human revolutionary program, including that of communism, with God's purpose in history and insisted on the need to view Christian action in society – "sacramental service" – as the means through which God acts on behalf of the victims of exploitation. Neither *Docetism* – the old heresy according to which what is divine could not be manifest through what is human – nor *Ebionism* – the opposite heresy, according to which what is human finds meaning in its own internal development – are an adequate basis for the role of the church in society. The church is called to live on the basis of the Incarnation. If "our Lord is the incarnate Lord ... our obedience cannot be anything but incarnational obedience."[13]

González's was a valuable attempt to find a balance between two opposite positions adopted by evangelicals in the face of revolution. On the one hand, the position represented by North American fundamentalist theologian C. I. Scofield (whose study Bible, translated into Spanish, had wide distribution in Latin America), claimed that "The best help a pastor can bring to the social problems of the community is to humble himself before God, forsake his sins, receive the filling with the Holy Spirit, and preach a pure gospel of tender love."[14] On the other hand, there was the position represented by Cuban theologian Sergio Martinez Arce, who wrote: "All Revolutions always constitute the means through which the Kingdom of God is made real at a given time in history, and the revolutionaries are nothing else than 'servants of the Supreme God.' "[15]

The 1970s and the beginning of the 1980s were a dark period for human rights in Latin America. Repressive military dictatorships, buttressed by the doctrine of "national security" and oftentimes in complicity with the government of the United States, gave free rein to state terrorism as a means to prevent revolutionary change. Unauthorized surveillance and detention of common citizens, concentration camps, torture, and the "disappearance" of persons became the order of the day. Quite a number of Christians – Roman Catholic and Protestant – who had made an "option for the poor" were silenced or killed. An outstanding example of these victims of repression was Mauricio Lopez, a well-known Protestant leader, Professor at the National University of Cuyo and Rector of the National University of San Luis, Argentina, who was kidnapped by a military squad and later assassinated in 1977. Another important example was Archbishop Oscar Romero of El Salvador, who was shot dead while celebrating mass in 1980. Both of these men, like many other men and women during those dismal years, paid the price of *doing* – not just writing – theology in a revolutionary situation.

EVANGELICAL CHURCH GROWTH

The amazing numerical growth of Protestant (especially Pentecostal and neo-Pentecostal or Charismatic) churches in Latin America during the last three decades has become a matter of concern to Roman Catholics and has attracted the attention of students of contemporary religious phenomena. It may be an exaggeration to say that within a few years this region of the world will be Protestant, as some observers have predicted. There seems to be enough evidence, however, to suspect that David Stoll's forecast – that "if the growth of the last few decades continues, Latin Americans claiming to be *evangélicos* could still become a quarter to a third of the population early in the twenty-first century" – has been fulfilled.[16] To be sure, not all the Latin American countries can provide reliable figures on the multiple religious affiliations represented in their population. Furthermore, it must be recognized that the picture varies from country to country. The fact remains that even in countries where evangelical church growth is considerably slower than in others, the growth is significant enough to enable us to state that the number of evangelical Christians is definitely a new constituent factor of the context in which theologians are summoned to think on the nature and the mission of the church.

Before discussing the questions that the numerical growth of the church poses to theology with regard to her nature and mission, however, mention should be made of the Latin American Theological Fraternity (FTL, the Spanish acronym), whose local chapters have oftentimes dealt with these. Some of the members of the FTL have become internationally known: for instance Orlando Costas of Puerto Rico; Edesio Sánchez-Cetina of Mexico; Elsa Tamez and Arturo Piedra of Costa Rica; H. Humberto Bullon of Peru/Costa Rica; Samuel Escobar, Pedro Arana, and Tito Paredes of Peru; Emilio A. Nuñez of El Salvador/Guatemala; Valdir Steuernagel and Ricardo Barbosa Souza of Brazil; Esteban Voth, Daniel Schipani, and Ruth Padilla of Argentina; and Nancy Bedford of Argentina/United States. Founded in 1970, this "evangelical renewal" movement – as José Míguez-Bonino has called it – has made a significant contribution to the development of a contextual theology arising "from the very heart of evangelical piety."[17] It started with a strong affirmation of the authority of Scripture for Christian faith and praxis, coupled with the recognition that, for the sake of faithfulness to the gospel, the Latin American socio-economic, political, cultural, and religious situation should be seriously taken into account. It was assumed that the focus of theology is not doctrine and orthodoxy *per se*, but life and orthopraxis.

With regard to the nature of the church, there are at least two critical questions that numerical church growth poses to theology – more specifically, to pastoral theology: how can numerical growth be kept in balance with other dimensions of church growth? What is the place of Christian discipleship in relation to numerical church growth?

In 1982, Orlando Costas,[18] one of the most prolific Latin American theologians related to the FTL, wrote an article entitled "Dimensions of integral church growth" in which he claimed that, although growth is a sign of life, it can also be dysfunctional, as is the case with cancer. As a living organism, the church is meant to grow, but her growth needs to be theologically tested on the basis of three qualities that she is expected to have as the church of the triune God: (a) faithfulness, because she is the people of God; (b) incarnation, because she is the body of Christ; and (c) spirituality, because she is the community of the Spirit. These three qualities are essential to church growth. For this growth to be truly integral, it must take place in four dimensions. The first dimension is *numerical growth* – the multiplication of believers resulting from the mission of the church, which includes the proclamation of the gospel to men and women everywhere. The second dimension is *organic growth* – the strengthening of personal relationships and mutual complementation of the members within the body. The third dimension is *conceptual* (or theological) *growth* – the increasing understanding of the faith and its practical implications for life. The fourth dimension is *diaconal* – the intensification of service to the world as an expression of God's love. For Costas, there is integral church growth when these four dimensions are kept in balance with one another: "It may be said that the church grows *integrally* when she receives new members, expands internally, deepens her knowledge of the faith and serves the world, but it grows *qualitatively* when in each dimension it reflects spirituality, incarnation, and faithfulness. By itself, numerical growth becomes fatness; organic growth, bureaucracy; conceptual growth, theoretical abstraction, and diaconal growth, activism."[19]

In conclusion, numerical growth – the obsession of many church leaders in Latin America – for the sake of the gospel needs to be balanced with the other dimensions of growth.

This conclusion is closely related to the insistence on the part of FTL-related theologians on the priority of Christian discipleship over numerical growth. Jesus' Great Commission to the church (represented by the eleven disciples in Galilee), right before his exaltation, was: "Go . . . and make disciples of all nations, baptizing them . . . and teaching them to obey everything that I have commanded you" (Matt. 28:19–20). No reference was made to numbers of converts! The criterion for faithfulness to the Lord's intention regarding the life and mission of the church was thus clearly defined at the very beginning of church history – not success measured in terms of numbers, but faithfulness in the making of disciples who would take upon themselves the yoke of obedience to the law of Christ in every aspect of life.

With this understanding, quite early in the history of the FTL several of its members engaged in open debate with advocates of "Church Growth" related to the School of World Mission of Fuller Theological Seminary in Pasadena, California, for whom the basic question that an evangelistic church had to ask was: how can she increase the number of converts?

Along these lines, "Church Growth" proposed that the best way for the church to "win over" an ethnic, a linguistic, or a social-class group is, according to the "homogeneous unit principle," to enable people to become Christians without crossing barriers.[20]

This position was strongly criticized by FTL theologians as an attempt "to accommodate the gospel to the world for the sake of numbers, a presumption that the message must be reduced to a minimum in order to make it possible for all men [and women] to want to become Christian."[21] In contrast with this pragmatic approach, which they regarded as reflecting what Jacques Ellul described as the "technological mentality," they claimed that "The task of the evangelist in communicating the gospel is not to make it easier, so that people will respond positively, but to make it clear."[22] One aspect of making the gospel clear is proclaiming that, because of Jesus Christ's work, "There is no longer Jew or Greek, there is no longer slave or free, there is no longer male or female, for all of you are one in Christ Jesus" (Gal. 3:28). If the dividing lines have been erased in Jesus Christ, how can it be claimed that racial and class segregation should be infused into the strategy of world evangelization for the sake of numerical growth?

With regard to the mission of the church, two questions are unavoidable in light of the numerical growth of evangelical churches in Latin America: what is the mission of the church in this region of the world today? What is the role of the church in relation to the state?

Several FTL theologians have pointed out the incongruity between the fantastic numerical growth of churches and the parallel growth of corruption and exploitation, injustice and poverty in Latin America. Many years ago, W. Stanley Rycroft, a missionary to Peru, claimed that "The gospel of Christ is related to the whole of life, and whether it be relieving human suffering through medical care, improving home and family life, redeeming the land, or educating the young, the church has a responsibility."[23] Sadly, the historical record of evangelical churches since he wrote shows that the large majority of them would not have agreed with him but rather with many other (especially North American) missionaries, according to whom the mission of the church was defined exclusively in terms of "saving souls" and planting churches. One of the consequences of this view has been the common lack of concern for human needs on the part of evangelical Christians in Latin America.

The memorable speech on "The Social Responsibility of the Church" delivered by Samuel Escobar at the First Latin American Congress on Evangelism held in Bogota, Colombia, in November 1969, threw into relief one of the basic themes that were to receive deliberate attention by the FTL in the succeeding years. As a result, one of the most significant contributions of this movement to the cause of God's Kingdom has been a rich body of literature in which the mission of the church is viewed in terms of integral mission – a mission that maintains the unity between justification by faith and the struggle for justice, between faith and works, between spiritual needs and material and physical needs, and between the personal and the social dimensions of the gospel. The practical result is that a growing number of evangelical Christians in Latin America today are experiencing that "The church is the community that lives by the biblical vision. The church proclaims in her worship as well as in her service, message and lifestyle that the existence of the universe and human history can only be understood and make sense within the purpose of God, manifested in Jesus Christ by the power of the Holy Spirit."[24]

It has been estimated that at the beginning of the 1940s there were in Latin America 2,000,000 evangelicals out of a total population of 128,000,000.[25] As a small (often persecuted) minority, they could not aspire to have access to political power and had to limit their action in the political arena mainly to the struggle for religious freedom. The situation since then has drastically changed. Even if David Stoll's estimate[26] is off target, the fact remains that in most of the countries in this region evangelical Christians are presently able not only to elect members from their congregations to public offices, but also to form political parties. The time seems to have arrived when the biggest and most dangerous temptation for Latin American evangelical Christians is to try to replace the Roman Catholic Church as *mater et magistra* in society.

From this perspective, Protestant numerical growth poses to theology an urgent question regarding the relationship between the church and the state. After the damaging effects that Roman Catholic Constantinianism has had in Latin America for both the church and society, Protestant Constantinianism is by no means a desirable option. As Míguez-Bonino has put it, "What we Protestants reject is not that there has been established, or may be reestablished, a 'Roman Catholic Christendom,' but that a 'Christendom' be established at all."[27]

THE CHALLENGE OF GLOBALIZATION

Might globalization in some sense be today's new form of Christendom? No full discussion of this phenomenon is here possible. In light of its influence on humankind everywhere, however, it should at least be mentioned as a constituent element of the socio-economic and political context with which theology in Latin America has to cope.

The dominant form of globalization at the beginning of the twenty-first century is that of so-called neo-liberal capitalism. According to Leslie Sklair, capitalist globalization, which emerged in the second half of the twentieth century, is "a particular way of organizing social life across existing state borders" and includes three interrelated transnational elements or (as he calls them) practices: (1) the transnational corporation, "the major locus of transnational economic practices"; (2) the transnational capitalist class, "the major locus of transnational political practices"; and (3) the transnational culture-ideology of consumerism, "the major locus of transnational culture-ideology practices."[28] After a careful analysis of each of these three elements, Sklair concludes that global capitalism, "driven by the TNCs [transnational corporations], organized politically through the transnational political class, and fueled by the culture-ideology of consumerism, is the most potent force for change in the world."[29] The damaging effects that global neo-liberal capitalism is having on the poor can hardly be exaggerated. The net result of this system of institutionalized injustice is that the rich are becoming richer and the poor are becoming poorer everywhere.

At the same time, there is another type of global reality that Christians must reckon with – the reality of the global Christian community. At the beginning of the twentieth century, the large majority of Christians lived in Europe and the Western hemisphere; approximately half of all Christians were Europeans. By contrast, at the beginning of the twenty-first century the seeds of the Christian faith planted in the southern hemisphere are bearing abundant fruit and the center of gravity of the Christian world is moving southward. As Andrew F. Walls has expressed it, "the European hegemony of the world is broken; the recession of Christianity among the European peoples appears to be continuing. And yet we seem to stand at the threshold of a new age of Christianity, one in which the main base will be in the Southern continents."[30] From a Christian perspective, the global church with the main base in the South is the most important fact of our time.

With these two types of globalization in view, theology has the task of exploring the meaning of true Christian partnership across national borders.

On the one hand, partnership is essential in the communication of the gospel. If the church is to be relevant to the large majority of people in the world, she needs to learn what it means to communicate Jesus Christ's good news to the poor not only through what she *says* but also through what she *is* and what she *does*. Integral mission is not an option among many others – it is the only way for the church everywhere, in the North and the South, in the East and the West. It means, among other things, practical solidarity with people in need – not only the sinners but also the "sinned against," that is, the victims of injustice, the marginalized, the poor.

On the other hand, partnership is essential in the theological field itself. Already at the International Congress for World Evangelization held in Lausanne, Switzerland, in 1974, a Latin American speaker made a plea for "the recognition of a problem and a change of attitude," which he defined in the following terms:

> The problem is that one version of culture Christianity based on an inadequate theological foundation and conditioned by "fierce pragmatism". . . is being regarded by some as the official evangelical position and the measure of orthodoxy around the world. The change of attitude being called for involves the renunciation of ethnocentrism and the promotion of theological cross-fertilization among different cultures. Under the Spirit of God, each culture has something to contribute in connection with the understanding of the gospel and its implications for the life and mission of the church. North American culture Christianity should not be allowed to deprive us of the possibility that we *all* – whatever our race, nationality, language, or culture – as equal members of the body of Christ "attain the unity of the faith and of the knowledge of the Son of God, to mature manhood, to the measure of the stature of the fullness of Christ" (Eph 4:13). The key here is *cross-fertilization*.[31]

This rather lengthy quotation from a paper read at an international conference that took place over three decades ago is made because of its boldness and because the call to engage in theological cross-fertilization remains as relevant today as it was at that time. The mark of a truly evangelical theology is faithfulness to the Word of God, but its relevance depends on the extent to which it responds to human needs in a particular context. What we may call a "universal theology" can only be the final result of the search for both faithfulness and relevance in multiple contexts. "For now we see in a mirror, dimly, but then we will see face to face. Now [we] know only in part; then [we] will know fully, even as [we] have been fully known" (1 Cor. 13:12).

Further reading

Alves, Rubem. *A Theology of Human Hope*. Washington, DC: Corpus, 1969.
Escobar, Samuel. *A Time for Mission: The Challenge for Global Christianity*. Leicester: InterVarsity, 2003.
Garrard-Burnett, Virginia, and David Stoll (eds.). *Rethinking Protestantism in Latin America*. Philadelphia, PA: Temple University Press, 1993.
González, Justo. *Christian Thought Revisited*. Nashville, TN: Abingdon, 1989.
Gutiérrez, Gustavo. *A Theology of Liberation: History, Politics, and Salvation*. Translated and edited by Sister Caridad Inda and John Eagleson. Maryknoll, NY: Orbis, 1973.
Mackay, John A. *The Other Spanish Christ: A Study in the Spiritual History of Spain and South America*. New York: Macmillan, 1933.
Miguez-Bonino, José. *Faces of Latin American Protestantism*. Grand Rapids, MI: Eerdmans, 1995.
Padilla, C. René. *Mission Between the Times: Essays on the Kingdom*. Grand Rapids, MI: Eerdmans, 1985.
Sklair, Leslie. *Globalization: Capitalism and Its Alternatives*. 3rd edition. Oxford: Oxford University Press, 2002.
Walls, Andrew F. *The Missionary Movement in Christian History: Studies in the Transmission of Faith*. Maryknoll, NY: Orbis, 2000.

Notes

1. John A. Crow, *The Epic of Latin America*, 4th edition (Los Angeles: University of California Press, 1992), p. xvi.
2. Cf. Gustavo Gutiérrez, *Las Casas: In Search of the Poor of Jesus Christ*, translated by Robert R. Barr (Maryknoll, NY: Orbis, 1993).
3. John A. Mackay, *The Other Spanish Christ: A Study in the Spiritual History of Spain and South America* (New York: Macmillan, 1933), p. 101.
4. *Ibid.*, pp. 110–11.
5. *Ibid.*, p. 96.
6. *Ibid.*, p. 124.
7. *Ibid.*, p. 161.
8. *Ibid.*, p. 263.
9. *Ibid.*, p. 262.
10. Rubem Alves, *A Theology of Human Hope* (Washington, DC: Corpus Books, 1969).
11. Justo L. González, *Revolución y encarnación* (Rio Piedras, Puerto Rico: Librería La Reforma, 1965), pp. 45–54 (my translation).
12. *Ibid.*, p. 48.
13. *Ibid.*, p. 74.
14. Quoted by George Marsden in *Fundamentalism and American Culture: The Shaping of Twentieth-Century American Evangelicalism 1870–1925* (Oxford: Oxford University Press, 1980), p. 255.
15. Quoted in C. René Padilla, "Iglesia y Sociedad en América Latina," in C. René Padilla (ed.), *Fe cristiana y Latinoamérica hoy* (Buenos Aires: Ediciones Certeza, Padilla, 1974), p. 134 (my translation).

16. David Stoll, "Introduction," in Virginia Garrard-Burnett and David Stoll (eds.), *Rethinking Protestantism in Latin America* (Philadelphia, PA: Temple University Press, 1993), p. 2.
17. José Miguez-Bonino, *Faces of Latin American Protestantism* (Grand Rapids, MI: Eerdmans, 1995), p. 48.
18. Orlando E. Costas, "Dimensiones del crecimiento integral de la iglesia," *Misión* (July–September 1982): 8–14 (my translation).
19. *Ibid.*, p. 14.
20. Cf. Donald McGavran, *Understanding Church Growth* (Grand Rapids, MI: Eerdmans, 1970), pp. 198–215.
21. C. René Padilla, *Mission Between the Times: Essays on the Kingdom* (Grand Rapids, MI: Eerdmans, 1985), p. 39.
22. *Ibid.*, pp. 39–40.
23. W. Stanley Rycroft, *Religion and Faith in Latin America* (Philadelphia, PA: Westminster, 1958), p. 170.
24. Samuel Escobar, *A Time for Mission: The Challenge for Global Christianity* (Leicester: InterVarsity, 2003), p. 168.
25. Cf. W. Stanley Rycroft, *On This Foundation: The Evangelical Witness in Latin America* (New York: The Friendship Press, 1942), p. 75.
26. Stoll, "Introduction," p. 2.
27. Míguez-Bonino, *Faces of Latin American Protestantism*, p. 111.
28. Leslie Sklair, *Globalization: Capitalism and Its Alternatives*, 3rd edition (Oxford: Oxford University Press, 2002), p. 8.
29. *Ibid.*, p. 47.
30. Andrew F. Walls, *The Missionary Movement in Christian History: Studies in the Transmission of Faith* (Maryknoll, NY: Orbis, 2000), p. 22.
31. Padilla, *Mission Between the Times*, p. 16.

18 Evangelical theology in North American contexts

TIMOTHY GEORGE

In July 2000, some 10,000 evangelists, theologians, mission strategists, and church leaders from more than 200 countries – more than belonged to the United Nations at the time – came together in Amsterdam at the invitation of Billy Graham to renew their commitment and formulate new strategies for world evangelization in the twenty-first century. The theologians' track at this meeting was chaired by James I. Packer, a British theologian based in North America,[1] whose writings had been translated into many languages and whose influence was widely recognized throughout the world evangelical movement. This gathering produced a theological statement, the Amsterdam Declaration, which defined Christian theology as "the task of careful thinking and ordering of life in the presence of the triune God," and also asserted that "theologians can help to clarify and safeguard God's revealed truth" by "providing resources for the training of evangelists and the grounding of new believers in the faith."

Amsterdam 2000, as this conference was called, was a mosaic of global, transdenominational evangelicalism, a religious current identified by Wolfhart Pannenberg as one of three (along with Orthodoxy and Roman Catholicism) vital, ascendant forces within the world Christian movement. The four preceding chapters in this book explore the distinctive voice of evangelical theology as it has emerged in its African, Asian, European, and Latin American contexts. Our purpose here is to review some of the major issues, themes, and leaders that have shaped evangelical theology in North America. Perhaps this chapter will also allow readers of the whole volume to evaluate the degree to which North American evangelicalism is or is not like evangelicalism in other parts of the world and also the degree to which North American evangelicalism does or does not set the tone for discussions and practice in other parts of the world.

SHAPING A TRADITION

Historian William McLoughlin once said that it is as difficult to unscramble eggs as it is to separate evangelicals from nineteenth-century American culture.[2] If 1800–1900 was "the evangelical century" in American history, proponents of this movement look to earlier precedents including the coming of the Pilgrims to Plymouth Bay, the Puritan founding of New England, and a kind of civic righteousness marked by election day sermons and special public occasions, "solemn assemblies," for prayer, fasting, and repentance. Also important was the establishment of centers of learning such as Harvard College, which was intended to be a "seminary in the wilderness" to prepare ministers of the gospel for the service of the church – *pro Christo et ecclesiae*, as an early Harvard seal put it. Also important was a pervasive populist piety shaped by Protestant classics such as John Bunyan's *The Pilgrim's Progress*, John Foxe's *Acts and Monuments of the Christian Church* (Book of Martyrs), and, above all, the King James Version of the Bible.

Among the books brought to the New World on board the *Mayflower* were the Geneva Bible (the KJV was too recent and "liberal" for the separatistic Pilgrims) and the collected works of William Perkins, a Cambridge Puritan theologian who specialized in practical divinity by applying the principles of Calvinist theology to individual "cases of conscience." William Ames, one of Perkins's students, also emphasized the experiential dimension of Christian thinking, defining theology as "the knowledge of living in the presence of the living God."[3] Ames's *Marrow of Sacred Theology* was the first theology textbook used at Harvard College. His synthesis of doctrinal content and spiritual application – head and heart – would characterize the development of theology among evangelical Christians in America.

To a great extent theological development in colonial America extended patterns already adumbrated in the Old World. Roger Williams debated with Quakers in Rhode Island as John Bunyan did in England. The antinomianism of Anne Hutchinson recalled earlier disputes among Lutherans on the Continent and Presbyterians in Scotland. Likewise, the major Reformation standards were adopted by the fledgling denominations in North America: Lutherans in America were loyal to Augsburg, Reformed Christians followed Dort and Westminster, while Anglicans used the Book of Common Prayer with its Thirty-nine Articles of Religion. When the Baptists of Philadelphia hired Benjamin Franklin to publish their first confession of faith in 1742, they adopted as their own the

Second London Confession of 1689 with two additional articles allowing for hymn singing and laying hands on all baptized believers.[4] Despite these continuities, however, the North American context of Protestant Christianity would decisively shape its theology and piety as became clear in the era of the Great Awakenings.

The Awakenings were international, transatlantic movements of ecclesial and spiritual renewal embracing Pietism in Germany, Methodism in Great Britain, and revivalism in the American colonies. A key figure in this development was George Whitefield, a dramatic preacher who made seven trips across the Atlantic and is said to have preached 15,000 times during his thirty-three year career. Whitefield preached up and down the eastern seaboard from Savannah, Georgia to York, Maine, making thousands of converts and stimulating local revivals wherever he went. Whitefield was a Calvinist in theology and quarreled with John Wesley over the doctrine of predestination, though the two were reconciled before Whitefield's death in 1770. The roots of evangelicalism in Canada can also be traced to a series of revivals that swept the Maritimes under the preaching of Nova Scotian evangelist Henry Alline.

The great theologian of the Awakenings, and arguably the most substantial theologian America has yet produced, was Jonathan Edwards. Best remembered for his revival sermon, "Sinners in the Hands of an Angry God," Edwards was a Yale-educated thinker of enormous intellectual range and creativity. Well acquainted with the works of John Locke and Isaac Newton, Edwards sought to present the grand themes of Calvinist theology – divine sovereignty, human depravity, election by grace leading to a life of holiness – in fresh, compelling ways that would make sense to his contemporaries. His books on *Freedom of the Will* (1754) and *Original Sin* (1758), together with his earlier *Treatise Concerning Religious Affections* (1746), reveal his theological depth and insight. In the century after his death, Edwards's legacy became a matter of dispute as some of his theological heirs, notably Lyman Beecher and Nathaniel Taylor, modified Edwards's unique synthesis of Calvinism and revivalism, while others, especially Charles Hodge and his colleagues at Princeton, warned against such devolution. Mark Noll has summed up this development well: "In later generations, American revivalists were more likely to follow Edwards in appealing for the new birth than were American theologians in defending the broadly Calvinistic themes so central to his concern."[5]

When Edwards died in 1758, the energies of the First Great Awakening were largely spent, but new vitalities and new ideas would emerge in the period 1790 to 1830, the era of the Second Great Awakening, which Gordon

S. Wood has called "the time of greatest religious chaos and originality in American history."[6] The ferment of this period decisively shaped the evangelical story and accounts for what historian Timothy L. Smith, also a Nazarene minister, has called "the kaleidoscopic diversity of our histories, our organizational structures, and our doctrinal emphases."[7] Not only did the Awakenings bring new life into some older denominational structures – producing, for example, New Light Congregationalists, New Side Presbyterians, and New Connection Baptists – it also produced a variety of new movements, including Adventist, Holiness, Restorationist, and (in the early twentieth century) Pentecostal churches. In an age that loved religious debate, each new permutation of the evangelical tradition introduced ardent polemics and novel theological emphases based on distinctive appeals to the Bible refracted, to be sure, through the prism of personal religious experience.

At the same time, however, beyond the cacophony of diverse (and sometimes strident) voices, there was an assumed consensus shared by most Protestant Christians in North America. Not even the seismic divide of the Civil War could obliterate this sense of a shared theological heritage. Thus Baptist theologian Francis Wayland, writing in 1861, could claim for his denomination what others could also say about their own: "The theological tenets of the Baptists, both in England and America, may be briefly stated as follows: they are emphatically the doctrines of the Reformation, and they have been held with singular unanimity and consistency."[8] During this time, historians of Christian doctrine begin to speak about the formal and material principles of the Reformation. The formal principle referred to the normativity of Holy Scripture as "the only rule of faith in practice," while the material principle focused on the soteriological doctrine of justification by faith alone. Significantly, subscription to this doctrine was required for all who worked at the Young Men's Christian Association, when shoe salesman-turned-evangelist Dwight L. Moody became affiliated with this organization in Chicago in the 1850s.

Not everyone, of course, was included in this evangelical consensus. Mormons, Christian Scientists, and Jehovah's Witnesses all held to doctrines deemed heterodox from an evangelical perspective. New England transcendentalists and Unitarians denied core Christian doctrines about the Trinity and the deity of Christ. Ecclesiological exclusivism also set apart Baptist Landmarkists, some of the Restorationist followers of Alexander Campbell, and, of course, Vatican I-era Roman Catholics. But the evangelical consensus was sufficiently strong to spawn a host of interdenominational ministries, including orphanages, Bible societies, publication boards, colleges and academies, and above all, an evangelical missionary movement of global proportions. On one occasion, Whitefield, while preaching from a balcony in Philadelphia, looked up to heaven and cried out these words:

> Father Abraham, whom have you in heaven? Any Episcopalians?
> No!
> Any Presbyterians?
> No!
> Any Independents or Methodists?
> No, no, no!
> Whom have you there?
> "We don't know those names here. All who are here are Christians . . ."
> Oh, is this the case? Then God help us to forget party names and to become Christians in deed and in truth.[9]

Without denying denominational distinctives or doctrinal angularities, North American evangelicals embraced a version of what C. S. Lewis would call (reclaiming a term used by the Puritan Richard Baxter) "mere Christianity." Another term for mere Christianity might be *core Christianity*. In an era when, with some exceptions, most Protestant theologians, denominations, and institutions affirmed the Reformational core of classical Christian theology, however informed by current philosophical construals and shaped by the spirituality of the Awakenings, evangelical theology was not sharply distinguished from that which obtained in mainstream Protestant culture as a whole. In the meantime, the evangelical consensus supported numerous movements for social reform, including the abolition of slavery, suffrage, temperance, child labor laws, fair wages for workers, and many other progressive issues to which many theologically conservative Christians were once committed – before what David Moberg has called "the great reversal," an evangelical withdrawal from such concerns.[10]

PROTEST AND RETREAT

When D. L. Moody died in 1899, the evangelical vision of America as a nation imbued with orthodox Christian values still appeared to be intact. Two years before Moody was born, Alexis de Tocqueville published *Democracy in America* (1835) in which he wrote that "there is no country in the world where the Christian religion retains a greater influence over the souls of men than in America."[11] This still seemed to be the case as the new century dawned, but there were troubling signs that evangelical theology would face new challenges in the era ahead. Already several major denominations had faced internal struggles over historicist methods of biblical criticism that seem to impugn the integrity of the Bible. Theological liberals de-emphasized the supernatural origin of Scripture and with it many of the classical teachings of Christianity. At the same time, the growing acceptance of Darwinism in the natural sciences seemed to place the historic orthodox understanding of creation on a collision course with the dominant trend of modern thought. Though some conservative theologians, such as Benjamin Warfield, found Genesis 1 and 2 compatible with certain forms of theistic evolution, many others believed that such views required a more defiant theological response.

In 1910 the general assembly of the Presbyterian Church adopted the "Five Fundamentals" that were to become a rallying cry for conservative Protestants: the virgin birth of Christ, the inerrancy of Scripture, objective substitutionary atonement, bodily resurrection, and authenticity of the biblical miracles. Over the next five years a series of twelve paperbacks appeared called *The Fundamentals*. These pamphlets were sent free of charge to Protestant ministers and Christian workers across America and helped to consolidate a coalition of protest against the rising tide of "Modernism," the name given to the impulse of accommodation on the part of those who sought to revise traditional Christian doctrines in the light of evolution, biblical criticism, and a more optimistic view of the human condition. In 1920, Curtis Lee Laws, a Baptist editor, called on his fellow conservatives "to do battle royal for the Fundamentals." Laws defined fundamentalism as "a protest against that rationalistic interpretation of Christianity which seeks to discredit supernaturalism."[12]

Fundamentalism was largely a populist movement supported by zealous pastors, itinerant Bible teachers, and evangelists such as Billy Sunday, who once boasted that he knew no more about theology than a jack-rabbit knew about ping-pong! However, among those who contributed to *The Fundamentals* was a cadre of serious scholars that included the Scottish theologian James Orr, Anglican bishop H. C. G. Moule, Southern Baptist educator E. Y. Mullins, and the Princeton stalwart, B. B. Warfield. One of Warfield's younger colleagues, J. Gresham Machen, who commanded the respect of such notable liberals as H. L. Mencken and Walter Lippmann, was a New Testament scholar of note who had studied in Germany and published impressive studies on the virgin birth of Christ and the origin of Paul's religion. In 1923 he published *Christianity and Liberalism*, a classic statement of evangelical theology in which he contrasted orthodox and

Modernist views on God, Christ, the Bible, sin, salvation, and the church. His main point was as simple as it was drastic: through its compromise of historic Christian teaching on these crucial issues, liberalism had "evolved" into a new and different religion. Though Machen was a stout Presbyterian who appreciated the depth of the historic divide between Catholicism and his own Protestant confessional tradition, he was willing to say that the gulf between Rome and Geneva was negligible compared to the gaping chasm – he used the word *abyss* – separating classic Christians from those who eviscerated the historic Christian faith.

During the later 1920s and 1930s, the fundamentalist–Modernist conflict shifted from a battle over ideas to a struggle for control of denominations and church institutions. In the white Southern and African American denominations, liberal inroads were minimal and the conflict was subdued. However, there were major splits among Baptists and Presbyterians in the North and fractious infighting among Methodists, Congregationalists, and Disciples of Christ as well. Augustus H. Strong, a major theological voice among Baptists in the North, reluctantly sided with the fundamentalists because he saw the rise of Modernism as a threat to the gospel itself. A mediator by temperament, however, Strong criticized both sides. The fundamentalists were not fundamental enough, he said, for they failed to appreciate the culture-transforming aspect of Christ's incarnation. Liberals, on the other hand, with telescopes in hand, can "see a fly on a barn door a half mile off, but they cannot see the door."[13] More typical of the militancy of the fundamentalist movement was Canadian pastor T. T. Shields, the "battling Baptist," who declared at the height of the controversy, "As far as I am concerned, I will have no compromise with the enemy. I have declared again and again that I have resigned from the diplomatic corps; I am a soldier in the field, and as God gives me strength, everywhere, as long as I live, in the name of the Lord, I will smite [Modernism]."[14]

Future developments in North American evangelical theology were affected by three aspects of the early twentieth-century fundamentalist movement.

(1) Its ecumenical character. Like the Awakenings and missionary movements that preceded it, fundamentalism was a transdenominational phenomenon that transcended many confessional and theological divides. For example, the fundamentalist coalition included staunch Calvinists and consistent Arminians, dispensational premillenialists and others with contrasting eschatologies, advocates of perfectionist and holiness views of sanctification, as well as those who were skeptical of such doctrines of the Christian life. What united such disparate groups were a common

commitment to the inspiration and unique authority of the Bible, usually embracing a view of biblical inerrancy, and a concern, exemplified by Machen, that the Christian faith itself was under attack.

(2) Its patriotic context. While the theological issues debated in this conflict were not unique to North America, the political and social setting in which they took place gave them a more prominent role in the unfolding evangelical story. During World War I, fundamentalists often equated liberal criticism of the Bible and its roots in German rationalistic theology with the Kaiser's imperialistic policies. Evangelical theology in North America (more so in the United States than in Canada where the fundamentalist movement was always a much tinier minority) would be marked by tension between global mission and national revival on the one hand and a turned-in-on-itself piety and exclusivism on the other.

(3) Its separatistic thrust. In the years following the Scopes Trial (1925), a public relations disaster for conservative Protestants, fundamentalism seemed to be in full retreat, having lost control of major denominations and theological institutions. Ideologically displaced and culturally homeless in their own country, such fundamentalists resembled in some ways the numerous communities of immigrants flooding into the major cities of America at the time. "Wherefore come out from among them, and be ye separate, saith the Lord," as 2 Corinthians 6:17 reads in the KJV, could be regarded as the key Bible verse of this movement which made a virtue out of its quarantined ecclesiology. At the same time, as Joel Carpenter has shown, although sequestered from the mainstream religious currents of the time, these believers were not idle.[15] They were busy developing a host of agencies, Bible schools, mission societies, publishing houses, and the like, that would spawn a revival of conservative evangelicalism following the Second World War.

FROM THE MARGINS TO THE MAINSTREAM

A new phase of the evangelical saga in North America began during the ferment of World War II and the first decade of the Cold War that followed. This movement was dubbed "neo-evangelicalism" by Harold John Ockenga, an erudite Boston pastor and a major force in three institutions that would take the lead in this new approach: the National Association of Evangelicals (1942), Fuller Theological Seminary (1947), and Christianity Today (1956). What these new reformers sought was a kind of progressive fundamentalism that would be "anchored to the Rock, but geared to the times," to quote the motto of Youth for Christ, an organization that launched the ministry of Billy Graham, the world's most famous evangelical and the public face and voice of the movement for millions.

A number of new theological voices gave shape to North American evangelical thought during this period.

Carl F. H. Henry (1913–2003)

Henry, a member of the founding faculty of Fuller Seminary and the first editor of *Christianity Today*, published in 1947 a small book, *The Uneasy Conscience of Modern Fundamentalism*, in which he called on fellow conservatives to come out of their intellectual ghetto in order to pursue vigorous social and cultural engagement for the sake of the gospel. Henry was not proposing a revisionist version of evangelical theology. As he would later say, he and his colleagues were seeking "to restate where fundamentalism ought to be in the light of its own heritage."[16] Henry rejected liberal versions of the social gospel that tended to be all social and no gospel, but he appealed to the earlier evangelical consensus of cultural engagement and social reform. This theme would echo through Henry's later writings including *Christian Personal Ethics* (1957) and *Aspects of Christian Social Ethics* (1963). For Christian social activism to be effective, he said, it had to be supported by solid theological reflection based upon biblical revelation. Metaphysics and ethics go together, Henry believed, and this assumption shaped his persistent critique of contemporary trends in philosophy and theology. From his *Remaking the Modern Mind* (1946) through his massive six-volume theological epistemology, *God, Revelation and Authority* (1976–83), Henry challenged and debated with competing worldviews and alternative theological construals in the name of historic biblical theism which accepted the authority of Scripture as the inerrant Word of God. Through his pivotal leadership at *Christianity Today* and his close association with Billy Graham, Henry influenced evangelical thought beyond North America. In 1966 he co-chaired with Graham the World Congress on Evangelism in Berlin, the precursor of the 1974 International Conference on World Evangelization at Lausanne. In recent years, Henry's theology has been criticized by younger evangelicals who find his emphasis on the propositional nature of biblical revelation and a deductive theology based on rationally justifiable truth claims inadequate for the present postmodern situation. But Henry's theological work, both in scope and depth, remains unparalleled, despite his waning influence among contemporary thinkers. As a scholar outside the evangelical community has put it, Henry "has championed evangelical

Christianity with clarity of language, comprehensiveness of scholarship, clarity of mind, and vigor of spirit."[17]

E. J. Carnell (1919–1967)

Edward John Carnell was one of Henry's colleagues at Fuller Seminary, an insightful thinker who held doctorates from both Harvard and Boston University. Both Henry and Carnell had studied with the Calvinist philosopher Gordon H. Clark at Wheaton College and his rigorous Christian rationalism left its imprint on both men. Carnell's first book, *An Introduction to Christian Apologetics* (1948), set the direction for his life's work over the next two decades. Carnell once remarked that in his view evangelicals were desperately in need of prestige, and he did his best to give them some in the world of academic theology. In addition to *A Philosophy of the Christian Religion* (1952), Carnell published *Critical Studies of the Theology of Reinhold Niebuhr* (1951) and *Soren Kierkegaard* (1965), as well as a major statement of evangelical belief, *A Case for Orthodox Theology* (1959). Carnell also participated in a public dialogue with Karl Barth during the latter's only visit to North America in 1962. Many of the tensions that course through evangelical thought were present in the troubled life of E. J. Carnell. For example, he remained strongly committed to biblical inerrancy even though his own school removed that doctrinal distinctive from its statement of faith. At the same time, Carnell drew (not so) friendly fire from fellow conservatives when he referred to fundamentalism as "orthodoxy gone cultic." Perhaps Carnell is best interpreted as a forerunner of emerging trends within North American evangelicalism. Anticipating a technological revolution that would play a major role in evangelical outreach, Carnell published in 1950 *Television: Servant or Master?* His interest in Barth, whom he called an "inconsistent evangelical," and his openness for ecumenical dialogue also presaged future developments. Carnell's emphasis on the church as a community of love has led one scholar to refer to his later works as "apologetics for the tender-minded."[18] Carnell's Christ-centered piety is well expressed in this reflection on the Christian's hope for eternal life:

> We are alone when we enter the world, but when we leave it we shall feel the abiding presence of the Lord. As death draws near and we dread the dark journey ahead, the Lord will assure us that our lives are precious in the sight of God. He will gently say, 'Child, come home.' Jesus has given his word that he will never leave us or forsake us, and his word is as firm as his character.[19]

Bernard Ramm (1916–1992)

A native of Montana, Ramm studied at Eastern Baptist Theological Seminary and took graduate degrees in the philosophy of science at the University of Southern California. His teaching career, which began at the Bible Institute of Los Angeles, took him across a large swath of the American evangelical landscape. One of his most important books was *The Christian View of Science and Scripture* (1954). Like Carnell, Ramm was concerned with how evangelical theologians could present effective apologetics in the face of challenges posed by the Enlightenment and modern science. Like Henry, Ramm worked within the main lines of Reformed theology, but he came to a more positive appreciation of Karl Barth than either of his contemporaries. Barth's theology, he believed, was "a restatement of Reformed theology written in the aftermath of the Enlightenment but not capitulating to it."[20] Ramm did not accept Barth's theology *tout court*, challenging, for example, its tilt toward universalism. But in his influential book *After Fundamentalism* (1983), Ramm encouraged North American evangelicals to engage Barth as a constructive discussion partner in their own theological work. Having read through every page of the massive *Church Dogmatics* during a sabbatical with Barth in Basel, Ramm believed that such a close encounter with this major thinker would clear away many popular misconceptions of his theological method and content. Ramm's later books, *An Evangelical Christology* (1985) and *Offense to Reason: A Theology of Sin* (1985), both betray the Barthian turn in Ramm's development, though he was never able to synthesize Barth's work and the major themes of evangelical theology in an entirely satisfactory way.

Donald Bloesch (1928–)

Unlike the other thinkers we have reviewed here, Donald Bloesch did not emerge from the neo-evangelical matrix of post-fundamentalist conservative struggles. Rather, his spiritual and theological roots lie in the traditions of German and Swiss Pietism. For thirty-five years he taught at the University of Dubuque Theological Seminary, affiliated with the mainline Presbyterian denomination. Bloesch himself, along with Gabriel Fackre, an evangelically friendly ecumenical theologian, has been a major force for theological renewal within the United Church of Christ, one of the most liberal denominations in North America. At the same time, through his prolific writings, Bloesch has had a significant influence within the evangelical community and beyond. Like Ramm, but perhaps with more acuity and critical comprehension, Bloesch has appropriated the theology of Karl Barth. His book *Jesus is Victor!: Karl Barth's Doctrine* of Salvation (1976) is an important study of Barth's soteriology. Mindful of the strengths of Pietism and standing squarely within the major stream of Reformation theology, Bloesch has mined the wider Christian tradition in his irenic restatement of classical theology. This spirit is evident in his two-volume *Essentials of Evangelical Theology* (1978–79), as well as his major seven-volume systematic theology, *Christian Foundations* (1992–2004), a wide-ranging compendium that some have called the evangelical summa of the twentieth century. Bloesch has been described as a "progressive" evangelical theologian, but he has issued strong warnings against the kind of uncritical accommodation evident in radical feminism (*Is the Bible Sexist?*, 1982), therapeutic spiritualities (*The Struggle of Prayer*, 1980), and challenges to traditional Trinitarian theology (*The Battle for the Trinity*, 1985). And, while appreciative of certain emphases in both narrative theology and open theism, Bloesch has demurred on both fronts, affirming "the propositional dimension of biblical revelation" on the one hand, and "the sovereignty of divine grace as well as human freedom on the other."[21] Bloesch is best interpreted as a bridging figure whose work spans many of the creative tensions within evangelical theology as well as several trajectories of the historic Christian tradition.

Clark H. Pinnock (1937–)

A Canadian theologian with wide-ranging experiences and an uneven trajectory, Clark H. Pinnock represents those North American evangelicals who want to work within the tradition but whose ideas have led them to challenge some of its most cherished assumptions. Brought up in a liberal Baptist congregation in Toronto, Pinnock was converted to Christ at age twelve, and, as a new believer, was influenced by both Youth for Christ and the Keswick movement. As a young theologian, his two mentors were F. F. Bruce, with whom he studied New Testament at Manchester University, and Francis Schaeffer, who confirmed Pinnock's early interest in apologetics and Reformed theology. His first teaching job was at a Southern Baptist seminary in New Orleans where he defended biblical inerrancy and militantly attacked Southern Baptist theologians who denied it. Pinnock's book *Biblical Revelation* (1971) best represents this period of his career. Over the years, however, Pinnock came to question a number of his earlier views. In *The Scripture Principle* (1984), Pinnock presented a much more nuanced view of inerrancy. In a number of books he wrote or edited, including *Grace Unlimited* (1975), *The Grace of God, The Will of Man: A Case for Arminianism* (1989), *Tracking the Maze* (1990), and *A Wideness in God's Mercy* (1992), Pinnock abandoned his early

Augustinian–Calvinist soteriology in favor of more Arminian construals of grace and conversion. More recently, Pinnock (along with John Sanders) advocated a more inclusivist view of salvation among the unevangelized, and (with Gregory Boyd and Richard Rice) he has argued for a form of open theism which questions God's comprehensive knowledge of future contingents. Pinnock's revisionist theology has influenced a number of younger evangelical theologians who push the boundaries of evangelical thought in a more liberal or progressivist direction. At the same time, he strongly claims the evangelical heritage as his own and, in a raucous row over open theism, the Evangelical Theological Society voted in November 2003 to retain him in its membership. Reiterating his commitment to the historic truths of the incarnation and atonement, and of salvation by grace through faith in Jesus Christ, as well as the infallibility of the Bible as the norm of the evangelical message, Pinnock described what it means for him to write as an evangelical theologian:

> I am not writing theoretically or abstractly. I feel keenly about my subject matter here. As a theologian I work where the battle for the Gospel truth rages fiercely. As a church member and deacon, I long for the church to come alive under God. As a Canadian citizen I grieve over the decline of North America into the secular abyss and thirst for its Christian reconstruction.[22]

Thomas C. Oden (1931–)

If the trajectory of Pinnock's theological pilgrimage has been from a strict conservative pole to a more open-ended position, then that of Thomas C. Oden has been in the opposite direction. In what he has called his "long journey home," Oden traces his trek from modern theology (especially its Freudian and Bultmannian mutations) to an embrace of the classic Christian faith or what he has called paleo-orthodoxy. In two books, *Agenda for Theology* (1979) and *After Modernity – What?* (1990), Oden described this transformation and set forth his program for the retrieval of the classic orthodox tradition. One of Oden's teachers, Will Herberg, once chided him for neglecting the writings of the patristic and medieval eras; Oden's decisive theological turn was aimed at a recovery of the consensual wisdom of the apostolic witness as reflected in this literature. This involved taking seriously, in the words of Lancelot Andrewes, "one canon, two testaments, three creeds (the Apostles', Nicene and Athanasian), four (ecumenical) councils, and five centuries along with the fathers of that period."[23] These principles have undergirded Oden's prolific writings including his works on pastoral theology, biblical exegesis, ecclesiology, and a major three-volume systematic theology. Perhaps more than anyone else, Oden has worked assiduously to bring the evangelical community into creative dialogue with the Great Tradition and this is nowhere better seen than in the *Ancient Christian Commentary on Scripture*, an impressive twenty-seven volume series of the early church's exegetical work arranged in canonical order. A loyal member of the United Methodist Church, Oden has served as a theological advisor to the Confessing Movement within his denomination and, in an effort to reverse liberalizing trends of recent decades, he has encouraged similar renewal movements in other mainline Protestant denominations as well. In doing so, Oden has called for a "new ecumenism" that cuts across traditional confessional and denominational lines in favor of a deeper unity derived from the biblical and classical sources of the Christian faith.

Millard J. Erickson (1932–)

With deep roots in the Swedish Baptist tradition, Millard J. Erickson majored in philosophy at the University of Minnesota before completing theological and graduate studies at three institutions in Chicago – Northern Baptist Theological Seminary, the University of Chicago, and Northwestern University. His dissertation was an analysis of the theology of Henry, Ramm, and Carnell. Erickson's trilogy of primary sources, *Readings in Christian Theology* (1973–79), and his three-volume systematic work, *Christian Theology* (1983–85), have been translated into several languages and are widely used as college and seminary textbooks. His doctoral mentor, William Hordern, has claimed that Erickson's systematic theology did for North American evangelicalism what Karl Barth's *Church Dogmatics* did for neo-orthodoxy. Erickson is well acquainted with biblical theology and the history of doctrine, drawing heavily on these sources in his creative synthesis of evangelical theology. Erickson affirms the inspiration and inerrancy of Scripture but pays close attention to its phenomenological language. He follows the main lines of Reformed soteriology but affirms the universal extent of the atonement. He writes as a Baptist theologian but is sensitive to wider evangelical and ecumenical concerns. Erickson is fully supportive of the role of women in ministry but does not accept the revisionist conclusions of much contemporary feminist theology. Erickson writes with analytical precision and is well aware of wider theological currents, including the work of Continental theologians such as Wolfhart Pannenberg. He is also a theological trend-watcher and has carefully analyzed both the promise and the perils of postmodernism, postconservatism, and other trajectories of "the evangelical left." Both in his *Truth or Consequences* (2001) and in his contribution to *Reclaiming the Center* (2004), he criticized the narrow focus and largely reactionary bent of much recent so-called progressive evangelicalism. The burden of Erickson's own theological contribution, however, is more constructive than critical, as can be seen in his writings on Christology (*The Word Became Flesh*, 1991), Trinitarian theology (*God in Three Persons*, 1995), and soteriological inclusivism (*How Shall They Be Saved?: The Destiny of Those Who Do Not Hear of Jesus*, 1996).

J. I. Packer (1926–)

James Inell Packer, who turned 80 in 2006, is a British-born Anglican theologian who has taught at Regent College, Vancouver, since 1979. Well versed in Reformation theology and the classics of the Puritan tradition, Packer writes theology with an eye toward spiritual nurture, pastoral application, and evangelistic outreach. His *Knowing God* (1973) is one of the most popular theological studies of the twentieth century and has become a classic within the world evangelical community. In this and many other books, some with intriguing titles such as *Keep in Step with the Spirit* (1984) and *Hot Tub Religion* (1987), Packer has become the leading catechetical theologian of the evangelical movement. Together with Oden, he published *One Faith: The Evangelical Consensus* (2004), a series of extracts from evangelical statements of faith produced since 1950. Oden the Arminian and Packer the Calvinist collaborated to show how both major streams of evangelical history converge to nurture contemporary evangelical theology. Evangelical Christians differ over issues such as the proper form of church government, the meaning and mode of baptism, glossolalia, millennialism, theological epistemology, forms of worship, and others, but most will recognize themselves in the definition this book presents –

> those who read the Bible as God's own Word, addressed personally to each of them here and now; and who live out of a personal trust in, and love for, Jesus Christ as the world's only Lord and Savior. They are people who see themselves as sinners saved by grace through faith for glory; who practice loyal obedience to God; and who are active both in grateful, hopeful communion with the triune God by prayer, and in neighbor-love, with a lively commitment to disciple-making according to the Great Commission.[24]

Packer has garnered further attention through his participation in and advocacy for the project known as Evangelicals and Catholics Together, an ongoing theological workgroup convened by Charles W. Colson and Father Richard John Neuhaus for the purpose of exploring greater unity and cooperation between Roman Catholics and evangelical Christians in North America. Packer's transatlantic career demonstrates the way in which theology in North America, a continent peopled by immigrants, has received and contextualized various currents of thought from abroad, even as theologies wrought in the crucible of North American conflicts and developments have been exported to nearly every nation through the global missionary movement and, increasingly, through the universalizing reach of information technology and new media resources.

PROSPECT FOR THE FUTURE

The thinkers summarized here are by no means a complete list of significant theological voices among evangelicals in North America. Further discussion would need to include the late Stanley Grenz, whose untimely death in 2005 deprived the evangelical community of one of its most prolific theologians; Kevin J. Vanhoozer, whose book *Is There a Meaning in this Text?* (1998) deals in a nuanced way with hermeneutical issues raised by postmodernism; Steven Land, Cheryl Bridges Johns, and Frank Macchia, who write from Pentecostal perspectives; David Wells, who in a series of important studies (*No Place for Truth*, 1993; *God in the Wasteland*, 1994; *Losing Our Virtue*, 1998; *Above All Earthly Pow'rs*, 2005) has warned the North American evangelical church about the theological consequences of accommodating to a consumerist culture; and Miroslav Volf, a Yale theologian with European roots, who has made significant contributions to ecclesiology and pneumatology. Evangelical scholars in North America who work in the disciplines of philosophy and history have made more notable contributions to the wider academy than those engaged in theological studies. In part, this is because religious studies displaced theology in many academic institutions and those scholars who take theological commitments seriously are a shrinking minority within an increasingly secularized academy. Evangelical theology, however, is flourishing where evangelicals have always been strongest – at the grassroots, among new believers, in local communities of faith. The theologians of choice among such evangelicals are not guilded scholars but pastors. Three pastors – Rick Warren, John Piper, and Brian McLaren – are arguably more influential among North American evangelicals today than any academic theologian.

While some interpret current tensions within evangelical theology as a sign of its fracturing and demise, they are better seen as indications of vitality and renewed strength, if not quite yet another awakening.

Evangelical theology of the future will have different demographics from that of today, with the voices of women and persons of color more prominent than they have been thus far. Though new ideas will doubtless continue to bubble up, elitist issues that sometimes stir academic debate, such as open theism or the niceties of postmodern theory, will not likely find deep root among believers in local congregations or on the mission fields. There, evangelicals will be more concerned about how to live the Christian life and bear faithful witness in a culture no longer normed by the standards of truth, beauty, or goodness. Future evangelicals in North America will also need to listen more carefully than they have done in the past to the vibrant voices of the global evangelical family. This, in turn, will lead North American evangelicals to find solidarity with Christians in other ecclesial traditions who take seriously the core theological commitments of biblical faith.

Further reading

Bloesch, Donald G. *Christian Foundations* series. Downers Grove, IL: InterVarsity, 1992–2004.

Erickson, Millard J. *Christian Theology*. Second edition. Grand Rapids, MI: Baker, 1998.

Erickson, Millard J., Paul Kjoss Helseth, and Justin Taylor (eds.). *Reclaiming the Center: Confronting Evangelical Accommodation in Postmodern Times.* Wheaton, IL: Crossway, 2004.

Grenz, Stanley J. *Renewing the Center: Evangelical Theology in a Post-Theological Era.* Grand Rapids, MI: Baker, 2000.

Henry, Carl F. H. *God, Revelation, and Authority.* 6 vols. Waco, TX: Word, 1976–83.

Lints, Richard. *The Fabric of Theology: A Prolegomenon to Evangelical Theology.* Grand Rapids, MI: Eerdmans, 1993.

Olson, Roger E. *The Westminster Handbook to Evangelical Theology.* Louisville, KY: Westminster John Knox, 2004.

Packer, J. I., and Thomas C. Oden (eds.). *One Faith: The Evangelical Consensus.* Downers Grove, IL: InterVarsity, 2004.

Pinnock, Clark, et al. (eds.). *The Openness of God.* Downers Grove, IL: InterVarsity, 1994.

Ramm, Bernard. *The Evangelical Heritage.* Reprint with a foreword by Kevin J. Vanhoozer. Grand Rapids, MI: Baker Academic, 2000.

Stackhouse, John G., Jr. (ed.). *Evangelical Futures: A Conversation on Theological Method.* Grand Rapids, MI: Baker Academic, 2000.

Notes

1. From the editors: for cultural reasons, it made more sense to include Mexican theology in the article on the Latin American context, rather than here.
2. William G. McLoughlin, *The American Evangelicals, 1800–1900, and Anthology* (New York: Harper Torchbacks, 1968), p. 26.
3. My translation of Ames's dictum: *Theologia est scientia vivendo deo*. See Keith L. Sprunger, *The Learned Dr. Ames* (Champaign: University of Illinois Press, 1972).

4. The first "indigenous" confession of faith among Baptists in America was the New Hampshire Confession of 1833. See William H. Brackney, A Genetic History of Baptist Thought (Macon, GA: Mercer University Press, 2004).

5. Mark A. Noll, A History of Christianity in the United States and Canada (Grand Rapids, MI: Eerdmans, 1992), p. 97.

6. Gordon S. Wood, "Evangelical America and Early Mormonism," New York History 61 (1980): 359–86, p. 362.

7. Timothy L. Smith, "The Evangelical Kaleidoscope and the Call to Christian Unity," Christian Scholar's Review 15 (1986): 125–40, p. 126.

8. Francis Wayland, The Principles and Practices of Baptist Churches (London: J. Heaton and Son, 1861), pp. 15–16.

9. Quoted in Winthrop S. Hudson, American Protestantism (Chicago: University of Chicago Press, 1961), p. 45.

10. David O. Moberg, The Great Reversal: Evangelism Versus Social Action (London: Scripture Union, 1972).

11. Alexis de Tocqueville, Democracy in America (New York: P. F. Collier and Son, 1900).

12. Curtis Lee Laws, "Convention Side Lights," Watchman–Examiner 8 (1 July 1920), p. 834, cited in George M. Marsden, Fundamentalism and American Culture: The Shaping of Twentieth Century Evangelicalism, 1870–1925 (New York: Oxford University Press, 1980), p. 159 fn. 19.

13. Augustus H. Strong, What Shall I Believe? (New York: Revell, 1922), pp. 62–63. See also Grant Wacker, Augustus H. Strong and the Dilemma of Historical Consciousness (Macon, GA: Mercer University Press, 1985).

14. T. T. Shields, in Gospel Witness 2 (31 May 1923); quoted in John G. Stackhouse, Canadian Evangelicalism in the Twentieth Century (Toronto: University of Toronto Press, 1993), p. 23.

15. Joel Carpenter, Revive Us Again: The Reawakening of American Fundamentalism (Oxford: Oxford University Press, 1997).

16. Carl Henry and Kenneth Kantzer, "Standing on the Promise," Christianity Today (16 September 1996): 28–36.

17. E. G. Homrighausen, review of A Plea for Evangelical Demonstration by Carl F. H. Henry, Princeton Seminary Bulletin 65 (July 1972): 96–97, p. 96.

18. Kenneth C. Harper, "Edward John Carnell: An Evaluation of his Apologetics," Journal of the Evangelical Theological Society 20 (1977): 133–45.

19. E. J. Carnell, "Fear of Death and the Hope of the Resurrection," in Ronald H. Nash (ed.), The Case for Biblical Christianity (collected writings of Carnell) (Grand Rapids, MI: Eerdmans, 1969), pp. 181–82.

20. Bernard Ramm, After Fundamentalism: The Future of Evangelical Theology (San Francisco: Harper and Row, 1983), p. 14.

21. "Donald Bloesch Responds," in Elmer M. Colyer (ed.), Evangelical Theology in Transition (Downers Grove, IL: InterVarsity, 1999), p. 184.

22. Clark H. Pinnock, Three Keys to Spiritual Renewal (Minneapolis, MN: Bethany, 1985), p. 11.

23. Quoted in Thomas C. Oden, "Back to the Fathers," Christianity Today (24 September 1990): 28–31, p. 28.

24. J. I. Packer and Thomas C. Oden (eds.), One Faith: The Evangelical Consensus (Downers Grove, IL: InterVarsity, 2004), p. 19.

Index

Abelard, Peter, 81–82
activism, 2, 10, 12, 29, 155, 247, 248, 252, 255, 279, 283
Adeyemo, Tokunboh, 214, 218
Adventists, 278
African Americans, 177, 253–54, 281
Agamben, Giorgio, 179, 180–86
Alline, Henry, 277
Alves, Rubem, 263, 264
Ames, William, 276
Amsterdam, 275
Anabaptists, 83, 86, 146, 155
Anderson, Allan, 231
Anderson, Norman, 199, 204, 207
Andrewes, Lancelot, 287
Anglican Communion, 242, 243, 246, 276
    restoration of, 247, 248, 252, 278
Anglo-Catholic, 127, 246–47
Anselm (of Canterbury), 59, 81–82, 88–89, 180
apologetics, 59, 247, 253, 285
Aquinas, Thomas, 19–20, 88, 89
Arana, Pedro, 266
Aristotle, 167, 183
Arius, 171
Arminianism, 18, 24, 25, 30, 115–16, 117, 242, 246, 287
Arminius, Jacobus, 115
arts, 155
Athanasius, 89, 94–95, 171
atonement, 79, 81–83, 244, 245, 255
    and the wrath of God, 82–83
    moral influence, 82
    objective, 81–82
    (penal) substitution, 9, 10, 81, 82–83, 244, 248, 250, 253, 255, 259–63
    satisfaction, 82, 89
    subjective, 81–82
Augustine, 71, 79, 95, 109, 117, 180, 204

Bacon, Francis, 147
Baéz-Camargo, Gonzalo, 262
Bajeux, J. C., 217
Baldwin, H. Scott, 165
baptism, 117, 232, 234
Baptists, 252, 276, 278, 281
Barbosa Souza, Ricardo, 266
Barreiro, Julio, 263
Barron, Bruce, 128
Barth, Karl, 26, 39, 58–59, 202, 249, 250, 252, 255, 284, 285, 288
Bartolomé de Las Casas, 260
Bauman, Zygmunt, 253
Baur, F. C., 52
Baxter, Richard, 233, 279
Beasley-Murray, George, 251
Bebbington, David, 1–2, 128, 225, 228, 241, 249, 254
    Quadrilateral, 1, 2, 128, 225, 228, 254
Bedford, Nancy, 266
Bediako, Kwame, 27, 219–20
Beecher, Lyman, 277
Berkhof, Hendrikus, 131
Berkouwer, G. C., 53
Bérule, Pierre de, 193
Bible, 1, 7–9, 21, 26, 54, 135, 247, 255, 278
    authority of, 35–36, 54, 156, 164–67, 218, 228, 244, 254, 255, 266, 271, 278
    criticism of, 38, 52, 56, 60, 244, 251, 280
    inerrancy of, 8, 38–40, 228, 254, 255, 282, 284, 286
    infallibility of, 38–40, 228

293

Bible, (cont.)
   inspiration of, 9, 36–38, 247, 254, 282
   interpretation of, 40–45, 60–61, 165, 233
   narrative of, 26–27, 71, 76, 110
   Sola scriptura, 8–9, 35, 200, 201, 244
Biel, Gabriel, 84
Birks, T. R., 247, 248
Blocher, Henri, 251
Bloesch, Donald, 99, 285–86
Boethius, 167
Boff, Clodovis, 263
Boff, Leonardo, 263
Booth, Catherine, 248
Booth, John, 248
Boyd, Gregory, 287
Braga, Erasmo, 262
Bridges Johns, Cheryl, 290
Briner, Bob, 155
Bruce, F. F., 251, 286
Buber, Martin, 168
Bujo, Bénézet, 216
Bulgakov, Sergei, 95
Bullon, H. Humberto, 266
Bultmann, Rudolf, 56
Bunyan, John, 276
Butler, Joseph, 244
Butler, Judith, 178

Calvin, John, 21, 72, 87–88, 100–01, 136,
   145, 167
Calvinism, 18, 24, 30, 86–87, 242, 243, 246,
   248, 277
Campbell, Alexander, 278
Canclini, Santiago, 262
Carlson Brown, Joanne, 89
Carnell, E. J., 284
Carpenter, Joel, 282
Casas, Bartolomé de Las, 260
Catholic, 28, 130
Chalke, Steve, 255
Chalmers, Thomas, 4, 244–45, 246,
   248, 253
Chan, Simon, 129
charismatic, 10, 120, 225, 227, 251,
   252, 265
Charles, Thomas, 244
Clark, Gordon H., 284
classical theism, 19–21, 23–24, 171
Coleridge, Samuel Taylor, 244, 246, 254
Colson, Charles W., 290
Columbus, Christopher, 259
common sense realism, 147–49

community, 72, 75, 95, 96, 97, 101–02,
   118–19, 120, 121, 164, 173
Congregationalists, 278, 281
contextualization, 44, 154, 229, 234
conversion, 1, 10–12, 109–19, 148–51, 154,
   226, 227, 228, 255
Costas, Orlando, 266–67
Crawford, T. J., 248, 251
creation, 66–67, 74–75, 96, 254, 255
creed, 4, 28, 44–45, 171
   Apostles', 4
   Nicene, 4, 28, 93, 130–31
cross (or crucicentrism), 1, 9–10, 187, 193,
   228, 231
Crow, John A., 259
culture, 145, 154, 155, 206, 219, 249, 252,
   266, 271

Dabney, Robert Lewis, 98
Dain, Jack, 153
Dale, R. W., 248
Daly, John Patrick, 189
Darby, John Nelson, 150, 246, 247, 248, 252
Darwin, Charles, 149, 247, 280
Dawn, Marva, 18
Del Colle, Ralph, 98
Denney, James, 52, 248
denominations, 127, 246, 247, 252, 275, 276
   mainline, 133, 199, 214, 225, 227, 229,
      280–81
   renewal of, 288
   separation from, 251, 282
Descartes, René, 167
Dickson, Kwesi, 218
dispensationalism, 150
Dissenters, 243, 246
doctrine, 203, 214–15, 220, 226, 242, 251, 252,
   255, 275, 276, 277
Don Francisco Giner de los Ríos, 261
Don Miguel de Unamuno, 262
Douglass, Frederick, 190
Drummond, Henry, 247
Dunn, James D. G., 57
Dussell, Enrique, 263
Dyrness, William, 231

Eastern Orthodoxy, 4–5, 35, 88–89, 94
ecclesiology, 102, 103–04, 125–38, 215,
   263, 269
   black, 254, 280
   church growth, 265–69
   incarnational, 135–36, 264

missional, 133–34, 137, 267
transdenominational, 281, 284, 288
Trinitarian, 136, 208
economics, 260, 263, 266, 270
Edwards, Jonathan, 5, 148, 149, 243, 244,
   251, 277
Ela, Jean-Marc, 215
Ellacuria, Ignacio, 264
Ellingworth, Paul, 218
Ellison, Ralph, 177
Ellul, Jacques, 268
embodiment, 71, 72
emergent church, 132–33, 252–53
Enlightenment, 147, 148, 168, 227, 254
Erickson, Millard, 96, 202, 215, 288–89
Erskine, Ebenezer, 242
Erskine, John, 242, 245, 248
Erskine, Ralph, 242
eschatology, 70, 72–73, 100–03, 113–14, 118,
   137–38, 201, 234, 261
   postmillennial, 147, 150
   premillenial, 149–51, 247
Escobar, Samuel, 266, 268
Eucharist, 232
Evangelical Alliance (UK), 2, 3, 4, 9, 10, 249
Evangelical Theological Society (USA), 25,
   33, 287
"Evangelicals and Catholics Together,"
   83, 289
experience, 126, 148, 233, 243, 276, 278

Fackre, Gabriel, 285
faith, 111–12, 113–14, 157, 200, 204, 262
Farley, Edward, 23
federal theology, 60
Fee, Gordon, 117, 164
feminism, 74, 100–01
feminist theology, 100–01, 163
Festus, Pompeius, 181–82
Finney, Charles, 127, 148, 249
Finney, Elizabeth, 249
Fitch, David, 129
Forsyth, P. T., 9, 52, 250
Foucault, Michel, 184
Foxe, John, 276
Frame, John, 17
Francis of Assisi, 2
Franklin, Benjamin, 276
free church, 127, 131, 232
Freston, Paul, 225, 231
Freud, Sigmund, 152
Fueter, Paul D., 217

Fuller, Andrew, 243–44
Fuller Theological Seminary, 39, 267, 282,
   283, 284
fundamentalism, 38, 128, 149–51, 157, 214,
   249, 280–81

Gatwa, Tharcisse, 215
Gaussen, Louis, 247
gender, 71, 164, 166
   and ordination, 128
   complementarian views of, 165–66
   egalitarian views of, 74, 165–66
   in the Bible, 164–67
   of God, 163, 171–73
George, Timothy, 81, 213–14
Getui, Mary, 215
Gibellini, Rosino, 217
Giles, Kevin, 171
Gill, John, 243
globalization, 27–28, 36, 43, 153–54, 199, 217,
   229, 260, 269–71, 290
Gnanakan, Ken, 228, 230
González, Juan Orts, 262
González, Justo, 262, 264
gospel, 9–10, 17, 29, 35, 60, 100–01, 109,
   219–20, 229, 230
"Gospel of Jesus Christ: An Evangelical
   Celebration," 82, 83
Graham, Billy, 127, 151, 153, 249, 275, 283
Great Awakenings, 126, 151, 157, 214, 277–78
Gregory of Nyssa, 89
Grenz, Stanley, 27, 42, 125, 131, 169, 290
Grudem, Wayne, 166
Gunton, Colin, 95, 250
Gutiérrez, Gustavo, 263, 264

Haldane, James, 247
Haldane, Ralph, 247, 248
Harris, Howell, 5, 243
Hart, Darryl G., 127
Hart, David Bentley, 88–89
Harvey, Thomas, 231
Hatch, Nathan, 127
Hauerwas, Stanley, 155, 234
Haye, Sophie de la, 218
Hays, Richard, 90
Hendry, George, 93
Henry, Carl F. H., 39, 53, 151, 155, 283–84
Herberg, Will, 287
hermeneutics, 43–45, 162, 164, 165, 166–67,
   207, 221
Hick, John, 27, 202, 204

Hirsch, E. D., Jr., 41
history of religions, 56–58, 208
Hodge, Charles, 20, 52, 147, 167–68, 277
Holiness, 119, 130, 249, 278
Holy Spirit, 1, 10–12, 41–42, 69–70, 93–104,
    116, 117–19, 120, 156, 172, 205,
    208, 232
    baptism of, 120, 148
    "second blessing" of, 120
Hordern, William, 288
Horton, Michael, 59–60
house church, 231, 252
Houston, James, 170
Howard, Jorge, 262
humanity, 65–66, 157, 164, 167–69, 194, 215
    image of God, 65, 66–70, 173
    relational, 167–69, 208
Humphrey, Edith, 130
Hutchinson, Anne, 276
hymns, 157

inclusivism, 199, 200, 287
Inman, Samuel Guy, 262
International Council on Biblical
    Inerrancy, 39, 40
    "Chicago Statement," 39, 40
Irenaeus, 193
Irving, Edward, 243, 244, 245, 246, 247,
    248, 252
Israel, 66–68, 110–13, 187, 188

Jacobs, Harriet A., 177, 180, 187
JanMohamed, Adbul M., 179, 183–85
Jenkins, Philip, 43
Jesus Christ, 1, 21, 28, 68, 73, 75–76, 97–100,
    135, 171, 172, 203
    Chalcedon, 59, 204, 206, 207–08
    "from below," 57, 172
    Holy Saturday of, 186, 189, 192
    Logos Christology, 97
    Solus Christus, 51, 135, 200, 201, 206
    Spirit Christology, 97, 98–100
    work of, 9–10, 52, 87, 193–94
John (of Damascus), 89
John XXIII (Pope), 152
Jones, Serene, 100
Julio de Santa Ana, 263
justice, 103–04, 136, 153, 154, 248
justification, 79, 83, 98
    by faith alone, 84, 89–90, 278
    by imputed righteousness, 81, 83
    by inherited righteousness, 81

Kant, Immanuel, 52, 58
Kato, Byang, 213, 218–20
Kelsey, David, 42
Kenzo, Mabiala Justin-Robert, 220–21
Keswick, 148, 149, 249, 286
Kierkegaard, Søren, 193
King, Martin Luther, 152
Kreider, Alan, 252
Kreider, Eleanor, 252
Kuyper, Abraham, 155, 249, 253

LaCugna, Catherine, 96
Land, Steven, 290
Lausanne Movement, 157
    International Congress on World
        Evangelization, 11, 153–54, 229,
        271, 283
    Lausanne Covenant, 11, 153, 201, 246
Laws, Curtis Lee, 280
Lefebvre, Marcel, 216
Lewis, C. S., 153, 156, 199, 279
Lewis, Donald M., 1
liberalism, theological, 6, 53, 199, 200, 203,
    227, 230, 250–51, 280, 281
liberation theology, 100, 230, 263–65
Lippmann, Walter, 280, 281
Lloyd-Jones, Martin, 251
Locke, John, 277
London Missionary Society, 246, 247, 248
Lopez, Mauricio, 265
Lull, Raymond, 261
Lundin, Roger, 149
Luther, Martin, 21, 79–81, 83–84, 145
    "Finnish Interpretation" of, 88
Lutheran, 51, 84, 85, 119, 127, 276

Macchia, Frank, 290
Machen, J. Gresham, 52, 154, 155, 280–81
MacIntyre, Alasdair, 255
Mackay, John A., 261–62
Macleod, Donald, 55
Mangalwadi, Vishal, 228
Marsden, George, 127
Martinez Arce, Sergio, 265
Marx, Karl, 152, 186, 230, 253
Mathews, Shailer, 128
Mbembé, Achille, 177, 181–86
McKim, Donald, 39
McLaren, Brian, 290
McLeod Campbell, John, 245, 248, 252
McLoughlin, William, 276
McPherson, Aimee Semple, 127

Melancthon, Philip, 51
Mencken, H. L., 280, 281
Mennonite, 85–86, 155
Mergal, Angel M., 262
metaphysics, 162, 167, 169, 208
Methodist, 6, 86, 126, 277, 281, 288
Meye Thompson, Marianne, 166
Migliore, Daniel, 97
Miguez-Bonino, José, 263, 266, 269
Mingdao, Wang, 231
miracles, 232
Miranda, José, 263
missions, 8, 11, 12, 97, 133–34, 137, 146, 154,
    155, 199, 204, 207, 226, 229–30,
    243, 246, 247, 252, 253, 259, 268,
    271, 279
Moberg, David, 279
modern(ism), 6, 21–22, 38, 71–72, 128, 147,
    202, 227, 229, 280, 281
Moltmann, Jürgen, 100, 168, 170
Moody, Dwight, 127, 249, 278, 279
More, Hannah, 246, 253
Moule, H. C. G., 249, 280
Mouw, Richard, 155
Mullins, E. Y., 280
Murray-Williams, Stuart, 252

National Association of Evangelicals
    (USA), 3, 10, 282
nationalism, 75, 253, 282
naturalism, 38, 52
Netland, Harold, 202–03
Neuhaus, Richard John, 290
Newbigin, Lesslie, 230
Newman, John Henry, 246–47
Newton, Isaac, 277
Newton, John, 22
Nietzsche, Friedrich, 152
Noll, Mark A., 2, 146, 155, 241, 242, 255, 277
Nuñez, Emilio A., 266

Ockenga, Harold John, 282
Oden, Thomas, 55, 287–88, 289
Olson, Roger, 79
open theism, 24–25, 28, 286, 287
Orr, James, 52, 280
orthodox(y), Christian, 3–5, 17–19, 35, 36, 51,
    81, 130–31, 171, 203, 213, 242, 252,
    271, 278, 279, 286, 288

Packer, J. I., 251, 255, 275, 289–90
Padilla, Ruth, 266

Palamas, Gregory, 89
Paley, William, 244
Palmer, Timothy, 219
Panikkar, Raimon, 208, 230
Pannenberg, Wolfhart, 59, 275, 288
parachurch, 125, 226
Paredes, Tito, 266
Parker, Rebecca, 89
Parsons, Talcott, 161
Pénoukou, Efoé Julien, 215, 216
Pentecostal, 6, 10, 93–94, 120, 153–54, 205,
    214, 225, 227, 231, 232, 234, 254, 265,
    278, 290
    Oneness, 4
Perkins, William, 276
philosophy, 19, 24, 168, 280, 290
Piedra, Arturo, 266
Pieris, Aloysius, 230
pietism, 18, 29, 277, 285
piety, 11, 36, 51, 71, 214, 255, 276, 277, 282, 284
Pinnock, Clark, 25, 204–05, 207, 230, 286–87
Piper, John, 290
Plantinga, Cornelius, 103
pluralism, 27, 154, 201, 202, 203, 207, 229–30
Plymouth Brethren, 150, 252
politics, 181–86, 217, 230, 231, 234, 245, 266,
    269, 270
post-Reformation, 51–52, 126
postmodern, 27, 42, 132, 164, 221, 230, 233,
    283, 288
poverty, 263, 268
pragmatism, 147, 227, 247, 271, 276
preaching, 137, 229, 243, 252
Presbyterians, 278, 280–81
Princeton Theological Seminary, 38, 52
process theology, 23, 25
prophecy, 134, 136
Protestant, 1, 2, 3–5, 35–36, 79–81, 226, 260,
    262, 263, 277, 278, 279
Puritans, 147, 149, 188, 214, 242, 251, 276, 289

race, 177–94, 268
Ramachandra, Vinoth, 202, 203–04, 230
Ramm, Bernard, 285
reason, 168, 283
reconciliation, 1, 9–10, 68–69, 75, 96, 112–13,
    136, 164, 173, 205
Reformation, 20–21, 35–36, 79–81, 145, 147,
    213, 276, 278
    radical, 115, 127
Reformed, 51, 86–87, 115, 120, 127, 149, 155,
    276, 285

regeneration, 117
  baptismal, 117
religions, 199–200, 216, 220, 227, 232
Rembao, Alberto, 262
resurrection, 59, 98, 121, 189, 190–94
revelation, 206, 207, 214, 283
  propositional, 37, 283
revival, 1, 51, 145, 146, 148–49, 249, 277
Rice, Richard, 287
Richard, Pablo, 263
Ricoeur, Paul, 118
Ritchie, John, 262
Robertson, Pat, 156
Rogers, Jack, 39
Roman Catholicism, 4–5, 6, 35, 54, 83–84,
    85, 133, 199, 255, 259–63, 269, 278
  Council of Trent, 84
  Second Vatican Council, 152
romanticism, 147–49
Romero, Oscar, 265
Rookmaaker, H. R., 152
Runia, Klaas, 55
Rycroft, Stanley, 262, 268

sacraments, 135, 136–37, 232
Sáenz, Moisés, 262
salvation, 59, 206, 243
  ordo salutis, 115–16
  sola fide, 200, 278
Salvation Army, 12, 157
Samartha, Stanley J., 203
Sánchez-Cetina, Edesio, 266
sanctification, 85, 95, 118–21
Sanders, John, 206, 287
Schaeffer, Francis, 151–54, 156, 286
Schipani, Daniel, 266
Schleiermacher, Friedrich, 148
scholasticism, 18, 29
Scofield, C. I., 150, 265
Segundo, Juan Luis, 263
Shedd, W. G. T., 52
Shields, T. T., 281
Shults, LeRon, 27
Simeon, Charles, 248
Simons, Menno, 85–86
sin, 67, 72, 110, 117, 136, 201, 228
Sklair, Leslie, 270
slavery, 177, 180, 190, 191
  abolition of, 190–94, 245, 246, 279
Smeaton, George, 248, 251
Smith, Pearsall, 249
Smith, Timothy L., 278

Snyder, Howard, 126, 127
Sobrino, Jon, 264
Song, C. S., 230
sovereignty, divine, 23–24, 30, 157
Spillers, Hortense, 184
spirituality, 8, 229, 232
Spurgeon, Charles, 248
Stendahl, Krister, 90
Steuernagel, Valdir, 266
Stoll, David, 265, 269
Stott, John, 153, 155, 230, 251, 255
Strauss, D. F., 52
Strong, Augustus H., 281
suffering, 89, 134
Sunday, Billy, 280
Surin, Kenneth, 182

Tamez, Elsa, 266
Taylor, Dan, 242
Taylor, Nathaniel, 277
Tetzel, John, 83
theology, 23, 286, 289
  dogmatic, 55, 61, 251, 275
  historical, 54, 61
Tidball, Derek, 2
Tillich, Paul, 87
Tocqueville, Alexis de, 279
Tomlinson, Dave, 252
Torrance, Alan, 166, 167, 170
Torrance, James, 172
Torrance, T. F., 250
tradition, 35, 44–45, 127, 246, 279, 288
translation, 44, 221, 268, 271
Trinity, 25–27, 28, 65, 70, 94–97, 136, 169–71,
    207–08
  participation in the, 97, 136, 208
  social, 27, 102, 169–70
  subordination in the, 99, 100,
    170–71

Vanhoozer, Kevin J., 290
Varetto, Juan C., 262
Visser't Hooft, Willem, 131
Voth, Esteban, 266
Volf, Miroslav, 27, 166, 290

Walls, Andrew, 43, 270
Warfield, B. B., 52, 128, 168, 280
Warren, Rick, 290
Watts, Isaac, 251
Wayland, Francis, 278
Webber, Robert, 129, 133

Webster, John, 132, 135
Welker, Michael, 103
Wells, David, 17, 129, 131–32, 290
Wells, Samuel, 83
Wesley, Charles, 242
Wesley, John, 1, 5–6, 10, 86, 88, 116, 126, 241,
    242, 244, 254, 256, 277
Wesleyan, 18, 83, 115, 120, 249
Whitefield, George, 1, 5–6, 10, 126, 242, 244,
    277, 279
Wilberforce, William, 12, 43, 148, 245–46,
    248, 251
Williams, A. N., 89
Williams, Roger, 276
Witherington, Ben, 57

Wolterstorff, Nicholas, 103, 155
Woodbridge, John, 39
World Evangelical Fellowship (now
    Alliance), 8, 9, 43, 44, 225
worldview(s), 202, 227, 229, 283
worship, 18, 120, 136, 137, 252
Wright, N. T., 41, 57
Wright, Nigel, 252
Wright, Richard, 180, 183–89

Yoder, John Howard, 131, 155
Yong, Amos, 205
Youth for Christ, 151, 282

Zokoué, Isaac, 220

Scripture Index

Genesis
  1:2–9   67
  1:26   74
  1:26–27   67
  3   110, 111
  3:17–18   67
  5:1–2   74
  6:6   21
  18:22   110
Exodus
  3:14   20
  14:19–21   67
  14:19–31   67
  19:6   68
  20:2   26
Leviticus
  19:2   119
  19:12   111
  20:26   119
  22:13   110
  26:40–42   111
Numbers
  21:4–9   112
Deuteronomy
  3:24   69
  4:24   111
  4:30   112
  4:34   69
  30   111
Joshua
  24:33   111
1 Samuel
  7:3   111
  15:35   21

1 Kings
  8:33   111
  8:35   111
2 Kings
  23:25   122
2 Chronicles
  7:14   111
Nehemiah
  9   122
Psalms
  16:11   96
  32:3–5   110
  65:6   69
  68:5–6   73
  80:14   122
  93   67
  99:5   119
  107   122
  107:24   69
  115   68
  132:9   68
  132:16   68
  132:18   68
  135   68
Proverbs
  28:13   110
Ecclesiastes
  7:20   114
Isaiah
  6:9–10   68
  6:10   112
  6:11–12   68
  6:11–13   112
  10:20–21   112

Isaiah (cont.)
11:1–5   112
11:10   112
23:18   68
25:7   192
28:16   112
30:15   122
32:15   68
33:3–16   112
35:5–6   68
36:24–27   112
42:16   69
44:3   68
44:22   112
45:8   68
45:17   68
46:13   68
51:3   68
52:1   68
53:2–12   112
55:11   38
59:21   68
61   68
61:10   68
63–64   112
63:17   112
66:1a   67
Jeremiah
4:4   111
13:23   112
26:3–4   122
31:31   112
31:31–34   112
34:5   122
Lamentations
5:21   112
Ezekiel
10   68
11:19   113
11:19–20   118
18:15–17   119
18:31   113
33:8–11   111
36:24–26   111
36:35   68
37:1–14   187
37:5–6   68
37:14   68, 113
Daniel
7   68

9:25   112
Hosea
3:5   112
5:4–14   112
5:15   112
6:1–6   111
6:6   111
Joel
2:3   68
Amos
7:8–8:2   112
9:14   122
Jonah
3:10   122
Zechariah
3:3–5   68
12:10   112
14:14   68
Malachi
3:6   21
4:5–6   112
Matthew
1:1–17   68
3:1–12   113
3:2   113
4:17   113
4:23–6:10   69
5:1–7:29   114
5:20   114
5:48   20
6:9   119
6:10   73
8:27   69
9:12–13   114
11:20–24   113
11:28–30   113
12:28   97
18:3   114
22:37–39   102
23:9–11   172
23:37   115
24:37   68
28:19   11
28:19–20   267
Mark
1:4   113
1:4–8   113
1:15   113
1:24   119
4:14   69

8:14–10:52	69	17:17	120
9:33–10:45	69	19:30	109
10:27	114	Acts	
14:36	31	1	109
Luke		1:8	11, 119
1:1–4	38	2:1–12	119
1:5–25	113	2:14–36	69
1:35	97	2:37	118
1:41	113	2:38	122
1:54–55	68	2:40–47	118
1:57–80	113	3:19	122
2:4–11	68	5:3–4	11, 94
3:1–18	113	5:31	122
4:1	97	8:22	122
4:16–21	114	9–10	118
4:18	97	11:18	122
5:32	113	20:21	122
11:17–20	118	20:32	119
11:20	97, 113	26:20	122
14:16–17	115	Romans	
15	101	1:4	97
20:36	72	1:6–7	115
John		2:4	113
1:1	68	2:13	80
1:1–18	37	3:23	114
1:4	68	3:23–25	82
1:9	115	3:24–26	81
1:12	172	3:25	82
1:12–13	117, 118	3:28	81
1:13	80	3:31	80
1:14	68	4:25	98
3:3–8	114	5:1	81
3:6	117, 118	5:1–2	80
3:16	114, 115	5:5	96, 102
3:16–17	120	5:6–8	109
4:14	120	5:12–21	68
4:24	20	5:14–21	118
5:15–23	69	5:20	117
5:26	20	7:1–8:4	117
10:10	114, 120	8:2	120
11:38	69	8:4–5	120
14:8–11	69	8:6	120
14:16–26	119	8:9	117, 118
14:26	99	8:9–14	120
15	165	8:9–17	117
15:13	120	8:11	97, 98, 109
15:26	93, 99	8:14–35	70
16:13	93	8:15	31
16:14	93	8:17	70
17	121	8:19–25	73

Romans (cont.)
8:20–23	67
8:27	119
8:29	69, 73
8:29–30	114
9	116
9–11	192
10:14–15	117
12:1	121
12:1–21	120
12:3–8	118
14:17	104
15:16	118
16	165

1 Corinthians
1:9	115
1:10	96
1:13–2:5	117
1:18–25	29
1:26	115
2:13	116, 117
3:3	96
3:16–17	70
4	165
6:11	118
6:19–20	70
9:22	256
11	170
12–14	70
12:4–7	118
13:12	271
15	72
15:21–22	68
15:45–49	68
15:49	73
15:54–55	120

2 Corinthians
1:22	232
3:6	120
3:18	69, 72
4:4	69
5	68
6:17	282
13:14	94

Galatians
2:16	81
3:26–29	73
3:28	70, 268
4:6	31
5:16	120

5:22	96, 102
5:25	120
6:7	193

Ephesians
1:3	70
1:4–5	114
1:5	71, 120
1:9–10	73
1:13–14	232
1:14	102
1:17	100
1:18	119
1:18–23	69
2:6	69
4:2	96
4:13	271
4:14–16	102
4:23–24	72
5:26	119
5:27	119

Philippians
2:1–18	69, 120
2:5–11	171
3:8–10	121
3:12	104

Colossians
1:15	68, 69
1:18	68, 72
2:3	45
3:10	69
3:14	96

2 Thessalonians
| 2:13 | 118 |

1 Timothy
| 2 | 165 |
| 3:16 | 98 |

2 Timothy
| 3:15 | 37, 45 |
| 3:16–17 | 36, 37, 40 |

Titus
2:14	119
3:5	117
3:7	81

Hebrews
1–4	69
1:1–3	37
1:3	100
1:4	69
2:11	73
2:14	118

6:1	122	2 Peter	
6:4	102	1:4	88
6:5	102	3:6–7	68
9:4	97	3:16	37
10:10	119	1 John	
10:29	119	1:3–4	96
13:20–21	119	3:2–3	73
James		4:2	120
2:26	120	4:18	116
1 Peter		Revelation	
1:2	119	2:21	122
1:15	119	2:22	122
2:4–5	70	16:9	122
2:9	70, 115, 121	21:1–22:5	66
3:18	109	22	70
4:14	100		